GLOBAL COMPETITION AND LOCAL NETWORKS

T0303961

Global Competition and Local Networks

Edited by
ROB B. McNAUGHTON
University of Waterloo, Canada
MILFORD B. GREEN
University of Western Ontario, Canada

Routledge
Taylor & Francis Group

LONDON AND NEW YORK

First published 2002 by Ashgate Publishing

Reissued 2018 by Routledge
2 Park Square, Milton Park, Abingdon, Oxon OX14 4RN
711 Third Avenue, New York, NY 10017, USA

Routledge is an imprint of the Taylor & Francis Group, an informa business

Publisher's Note
The publisher has gone to great lengths to ensure the quality of this reprint but points out that some imperfections in the original copies may be apparent.

Disclaimer
The publisher has made every effort to trace copyright holders and welcomes correspondence from those they have been unable to contact.

A Library of Congress record exists under LC control number: 2002100329

ISBN 13: 978-1-138-71681-0 (hbk)
ISBN 13: 978-1-138-71679-7 (pbk)
ISBN 13: 978-1-315-19683-1 (ebk)

Contents

PART I:UNDERSTANDING LOCAL NETWORKS AND THEIR LINKS
    TO COMPETITIVENESS

PART II: INNOVATION IN LOCAL NETWORKS

PART III: THE CONSTRAINTS OF LOCAL NETWORKS

PART IV: CONTEXTS OF NETWORK STRATEGIES

List of Figures

List of Tables

List of Contributors

Andersson, Ulf. Department of Business Studies, Uppsala University, PO Box 513, 751 20 Uppsala, Sweden. Ulf.andersson@fek.uu.se

Bramanti, Alberto. Department of Economics, Bocconi University, Milan, Italy. Alberto.bramanti@uni-bocconi.it

Bratl, Hubert. Institut für Regionale Innovation, Lederergasse 35/5/1, A-1080 Wien, Austria. Bratl@invent.or.at

Brown, Les. Department of Marketing, University of Southern Queensland, Toowoomba, Queensland, Australia, 4350. Brownl@usq.edu.au

Brown, Peter. City Marketing and Development, Dunedin City Council, 50 The Octagon, PO Box 5045, Dunedin, New Zealand. Peter.brown@dcc.govt.nz

Burlat, Patrick. Ecole des Mines de Saint-Etienne – Centre SIMMO, 158 Cours Fauriel, 42023 Saint-Etienne Cedex 2, France. Burlat@emse.fr

Coe, Neil M. School of Geography, University of Manchester, Oxford Road, Manchester, UK, M13 9PL. Neil.coe@man.ac.uk

Deans, Mae. Legislative Assembly of Alberta, 201 Legislature Annex, 9718-107 Street, Edmonton, Alberta, Canada, T5K 1E4. Mdeans@planet.eon.net

Edgington, David W. Department of Geography, University of British Columbia, Vancouver, British Columbia, Canada, V6T 1Z2. Edgingtn@geog.ubc.ca

Feser, Edward J. Department of City and Regional Planning, University of North Carolina, CB 3140, New East Building, Chapel Hill, North Carolina, USA, 27599-3140. Feser@email.unc.edu

Forsgren, Mats. Department of Business Studies, Uppsala University, PO Box 513, 751 20 Uppsala, Sweden. Mats.forsgren@fek.uu.se

Gentzoglanis, Anastassios. Center for the Study of Regulatory Economics and Finance, Department of Economics, University of Sherbrooke, Sherbrooke, Quebec, Canada J1K 2R1. Agentz@courrier.usherb.ca

Green, Milford B. Department of Geography, University of Western Ontario, London, Ontario, Canada N6A 5C2. Mbgreen@uwo.ca

Izushi, Hiro. Center for Local Economic Development, Coventry Business School, Coventry University, Priory Street, Coventry, UK CV1 5FB. H.izushi@coventry.ac.uk

Maggioni, Mario A. DISEIS, Department of International, Institutional and Development Economics, and Faculty of Political Science, Catholic University of Milan, Milan, Italy. Maggioni@mi.unicatt.it

Matear, Sheelagh. Department of Marketing, University of Otago School of Business, PO Box 56, Dunedin, New Zealand. Smatear@business.otago.ac.nz

McCarroll, Andrew. Farming Systems Institute, Department of Primary Industries, PO Box 102, Toowoomba, Queensland, Australia, 4350. McCarr@prose.dpi.qld.gov.au

McDonald, Frank. International Business Unit, Manchester Metropolitan University, Aytoun Street, Manchester, UK, M1 3GH. F.McDonald@mmu.ac.uk

McNaughton, Rod B. Department of Management Sciences, University of Waterloo, Waterloo, Ontario, Canada, N2L 3G1. Rmcnaugh@engmail.uwaterloo.ca

O'Hagan, Sean B. Department of Geography, University of Western Ontario, London, Ontario, Canada, N6A 5C2. Sbohagan@uwo.ca

Peillon, Sophie. Ecole des Mines de Saint-Etienne – Centre SIMMO, 158 Cours Fauriel, 42023 Saint-Etienne Cedex 2, France. Speillon@emse.fr

Sweeney, Stuart H. Department of Geography, University of California, Santa Barbara, California, USA 93106-4060. Sweeney@geog.ucsb.edu

Tödtling, Franz. Department of City and Regional Development, Vienna University of Economics and Business Administration. Roßauer Lände 23, A-1090 Wien, Austria. Franz.Toedtling@wu-wien.ac.at

Townsend, Alan R. Department of Geography, University of Durham, South Road, Durham, UK DH1 3LE. Alan.townsend@durham.ac.uk

Trippl, Michaela. Institut für Regionale Innovation, Lederergasse 35/5/1, A-1080 Wien, Austria. Trippl@invent.or.at

Tucker, Brett. Rural Industry Business Services, Department of Primary Industries, PO Box 1143, Bundaberg, Queensland, Australia, 4670. Tuckerb@dpi.qld.gov.au

Vertova, Giovanna. Department of Economics, University of Bergamo, Piazza Rosate 2, 24129 Bergamo, Italy. Vertova@unibg.it

Walcott, Susan M. Department of Anthropology and Geography, Georgia State University, 33 Gilmer Street, University Plaza, Atlanta, Georgia, USA, 30303-3083. Swalcott@gsu.edu

Preface

The globalization of finance, communication, technology and markets has resulted in unprecedented business competition. The forces of globalization would at first thought logically reduce the importance and relevance of firm location. Yet the regional clustering of leading firms continues, and successful clusters are universally attributed with contributions to economic growth at a national level. While it may seem paradoxical, competitiveness in global markets is linked to the development of local clusters of firms. Many academic researchers and business commentators view local clusters as a means to lever home-based competitive advantage into international markets. Policy makers have adopted this logic, designing programs to facilitate development of local networks of firms "clustered" in a distinct geographical region. It is thought that firms within these clusters derive support and competitive advantage through their local relationships, place-specific history, economic factors, values and common culture.

Global Competition and Local Networks is the second book we have edited on the theme of local networks. The first, *Industrial Networks and Proximity*, published in 2000 by Ashgate Publishing Limited is a collection of ten chapters that explore the proposition that firms located close to each other are more likely to know about each other, and to be able to co-operate for mutual advantage. The chapters include discussions of theory, development of techniques for measuring the clustering phenomenon, and empirical examples of the role of proximity in industrial organisation and economic exchange.

Global Competition and Local Networks begins where the first *Industrial Networks* ends. It addresses the issue of how participation in local networks helps firms to be globally competitive. Academic researchers in a number of disciplines are very interested in how small and medium sized firms in local business communities can be globally competitive.

A variety of theories have emerged to explain aspects of the phenomenon: economists and economic geographers have developed sophisticated models of agglomeration, organisation theorists have focused on the vertical disintegration of the firm, business writers have seen it as a response to competitive pressure, and social network theorists have pointed to the role of relationships between actors and their communities as the underlying reasons for clustering. All these efforts at explanation agree that clusters create externalities such as technological spillovers, specialised and flexible labour pools and intermediate inputs and outputs that provide a competitive advantage for firms within a cluster.

Our goal was that the contributors to this book would begin to synthesise the diverse literature as well as report the results of original research. *Global Competitiveness and Local Networks* contains fifteen chapters contributed by 28 researchers from North America, Europe, and Australasia, representing a range of disciplines including economics, geography, marketing, and international business. The chapters are organised into four sections: understanding local networks and their links to competitiveness, innovation in local networks, the constraints of local networks, and the contexts of network strategies. What follows is a brief synopsis of the chapters within these sections:

The first chapter by Peter Brown and Rod McNaughton provides an extensive review of the literature on local clusters of firms. The review begins by tracing the evolution of geographical concentration of production and discusses important preconditions in the development of a cluster. It then examines externalities that underpin this concept before discussing the positions of various schools of thought and factors contributing to cluster development. The chapter concludes by discussing negative cluster externalities and cluster types. A key contribution of this chapter is a model (Figure 1.1) of a continuum of cluster types, distinguished by the degree of networking between firms, and the extent to which there is active management of potential benefits that can be realised from cluster externalities.

In the second chapter, Frank McDonald and Giovanna Vertova provide definitions of geographically based networks. Their taxonomy includes Clusters and two different types of Industrial Districts (the distinction is made on the basis of the type of networks that can exist within the Industrial Districts). The definitions stem from a model based on the works of Marshall, Porter, Krugman and North. North's work in particular, is used to highlight the importance of history and institutional frameworks in the formation and development of the various types of geographically based networks.

McDonald and Vertova's model suggests that geography, history and institutional frameworks are crucial to the formation and development of geographically based networks, with their development path determined by these factors. Socio-economic factors within Clusters and Industrial Districts are also included in the model and are used to explain how local trust-based networks may be constructed, particularly in societies that have national institutional frameworks that are not conducive to lowering uncertainty and transaction costs. The connection between these networks and competitiveness is considered by examining the effect of the development of geographically based networks on transaction and production costs. Clusters and Industrial Districts are defined by reference to the type of networks that emerge from proximity between firms, institutions and socio-economic structures. The possible competitive advantages that can be created by proximity are then classified.

Anastassios Gentzoglanis' chapter presents an analytical framework with some theoretical elements that analyse networks as a means of increasing flexibility. Flexibility refers to the adaptation capability of the firm and its learning ability. Its adaptation capability protects the firm from external shocks while its learning ability enables the network to create resources through a collective learning process. There are benefits and costs of interactive learning, which depend on the "cultural" distance between the two entities. Gentzoglanis argues that distance may not have a geographical dimension but it may be more associated with differences in knowledge. The more distant (different) firms' knowledge base is, the greater the learning potential. Once the network is set up, interactive learning becomes possible through the establishment of shared information channels and codes of information. The initial process of mutual understanding is becoming more costly as the cultural distances are great.

Gentzoglanis uses the concept of *knowledge proximity* rather than of geographical distance to better explain the formation of networks (both vertical and horizontal) as a means of increasing partners' flexibility. He demonstrates how networks are more likely to form between firms situated at some distances on the continuum of knowledge (e.g., firms having complementary technologies - vertical networks - or firms being in the same stream of the production process but having different knowledge bases - horizontal networks). Case studies from the car industry (Ballard Power System) and the telecommunications industry (Bell Canada) serve as examples of his approach.

In the fourth chapter Sean O'Hagan and Milford Green continue the theme of knowledge within local networks. Their chapter begins by reviewing the different types of knowledge typically identified within the literature, and then summarising the literature on the relationship between knowledge and the region. O'Hagan and Green argue that today knowledge instead of land, labour, and capital, is the key to competitive advantage. Knowledge allows the firm to develop superior technological know-how and create innovative products better than their rivals. The ultimate challenge to management for sustained growth is to create knowledge that is not easily imitated by competitors and to use this knowledge for innovative purposes. An important contribution of this chapter is the explicit identification of the geographic implication of knowledge forms. Namely:

- The codified nature of explicit knowledge allows it to be imitated relatively easily by competitors. The firm must therefore use tacit knowledge if sustainable competitive advantage is to be created.
- Geographic proximity is important for tacit knowledge transfer. Since face-to-face contact is necessary for tacit knowledge transfer, localized relationships are essential.

Therefore, when attempting to explain the competitive advantage of firms, not only should the transfer of tacit knowledge be studied, but the geographical implications for tacit knowledge need to be considered as well.

The chapter contributed by Edward Feser and Stuart Sweeney extends the existing literature by outlining a method for identifying spatially binding ties within clusters of firms. The idea is that within a given network or cluster, some linkages depend on proximity while others do not. Using a combination of data reduction methods and point process modelling techniques, they identify which sectors within a broader economic cluster encourage spatial concentration. The method is illustrated by application to the printing and publishing production chain.

Feser and Sweeney point out that firms form linkages that are both spatially determinant and non-local or global in nature. This means that observed economic clusters (firms linked within supplier chains, as a result of technological complementarities, or within networks) may or may not appear clustered in space. More accurately, economically linked firms are likely to exhibit a greater or lesser degree of spatial clustering depending on the specific nature of the linkage

The sixth chapter by Patrick Burlat and Sophie Peillon notes that corporate restructuring over the past two decades has led firms to adopt vertical disintegration strategies which have deeply transformed the nature of relationships between firms, and led to a new organisational form: the network. This chapter addresses the "network of firms", i.e., industrial structures linked by horizontal agreements (unlike the "firm network" managed by a focal firm). These dynamic networks are able to make use of the skills and know-how distributed between independent firms. This leads to a new conceptualization of the frontier of the firm – "firms without borders". Burlat and Peillon argue that because of disintegration, traditional borders, which defined the firm as a place of production, are not relevant anymore. The benefits of dynamic networks of firms mainly lie in the fact that they constitute a preferential way to acquire external skills while preserving each partner's **independence**.

Burlat and Peillon illustrate their argument with an examination of firms in the Rhône-Alpes region in France. In this area, a multitude of small subcontractors account for the most significant industrial activity. They observe the emergence of dynamic networks intended to mobilize distributed skills and know-how, and conclude that unlike information, which forwards instantaneously, skills sharing within a non-hierarchical framework of co-operation is not easily freed from cultural barriers and linguistic borders. The process of constitution of non-hierarchical networks, founded on the exchanges of skills and on the establishment of trust, is thus fully carried out only in a context of geographical and cultural proximity.

The next chapter, authored by Susan Walcott, contrasts biomedical clusters in two dynamic Sunbelt sites of approximately the same size - metropolitan Atlanta, Georgia and San Diego, California - to show the critical role of place components in nurturing a nascent economic complex. Her examination of the structure and nature of biomedical firms tests theories on high tech industry characteristics and the match with place characteristics predicted to be most conducive to innovative firm growth. Walcott shows that a synergistic relationship exists between San Diego's Western openness and Atlanta's Deep South relational connectivity, and the health of their respective milieus.

San Diego is the more stereotypical innovative milieu, which reveals the importance of Universities and the organisational prowess of savvy individuals in creating dynamic organisations that foster and promote the cluster. Atlanta, on the other hand, lacks the concentration of flagship universities present in California. Atlanta trades on other market factors: airport connections, international visibility, labour base and quality of life. Indeed, the exact locations of Atlanta's clusters are more a reaction to negative externalities: long commute, inadequate schools, and real estate shortages leading to north side concentrations defined by specific highway access.

Franz Tödtling, Michaela Trippl and Hubert Bratl contribute the eighth chapter. They argue that networks are important not only for high-technology regions or innovative milieux, but that they are also important for traditional industrial regions and their reconversion process. This chapter investigates such networks on the basis of a firm survey and interviews for an old Austrian industrialised region (Styria) undergoing restructuring since the 1980s. Styria is analysed to discover to what extent firms engage in innovation activities relying on external partners in this process.

Tödtling and his colleagues show that, overall, the most important innovation networks are along the value chain (customers, suppliers) as well as those networks with knowledge suppliers (universities, consultants). In the geography of those networks they find that regional, national and international (European) levels are complementary rather than substitutes, since firms that are networking at a local/regional level are also more actively engaged in international technology co-operation. The role of policy actors is analysed in particular for the automotive cluster in the region. It is shown that the strengthening of innovation support institutions, and the setting up of coordinating institutions were highly important for the stimulation of networks in the cluster.

The next chapter is by Hiro Izushi, and is the first of four chapters that discuss the limitations of local networks, and their negative externalities. Izushi argues that local networks can be a liability in the process of adaptation and may disintegrate as some firms enter external networks in the search for advanced knowledge. Firms in traditional districts are often locked into their local networks and are unable to access the knowledge required to enter an area of more advanced technology. Adaptation of traditional industry to high technology is often a leap rather than a gradual change, requiring scientific and technical knowledge in another discipline. Content with their local tried-and-true methods of knowledge acquisition, small and medium-sized firms in mature industries often fail to explore sources of such knowledge outside of their districts.

Further, even if firms access sources of knowledge outside their districts, those external links do not always encourage them to diffuse such knowledge within the districts. While networks by nature facilitate diffusion of knowledge within, they vary in the degree to which they keep their knowledge from diffusing to others. Unlike links to universities and research institutes, some inter-firm networks are found to keep tight control over information flows. When firms in industrial districts establish external links to such tight networks in their search for advanced knowledge, they cease to co-operate with others in their local networks. This has adverse effects upon the local networks and hampers their district-wide entry into an advanced area of technology.

This chapter demonstrates these points by examining the district of traditional ceramics manufacturing in Seto, Japan. Against the background of its failed district-wide shift to advanced ceramics, it provides cases of those firms which succeeded and those that failed in their entry into advanced ceramics, and analyses their use of networks, both local and external as well as with firms and with universities and research institutes. The chapter also suggests that successful district-wide transformation partly hinges upon the ability of local research institutes to liaise with firms in their locality, keeping a close eye on their technological needs and drawing on knowledge in an appropriate discipline from universities and research institutes in other regions.

David Edgington continues the theme of the limits to networks by examining the lean production system used by Toyota in the Chukyo region of Japan. Toyota itself geared up to mass-production in the 1950s, at which time it recognised the need for at least a core of subcontractors which could guarantee to supply cheap parts of high quality at high volumes and implement rapid changes. The vertical structure of the local automotive parts supply industry, organized in a pyramid structure was a major feature pioneered by Toyota. This chapter examines that extent to which proximity is important to innovation in the Chukyo region. Dense assembler-supplier relationships were certainly important to Toyota's competitiveness up to the late-1980s. From then on, however, the dense agglomeration, rising land prices and a tight labour market proved to be a disadvantage, causing Toyota to search for sites for its new factories in the peripheral regions of Japan (Kyushu, Tohoku and Hokkaido). Moreover, during Japan's economic recession of the 1990s automobile production has ceased to be a propulsive industry in Chukyo, and Toyota is now looking to diversify, possibly out of the region.

Edgington illustrates his argument about the "limits of lean" using data from interviews with a wide range of private sector and public sector actors in Chukyo - including Toyota and other major assembly firms, subcontractors and government agencies. The research suggests that Chukyo is an example of a "learning region", one that exemplifies an interesting mix of public and private sector actors, local and central government, and suppliers and assembly firms. The implication for network formation theory is that "local" production links and proximity in industrial systems work best when complemented by "organisational proximity" among organisations committed to the long-term future of industrial regions.

Mario Maggioni and Alberto Bramanti are the authors of the eleventh chapter. This chapter provides a theoretical justification and an empirical test of the hypothesis that local identity is only one of the two intertwined and mutual reinforcing engines that drive the development of spatial systems of production and innovation (SPSIs). The second engine is the existence of an efficient network of global relationships.

This hypothesis is based on a rich set of empirical evidence and case studies showing a high correlation between the performance of a particular SSPI (in terms of survival and growth) and proper mix of the two above mentioned dimensions: internal cohesion and external linkages. The balance between local and global aspects of inter-firms relationship is thus essential in providing a stable path of sustainable growth and endogenous development. The last two terms refer to two essential features of the patterns of evolution of a local productive system. The first feature, (sustainable growth) concerns the existence of conditions for the re-production of (human, technological, natural social) resources, which can grant the persistence of positive performances of the system in the long run. The second feature, (endogenous development) refers to the capability of the local agents (these being firms, entrepreneurs and/or local authorities) to control and guide the patterns of quantitative and qualitative expansion of the local system and to escape external influences.

The hypothesis is tested on a sample of Italian "industrial districts" to show its empirical as well as theoretical relevance. Further evidence comes from two databases originally built by these authors on the location strategies and decisions of high-technology firms in four OECD countries, and the determinants of economic performance in Italian high-growth enterprises.

Neil Coe and Alan Townsend contribute the final chapter in the section on the constraints of local networks. This chapter explores the nature of agglomeration in fast growing producer service sectors. Many contemporary accounts of economic change suggest that the co-location of firms with their suppliers, partners and clients enables the development of dense networks of both traded and un-traded interdependencies that have a powerful impact on economic growth. However, the analysis presented in this chapter suggests that these accounts over emphasise the importance of such networks as the main causal factor behind the development of agglomerations, when in fact powerful processes of cumulative causation (i.e., self reinforcing processes) are simultaneously at work. For example, a large proportion of service sector entrepreneurs establish new businesses in the same locality as they were previously working, thereby reinforcing the dominance of leading regions. Similarly, foreign investment in producer service industries is overwhelmingly attracted to core regions that have established a reputation for excellence in those activities. It would be a mistake, therefore, to simply "read-off" from the resulting co-location of activity that such businesses are necessarily heavily embedded in local networks with other similar firms, clients and suppliers. On the contrary, intra-regional, inter-regional, and to a lesser extent, international network linkages are also of importance.

The chapter suggests those accounts of networks and producer service sector agglomeration need to be more historically, geographically and sectorally nuanced. Existing categorizations of service activity mask great structural variations both between, and within many sectors, which in turn influence the nature and spatiality of growth in these industries. The example of South East England illustrates the need to fully account for the geographically and historically specific antecedents of contemporary growth.

The final section of *Global Competition and Local Networks* contains three chapters that illustrate three very different contexts in which local networks influence international competitiveness: the case of rural entrepreneurs, the development of a network that aids the export of agricultural products, and the local subsidiaries of multinational corporations.

In chapter thirteen, Mae Deans describes how rural agribusiness owners operate their firms in a complex web of social relationships. This chapter emphasizes the importance of the relationship between social structures and entrepreneurial activity of rural agribusiness owners. Social relationships of these owners are not fully understood, yet an extensive body of literature does exist on networks and entrepreneurial activity. However, little of this research concerns the networking activities of agribusiness entrepreneurs located in rural areas. Deans contributes to this relatively unexplored area by focusing on three networks used by agribusiness owners: family and friendship networks, broker networks, and volunteer networks. The research draws upon the theoretical work of Granovetter and Aldrich, particularly their work on the "strength of weak ties" and the embeddedness of economic activity in social action.

More specifically, Deans explores the question of how the proximity to personal networks, chosen by an owner, constrain or augment the ability of a firm to export regionally, nationally, and internationally. The answer to this question comes from 40 face-to-face interviews using a questionnaire that collected both quantitative and qualitative responses. She compares two types of farm diversification activities: those businesses generating value-added products, but skewed toward manufacturing firms; and businesses engaged in a niche-market agricultural operation.

The study provides several insights. First, relationships deemed to have close proximity - spouses and friends - inhibit the business operations by stifling an owner's initiative and risk-taking desires. Secondly, children - whether they are still at home or pursuing other career interests - are excluded from all aspects of the business operation. Thirdly, broker networks with less personal proximity (customers, trade shows, and journals) bring additional market knowledge to the owner and contribute to exporting opportunities that otherwise would be unavailable. Fourthly, broker networks vary from industry to industry. Thus, some owners unwittingly use networks that restrict their business activity by providing inappropriate or spurious information. Finally, owners who become dependent upon a particular set of social networks are less likely to increase sales or exporting potential.

The penultimate chapter by Sheelagh Matear, Brett Tucker, Andrew McCarroll and Les Brown adopts a markets-as-networks perspective to examine the development of internationalization among a group of small agribusiness firms in Queensland, Australia. These exporters have adopted a collaborative approach to overcome problems of critical mass, multiple contact points and product quality specifications. However, the network extends beyond the immediate group to create an inter-regional network, which further increases the volume of product available and, in the case of fresh produce, the time period for which it is available. A further unique feature of this case is the alignment of the network with the category management system adopted by one of the major customers. The collaborative efforts and network development have enabled these firms to compete successfully in international markets, in particular establishing supply relationships with major food retail conglomerates in Asia.

Matear and her colleagues adopt a unique research method. Arguing that the processes through which relationships, and therefore networks, develop are complex and difficult to appreciate from an external analyst's perspective, they draw from the action research report of the Senior Trade Development Officer who played a key role in facilitating the development of the network, plus archival files of the project, interviews with alliance members and multiple interviews with the trade development officer.

In this final chapter, Ulf Andersson and Mats Forsgren address the management problem of finding the right balance between local adaptation and global integration for the subsidiaries of multinational companies. Local capabilities at the different subsidiaries are seen as important resources that should be employed on a global scale to achieve competitive advantage. Although different scholars emphasise, the importance of integration within the MNC, Andersson and Forsgren point out that little attention is paid to the problem of transforming capabilities developed at the subsidiary level into competitive advantage for the whole corporation.

Multinational corporations belong to multiple business networks. These networks are first of all sets of exchange relationships in which the subsidiaries are embedded. The counterparts in terms of customers, suppliers, competitors, governments, and trade unions exert influence on the separate subsidiaries through these relationships. This influence can or cannot be in accordance with integration and a coherent strategy at the headquarters level. Andersson and Forsgren argue that an analysis of both the needs and possibilities of integrating different units in a multinational corporation must take networks of business relationships on the subsidiary level into account. Thus, the issue of integration in the multinational corporation needs to be reformulated. It is not only a question of designing the organisation in such a way that sufficient integration and co-operation between units is reached, but also of obtaining flexibility and economy of scale and scope among a set of subsidiaries, which are embedded in different business networks. The question of integration should be extended to a question of embeddedness in networks *both* inside and outside the multinational corporation. The degree of a subsidiary's integration into a corporate system must be evaluated against its embeddedness in the external network of specific relationships.

This chapter discusses the concepts of embeddedness and integration within multinationals. A measurement of the degree of embeddedness in a subsidiary's network is developed which is used to analyse external and corporate embeddedness in a large number of subsidiaries belonging to Swedish multinationals. It is found that the degree of embeddedness varies considerably among the subsidiaries, from more or less "market-like" situations to highly structured networks with a high degree of embeddedness. The empirical results also indicate that the external embeddedness is at least as important as the corporate embeddedness for the subsidiaries, or expressed differently, the "integration" with external counterparts is as important as integration within the multinational corporation.

Andersson and Forsgren suggest four archetypes of integration based on the configuration of a subsidiary's supplier and customer relationships. The classification is based on an identification of a subsidiary's counterparts in terms of business relationships and to what extent these relationships are with external or corporate units. It is found that the average degree of external embeddeness in each relationship increases as the archetypes get more integrated. This means that the more a subsidiary is integrated into the corporate system of flows of goods and knowledge, the higher the external embeddedness, and the more it is stuck in the middle, between two forces influencing its behaviour.

In sum, *Global Competition and Local Networks* is a collection of fifteen chapters that bring a variety of theoretical perspectives and empirical evidence to the question of how participation in local networks can help a firm to be globally competitive. The material well illustrates the diversity of thought and research that characterise this important area of business research. We hope this volume will spur others on to research this challenging topic.

Rod B. McNaughton   Milford B. Green
Waterloo, Canada   *London, Canada*

PART I:
UNDERSTANDING LOCAL
NETWORKS AND THEIR
LINKS TO COMPETITIVENESS

1 Global Competitiveness and Local Networks: A Review of the Literature

PETER BROWN AND ROD B. McNAUGHTON

The globalization of finance, communication, technology and markets has resulted in unprecedented business competition, especially for small firms. The tendency towards globalization appears to reduce the importance and relevance of local regions and yet, regional clustering of leading firms is found in almost every national economy in the world. As the phenomenon of globalization, and global competition has increased, interest in local regions and regional clusters of firms has also increased. Researchers have begun to discuss the phenomenon of regional clusters in the context of home-base competitive advantage in an international market. Where general network strategies once formed the basis of government programs designed to address issues of growth and internationalization, there is now a growing interest in *localized* networks, where many firms within a particular sector are "clustered" in a distinct geographical region. Firms within these clusters apparently derive support and competitive advantage through highly localized inter-firm relationships, place-specific history, economic factors, values and culture. Clusters are increasingly seen as the driving force of international trade. They are credited with providing the environment for developing leading-edge technology, the acquisition and use of information and innovation through co-operation and competition between firms within the cluster.

The literature on industrial location suggests a number of possible explanations for the phenomenon of local clusters. Urban economists and economic geographers have developed sophisticated models of agglomeration while the field of industrial organization has focused on the vertical disintegration of firms. Researchers in business disciplines see clusters as a response to competitive pressure, and social network theorists have pointed to the role of relationships between actors and their communities as the underlying *raison d'être* of industrial clusters. All these efforts at explanation agree that clusters create externalities such as technological spillovers, specialized and flexible labor pools and intermediate inputs and outputs that provide a competitive advantage to firms within the cluster.

This chapter provides a literature review that traces the evolution of the geographical concentration of production and discusses important preconditions in the development of a cluster. It then examines the externalities that underpin clusters before discussing the positions of various schools of thought and factors contributing to cluster development. The chapter concludes by proposing a model of the types of clusters that helps distinguish between the concepts of networks, clusters and industrial districts.

The Evolution of Geographical Concentration of Production

Many analyses of the cluster phenomenon begin with Marshall and his work on industrial districts. Marshall's explanation of the evolution of industrial districts begins with the earliest stages of civilization when "...every place had to depend on its own resources for most of the heavy wares which it consumed" (Marshall 1910, p. 267). Marshall cited the chief causes of industry localization as physical conditions such as the character of the climate and the soil, the existence of mines and quarries in the neighborhood, or easy access by land or water. Thus the great iron industries in England first established themselves in districts where charcoal was plentiful, afterwards moving to be near collieries. The Sheffield cutlery industry, for example, was founded on the excellent grit available for its grindstones. Heavy industry that required large resources to operate was sited near coalmines for production efficiencies. As access to raw materials, production resource needs, transportation networks or market servicing costs changed, so the location of these heavy industries changed.

Another cause of localization suggested by Marshall was the patronage of a Court, which, by demand or importation of skilled artisans, caused a specialized industry to develop in a particular town. Marshall also acknowledged that accidents of history, combined with the character of people and their social and political institutions, have determined whether any particular industry flourished in any one town (Marshall 1910). This organization of geographic space can be simply understood in terms of the distribution of physical resources and transportation issues but this does not fully explain the intensity or density of varying types of experiences in different countries.

Prior to Marshall, Adam Smith (1776, republished 1979) had already focused on a different underlying principle of clusters, the technical division of labor within individual workshops. He argued that the greater the volume of output from any workshop, the more feasible it became to reorganize production by dividing the elements of production into a series of simple tasks. Thus production becomes increasingly streamlined and overall productivity tends to rise. This argument could be extended to communities of production where independent workshops specialized in specific tasks and became production units in their own right. These discreet units inter-linked with other production units clustered together in one location creating a vertically disintegrated system of organization that led to individual regions specializing in particular types of products.

Ricardo (republished 1971) elaborated on this theory in the early nineteenth century by stating that trade occurred between countries or regions on the basis of their comparative advantages in production. He argued that trade would occur even though one of the countries may not enjoy an absolute cost advantage in any commodity it produces. As long as it had a relative or *comparative* advantage in relation to its prospective trading partner, trade would occur to the mutual benefit of both. "It is this principle which determines that wine shall be made in France and Portugal, that corn shall be grown in America and Poland, and that hardware and other goods shall be manufactured in England" (Ricardo 1971, p. 152).

The underlying premise on which this is based is that different countries, cities and regions have distinctive kinds of resources or factor endowments that manifest themselves in efficient forms of local specialization and trade. But the industrial concentration observed in Europe and North America can only be partially accounted for in terms of pre-given natural endowments. The presence of resources like coal, iron ore, or natural harbors certainly influenced the location of industry. But many sectors, such as the cotton spinning and weaving of Manchester or the shoe and leather industries of southern New England, are only tenuously associated with underlying physical conditions. They were certainly linked to pools of skilled labor but was the labor pool a cause or effect of industrial development? Did regions create industrial development or did industrial development create regions?

The relationship between geographic location and the existence of natural endowments is even more tenuous in the twentieth century. There is nothing in the early historical geography of Detroit, Silicon Valley or Seattle that would foreshadow their emergence as world centers for car, computer or aircraft industries (Scott 1998, p. 64).

The answer lies beyond the production system generated by the Industrial Revolution where activity was, by necessity, located close to sources of materials and energy. From the beginning of the nineteenth century, small, vertically disintegrated workshops and factories began to accumulate around large urban areas that provided pools of labor. From the 1920s, increasing competition and scale economies led to the Fordist system of mass production and a significant transformation of the economic landscape. This development gave rise to massive industrial metropolitan areas around the globe, with large lead companies and a complex network of supplier firms.

The competitive edge of Fordist mass-production systems had waned by the 1980s, because of diseconomies resulting from congestion, excessive growth and the development of multi-regional and multi-national companies (Massey 1984). Production processes were split into independent stages and often scattered through different areas or countries with appropriate labor market conditions. Eventually this led to the de-industrialization and economic decline of many of the metropolitan areas that had grown out of the developmental thrust of the previous sixty years.

Since 1980, what is described as post-Fordist industrialization - or flexible specialization - has ignited a resurgence of industrial districts around the world in industries as diverse as fashion clothing, footwear, furniture, films and biotechnology. Piore and Sabel (1984) claim that the growth of consumer sophistication, along with volatile markets and shorter product life cycles, call for more flexibility in production. It is more difficult to meet consumer demand for differentiation and quality through mass production that is constrained by the rigidity of vertical integration and hierarchical control. Piore and Sabel argue that the re-emergence of Marshallian industrial districts, particularly in Italy but also elsewhere in the world, is a direct response to the new demands of the market and the need to co-operate within vertically disintegrated clusters of flexible but specialized firms.

Agglomeration and Externalities

Economies of Scale

Underlying the discussion of clusters is the orthodox economic analysis of why concentrations of industries or economic activity occur. This begins with the theory of economies of scale, internal to the producing firm (Harrison 1991; Feser 1997). Unit costs of production are presumed to fall as the scale of the production facility increases (up to a certain point). That is, economies of scale, or increasing returns, occur when the increase in scale of a plant generates a proportionally greater increase in output from the plant. Individual firms can experience economies of scale internally through growth of input-output ratios, increased division of labor and eventual vertical integration. The potential of internal economies of scale provides an explanation as to why firms might increase or concentrate production at one facility rather than produce at several smaller factories in different locations.

The efficiencies that are usually associated with large firms and internal economies of scale are also apparently available to smaller firms when they co-locate (Marshall 1910; Harrison 1991). However, the economies of scale are not internal, but *external* to the firm. An externality is any factor, occurrence or activity that lies outside the control of an individual firm but has some impact on the firm's internal production or performance.

Firms in the normal course of business internalize some externalities when they purchase, as inputs for their own production, the outputs of other firms. But beyond simple physical buyer-supplier transactions, there are potent externalities that arise from the economic space or co-location of firms that do not fit within the logic of the pricing system (Scott 1998). These externalities can take the form of information spillovers (that provide information to firms when they did not participate in its creation), labor pool advantages or infrastructure provision.

Marshallian Externalities

Marshall was perhaps the first to identify external economies - what he defined as "being dependent on the general development of the industry" (Marshall 1910, p. 266) - that provide benefits to individual firms from the growth of pools of common factors of production. According to Marshall there are four specific externalities that explain why, once an industry has chosen a locality for itself, it is likely to stay there. The first three have provided the basis for much of the recent discussion of this area, while the fourth has been largely ignored. However, it is an integral part of this discussion and will be examined more fully.

Firstly, because information flows more easily over short distances, an industrial center generates what the modern literature calls technological spillovers. Marshall claimed that proximity allowed the observance, adoption and adaptation of new techniques or innovations by other individuals and firms. "The mysteries of the trade become no mysteries; but as it were in the air, and children learn many of them unconsciously. ...if one man starts a new idea, it is taken up by others and combined with suggestions of their own; and thus it becomes the source of new ideas" (Marshall 1910, p. 271).

Secondly, a concentrated industry can support more intermediate or localized suppliers, which in turn makes the industry more efficient, reinforcing the concentration. Marshall identified that subsidiary trades would develop around clusters of firms providing inputs and opportunities for outputs through specialization. Firms were likely to devote themselves to one small branch of the process of production and contract their service to a wide number of other firms allowing economic use of expensive technical machinery (Marshall 1910).

The third factor Marshall cites is a local market for special skill - what has since been dubbed a labor pool - "...a localized industry gains a great advantage from the fact that it offers a constant market for skill" (Marshall 1910, p. 271). Employers were considered likely to opt for locations where they could find a good choice of skilled workers, while those seeking employment were likely to locate where there were many employers who needed their particular skills. Marshall also refers to an interaction between social and economic forces in discussing this concept of a labor pool. He suggests there are often strong social relationships between the employer and the employed and the availability of a pool of labor (or conversely, other employment opportunities) prevents a breakdown of this important social relationship.

Marshall makes an important distinction between industries that require massive material and skills that can be easily acquired and industries that require less massive material but relies on skills that can not be quickly acquired. It is these industries which would be "loth (sic) to quit a good market for its labor" because they acquire "industrial atmospheres" which yield great advantages to manufacturers (Marshall 1919, p. 284). And it is this distinction that sets specialized industrial districts apart from cities that contain large industrial and trading activity of many kinds where "artisans ceased to completely dominate the town as of yore" (Marshall 1919, p. 286).

So far, the three factors outlined have centered on economy of *production*. The fourth factor Marshall considers is *market*-related. Marshall suggests that the convenience of the customer must also be considered. "He will go to the nearest shop for a trifling purchase; but for an important purchase he will take the trouble of visiting any part of the town where he knows that there are specially good shops for his purpose. Consequently, shops that deal in expensive and choice objects tend to congregate together; and those which supply ordinary domestic needs do not" (Marshall 1910, p. 273). This implies three things. First, that it is valuable to be part of a congregation so a firm can compete equally in the marketplace. Second, that being part of the congregation may enhance customers' perceptions of manufacturer credibility. And third, it implies the creation of customer value through reduced search costs. In effect, Marshall linked the concept of shared knowledge and information with marketing (Zaratiegui 1997). He expressly predicted increasing marketing activity by firms that would be "facilitated by association with others engaged in the same industry" (Marshall 1919, p. 511).

Many producers sharing access enhance these external factors. And because capital and labor will migrate to such areas to take advantage of the larger markets for their services, externalities are more likely to achieve some sort of critical mass and come to include a wider specialization. The enhanced supply of external factors and the greater specialization present will tend (according to Marshall) to drive down factor prices or raise productivity. That eventuality is the external benefit to the firm - each firm's cost of production will be lower in the presence of externalities such as specialized pools of labor, infrastructure, capital and knowledge. This is because each firm does not have to create these same factors for and by itself as it would if located apart from other firms.

Urbanization and Localization

Hoover (1937 pp. 90-91), writing after Marshall, drew a distinction between urbanization and localization, isolating these two concepts from economies due simply to scale of plant. Losch (1954) and Isard (1956) also discussed this distinction. Hoover classified agglomeration factors into three discreet areas - large-scale economies within a firm, localization economies where all firms in a single industry were situated in a single location and urbanization economies where all firms in all industries were situated in a single location.

Urbanization economies reflect externalities associated with the presence of firms from diverse industries. Larger, more populated areas are also more likely to house universities, research laboratories, trade associations and other information/knowledge generation institutions. Diversity of industry mix and close proximity generates benefits for everyone in the region and allows cross-fertilization of industry practices from one industry to another. It also offers a work force with a broader skill-base, which may be advantageous to emerging technologies (Harrison 1991). This local diversity has led to considerable work on urban growth theories based on diffusion of technical information spillovers, supportive public and private services, distribution networks and supply arrangements within the cluster or district (e.g., Saxenian 1994; Scott 1986, 1996, 1998; Harrison 1991). This almost Marshallian idea of collective services is common to industrial parks, shopping malls, and warehousing districts where potential benefits are attributable to the realization of scale economies in service provision.

Localization economies, on the other hand, are externalities that arise from firms in the same industry being located in one geographic place. These externalities may be as simple as the possibility of economies of scale in production and availability of shared inputs. There may also be knowledge spillovers, either informally or through backward and forward linkages such as subcontracting or technology agreements (Saxenian 1994) Since these firms face similar problems and use similar technologies, they are likely to closely observe each other's activities.

Pecuniary and Technological Externalities

Marshall's writing about externalities was later re-interpreted by Scitovsky (1963). Scitovsky suggested that there were other kinds of externalities that arose when certain firms invested in new plant and equipment and where that new plant actually enhanced the profitability of other firms' existing operations - that is, they gained benefit without incurring cost. Scitovsky labeled that phenomenon *pecuniary* externalities, referring to the dynamic impact of one firm's new investments on the possibilities for enhanced profitability of, and therefore expansion by, other firms (Harrison 1991). These differed from what Scitovsky called *technological externalities* such as spillovers that come from non-market interactions.

Pecuniary externalities can be demonstrated on a practical level if two firms are considered, where the output of one is used as the input of the other. If the first factory, by investment or organizational change, begins to produce a cheaper or better quality output this presents an advantage to the firm using it as input. That is, at least some of the benefit of the new plant is passed on to another firm without cost to that firm. Marshall's externalities turn out to be a mix of technological and pecuniary externalities but the basic thrust of his argument is consistent - each type of externality may lead to the agglomeration of economic activities (Fujita and Thisse 1996).

Location Theory and Agglomeration

Location theory has a long intellectual history ranging from early classical formulations by Weber (1929) through the central-place constructs of Christaller (1933) and Losch (1954), to the "new" economic geography based on a historical-structural agenda that examines the interrelationship of transaction costs, externalities and location (Rabellotti 1995; Scott 1998). Much of the classical approach examines the effects of physical transportation costs on locational decision-making and behavior and attempts to provide a general geometric model of the economic landscape.

In the first major examination of industrial location and agglomeration, Weber (1929), proposed three general location factors - transportation cost differentials, labor cost differentials and economies of scale (agglomeration economies). The first two determined where industry might be distributed between regions, while the third tended to influence the concentration of industries within a region. Weber's analysis concentrated on achieving minimum transportation costs that, in a simple resource versus market scenario would require the firm to locate either near the resource or near the market. By introducing labor cost differentials and economies of scale, cost-savings could be generated by the firm moving away from a location determined solely by input and product transportation considerations. But While Weber drew on the idea of externalities; he did not supplement the analysis of transport costs with an analysis of the firm's expenditure on information (Benko and Dunford 1991).

Criticism of the Weberian approach has centered on the narrow assumption of fixed prices for inputs and outputs, limited production sites and no cognizance of market structure. Losch (1954) was the first to relax these assumptions when he proposed a general equilibrium analysis for networks of producers and consumers, allowing for variations in demand and cost parameters. His central-place theory (following from the work of Christaller) discussed how a trade-off between economies of scale and transportation costs leads producers to cluster together into a hierarchy of cities serving nested, hexagonal market areas.

Later theorists have focused more on the relationship between the firm and the market, arguing that the determination of internal versus external division of labor is more important than simple economies of scale in explaining locational agglomeration. For example, Stigler (1951) suggested that changes in market demand influenced division of labor within and between firms.

Williamson (1985) explained division of labor and the vertical integration or disintegration of the firm in terms of transaction costs, and the explicit and implicit contracts govern interaction between firms and individuals. Emphasis remains on the transaction itself and opportunistic behavior by buyers and sellers (Uzzi 1997). Scott (1986) has drawn heavily on Coase (1937) and Williamson (1985) for his agglomeration theory, which is based on the notion of flexible specialization. The need to be flexible encourages vertical disintegration that in turn encourages clustering with key suppliers and service providers to reduce the spatial costs of external transactions. This, in turn, encourages further vertical disintegration.

Summary

The central tenet within these theoretical approaches is cost minimization (where particular local or social factors are seldom considered) and the necessary existence of a rational "economic man". These models usually predict a concentration of firms or related industries (where some firms' outputs are used as a resource for others) based on the existence of perfect knowledge, rational decision-making and the motive of profit. In summarizing the contribution of these economics-based concepts to the theory of location, Krugman states:

> There are costs to transactions in space; there are economies of scale in production. These two facts are the key... Because of economies of scale, producers have an incentive to concentrate production of each good or service in a limited number of locations. Because of the costs of transacting across distance, the preferred locations for each individual producer are those where demand is large or supply of inputs is particularly convenient – which in general are the locations chosen by other producers. Thus concentrations of industry, once established, tend to be self-sustaining; this applies both to the localization of individual industries and to such grand agglomerations as the Boston-Washington corridor (Krugman 1991, p. 98).

While Krugman's comment about the self-sustainability of clusters may be accurate, issue can be taken with the logic of his other claims. At best they represent only a partial answer to why firms cluster in space. As Baptista suggests, "...transport costs are not the sole determinant of a firm's location decision and a fuller analysis must examine the intrinsic characteristics of each location" (1998, p. 21). Certainly, greater efficiencies in the international market for technology and management expertise mean the concept of transaction costs is now seen as sometimes only a small cost among many other costs and benefits (Contractor 1990).

Going beyond this, there is criticism of the absence of social awareness in explanations of economic or locational behavior, a point not lost on Marshall (1910, p. 272). A decisive response to this economic approach comes from Pred (1969) who points to the underlying optimum-seeking philosophy of the economic location agglomeration theory tradition – minimization of cost (Weber 1929; Hoover 1948; Williamson 1985), or maximization of profit and maximization of space utility (Losch 1954; Isard 1956). Pred points out that the basic unit of action has been consistently perceived as atomistic, capable of acting with complete rationality and possessing perfect or near-perfect knowledge on which to base decisions. But reality is quite different to theory.

In addition to criticism of the logical consistency of assumptions involved in the theories discussed above, Pred (1969) points to the perceived motives of "economic man" and the knowledge level and mental acumen attributed to him. He claims it is logically inconsistent to argue that one firm will base its actions on the actions of other firms, relying on outguessing them while, in turn, not being outguessed themselves. He also dismisses the assumption of perfect knowledge, raising the *bounded rationality* problem identified by Simon (1957) and March and Simon (1958). Knowledge or information must be obtained (through search or experience) rather than being given, thus variations in information availability (and cost) will have considerable impact on decision-making. Pred (1969, p. 7) concludes that "It is logically impossible for any set of agricultural, industrial, or central place establishments acting as economic man in circumstances of imperfect competition to simultaneously arrive at locationally optimal decisions." Even Krugman acknowledges that economic location theories, like central-place theory, can only be useful if an imperfect market structure is described (Krugman 1996).

"Neo-institutionalists" such as Williamson and Scott (1985) struggle with the twin problems of bounded rationality - the inability to know all possible options for action - and opportunism - the tendency of one agent to take advantage of another (Harrison 1991). The transaction cost approach ignores technological, informational and social inter-dependencies that can lead to internalization or externalization of activities. Part of their response is an attempt to socialize their transaction-based theory by institutionalizing trust with contracts. But, these contracts are simply a substitute for trust and not a set of social arrangements or ongoing relationships that might really cultivate trust. Easton and Araujo (1994, p. 75) add that "...exchange processes are embedded in the dense fabric of social relations and economic exchange is rarely able to rid itself of non-economic exchange baggage such as social exchange, kinship and friendship networks, altruism and gift giving and a host of other psychological and sociological elements not liable to be reduced to the standardized metric of money."

If the purely economic explanation for clustering is flawed, there must be another explanation that either extends the purely economic argument or replaces it. This is discussed in the next section.

Beyond Economics-based Location Theory: Trust, Social Networks and Inter-dependency

The notion that the behavior of buyers and sellers must be subject solely to the pursuit of self-interest by rational atomistic individuals is central to orthodox economic theory. Relationships associated with production and distribution are assumed to be untouched by sociological, cultural, anthropological and political considerations such as size, location and history of community, family and ethnic ties, the presence or legacy of attachments to guilds, or commitment to place.

In an immensely influential article published in 1985, Granovetter challenged this orthodox view and posited that economic action is embedded in structures of social relations in modern industrial society. He accused neo-classical economic theorists of providing an under-socialized or atomised-actor explanation for action and ignoring the importance of on-going structures of social relations. His thesis of social "embeddedness" stresses the role of concrete personal relations and structures (or "networks") of such relations to explain why and how one individual interacts with another. Past experience and a build-up of relational knowledge creates a certain expectation of trust and abstention from opportunism. This personal experience and knowledge can, when involving dense networks of actors, "generate clearly defined standards of behavior easily policed by the quick spread of information about instances of malfeasance" (Granovetter 1985, p. 492).

Drawing explicitly from Granovetter and earlier work in economic and structural sociology, Coleman (1990) developed the concept of social capital to describe the positive benefits of networks within business communities. Social capital consists of obligations and expectations, information channels and a set of norms and effective sanctions that constrain or encourage certain types of behavior. Close social networks and organizational arrangements that allow for multiple relations help social capital to develop. Putnam (1993) also utilizes the social capital concept claiming it facilitates co-ordination and cooperation within networks. Social capital is created when positive relationships are formed and it appreciates through repeated interaction and development of trust. While Putnam talks of civic engagement and complex and deep social ties, social capital can also be applied to a vastly different economic space like Silicon Valley where there is little or no history, family ties and structured community. The main networks of social capital in Silicon Valley are focused, productive interactions among social institutions and entities like Stanford University and the University of California, government agencies, venture capital firms and business networks (Cohen and Fields 1999).

A further theoretical development in this process of understanding clustered economic activity has been the fusion of new growth theory with agglomeration (Weber 1929; Hoover 1948), regional development (Krugman 1991a, 1991b) and innovation diffusion (Feldman 1994) theories. New growth theory identifies human capital as the engine of growth; where that growth is driven by the influence economic actors have on the productivity of each other (Lucas 1988; Martin 1999). The ways people interact determines the extent externalities and spillovers will advantage firms in proximity to each other. Lucas (1988) stresses that the economic mechanism at the heart of growth requires social interactions and external effects, which are mostly local in nature.

It is possible to link this aspect of new growth theory with the social capital theorists by thinking of the two as twin elements in explaining monetarily uncompensated information exchanged between firms (Feser and Sweeney 1998). The social capital concept provides the social structures that determine who is going to interact, while the human capital concept determines how they interact. Along with new growth theory, Granovetter's influence and that of social capital theorists such as Coleman, Putnam, and Bourdieu has been significant in cluster literature, particularly that related to industrial districts.

In the mid-to-late 1970s, interest turned towards Italy and specifically the Northeast-Center of the country, dubbed the "Third Italy" by scholars (Bagnasco 1977; Piore and Sabel 1984; Storper 1997). There, the existence of industrial districts made up of large numbers of interdependent, flexible yet specialist, small firms was hailed as proof of an "industrial divide" between post-war mass production and what was called *flexible specialization* (Piore and Sabel 1984). The success of this "Third Italy" has been attributed to the high level of collaboration among networks of small firms making economies of scale possible and the development of industrial districts of firms covering all phases of production to

"...collectively dominate markets and, through competition, spur innovation" (Rosenfeld 1992, p. 163).

The research conducted by Piore and Sabel (1984) paralleled that of Giacomo Becattini (1990) who was one of the major contemporary students of Marshall. Becattini had applied Marshall's concept to that found in the third Italy focusing on the economic basis (externalities linked to division of labor) and social environment supporting interaction between firms. The modern concept of industrial districts is a dynamic version of Marshall's industrial district, which advances the understanding of why firms might cluster together for more than just economic reasons.

There is general agreement that industrial districts are "geographically defined productive systems characterized by a large number of firms involved at various stages, and in various ways, in the production of a homogeneous product." (Pyke, Becattini and Sengenberger 1990, p. 2) These districts display hallmarks of adaptability and innovation via a flexible workforce and production network. Organization and leadership of these districts does not come from large, vertically integrated companies. Rather it comes from small, often family-owned firms grouped together by their particular specialization and stage of production or service. These small firms operate a kind of inter-dependency, which is more than the aggregate of productive units.

Some authors claim that a characteristic of the ideal or canonical industrial district is that it should be conceived as a social and economic whole (e.g., Bellandi 1989; Becattini 1990; Brusco 1990). The success of districts lies not just with economic factors, but also with broader social networks and inter-relationships as well. Rabellotti (1995) characterizes industrial districts as a spatially concentrated cluster of sectorally specialized firms, with strong forward and backward linkages, cultural and social commonality linking economic agents and creating a behavioral code, within a network of public and private supporting institutions. The influences of cultural background, trust and co-operation are key to maintaining transactional or economic links.

However, while some researchers have tended to treat the social embeddedness of firms as a defining characteristic of industrial districts or clusters, some suggest its causes and consequences are contingent on circumstances which may be highly place specific, or dependent on a firm's particular position within a cluster. Staber (1998) draws a distinction between stable, dense clusters such as those found in the Third Italy and clusters where Darwinian competitive pressure sees regular replacement of cluster partners, such as in the textile district of Baden-Wurttemburg. Social embeddedness can be defended in the former example, but not in the latter. Uzzi (1997) suggests that actors may respond to situations in differing ways depending on their position in a cluster and the circumstances of a situation. It is also important to note, "measurement problems mean that theoretical predictions concerning the role of social embeddedness in sustaining co-operation and inducing innovation are not easily refutable" (Staber 1998, p. 717).

While emphasizing the mutually shared benefits of co-location to individual firms - such as access to a larger and more specialized labor pool and the realization of external economies of scale - standard location agglomeration theory nevertheless follows traditional economics. Local economies are described as collections of atomistic competitors, formally aware of each other only through an input-output relationship mediated by price or cost signals.

By contrast, industrial district theorists emphasize the inter-dependence of firms, flexible firm boundaries, co-operative competition and the importance of trust - aspects of interaction, which lie outside the conception of independent arms-length transactional firms or vertically integrated corporations. This is the industrial district theorists' explanation for dynamic clusters - trust between actors, built up through repeated interaction that is likely to be facilitated through personal contact, which in turn is enhanced by geographical proximity.

The industrial district concept corresponds, to some degree, to the idea of *milieu* discussed by Aydalot and Keeble (1988) and Camagni (1991). The milieu is essentially a context for innovation and development that empowers and guides firms within its system of regional institutions, rules, and practices.

These concepts do not negate the importance of transactional systems or the economic logic of production to industrial organization and the concept of clustering. What they do suggest is that any economic or transactional system, where firms operate in a network situation, is necessarily embedded in historically determinate social conditions that are enhanced by spatial proximity. In turn, the relationship between firms determines the nature of the cluster, its development and performance.

History – Accident, Lock-in and Positive Feedback

A recurring theme in the study of location is that regional development is characterized by "path dependence" where historical accidents (chance locational events) can have long-run cumulative consequences. The basic competitive model of economic equilibrium implies inevitability about location decisions due to resource and factor endowments, and transportation costs. But uncertainty exists in industrial location and agglomeration, which means several alternative equilibriums are possible (Martin 1999). Which particular spatial pattern emerges will depend on history. The initial catalyst for a cluster may be an accident of history, but once it is established, it may become locked in through processes of cumulative causation based on increasing returns. "Thus 'irrational' economic decisions can generate sub optimal but equilibrium distribution" (Martin 1999, p. 70). Therefore, it can be argued that the establishment of early firms at a particular location is as much a matter of historical accident as anything else. The subsequent attraction of other firms depends on the existence of increasing returns, in the form of economies of scale and positive externalities.

The world's most examined cluster, Silicon Valley, was started by a mix of serendipitous events and watershed changes. Frederick Terman's desire to settle in California because of its climate meant he pursued an applied electrical engineering research and business start-up program as Stanford's vice-president rather than at a university on the East Coast. Military demands from the Korean War provided a stimulus to the nascent electronics industry (Saxenian 1990). Similarly, the United States call-center hub based in Omaha, Nebraska is a direct result of the US armed forces locating their strategic command center there. This required the installation of a huge communications infrastructure and capacity, which provided the opportunity for firms to establish national call-centers.

Clusters of firms can also originate from a single, successful start-up or parent firm. Thirty-one semiconductor firms were started in Silicon Valley during the 1960s and a majority could trace their origins back to one company (Saxenian 1994). The concept of lead firms, as the focal point in cluster and network development is common within the literature (e.g., Arthur 1990; Axelsson and Easton 1992; Humphrey and Schmitz 1996; Porter 1998a, 1998b; Scott 1998).

Once the initial location is determined (through historical conditions or accident, resource endowment or unique market demand) there are compelling reasons for firms to continue to locate near similar firms. As the first firms become successful, suppliers, workers and investors become available. This lowers the cost of entry for subsequent firms making the area relatively more attractive than other areas (Pouder and St. John 1996). If the net benefit of externalities increases with the number of firms in the region, positive feedback to other firms will see a predominant share of an industry cluster in a single region or location. (This holds up to a point where congestion and other negative externalities begin to adversely impact on firms.) Far from there being any intrinsic locational advantage, it is the attraction of subsequent firms that consolidates the location as an industry cluster (Storper 1997).

Arthur (1990) argues that the first firms to enter an industry choose their location either by chance or to maximize individual benefits (in line with economic theory discussed above). If benefits increase by locating near other similar firms then, over time, the industry becomes locked in to that location. New entrants then choose their location based on the positive feedback created by existing firms and they reinforce the geographic concentration of the particular industry.

Clusters, R&D, Learning and Innovation

A central tenet of geographical clustering is the concept of knowledge externality or spillover. Economic growth is driven by technological change (Romer 1990). Technological change is far from a random process as considerable conscious effort and investment drives research guided by market forces (Grossman and Helpman 1992). Castells (1989) contends that a cluster has the potential to become a milieu of innovation when certain fundamental elements of production converge. He argues that a cluster becomes a reservoir of innovative technological information through the activities of higher education institutions, and government or corporate sponsored research and development. This creates a pool of technical labor and attracts venture capitalists willing to risk capital on new ventures.

While research and the knowledge derived from it may originate with one firm, as soon as it is used in a productive way, it can be appropriated by other firms, at least in part (Arrow 1962). Patents may ascribe property rights to knowledge or innovation to an individual firm, but they also ensure the disclosure of that knowledge to the market and this impacts on the research activities of other firms. This might result in firms spending less on research, though firms may also have an incentive to still invest in research so their ability to identify and explore knowledge generated by other firms is maintained (Cohen and Levinthal 1989).

Considerable empirical evidence exists to support the conclusion that substantial spillovers are found between firms and industries, which lead to productivity gains and innovation (Jaffe 1986; Bernstein 1989). There is also strong evidence to suggest that geographic proximity plays an important part in this through the co-location of university and corporate research facilities (Porter 1998). Government financed research helps reduce average costs to industry (Baptista 1998) and specialized business services that provide expertise on government regulations, product testing, market research and financial services also play a crucial role in the knowledge infrastructure that supports innovation (Saxenian 1994). An area with specialized resources for innovation, such as a university or other research institutes has a comparative advantage and, because knowledge is cumulative, this advantage is self-reinforcing and leads to clustering of innovative activity (Arthur 1990). Further empirical data confirms that two major sources of new high technology entrepreneurs are higher-education institutions and well-established industrial firms that attract new firms (Dahlstrand 1999). This may lead to a growing disparity between regions that already possess indigenous high technology activities and those that do not. However, there are a large number of research universities around the world but "there is a much smaller number of Silicon Valleys..." (Storper 1997, p. 16). This suggests that there are other important conditions that influence the development of high-technology clusters at least.

The literature appears to indicate that research activity results in positive externalities for firms within clusters. These externalities lead to productivity gains and cost reductions, especially among smaller firms (Acs and Feldman 1994). The literature also suggests that networks of related innovating firms found in successful clusters make an important contribution to innovative effort and output (Freeman 1991). These networks, in tandem with close user-producer relationships seem to distinguish successful clusters (Saxenian 1994; Nelson 1993). In some clusters, strong institutional support also plays an important part and social and cultural bonds made possible by proximity and frequent contact reinforce them (Debresson and Amesse 1991).

Integration between customers and suppliers also allows spillovers and feedback that stimulates innovation (Von Hippel 1988). In some cases users appear to be a better source of ideas to improve a product's technology than are the original producers of such technology (Baptista 1998). Moreover, firms within a cluster are often able to more clearly and rapidly discern new buyer needs (Porter 1998). Gertler (1995) suggests that proximity to demanding and technologically sophisticated customers represents a vital source of creative stimulus for producers who are more likely to be innovative when compelled to meet their customers' needs. He argues that a close and constructive relationship between users and producers reinforces development of innovation.

Innovation embodies an incremental, cumulative characteristic that cannot be solely attributed to the actions of individual entrepreneurs. Schumpeter (1939) posited that it was also dependent on technological and scientific knowledge trajectories. He observed that when one innovation had been successfully effected, the next wave of development was more likely to start in the same or neighboring field. Technological trajectories of a given industry often travel a parallel or complementary path to technologies in other industries. Thus, firms can depend on decisions made outside their borders by other firms in the technological space. These external economies create increasing returns for interdependent actors travelling along these pathways.

Building on the "economic spaces" work of Perroux (1950), Storper (1997) suggests there are technological inter-dependencies between firms that are non-tradable – knowledge or "common practice" spillovers that are not fully codifiable and which tie firms into networks with other firms. These ties can be formal exchanges or untraded inter-dependencies such as labor markets, public institutions and locally or nationally derived rules of action, customs, understandings and values. This concept links with the industrial district theories on embeddedness and social networks as it seeks to explain a process of *collective learning* by firms, whereby partly codified and partly tacit knowledge is interchanged and utilized in each of the participating firms (Maskell and Malmberg 1999). Codified knowledge (in the form of scientific and other forms of scripted or formal knowledge) is knowledge that can be reduced to symbols and language and thereby be transferred communicated or traded relatively easily (Von Hippel 1994). Tacit knowledge is specific knowledge that is embedded within a firm or geographical location and is not easily transferred beyond the context in which it is embedded (Dosi 1988).

Learning processes, which absorb information and generate and diffuse knowledge (of both sorts), are collective activities that form part of the background and experience of each firm (Amin and Wilkinson 1999). Shared social and cultural environment, common routines, norms and standards built on trust and co-operation underpin this collective learning process (Granovetter 1985; Nohria and Eccles 1992; Uzzi 1996; Kraatz 1998). As well, the existence of a mobile, highly skilled labor market, which diffuses tacit expertise and technological know-how, and the existence of a local specific technological resource base are key elements in collective learning of organizations (Camagni 1991; Keeble et al 1999; Longhi 1999). Empirical work suggests that at a local level, where firms share similar values, backgrounds and understandings of technical or commercial problems, an interchange of tacit information does take place (Von Hippel 1988; Maskell and Malmberg 1999).

The apparently cumulative nature of innovation is also relevant to the cluster concept. Knowledge spillovers or externalities are an important source of innovative output. The origins of these spillovers or knowledge inputs make up the technological infrastructure that supports innovation (Feldman 1994). As this infrastructure is place-specific, innovative activity tends to be geographically concentrated. It is interesting to note that as production has become more globalized, corporate research facilities have become more spatially concentrated, often located near a company's home base (Patel 1995).

While information can be easily transmitted across great distances, translating it into useable knowledge requires shared language and common frames of reference – a common culture (Harrison 1991). Feldman (1994) argues that innovation is an interactive process facilitated by face-to-face contact. Where technology is complex or subject to rapid change, proximity can be important for both users and producers. Personal communication within groups of individuals sharing common interests is considered to be a vital input to creativity (as distinct from productivity) and face-to-face contact is most effective for rapid product development (Fujita and Thisse 1996).

While the literature reviewed above indicates a clear link between clusters, research and development, learning and innovation, it does not confirm that a cluster will necessarily become a dynamic center for innovation or a "hotspot" of fast-growing innovative activity (Pouder and St John 1996). In fact, these kind of *dynamic* clusters arise infrequently, even when academic institutions, corporate research and development and innovative firms cluster (Meyer 1995). The key distinction between a cluster of firms where innovation may occur, and a cluster that becomes an innovative hotspot may be the existence of competition within the cluster. Competition is largely a function of the similarity in resource requirements among firms. As more and more firms join the cluster and compete for similar resources (human, financial and technological) industry-level innovation is intensified (Pouder and St. John 1996).

Clusters, Competition and Competitive Advantage

Along with Krugman, Porter was probably one of the first economists to regard geography as a central issue in the analysis of markets and competition. His book, *Competitive Advantage of Nations*, is one of the most cited works on the subject of clusters. Porter developed a framework to analyze the competitive advantage of different national economies involving a diamond of four components: factor conditions; demand conditions; firm strategy and rivalry; and supporting industries.

Porter argued that domestic rivalry and geographic concentration – clustering – are responsible for the dynamics of the system. Competition between firms clustered together stimulates investment in infrastructure, knowledge and skilled labor leading to a continual upgrading of these factors and eventual competitive advantage for the region (Porter 1990, 1998).

Rivalry and geographic concentration also have a favorable impact on local demand and the development of related or supporting industry. Through vertical and horizontal relationships between firms, specialized suppliers and users develop, reinforcing the cluster and its externalities. Thus strong competition between local firms leads to a competitive edge for the cluster. Local rivalry becomes a motivating factor, with peer pressure amplifying competitive pressure.

Porter sees clustering as crucial for organizational improvement and technological innovation. The interchange of information and knowledge between universities and other research centers and between customers and suppliers is facilitated by concentration. Specific knowledge concentrated in one area can act as a pull on labor and other resources such as capital. He also observes that the development of communications and reduction in transport costs do not negate locational advantages. In fact, they may heighten them as firms with a competitive advantage in one region or cluster can penetrate new markets more easily. The home base becomes more important in the face of globalization. Enright (1998) identifies home-based multi-nationals with a distinct center of gravity for their management and critical activities. He points out that even as competition and economic activity globalize, competitive advantage can be localized and that geographic sources of competitive advantage will become more, not less, important. Storper (1992) concludes that the clustering phenomenon places a fundamental limit on the process of globalization.

Porter provides an eloquent and persuasive case for the importance of clusters to national competitive advantage stating that they constitute a central influence on competition. The core of this influence is in productivity and the business environment that stimulates productivity growth. Clusters are seen as a manifestation of the interaction between Porter's four facets, which supports innovation, new business formation and industry expansion. But competitiveness is a result of clustered activity not a cause and Porter adds little new to the discussion on what causes clusters to occur or how to stimulate them. He merely articulates that a region or country well endowed with industrial clusters will experience some form of competitive advantage. Indeed, by ignoring cultural and historical factors, Porter's discussion of clusters and competitive advantage can be criticized as incomplete (O'Shaughnessy 1996).

Negative Externalities

Although the focus of this chapter has been on the positive externalities of clusters, there are negative externalities that must also be considered. Up to a certain point, the attractions of locating in a cluster may be compelling but the benefits can, eventually, be outweighed by negative conditions (Baptista 1998). Traditionally, the main concern regarding clusters is the impact of congestion and increased competition on firm costs (rents, labor and inputs) and subsequent performance (Swann and Preveza 1996). But there are also negative externalities that relate to labor, innovation, and the effective operation of network relationships within the cluster (see Table 1.1).

Table 1.1   Negative Externalities

Market related	Production related
• Congestion	• Congestion
• Increased output competition	• Increased input competition
• Loss of informational advantage	• Increased labor costs
• Groupthink	• Increased real estate costs
	• Loss of technological advantage
	• Groupthink

Demand for space in a particular locality can be responsible for driving up area rentals, which may impact on firm profitability. Space demand may also make it impossible to locate within the immediate cluster area. Increased competition on the supply side is likely to impact on availability of inputs and drive prices for inputs up as demand places pressure on input suppliers.

Both congestion and increased competition can impact on labor (Forester 1980) as demand for certain skills exceed supply and result in higher labor costs for firms. "Poaching" of trained staff can be a major problem in clusters where there is a shortage of qualified workers. Poaching enables a firm to save on productivity costs (little or no training down time for new staff) and there is minimal risk of retaliation. In some clusters poaching is a tacitly accepted rule of the local community (Paniccia 1998, p. 689). This practice can result in increasing the bargaining power of some workers, which ultimately drives up labor costs.

There is also a risk of losing an innovative or technological lead to other firms within a cluster. It is accepted that technological spillover occurs more rapidly within a close geographical area (Feldman 1994) and therefore there is always the possibility that research and development funded by one firm, may be used by another firm more effectively. While firms within a cluster usually hold a collective vision for the cluster, there is a danger in that vision becoming dominant and excluding alternate routes of development. It is possible for a cluster of firms to become locked in to what they have done well up to the present and to ignore market trends or new developments occurring outside the cluster's information sphere (Saxenian 1994; Porter 1998a). This problem is highlighted by the social capital literature, which suggests membership of a cluster could demand conformity and stifle creativity or entrepreneurship (Portes and Landolt 1996). It can also lead to a loss of objectivity where firms may try and keep networks together, or avoid change, at the expense of sound business practice (Locke 1999). Putting strong emphasis on personal relationships can lead to political activities where who you know and not what you know determine management responses to situations. Porter describes this situation as "groupthink" and cites it as a possible reason for the decline of a cluster (1998, p. 244).

The social capital literature suggests other problems, which may be associated with cluster networks. Strong ties between existing members of a cluster may be used to exclude newcomers or outsiders. This could be a barrier to start-up firms who are unable to access important resources controlled by the cluster network. Cluster membership may also reinforce poor management practices where they are common within the group and they may limit the extent to which firms have the resources or inclination to search them out (Portes and Landolt 1996). This could impact on firms' ability to identify new suppliers or import new technologies. It also impacts on their ability to seek out new markets or customers.

Positive externalities are more likely to occur early in the cluster's life cycle when there are fewer member firms. Negative externalities are more likely as the cluster matures and becomes increasingly congested (Swann, et al 1998). This implies that as more members are added to a cluster, transaction costs between cluster members increase sharply, thereby limiting the extent of cluster strategies (North 1991). Pouder and St. John (1996) echo this point by suggesting that an expanding cluster places pressure on managers' ability to store and retrieve information about other cluster members, which may limit a firm's choices in selecting appropriate partners within the cluster. Hochman (1992) identifies a number of social diseconomies of scale associated with agglomeration that he believes account for much of the real cost of congestion within a cluster. These negative externalities include the impact of entrepreneurial failure, and the mismatch of education and skill levels to available employment opportunities. These externalities contribute to unemployment, alienation and associated social problems. Hochman believes size matters too, with there being more likelihood of negative externalities being associated with larger, more congested clusters.

Clusters, Industrial Districts and Networks

There is still a degree of semantic ambiguity surrounding the term "cluster". Beyond the definitional difficulties of the cluster concept lies confusion over the distinction between a cluster and a network, and between a cluster and industrial district. In drawing together the various literature threads above to explain the evolution, theoretical underpinning and benefits of the cluster concept, it has become clear that there is a considerable inter-relationship between these terms. It has also become clear that it is possible to differentiate between them and propose the existence of a structural continuum that effectively defines the concepts. In the section that follows, definitions of the three terms are provided and the distinctions between them are discussed. A model that posits networks, clusters and industrial districts lie on a continuum is then introduced.

Clusters and Networks

A cluster is a sectoral and geographic concentration of enterprises. Specialization and cooperation are not subsumed in such a definition because firms can exist in a particular locality without moving beyond atomistic behavior. That is, they can exist without displaying network activity. However, once such a concentration exists, externalities such as those discussed above are likely to arise. Clusters have no formal membership requirements, foster implicit cooperation and often have a collective vision. They are often characterized by size, economic or strategic importance, products and services, vertical connections and common inputs (Rosenfeld, 1995). Many writers (e.g., Paniccia 1998; Prevezer 1997; Harrison 1991) acknowledge that spatially distant networks of firms can achieve certain externalities but that geographic co-location and face-to-face interaction enhance and enrich these externalities.

At the risk of confusing the issue further, Feser and Sweeney (1998) describe networks as economic clusters that are made up of firms linked through input and output relationships – transactions. They then go on to define geographic clusters as economic clusters that co-locate. This echoes Czamanski's (1974) industrial complex concept where firms in a cluster (network) actually locate together. Geographic clusters, as Feser and Sweeney acknowledge, go well beyond simple input-output transactions and depend on more than buyer-supplier relationships.

Enright (1998) categorizes the cluster concept in a different form. He writes about cluster "dimensions" where the degree of geographic scope, density, breadth, depth, activity, growth potential, innovative capacity, governance structure, coordinating mechanisms and state of development determine where the cluster sits on any development continuum. Enright's categorization is useful for describing clusters, but it ignores the type of network relationship between firms located in the cluster that might explain whether the "dimensions" above exist or can develop and where a cluster sits in terms of static or dynamic development.

In contrast to clusters, networks are generally based on a group of firms with restricted membership and specific, often contractual, business objectives designed to result in mutual financial gain. The members of a network choose each other; they agree explicitly to cooperate in some way and to depend on each other to some extent. Networks develop readily within clusters, particularly where familiarity and trust have been built through multiple business transactions.

Networking of firms is not necessarily tied to being in the same locality and can still lead to collective efficiency, although externalities tend to be small. The industrial districts in Italy have inspired other countries like Denmark, Canada, Australia and New Zealand to develop programs that will not necessarily replicate the Italian cluster experience but perhaps foster co-operation within their own specific cultural parameters. In Denmark, for example, it was impossible to duplicate the industrial district concept because of the absence of inter-firm cooperation in that country's culture and the absence of high concentrations of like firms (Humphrey and Schmitz 1996; Rosenfeld 1996). The network initiative that eventuated there was designed to foster co-operation between firms irrespective of their location or membership of a cluster. The success of this program, and that of others around the world, has not been fully evaluated but various observers have pointed to increases in firms forming networks, improved competitiveness through networking and benefits from joint action (Humphrey and Schmitz 1996; Ffowcs-Williams 1997a, 1997b).

Porter brings together the concepts of clusters and networks by stating that "a cluster is a form of network that occurs within a geographic location, in which the proximity of firms and institutions ensures certain forms of commonality and increases the frequency and impact of interactions" (Porter 1998, p. 226). Clusters that are dynamic and functioning well have moved beyond simple hierarchical networks to become characterized by numerous repeated connections between individuals, firms and institutions that constantly shift and expand. Porter (1998) observes that the level and strength of networks within a cluster determine its dynamism and innovation.

Clusters and Industrial Districts

The type of industrial concentration represented by industrial districts appears to be an extension of the cluster concept – a special case of cluster that emerges when it develops more than specialization and division of labor between firms. Humphrey and Schmitz (1996) make a clear distinction between the two by suggesting that specialization and co-operation need not be subsumed into the definition of a cluster. They argue that once a cluster concentration exists, external economies are likely to arise, notably from the emergence of suppliers of raw materials and components, or the emergence of a pool of skilled labor. (This argument assumes that clusters do not consciously arise because of externalities but generate them once the cluster is formed.) Clusters favor the emergence of specialized services in marketing, technical, financial and accounting matters (Humphrey and Schmitz 1996). Humphrey and Schmitz argue that the emergence of implicit and explicit forms of collaboration (network relationships) among local economic agents that enhance local production and, sometimes, innovation capability, and the emergence of strong sectoral associations distinguish industrial districts from clusters.

The key development in defining clusters lies in examining the nature of relationships between cluster members and the degree of networking that exists within the cluster (Humphrey and Schmitz 1996). Clusters are about networks and relationships. At the simplest level they consist of dyadic relationships. At a more advanced level, clusters are about nets of relationships, strengthened by geographic proximity. The degree of networking between cluster members determines a cluster's structure and distinguishes where a cluster sits on a continuum that extends from atomistic individual firms through to the industrial district model of complex historically and socially embedded relationships. Thus, we suggest that Porter's (1998, p. 197) original definition of a cluster should be elaborated to include delineation of cluster strength (dynamism) and structure:

"Clusters are geographic concentrations of interconnected companies, specialized suppliers, service providers, firms in related industries, and associated institutions (for example universities, standards agencies and trade organizations) in particular fields that compete but also co-operate." *The degree, or strength, of network relationships that exist between cluster members determines a cluster's structure, dynamism and benefits to member firms.* (Sentence in italics added by authors.)

Active and Passive Externalities: The Key to Distinguishing Networks, Clusters and Industrial Districts

Discussion of externalities has largely centered on describing the types of externalities that arise from geographical co-location. Hoover (1937), for example, distinguished their origins from urbanization or localization, and Scitovsky (1963) distinguished them as either pecuniary or technological. We assent that externalities can also be categorized in terms of *how* they arise.

Most externalities occur as a result of firms locating together, without any conscious effort on the part of individual firms. In fact, this is part of the definition of externalities – they occur outside the firm and provide positive benefits that have not been directly sought. So the traditional externalities of skilled labor pools, technological spillover and specialized inputs can be described as *passive* externalities – externalities that occur outside a firm's sphere of influence.

In contrast to these passive externalities, it is possible to think of externalities that arise directly through firm action. These are externalities that can only occur because firms are located in a cluster and these firms within the cluster actively work together in networks to progress an opportunity or situation. Examples of these *active* externalities might be joint sourcing of materials or other related joint-production activities, proactive implementation of infrastructure for developing clusters, or joint research and development. These active externalities result from the existence of familiarity and trust developed through experiencing passive externalities like input-output multipliers and the social networks that evolve around growing clusters.

As discussed earlier in this chapter, geographical co-location can range on a continuum from simple urban agglomeration of atomistic firms through to the intensive economic and social concept of an Italian industrial district. And at all stages there are degrees of network relationships that bind firms together moving from simple input-output transactional relationships to more involved networks embedded in some kind of social and historical environment. This is depicted in Figure 1.1. Applying this distinction, the inception and development of clusters can be traced by the degree of networking and dynamism that exists within the cluster. Inception appears to be a mix of consideration and chance, economic and social forces. Historical accident, resource endowment, existing infrastructure, social and political environment, economic factors and transaction cost minimization are all possible pre-conditions for cluster inception.

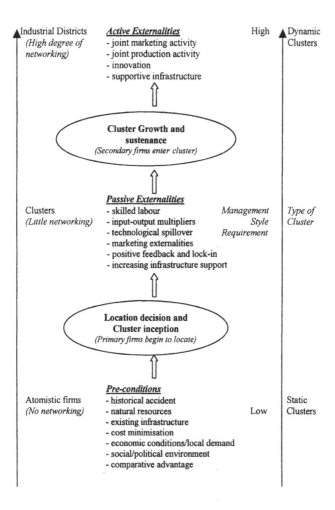

Figure 1.1   A Cluster Continuum Model

Once the cluster has begun to form, passive externalities reinforce and sustain the cluster, providing the conditions for it to be driven to a more dynamic phase depending on development of appropriate networks within the cluster. The externalities arising from this more dynamic cluster (based on trust and social inter-relationships) are active externalities, including those related to innovation, marketing and real competitive advantage for the cluster. This conceptualization has two immediate implications. First is that management style at the firm level must change as the sophistication of the cluster increases. The ability to maximize network opportunities, and to take advantage of active externalities, will rely on different management skills to those required at an earlier, production oriented stage. Second, there is an implication for economic development policy. The distinction between active and passive externalities might suggest that support structures and resources should be targeted at encouraging active externalities rather than passive, as these occur without direct intervention.

There is an identification and co-ordination role as well. Some form of cluster development agency (whether organized by the cluster alone or as a partnership between government and the cluster) may be required to identify specific firm needs within the cluster and co-ordinate action to satisfy those needs. But it is essential that assistance be rendered to firms as a part of the cluster, not just as individual firms. This collective approach is not only likely to be more cost-effective but it also may facilitate collective learning and reinforce the cluster concept.

Conclusion

The literature reviewed in this chapter reveals a rich vein of material from many different disciplines that seeks to explain the existence of industrial clusters, how and why they form and the impact they have on firms located within them. Theories of location decision and agglomeration range from purely economics-based through organizational to socio-historical models. There is broad agreement between researchers that external economies of scale are derived from co-location. Similarly, there is consistency on the necessary pre-conditions for clusters to form – historical antecedents or accident, resource endowment, economic or social conditions can all contribute to the decision for firms to locate in a particular area and create a cluster. It appears that to understand this phenomenon, one must combine wholesale locational agglomeration with specific kinds of social and political processes that shore up regional productive and competitive capabilities. Many over-lapping sub-systems (social divisions of labor, technologies, know-how, reputation effects, employment practices) all develop and grow in mutual interaction with one another creating competitive powers, as a whole, greater than the sum of the individual powers within each firm. And, perhaps, the historically important locational advantage of raw natural endowments has now been replaced by historically accumulated social and political structures instead.

An examination of the externalities that accrue from clusters reveals that these can be distinguished in terms of their active or passive nature. The traditional externalities cited (specialized labor pool, technological spillovers and intermediate inputs) are all passive externalities that occur upon co-location regardless of a firm's subsequent actions. But there are other externalities that result from co-location that can be defined as active externalities because firms within the cluster must actively seek out these externalities. Opportunities to engage in joint research, joint sourcing, joint production and proactive implementation of infrastructure for developing clusters exist within a cluster but are not realized until a firm actively pursues them with other firms. It is this distinction that enhances previous efforts to define clusters and provides a means to measure the dynamism or stage of development of a cluster. The existence of active or passive externalities and their relationship to a cluster's stage of development has significant implications for firms within the cluster, and government policy on economic development.

References

Acs, Z. and Feldman, M. (1994), "R&D Spillovers and Recipient Firm Size", *Review of Economics and Statistics*, vol. 76, pp. 336-340.

Amin, A. and Wilkinson, F. (1999), "Learning, Proximity and Industrial Performance: An Introduction", *Cambridge Journal of Economics*, vol. 23, no. 2, pp. 121-125.

Arrow, K. (1962), "The Economic Implications of Learning by Doing", *Review of Economic Studies*, vol. 29, pp. 155-173.

Arthur, W.B. (1990), "Silicon Valley Locational Clusters: Do Increasing Returns Imply Monopoly?" *Mathematical Social Sciences*, vol. 19, pp. 235-251.

Axelsson, B. and Easton, G. (1992), *Industrial Networks – A New View of Reality*, Routledge, London.

Aydalot, P., and Keeble, D. (eds), (1988) *High Technology Industries and Innovative Environments: The European Experience*, Routledge, London.

Bagnasco, A. (1977), *Tre Italie: La Problematica Territoriale Dello Sviluppo Italiano*, Il Mulino, Bologna.

Baptista, R. (1998), "Clusters, Innovation, and Growth: A Survey of the Literature", *The Dynamics of Industrial Clustering – International Comparisons in Computing and Biotechnology*, Swann, G.M. Peter, Prevezer, Martha, Stout, David, (eds) Oxford University Press, Oxford.

Becattini, G. (1990), "The Marshallian Industrial Districts as a Socio-economic Notion" In F. Pyke, G, Becattini et al (eds) *Industrial Districts and Inter-firm Co-operation in Italy*, International Institute for Labor Studies, ILO, Geneva, pp. 37-51.

Bellandi, M. (1989), "The Role of Small Firms in the Development of Italian Manufacturing Industry", in Goodman E, Bamford J. and Saynor P. (eds.) *Small Firms and Industrial Districts in Italy*, Routledge, London.

Benko, G. and Dunford, M. (eds) (1991), *"Industrial Change and Regional Development"*, Belhaven Press, London.

Bernstein, J.I. (1989), "The Structure of Canadian Inter-industry R&D Spillovers and the Rates of Return to R&D", *Journal of Industrial Economics*, vol. 37, pp. 315-328.

Bourdieu, P. (1986), "The Forms of Capital", pp. 241-258 in *Handbook of Theory and Research for the Sociology of Education*, John Richardson (ed.), Greenwood Press, New York.

Brusco, S. (1990), "The Idea of the Industrial District: Its Genesis", *Industrial Districts and Inter-firm Co-operation in Italy*, Pyke, F., Becattini, G. and Sengenberger, W. (eds), International Institute for Labour Studies, Geneva.

Camagni, R. (ed.) (1991), *Innovation Networks: Spatial Perspectives*, Belhaven Press, London.

Castells, M. (1989), *The Informational City: Information Technology, Economic Restructuring, and the Urban-Regional Process*, Basil Blackwell Ltd, Oxford.

Christaller, W. (1933), *Central Places in Southern Germany*, translated by C.W. Baskin (1966), Prentice-Hall, Englewood.

Coase, R.H. (1937), "The Nature of the Firm", *Economica*, vol. 4, pp. 386-405

Cohen, S. and Fields, G. (1999), "Social Capital and Capital Gains in Silicon Valley", *California Management Review*, vol. 41, no. 2, pp. 108-121.

Cohen, W.M. and Levinthal, D.A. (1989), "Innovation and Learning: The Two Faces of R&D", *Economic Journal*, vol. 99, pp. 569-596.

Coleman, J. (1990), *Foundations of Social Theory*, The Belknap Press, Cambridge, MA.

Contractor, F.J. (1990), "Contractual and Cooperative Forms of International Business: Towards a Unified Theory of Modal Choice", *Management International Review*, vol. 30, pp. 31-54.

Czamanski, S. (1974), *Study of Clustering of Industries*, Institute of Public Affairs, Halifax.

Dahlstrand, A.L. (1999), "Technology-based SMEs in the Goteborg Region: Their Origin and Interaction with Universities and Large Firms", *Regional Studies*, vol. 33, No 4, pp. 379-389.

Debresson, C. and Amesse, F. (1991), "Networks of Innovators: A Review and an Introduction to the Issue", *Research Policy*, vol. 20, pp.363-380.

Dosi, G. (1988), "Institutions and Markets in a dynamic world", *The Manchester School of Economics and Social Studies*, vol. 61, no. 2, pp. 119-146.

Easton, G. and Araujo, L. (1994), "Market Exchange, Social Structures and Time", *European Journal of Marketing*, vol. 28, no. 3, pp. 72-84.

Enright, M. (1998), *The Globalisation of Competition and the Localisation of Competitive Advantage: Policies Toward Regional Clustering*, Paper presented at the Workshop on Globalisation of Multinational Enterprise Activity and Economic Development, University of Strathclyde, May.

Feldman, M.P. (1994), *The Geography of Innovation*, Kluwer Academic Publishers, Dordrecht.

Feser, E.J. (1997), *The Influence of Business Externalities and Spillovers on Manufacturing Performance*, Unpublished Ph.D. Thesis, University of North Carolina.

Ffowcs Williams, I. (1997a), "Local Clusters and Local Export Growth", *New Zealand Strategic Management*, Summer 1997, 24 – 29.

Ffowcs Williams, I. (1997b), "Stimulating Local Clusters", A paper presented at the World Bank Workshop for Practitioners in Cluster Formation, Chihuahua, Mexico.

Forester, T. (ed.) (1980), *The Microelectronics Revolution*, Basil Blackwell, Oxford.

Freeman, C. (1991), "Networks of Innovators: A Synthesis of Research Issues", *Research Policy*, vol. 20, pp. 499-514.

Fujita, M. and Thisse, J. (1996), "Economics of Agglomeration", *Journal of the Japanese and International Economies*, vol. 10, pp. 339-378.

Gertler, M.S. (1995) "Being There: Proximity, Organization, and Culture in the Development and Adoption of Advanced Manufacturing Technologies", *Economic Geography*, vol. 72, pp. 1-26.

Granovetter, M. (1985), "Economic Action and Social Structure: The Problem of Embeddedness", *American Journal of Sociology*, vol. 91, no. 3, pp. 481-510.

Grossman, G., and Helpman, E. (1992), *Innovation and Growth in the Global Economy*, MIT Press, Cambridge, MA.

Harrison, B. (1991), "Industrial Districts: Old Wine in New Bottles?" *Regional Studies*, vol. 26, no. 5, pp.469-483.

Hochman, H.M. (1992), "New York and Pittsburgh: Contrasts in Community", *Urban Studies*, vol. 29, no. 2, pp. 237-250.

Hoover, E.M. (1937), *Location Theory and the Shoe and Leather Industries*, Harvard University Press, Cambridge, MA.

Hoover, E.M. (1948), *The Location of Economic Activity*. McGraw-Hill, New York.

Humphrey, J and Schmitz, H. (1996), "The Triple C Approach to Local Industrial Policy", *World Development*, vol. 24, no. 12, pp. 1859-1877.

Isard, W. (1956), *Location and Space Economy*, Wiley and Sons, New York.

Jaffe, A.B. (1986), "Technological Opportunity and Spillovers of R&D: Evidence from Firms" Patents, Profits and Market Value", *American Economic Review*, vol. 76, no. 5, pp. 984-1001.

Keeble, D., Lawson, C., Moore, B. and Wilkinson, F. (1999), "Collective Learning Processes, Networking and "Institutional Thickness"" in the Cambridge Region, *Regional Studies*, vol. 33, No 4, pp. 319-332.

Kraatz, M.S. (1998), "Learning by Association? Interorganizational Networks and Adaptation to Environmental Change", *Academy of Management Journal*, vol. 41, pp. 621-643.

Krugman, P. (1991a), *Geography and Trade*, MIT Press, Cambridge, Massachusetts.

Krugman, P. (1991b), "Increasing Returns and Economic Geography", *Journal of Political Economy*, vol. 99, no. 3, pp. 483-499.

Krugman, P. (1996), *Development, Geography and Economic Theory*, MIT Press, Cambridge Massachusetts.

Locke, E.A. (1999), "Some Reservations About Social Capital", *Academy of Management Review*, vol. 24, no. 1, pp. 8-9.

Longhi, C. (1999), "Networks, Collective Learning and Technology Development in Innovative High Technology Regions: The Case of Sophia-Antipolis", *Regional Studies*, vol. 33, no. 4, pp. 333-342.

Losch, A. (1954), *The Economics of Location*, Yale University Press, New Haven.

Lucas, R.E. (1988), "On the Mechanics of Economic Development", *Journal of Monetary Economics*, vol. 22, pp. 3-42.

March, J.G. and Simon, H.A. (1958), *Organizations*, Wiley, New York.

Marshall, A. (1910), *Principles of Economics (Sixth edition)*, McMillan and Co Ltd., London.

Marshall, A. (1919), *Industry and Trade*, McMillan and Co Ltd, London.

Martin, R. (1999), "The New "Geographical Turn" in Economics: Some Critical Reflections", *Cambridge Journal of Economics*, vol. 23, pp. 65-91.

Maskell, P. and Malmberg, A. (1999), "Localised Learning and Industrial Competitiveness", *Cambridge Journal of Economics*, vol. 23, no. 2, pp.167-185.

Massey, D. (1984), *Spatial Division of Labor: Social Structures and the Geography of Production*, Macmillan, London.

Meyer, D.R. (1995), "Formation of Advanced Technology Districts: New England Textile Machinery and Firearms, 1790-1820", *Economic Geography*, vol. 71, pp. 31-45.

Nelson, R.R. (1993), *National Systems of Innovation*, Oxford University Press, Oxford.

Nohria, N. and Eccles, R.G. (1992), *Networks and Organizations – Structure, form and action*, Harvard Business School Press, Boston.

North, D.C. (1991), "Institutions", *Journal of Economic Perspectives*, vol. 5, no. 1, pp. 97-112.

O'Shaughnessy, N.J. (1996), "Michael Porter"s *Competitive Advantage* Revisited", *Management Decision*, vol. 34, no. 6, pp. 12-20.

Paniccia, I. (1998), "One, a Hundred, Thousands of Industrial Districts. Organizational Variety in Local Networks of Small and Medium-sized Enterprises", *Organization Studies*, vol. 19, no. 4, pp. 667-699.

Patel, P. (1995), "Localised Production of Technology for Global Markets", *Cambridge Journal of Economics*, vol. 19, pp. 141-153

Perroux, F. (1950), "Economic Space: Theory and Applications", *Quarterly Journal of Economics*, vol. 64, No.1, pp. 89-104.

Piore, M. and Sabel, C. (1984), *The Second Industrial Divide: Possibilities for Prosperity*, Basic Books, New York.

Porter, M.E. (1990), *The Competitive Advantage of Nations*, The Macmillan Press Ltd, London.

Porter, M.E. (1998a), *On Competition*, Harvard Business School Press, Boston.

Porter, M.E. (1998b), "Clusters and the New Economics of Competition", *Harvard Business Review*, vol. 76, no. 6, pp. 77-90.

Portes, A. and Landolt, P. (1996), "The Downside of Social Capital", *The American Prospect*, no. 26, pp. 18-21.

Pouder, R. and St. John, C.H. (1996), "Hot Spots and Blind Spots: Geographical Clusters of Firms and Innovation", *Academy of Management Review*, vol. 21, no. 4, pp. 1192-1225.

Pred, A, (1969), *Behaviour and Location – Foundations for a Geographic and Dynamic Location Theory*, Royal University of Lund, Sweden.

Prevezer, M. (1997), "The Dynamics of Industrial Clustering in Biotechnology", *Small Business Economics*, vol. 9 pp. 255-271.

Putnam, R.D. (1993), *Making Democracy Work – Civic Traditions in Modern Italy*, Princeton University Press, Princeton.

Pyke, F., Becattini, G. and Sengenberger, W. (eds) (1990), "Industrial Districts and Inter-firm Co-operation in Italy", International Institute for Labour Studies, Geneva.

Rabellotti, R. (1995) "Is There an "Industrial District Model"? Footwear Districts in Italy and Mexico Compared". *World Development* vol. 23, pp. 29-41.

Ricardo, D. (1971), *Principles of Political Economy and Taxation*, Penguin Books, Middlesex.

Romer, P. (1990), "Endogenous Technological Change", *Journal of Political Economy*, 1990, vol. 98, pp. S71-S102.

Rosenfeld, S.A. (1994), "Danish Modern 1994 - Designing Networks in North America", *CMA Magazine*, April, pp. 24-26.

Rosenfeld, S.A. (1995), "Overachievers - Business Clusters that Work: Prospects for Regional Development", Regional Technology Strategies Inc.

Rosenfeld, S.A. (1996), "Does Cooperation Enhance Competitiveness? Assessing the Impacts of Inter-firm Collaboration", *Research Policy*, vol. 25, pp. 247-263.

Saxenian, A.L. (1990), "Regional Networks and the Resurgence of Silicon Valley", *California Management Review*, Fall issue, pp. 89-112.

Saxenian, A.L. (1994), *Regional Advantage: Culture and Competition in Silicon Valley and Route 128*, Harvard University Press, Cambridge, MA.

Schumpeter, J.A. (1939), *Business Cycles: A Theoretical, Historical and Statistical Analysis*, McGraw Hill, New York.

Scitovsky, T. (1963), "Two Concepts of External Economies", in Agarwala A.N. and Singh S.P. (eds) *The Economics of Underdevelopment*, Oxford University Press, Oxford.

Scott, A.J. (1986), "Industrial Organization and Location: Division of Labor, The Firm, and Spatial Process", *Economic Geography*, vol. 62, pp.214-231.

Scott, A.J. (1996), "Regional Motors of the Global Economy", *Research Policy*, vol. 25, pp. 391-411.

Scott, A.J. (1998), *Regions and the World Economy: The Coming Shape of Global Production, Competition and Political Order*, Oxford University Press, Oxford.

Simon, H.A. (1957), "The Compensation of Executives", *Sociometry*, vol. 20, pp. 32-35.

Smith, A. (1979), *The Wealth of Nations*, Penguin, Baltimore.

Staber, U. (1998), "Inter-firm Co-operation and Competition in Industrial Districts", *Organization Studies*, vol. 19, no. 4, pp. 701-724.

Stigler, G.J. (1951), "The Division of Labor is Limited by the Extent of the Market", *Journal of Political Economy*, vol. 59, pp. 185-193.

Storper, M. (1992), "The Limits to Globalization: Technology Districts and International Trade", *Economic Geography*, vol. 68, pp. 60-93.

Storper, M. (1997), *The Regional World*, The Guilford Press, New York.

Swann, P. and Prevezer, M. (1996), "A Comparison of the Dynamics of Industrial Clustering in Computing and Biotechnology", *Research Policy*, vol. 25, pp. 1139 -1157.

Swann, G.M.P, Prevezer, M., Stout, D. (eds) (1998), *The Dynamics of Industrial Clustering – International Comparisons in Computing and Biotechnology*, Oxford University Press, Oxford.

Sweeney, S.H. and Feser, E.J. (1998), "Plant Size and Clustering of Manufacturing Activity", *Geographical Analysis*, vol. 30, No 1, pp. 45-64.

Uzzi, B. (1996), "The Sources and Consequences of Embeddedness for the Economic Performance of Organizations: The Network Effect", *American Sociological Review*, vol. 61, pp. 674-698.

Uzzi, B. (1997), "Social Structure and Competition in Interfirm Networks: The Paradox of Embeddedness", *Administrative Science Quarterly*, 1997, vol. 42, pp. 35-67.

Von Hippel, E. (1988), *The Sources of Innovation*, Oxford University Press, New York.

Von Hippel, E. (1994), "Sticky Information and the Locus of Problem Solving: Implications for Innovation", *Management Science*, vol. 40, pp. 429-439.

Weber, A. (1929), *Theory of Location of Industry*, in Friedrich, C.J. (ed.) The University of Chicago Press, Chicago.

Williamson, O. (1985), *The Economic Institutions of Capitalism*, Free Press, New York.

Zaratiegui, J.M. (1997), "Twin Brothers in Marshallian Thought: Knowledge and Organization", *Review of Political Economy*, vol. 9, no. 3, pp. 295-312.

2 Clusters, Industrial Districts and Competitiveness

FRANK MCDONALD AND GIOVANNA VERTOVA

Geographical factors and their implications have been placed at the heart of the economic analysis only quite recently. Mainstream economics has tended to analyze geographical factors in terms of the trade-off between economies of scale and transport costs (Hoover 1948). Consequently, orthodox economic theory downplays the importance of geographical factors by focusing on the determinants of prices in relation to the characteristics of market structures. However, some economists, management theorists and economic geographers have pointed out the importance of *place* in influencing the costs and benefits associated with location (Amin and Malmberg 1992; Amin and Thrift 1994; Dicken 1998; Dunning 1998; Krugman 1991, 1995; Ottaviano and Puga 1998; Saxenian 1994). It has been widely recognized that economic activities are based in particular areas due to attractive characteristics in these locations. Therefore place matters, in the organization of economic activities. Furthermore, it has been argued that geographical proximity facilitates gains in efficiency and flexibility that individual producers, operating in isolation can rarely attain (Porter 1990). Geographical factors play, therefore, a crucial role as a source of competitiveness (Gertler 1995; Porter 1994; Porter and Solvell 1998; Ricci 1999; Saxenian 1991; Scott 1995). Geographical proximity can lead to the development of clusters and industrial districts that can lead to competitive advantage, through gains from external economies of scale, which are not available to firms operating in isolation. There is a large literature on Italian industrial districts that focuses on geographical factors as an important influence on the development of effective organizational structures for delivering high productivity and strong export performance by small and medium size enterprises (Brusco 1982; Goodman, Bamford, Saynor 1990; Pyke, Becattini, Sengenberger 1990; Russo 1985). There is also a literature on industrial districts in developing countries that focuses on benefits of geographical concentration as a means to achieve improved performance (Schmitz and Musyck 1994; Nadvi and Schmitz 1994; Cadène and Holmström 1998).

This chapter merges the theoretical tradition of Marshall (1890) on industrial districts with the socio-economic notion of industrial districts developed more recently (Becattini 1979, 1989, 1990). The synthesis of these two theoretical approaches provides a means to specify definitions of clusters and industrial districts. The chapter assesses the importance of these geographical concentrations for the competitiveness of firms by consideration of the mechanisms working inside clusters and industrial districts that enable them to achieve a high degree of competitiveness.

The Clustering Process

Although the terms cluster and industrial districts are often used interchangeable, they cover two distinct concepts. Clusters can be defined as "A group of producers making the same or similar things in close vicinity to each other" (Schmitz 1992, p. 65). Clusters have two defining characteristics, geographical concentration and sectoral specialization. The conditions that encourage firms to cluster in a particular geographical area are not fully understood. Nevertheless, three location and four industry specific factors provide the main influences on the development of clusters.

Geographical factors are the primary force leading to the creation of clusters. Standard location theory suggests that transport costs will limit geographical concentration. However, firms can benefit from geographical concentration when economies of scale are available. Therefore, transport costs must be assessed in relation to the gains from economies of scale. If the benefits of economies of scale outweigh transport costs, the incentive for firms to cluster will be high (Krugman 1991, 1995). It is often advantageous to locate in the region with the largest market when demand varies between geographical areas and when there are economies of scale (Krugman and Venables 1990, 1994, 1995). The main limits of these theories are their dependence on internal economies of scale and transport costs within a standard neo-classical framework (Martin and Sunley 1996). However, external economies of scale can stem from the existence of a specialized labor market and supporting services (Porter 1990) or from technological and knowledge spillovers that the clustering process encourages (Swann 1993). These proximity benefits rely on geographical concentration of firms and supporting organizations in the same or similar industries. Models based on the new economic geography focus on the importance of factor mobility and availability and congestion costs as limiting factors in the incentives to cluster (Ottavianno and Puga 1998). In these models, the process of clustering initially leads to cost advantages from internal and external economies of scale and from the expansion of the size of the market as concentration raises the income of factors of production within the cluster. The advantage of clustering induces inputs to migrate to clusters thereby creating a virtuous cycle of success breeding further success. However, as clusters develop, incentives to disperse operations increase because factor prices rise for those inputs that are immobile or that have inelastic supply. Congestion costs also increase as clusters develop and grow. A trade-off emerges between proximity benefits and the market size advantages of clusters compared to rising production costs associated with input supply and congestion. Although transport costs relative to proximity benefits are important sources of the attractiveness or otherwise of locations, the origin of clusters in a particular area is not fully explained by the existence of these cost advantages because these benefits arise from the clustering process. In order to reap the benefits of geographical concentration in a particular location, there must be conditions that favor concentration in a particular area. Historical events and institutional factors that are conducive to concentration provide the setting in which it is possible to reap proximity benefits.

Historical events can strongly influence the clustering process. The attraction of a particular location today often has its origins in historical accidents that occurred a long time ago. There are many examples of historical accidents leading to the development of clusters. The case of the US manufacturing belt displays the importance of historical accidents in determining the location of an industry and its remarkable persistence (Krugman 1991). Silicon Valley grew out of the few electronic companies gathered in that area, in order to take advantage of the proximity of the aerospace industry and from a concentration of computer scientists in Stanford University (Saxenian 1985). The historical development of financial services, in order to facilitate international commodity trade, is an important reason for the success of the City of London as an international center for finance (Casson and Cox 1993). Historically, the Italian ceramic tile industry in Sassuolo grew out of other related industries such as earthenware and crockery, which can be both traced back to the Middle Ages (Russo 1985; Vertova 2002). There are many other less famous examples of the importance of historical events in the development of clusters (Porter 1990). Moreover, when particular events generate business success and a cluster is created, it is likely to be maintained by its historical path-dependence and by the possibility to become locked-in into a particular pattern of specialization (Antonelli 1997).

Institutional factors are another important determinant of cluster formation and development. Institutions are the rules of the game in a society and, therefore, they shape human interaction. According to both the Old and the New Institutional Economics, institutions are routines, habits and social rules affecting the interaction among individuals (Hodgson 1998; Rutherford 1996; Samuels 1995; Stanfield 1999). There are different kinds of institutions, economic ones (e.g., the market, the firm, etc.), political ones (e.g., the government, political parties, etc.) and social ones (e.g., the family, the church, etc.). Furthermore, there are formal institutions, such as constitutions, laws, bills of rights, courts, regulations and standards, which form legal and political frameworks for social interactions. In addition, there are informal institutions, such as cultural norms, conventions, codes of conduct, norms of behavior, traditions, habits, attitudes and generally accepted, but informal, procedures for governing social interactions. Institutions carry out three basic functions for any economy to work: they reduce uncertainty, they manage co-operation and conflicts and they provide incentives that influence behavior in human interaction (Edquist and Johnson 1997). Institutional frameworks affect the transaction costs of doing business by influencing the time, effort and, especially, uncertainty associated with business activities. Institutional frameworks can be effective in reducing transaction costs because they affect levels of uncertainty in transactions and provide incentive systems for finding solutions to conflicts (North 1990). Moreover, some institutional systems have high levels of "adaptive efficiency" that permits quick and effective adjustment to new economic, political, market and technical conditions (North 1999). Countries, and some regions within countries, can develop institutional frameworks that are more capable of reducing uncertainty and transaction costs and have better "adaptive efficiency" than other countries or regions. In these cases, the decision to locate in such countries and regions will bring benefits in terms of lower uncertainty and lower transaction costs.

The characteristics of industries and markets also influence the formation and development of clusters. Clearly, geographical concentration is only beneficial for firms in industries that are capable of reaping proximity benefits. Moreover, firms in industries were labor costs are a low portion of total costs are likely to cluster because the harmful effects of increasing labor costs, resulting from geographical concentration, will be small (Krugman 1991; Ottaviano and Puga 1998). Firms in markets that have strong elements of non-price competition may also be more willing to cluster because the resources available to obtain quality advantages resulting from geographical concentration will help to offset the increase in labor costs arising from clustering (Porter 1990; Porter and Solvell 1998). The ideal industry for clustering would have low transport and trade costs, low labor costs relative to total costs, benefits from internal and external economies of scale and high technological externalities.

Some clusters may not deliver significant proximity benefits. For example, retail outlets of a particular type such as restaurants often cluster because of the benefits of reducing search costs for customers who may walk around a small area to select their preferred place to eat. This type of cluster can emerge through a process of a few restaurants initially finding themselves in close proximity and discovering the benefits of the low search costs for customers. This success leads to other restaurants locating in the same district. The competitive nature of these types of markets means that cooperation between firms is minimal, but some proximity benefits can arise from improved connections to supplier networks and other types of logistical and distribution issues. However, the main benefits of clustering arise from cutting down the search costs for customers and/or improvements in logistical and distribution operations.

The process of self-organizing clusters, arising from historical accidents, leads firms to locate in close proximity and to discover that proximity benefits can lead to the quick growth of clusters. This type of evolution appears to be prevalent in many cities where the existence of factors such as a natural harbor or navigable river leads to geographical concentration of firms engaged in activities that require low cost transport systems. These firms discover, by accident, the benefits of locating close to firms engaged in similar types of operations and a process of clustering spontaneously emerges (Krugman 1996; Fujita et al. 1999). This analysis suggests that clusters are not planned; rather they emerge from the uncoordinated and self-interested actions of agents responding to historical accidents and geographical conditions.

All these factors strongly influence the formation of clusters. Once clusters are established, they generate cost and quality advantages that are not available to firms not located in clusters. Firms in clusters, therefore, benefit from so-called *agglomeration economies* (Bellandi 1989). Figure 2.1 shows the main factors that influence the formation of and development of clusters.

Networking: From Clusters to Industrial Districts

Networks are the means by which clustered firms develop into industrial districts. According to Brusco, "A district comprises a cluster of firms producing something which is homogeneous in one way or another, positioning themselves differently on the market. Thus, the district could be defined as being a cluster, plus a peculiar relationship among firms" (Brusco 1990, p. 14). Networks involve relationship, which are neither purely market transactions nor hierarchies and are embedded in social and cultural conditions (Powell and Smith-Doerr 1994). Networks are, therefore, different institutional arrangements from the market or the internalized firm. Networks can be defined as "a set of high trust relationship which either directly or indirectly link together everyone in a social group" (Casson 1997, p. 4). Therefore, the basic element of network is trust, because networks are formed by relationships of mutual trust.

The principal task of networks is to gather, process and spread information. Economists have long accepted that information costs have a strong influence on the efficiency of exchange and that markets cannot handle information in a costless manner (Williamson 1985). Networks emerge as a coordinating mechanism for the transmission of information and, most important, they improve the quality of information because it flows between people who trust each other. Networks can be a more effective mechanism of co-ordination than traditional alternatives of the market and the vertically integrated firm (Casson and Cox 1993). Network linkages rely on trust between the parties, sustained by moral incentives, such as respect, reputation and sense of loyalty. Morality creates a climate of trust, thus avoiding opportunistic behavior. Face to face communications and contacts encourage information to be shared in a more co-operative and less competitive way, thus reinforcing the sense of mutual obligation. Moreover, the embedded argument shows the importance of networks in generating trust and discouraging malfeasance, by recognizing that human behavior is embedded in the structure of social relations, which are crucial for the production of trust in economic life (Granovetter 1985). Furthermore, continuous and repeated interaction has the tendency to build trust among parties.

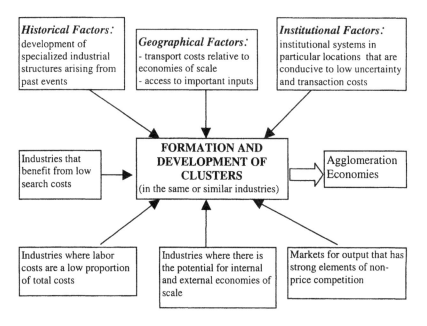

Figure 2.1   Formation of Clusters and Industrial Districts

Networks have been identified as crucial elements in the literature on local production systems. Perroux (1955), in his famous article on *growth poles*, recognizes the existence of external economies derived by the relationship among firms, when he explicitly identifies inter-industrial interactions and relationships as factors for local growth. Clusters of industrial complexes are geographically agglomerated and growing industries, producing *effets d'intensification* of economic activities and human contacts and generating uneven regional development within the national economy. The *milieu* approach focuses on the ways a territorial socio-economic network creates favorable conditions for technological innovation and, therefore, for economic growth (Aydalot 1986; Camagni 1991). The synergy created by the interactions among local factors is an important element of the *milieu innovateur* (Stöhr 1986; Maillat 1995). Local factors such as business services, public support, infrastructures, skilled labor and venture capital must be successfully woven together in order to sustain and support innovation. Regional synergy becomes therefore a more powerful explanation of innovation and, consequently, of local growth. The New Industrial Space approach identifies a network-base industrial system as a region (or a local economy) organized to adapt continuously to fast-changing markets and technologies (Piore and Sabel 1982; Storper and Allen 1989). Therefore, industrial systems based on networking can enable collective learning, thus leading to improved performance by firms located within such systems. Silicon Valley is a typical example of such a network (Saxenian 1994).

Two different kinds of networks can be identified, business and social networks, leading to the creation of different kinds of industrial districts.

Business networks are inter-firm relationships involving all firms within a district. Business networks identify the business groups as a collective of firms bound together in some formal and/or informal ways (Granovetter 1994). The main task of these networks is the gathering, processing and diffusion of information that helps in the operation of the system. Such networks require communication and coordination systems that provide low transaction costs and that deliver the required quality of outputs. Entrepreneurs, whose primary task is co-ordination, need to make decisions in a volatile environment and these networks help to obtain (at low cost) useful information on which to base the decisions. Moreover, the entrepreneur works in a constant state of flux and needs to update information constantly. Business networks speed up this upgrading process. The textile industry of Prato in Italy and the iron industry of Merthyr Tydfil in the South Wales are examples of the utilization of these kinds of networks for the internal co-ordination of districts (Casson and Paniccia 1995).

According to Brusco (1990), an industrial district is composed of different kinds of firms, organizations and agencies – "final-firms" producing for the final market (e.g., firms producing ceramic tiles), "stage-firms" involved in intermediate production (e.g., firms supplying materials for the decoration of ceramic tiles), and "others" firms and organizations working in a different industry to the one which defines the districts but, nevertheless, belonging to the same integrated sector as the final-firm (e.g., firms involved in the distribution of the final and semi-manufactured products). Firms, organizations, and government agencies providing technical and financial help also form part of others. Following this categorization, two types of integration can be identified in business networks:

- horizontal integration, among final-firms, between stage-firms and between final-firms, stage-firms and others. These networks are close inter-firm relations, supported by organizations and agencies that provide technical, business, financial and other services;
- vertical integration, between final-firms, stage-firms, and others. These networks are the so-called supply chain, formed by backward and foreword vertical integration.

A stylized example of a business network is given in Figure 2.2.

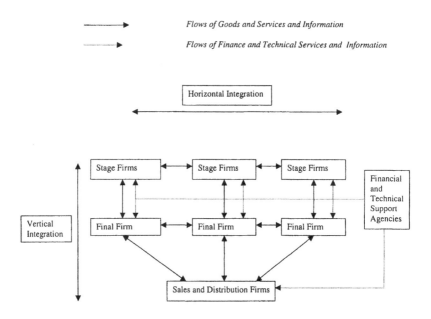

Figure 2.2   Business Networks

The attraction of geographical concentration for business networks stem from the existence of proximity benefits. Clearly, where proximity benefits are low, business networks will not be geographically concentrated. Furthermore, when clustering leads to rising costs due to high input costs and congestion, parts of the network that do not have high proximity benefits may be dispersed to lower cost areas. In this case, a geographically concentrated network would be linked to firms and organizations outside of the cluster. This could happen in vertical and horizontal networks and for final firms, stage firms and other firms and organizations. Geographical concentrations are also sometimes linked to other networks in different areas to gain benefits that are only available in particular areas. These types of networks have been found in the differentiated networks of multinational corporations. Multinational corporations sometimes create networks of subsidiaries that are given mandates to develop key activities such as production, product development and R&D that are used over all or large parts of the operations of the corporation (Birkinshaw and Hood 1998; Birkinshaw 2000). These subsidiaries are given such mandates because they are embedded in local networks that lead to benefits (from proximity) that are then used to enhance the overall effectiveness of the corporation. Figure 2.3 shows the main types of geographically concentrated business networks.

Successful business networks must evolve as technology, market conditions and political and economic circumstances change and thereby alter the conditions that are required to reap proximity benefits. Such changes may require the creation of new business networks based on dispersal of some operations to lower cost locations or the development of geographically differentiated business networks to take advantage of proximity benefits in other areas. Networks faced with changing market or technological conditions may have to adjust communication and coordination systems to ensure that they continue to deliver desired outcomes. When changing conditions require geographical concentrations to develop new linkages to dispersed firms and organizations or to geographical concentrations in other areas this is also likely to require adaptation of communication and coordination systems.

The balance between cooperation and competition within business networks must also be determined. In literature based on an analysis of competitiveness in geographical concentrations, a judicious mix of cooperation and competition is deemed to be essential to generate advantages (Porter 1990; Porter 1994; Markusen and Venables 1999). This literature typically advocates competition in final markets with cooperation

Self-contained Business Networks

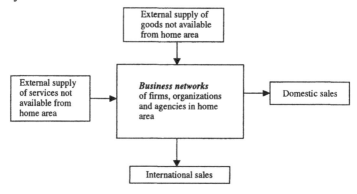

Business Networks with Geographical Dispersion

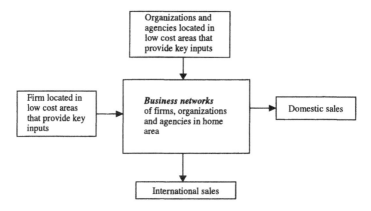

Figure 2.3   Geographical Concentrations and Business Networks

Business Networks with Differentiated Networks

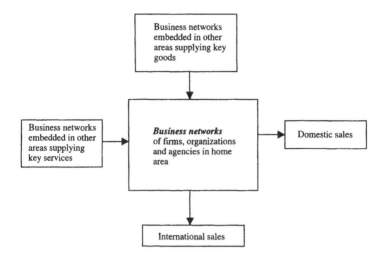

Figure 2.3   Geographical Concentrations and Business Networks (continued)

among firms and organizations to help solve common technical and economic problems. However, too much cooperation, especially among final-firms is thought to lead to high levels of x-inefficiency and slow responses to changing conditions. Much of the literature based on Italian industrial districts places considerably less emphasis on competition even among final-firms (Becattini 1990). Here the beneficial aspects of cooperation are deemed to outweigh any harmful outcomes arising from low competition within the industrial district. Italian industrial districts are often involved in highly competitive international markets where competition comes from firms located in other countries. Italian industrial districts are also underpinned by strong social networks that may mitigate against internal competition. It seems that the balance between competition and cooperation is influenced by market conditions and the nature of networks that sustain geographical concentrations.

Social networks are the second kind of networks identified in this chapter as important elements for the creation of industrial districts. Social networks are interpersonal relationships deriving from social factors and cultural characteristics, involving all the geographically concentrated firms and the local community. The literature about modern industrial districts refers to the importance of these kinds of networks (Becattini 1989, 1990; Pyke and Sengerberger 1990; Sengerberger and Pyke 1991). Becattini defines an industrial district as "a socio-territorial entity which is characterized by the active presence of both a community of people and a population of firms in one naturally and historically bounded area" (Becattini 1990, p. 38). Following this approach, this chapter argues that sociological as well as economic features are important in some industrial districts. When firms want to expand their business, important economic decisions must be taken and the more information that is available, the better. It becomes necessary to pool information from very different sources, in order to learn about prices, sources of inputs with the correct quality, access to financial resources and appropriate technology. In these circumstances, it is crucial to know the right people. Extended families, churches, educational organizations, local government authorities, local political parties and trade unions, professional associations and local banks can be involved in these networks. Since local actors share a strong homogeneous system of values, a sense of belonging encompasses the entire industrial community, thus giving the base for these social networks.

The creation of trust-based networks provides the basis for these social networks to reduce the time, effort and uncertainty associated with gathering and processing information, thus reducing transaction costs. Furthermore, these kinds of networks are more likely to be important in societies where the institutional structures have difficulties in institutionalizing trust across a wide band of society (North 1990). Therefore, people may be encouraged to form local social networks to compensate for the inadequacies of their national institutional frameworks. Moreover, some regions within nations may be more able to develop effective social networks than other regions. These differences are likely to be rooted in the historical development of regions. However, social networks may become an obstacle to economic growth. These kinds of networks may change only gradually and incrementally over time because of the commitment to a shared system of values, consequently, they may adapt slowly to new economic and social conditions. Nevertheless, social networks that can deliver high trust systems of cooperation and that are capable of fast response to economic, social, political, market and technical change are potentially able to provide competitive advantages, not available to firms located outside such environments. Social networks are likely to be more important in areas where institutional frameworks do not provide low uncertainty and transaction costs.

The composition of the major partners of social networks varies according to the historical determination of the roles and influence of groups with a given socio-economic environment. In the case of industrial districts, the social groups are closely linked to specific geographical areas. A schema of a social network is given in Figure 2.4. Within such a socio-economic environment, firms in the industrial district are able to call upon their social connections to gather and process information and to obtain services that are useful to the operations of the firms.

Links Between Business and Social Networks

There are differences between business and social networks. Business networks are *inter-firm relationships*, which can occur over long distance, especially with the increasing possibilities of using information and communication technologies to create and develop virtual business networks. However, geographical concentration is important for business networks when it is possible to acquire the benefits of external economies of scale based on proximity, such as access to a pool of skilled labor and to technical expertise that are largely based on tacit knowledge. Transactions in business networks are largely market-based rules governed by laws and institutional systems. These kinds of networks discourage the incentive to cheat because of the law and the institutions that govern market transactions. For example, laws that specify the rights and obligations of agreed transactions govern breaching of contract. Although there may be problems with opportunistic behavior in transactions covered by contracts, efficient organizational and institutional systems mitigate against these problems (Williamson 1979). However, institutional systems that generate high uncertainty and transaction costs may make greater use of non-market exchanges within business networks. These networks would have characteristics similar to "clans" (Ouchi 1981).

Social networks are *interpersonal relationships,* which normally need short distance to work, because they are based on face-to-face communications and contacts. Consequently, social networks require

Socio-economic Environment

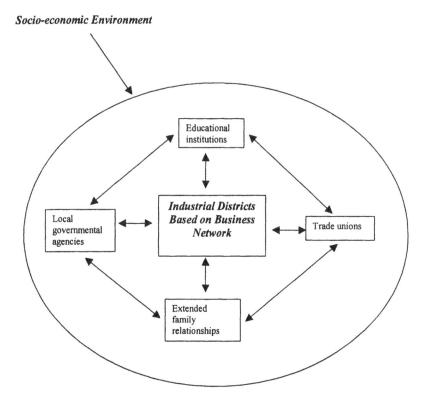

Figure 2.4   Social Networks

proximity between the actors that compose the network. In social networks, there are no laws against opportunistic behavior. Moral incentives are the strongest defense mechanisms. In this case, self-imposed moral and emotional sanctions discourage cheating because of the possibility of acquiring a negative reputation among the community and a sense of guilt and shame. The necessity of proximity for effective social networks is enhanced by the fact that moral mechanisms work better in small groups. Gelsin (1992) identifies two similar kinds of networks, "trade networks" as linkages between parties to trade goods and services and "knowledge networks" as flows of information and the exchange of knowledge irrespective of their connection to the flow of goods and services. The model presented in this chapter identifies business networks as trade networks and social networks as knowledge networks. Nevertheless, it is difficult to sharply distinguish and separate business and social networks, given that business relationships exist within a social context (Granovetter 1985).

The model developed in this chapter shows that the type of industrial district created depends upon the kind of networks firms are able to construct and develop. Clustered firms primarily based on business networks lead to the creation of what we term Industrial District Type 1 (ID1), which is very similar to the Marshallian district, described as a concentration of small business in the same or similar industries in a particular geographical area (Marshall 1890). Geographical concentrations that have extensive social networks, together with business networks, lead to the creation of what we call Industrial District Type 2 (ID2).

The Creation and Sustainability of Industrial Districts

The concept of industrial districts covers rather more than does the term cluster. The clustering process is regarded as the primary force, which drives firms to form geographical concentrations in certain areas. It is reasonable to assume that clustered firms operating in the same industry will engage in some kinds of business networks from the very beginning. However, the development of social networks has historical and institutional roots and, therefore, can take a long time to start and develop. According to this evolutionary process, a cluster is *something* that precedes an industrial district, but does not necessarily lead to it, unless some kind of network is created.

The formation and development of clusters and their evolution into industrial districts as networks leads to the emergence of different types of industrial districts. The majority of clusters are likely to evolve into ID1, where business networks are predominant. After all, the primary characteristic of industrial districts is business activity. However, some clusters may develop only very limited business networks of the type shown in Figure 2.2. In these cases, the limited business network connections would hardly warrant the title of an industrial district. Some clusters, especially those located in areas where institutional frameworks are not conducive to low transaction costs may develop important social networks to lower these costs. This would lead to the development of ID2. This process is illustrated in Figure 2.5.

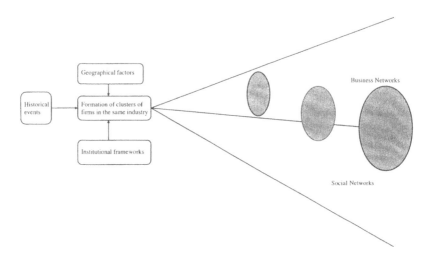

Figure 2.5   The Development of Clusters and Industrial Districts

The figure shows how industrial districts may become increasingly based on either business or social networks and that they might increase in size, where size is seen in terms of the number of agents involved in network relationships. An industrial district may expand over time, as more networks are created among an increasing number of economic agents. To be successful, industrial districts must seek an optimal size where the benefits from acquiring economies of scale and the advantages from the acquisition of knowledge from cooperation are maximized. This requires expansion of the size of networks until the marginal costs (including transaction costs) equals the marginal benefits secured from the networks. The size and composition of networks must also be effectively developed in the light of changing economic, political, social, market and technical conditions (Helpman 1997). In institutional systems that have high uncertainty and transaction costs for market-based transactions, the development of social networks may provide a means of reducing these costs (North 1990). Therefore, ID2 are more likely to be developed in such institutional systems. A summary of the generic factors influencing the development of industrial districts is given in Table 2.1.

Table 2.1   Generic Factors for the Creation, Development and Success of Industrial Districts

Conditions for the creation and development of industrial districts

	Well established business networks	Well established social networks	Industries capable of acquiring economies of scale	Firms that can acquire knowledge benefits from cooperation
ID1	Yes	No	Yes	Yes
ID2	Yes	Yes	Yes	Yes

Conditions for the success of industrial districts

Optimal balance between competition and co-operation	Optimal size of and spread of networks	Effective development of networks	Institutional systems with low TC for market transactions	Institutional systems with high TC for market transactions
Yes	Yes	Yes	Yes	No
Yes	Yes	Yes	No	Yes

The existence of industrial districts does not *per se* guarantee that proximity benefits will be reaped. Networks may be ineffective because the firms, organizations, agencies and social groups that compose the networks are not optimal in terms of the size of the network and/or the required range of participants is not created and developed. Furthermore, networks that have achieved optimal size and composition may not have appropriate communication and coordination systems. Additionally, geographical concentrations that have had effective networks may be unable to respond to changing conditions and thereby find that their proximity benefits begin to disappear. Indeed, the decline of Sheffield in the UK as an industrial district based on steel products (identified by Marshall) resulted from technological and economic changes that made the location advantages of Sheffield obsolete. The balance between competition and cooperation is also likely to influence the continuing effectiveness of geographical concentrations. Networks that lack competitive pressures may rapidly lose effectiveness in the face of unexpected changes if they have become locked into obsolete methods that cannot be quickly changed because of long experience of operating in an environment with few challenges.

Industrial Districts in Developing Countries

The identification of business and social networks as the foundations of industrial districts stems from Marshallian literature and the more recent research on industrial districts (Marshall 1890; Bellandi 1989; Becattini 1979, 1989, 1990). Marshall was so successful in theorizing about the success of local clusters of small firms, that they have been labeled *Marshallian industrial districts*. The main difference between these latter and the modern industrial districts is the role of institutional features. The modern approach considers institutions as key determinants for the formation of industrial districts, because sociological as well as economic conditions describe an industrial district. The presence of firms operating within the same industry, specific human resources, a distinguishable market supplying commodities with some special characteristics of their own, the way technological progress is introduced, the local credit system are the main economic features of the district. Moreover, the local community with its homogenous system of values, common rules and behavior are the social features of the district and give a sense of belonging to the local industrial community.

The Italian type of industrial district is not the only possible type of district (Markusen 1996). According to the model presented in this chapter (Figure 2.5), the typical Italian industrial district is the stereotype of ID2. However, there is much debate about the existence of Italian type industrial districts outside of northern Italy. "Whilst the validity of other areas in other countries to be called districts might sometimes be contested, the eligibility of localities in Italy is undisputed" (Pyke and Sengenberger

1990, p. 1). Finding ID2 in countries other than Italy has been a controversial matter. It has been suggested that this kind of industrial district is less likely to be found in developing countries due to the lack of an established industrial culture and to the insufficient development of local networks and embeddedness (Park 1996). However, social networks, such as extended families and personal relationships, exist in the newly emergent private entrepreneurs in the Chinese economy (Ping 1997). Moreover, Chinese business networks in Asia are characterized by extensive social networks based on extended families connections and tribal and linguistic groupings (Redding 1998). There is some evidence supporting the view that developing countries are benefiting from geographical concentration of firms based on social networks or may gain from creating such concentrations (Hilhorst 1998; McDonald, Sanchez, Vertova 2000; Li, McDonald, Vertova 2001; Nadvi and Schimtz 1994; Schimtz and Musyck 1994; Cadène and Holmström, 1998).

Geographical Proximity as a Source of Competitiveness

The new international economics has emphasized the role of the geography of a nation as a key determinant for trading and economic performance of national industries and as a way to enhance international competitiveness (Krugman 1991, 1995). In a world of imperfect competition and increasing returns, international trade is driven by internal and external economies of scale (Krugman and Venables 1994). Firms within clusters may obtain economic advantages by geographical proximity that could otherwise not be achieved. The importance of geographical proximity on international competitiveness is witnessed by the fact that regions with successful industrial districts performed particularly well in the global economic crisis of the 1970s and 1980s (Harrison 1992).

This chapter argues that the possibility to reap proximity benefits can be due to the presence of the two different kinds of networks, business and social networks. Both these kinds of networks can lead to a reduction in production costs and improvements in quality of outputs by reducing transaction costs.

Reduction in Transaction Costs

Transaction cost economics states that the firm is a hierarchical form of organization in order to internalize transaction costs (Coase 1937). These costs derive from three different failures - bounded rationality, opportunism and uncertainty (Williamson 1975, 1979, 1985). Bounded rationality is the result of human limits; opportunism is the result of self-interest; and uncertainty is the result of unforeseen difficulties embedded in every transactions. Under these circumstances, prices do not provide sufficient information to make decisions. Therefore, additional information is required to help make decisions that produce desirable outcomes. It is impossible to accurately define and estimate transaction costs because of the many different definitions of transaction costs and due to the difficulty in distinguishing transaction from production costs (Pitelis 1998; Pessali and Fernández 1999). It is, therefore, very difficult to calculate the benefits due to the reduction in transaction costs. However, reductions in transaction costs between cooperating agents enhance the possibilities of increasing the amount and level of beneficial exchanges. External economies of scale and quality improvements depend on the level and extent of exchanges between partners. Therefore, reducing transaction costs by forming appropriate networks provides opportunities to widen and deepen external economies of scale and enhances abilities to improve quality. When contract negotiation, monitoring and enforcement is expensive, exchange will be concentrated within groups that trust the members of the collective. By contrast, when information, measurement and enforcement costs are low, exchange can take place over greater distance and longer periods. Moreover, cultural, legal, political and institutional factors affect transaction costs by influencing levels on uncertainty in transactions (North 1990). Therefore, some institutional frameworks are better than others at reducing transaction costs. Hence, firms located in areas with institutional frameworks conductive to reducing transactions costs, will reap advantages that are not available to firms in areas with such favorable institutional conditions. Moreover, the concentration of business activities in these regions encourages the evolution of institutional frameworks, which help to maintain a low transaction costs environment, thus beginning a path dependent trend.

Reduction in Learning Costs

Evolutionary theory states that the firm is a learning organization and that the capacity for learning is related to individual skills, as well as the organization of the firm and the institutional set-up of the economy (Nelson and Winter 1982). Yet, individual skills are very difficult to transfer due to the tacit knowledge they incorporate (Howells 1995). However, personal contacts and interpersonal relationships may enhance the diffusion of this tacit knowledge among people sharing the same culture, traditions and history. When economic agents belong to the same "four spaces" - economic, organizational, geographical and cultural - the transmission of tacit knowledge becomes easier (Lundvall 1992). Industrial districts meet these requirements, because they geographically concentrate firms in an area where people share the same culture and the same economic and organizational system. Geographically concentrated firms support and enhance the feasibility of transmitting tacit knowledge. Furthermore, it is widely recognized that knowledge is the crucial resource and that the process of learning is the most important process within modern capitalistic societies (Lundvall and Johnson 1994). Network relationships are indispensable to transfer knowledge but, in particular, that part of knowledge which is tacit and difficult to codify. Indeed, one of the reasons why firms establish networks is to gain access to such knowledge (Lundvall and Johnson 1994).

The figure of the middleman, a merchant working in the textile industry of Prato in Italy, is a typical example of the way transaction and learning costs can be reduced in industrial districts (Casson and Paniccia 1995). The middleman co-ordinates material flows, both locally and over distance, within the district. He imports rags, gives the materials to independent subcontractors and exports the final products. The middleman creates important business networks, thus reducing transaction costs and enhancing the possibility to do business. Furthermore, if the middleman belongs to the same local community of the district, and he generally does, these business networks are strengthened by social networks. It becomes even easier to develop business activities because people belonging to the same social group can trust each other. The sense of belonging to the local community enables trust to be institutionalized and business becomes easier among people "speaking the same language".

Other Sources of Advantage

Two other factors enable the acquisition of competitive advantages by the development of clusters and industrial districts.

- *First mover advantage.* It gives cost advantage to producers enabling them to retain competitive advantage even if some other producers could potentially supply the same goods or services more cheaply. Since these potentially competitors are not first movers, it is difficult for them to compete because they cannot gain the agglomeration economies which are typical within clusters and industrial districts. Thus, a pattern of specialization established by, for example, historical accident might persist even when new producers could have lower costs if they could form geographical concentrations and thereby reap external economies of scale (Helpman and Krugman 1985). These advantages explain many examples of national export success as the result of self-reinforcing clusters or industrial districts, where first mover advantage of firms in some particular industries has led to continuing international competitiveness (Porter 1990).
- *Quality advantage.* In market where non-price competition is a crucial element, quality advantage is an important part of the competitive environment. In these markets, firms must provide the quality of products and services that is demanded. Firms are, therefore, obliged to obtain suitable factors of production in order to supply what the markets requires. In this case, proximity plays a crucial role because firms, organizations and people can procure suitable factors of production that convey advantages more easily than firms when they are geographically concentrated.

Figure 2.6 provides an outline of the links between the various types of geographical concentrations and competitive advantages.

The analysis of this chapter suggests that in industries subject to proximity benefits, the geographic concentration of firms and supporting organizations leads to competitive advantages. In areas where significant network benefits exist, the development of industrial districts will generate competitive advantages by reducing uncertainty and transaction costs leading to external economies of scale, learning benefits, first mover advantages and quality improvements. In areas where institutional systems are not conducive to low uncertainty and transaction cost market-based exchanges, these benefits are more likely to arise from ID2. However, in areas where institutional systems are conducive to low uncertainty and transaction costs market-based exchanges, ID1 are likely to be sufficient to generate competitive advantages. Where low network benefits exist, but when proximity advantages are available from low search costs for customers and from improvements in logistics and distribution operations, clusters that involve only limited network connections will delivery competitive advantages.

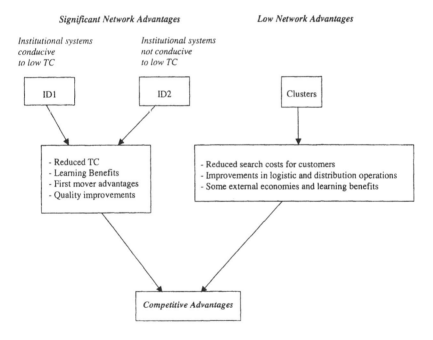

Figure 2.6   Clusters, Industrial Districts and Competitiveness

Conclusions

This chapter provides a conceptual framework to enable an analysis of the importance of *place* for competitiveness. Place often matters and where firms decide to locate can be crucial for the long-run prospects of survival and growth. The chapter argues that in industries capable of reaping proximity benefits, it is better to locate near other similar firms. This is especially true for small and medium size enterprises, for which the main problem is both to be small and to be isolated. Italian industrial districts and some parts of the German "Mittlestand" shed light on the advantages of geographical concentration as means of obtaining competitiveness for small and medium-sized enterprises. The possibility of proximity benefits gives advantages to geographically concentrated firms, enabling them to be more competitive in domestic and international markets. This chapter has shown that economic geography is a central part of the process by which national economic prosperity is achieved and maintained. However, to achieve sustainable competitiveness geographic concentrations must create and develop optimal networks that are capable of quickly responding to changing circumstances.

The theoretical framework suggests that clusters emerge from the influence of geographical factors, historical events and institutional frameworks and are, therefore, path-dependent. Consequently, it is not possible to copy the development of clusters outside their own environment. Policy makers should keep in mind that the development of clusters is constrained by past historical events, by specific institutional structures and by particular geographical conditions and, therefore, the particular form of existing clusters may not be transplanted from one geographical area to another.

Business and social networks are at the heart of industrial districts. Therefore, governments may help or hinder the development of industrial districts with policies that impact on the creation and development of networks. Governments could become facilitators of information networks by acting as sponsors of links between people, agencies and organizations that could provide valuable low cost information sources on market conditions, technology and sources of inputs. The development of appropriate networks may also help in the evolution of effective communication and coordination systems. Nevertheless, there are dangers in adopting such policies. Careful analysis is necessary to ensure that there are good grounds for encouraging the development of industrial districts by the development of business and perhaps social networks. The most sensible approach may be to identify those firms that are already clustering and help those that would benefit from extending their networks to develop into industrial districts.

The welfare implications of the development of industrial districts are not clear. Developing industrial districts may boost competitiveness in particular areas, but this could be at the cost of harming other parts of the economy. However, the tendency for geographical concentration to grow is likely to be strong. Therefore, if governments do not help to provide the conditions conducive to geographical concentration advantage will pass to other areas or countries that encourage these developments.

The framework presented in this chapter suggests that many important questions require answers. Clearly, the size, composition and evolution of networks is crucial to the ability of geographical concentrations to reap competitive advantage. However, the details of the factors that determine the effectiveness of networks vary from industry to industry, between locations and over time. The balance between competition and cooperation and the efficiency of communication and coordination systems are also subject to variation according to conditions that prevail within networks, market conditions and over time. The role of institutional factors in influencing the type of development of networks also requires further clarification. The impact of technical change on the creation and development of geographical concentrations is also an important factor that is not clearly understood. To answer these questions, analysis of empirical evidence on the operations of "real world" geographical concentrations is required to enable the development and clarification of our understanding of the links between clusters or industrial districts and competitiveness.

References

Amin, A. and Malmberg, A. (1992), "Competing Structural and Institutional Influences on the Geography of Production in Europe", *Environment and Planning in Europe*, vol. 24, pp. 401-416.

Amin, A. and Thrift, N. (1994) (eds), *Globalization, Institutions, and Regional Development in Europe*. Oxford University Press, Oxford.

Antonelli, C. (1997), "The Economics of Path-dependence in Industrial Organization", *International Journal of Industrial Organization*, vol. 15, n. 6, pp. 643-675.

Aydalot, P. (1986) (ed.), *Milieux Innovateurs in Europe*. GREMI, Paris.

Becattini, G. (1979), "Dal «settore» industriale al «distretto» industriale. Alcune considerazioni sull'unità di indagine dell'economia industriale", *Rivista di Economia Politica e Industriale*, vol. 5, pp. 7-21.

Becattini, G. (1989), "Sectors and/or Districts: Some Remarks on the Conceptual Foundations of Industrial Economics" in Goodman E., Bamford J., Saynor P. (eds), *Small Firms and Industrial Districts in Italy*. Routledge, London.

Becattini, G. (1990), "The Marshallian Industrial Districts as a Socio-economic Notion" in Pyke F., Becattini G., Sengenberger W. (eds), *Industrial Districts and Inter-firm Co-operation in Italy*. International Institute for Labour Studies, Geneva.

Bellandi, M. (1989), "The Industrial District in Marshall" in Goodman E., Bamford J., Saynor P. (eds), *Small Firms and Industrial Districts in Italy*. Routledge, London.

Birkinshaw, J. (2000), *Entrepreneurship in the Global Firm*. Sage Publications, London.

Birkinshaw, J. and Hood, N. (eds) (1998), *Multinational Corporate Evolution and Subsidiary Development*. Macmillan, London.

Brusco, S. (1982), "The Emilian Model: Productive Decentralisation and Social Integration", *Cambridge Journal of Economics*, vol. 6, no. 2, pp. 167-184.

Brusco, S. (1990), " The Idea of the Industrial District: its Genesis" in Pyke F., Becattini G., Sengenberger W. (eds) *Industrial Districts and the Inter-firm Co-operation in Italy*. International Institute for Labour Studies, Geneva.

Cadène, P. and Holmström, M. (1998), *Decentralized Production in India: Industrial Districts, Flexible Specialization and Employment*, Sage Publications, New Delhi.

Camagni, R. (1991) (ed.), *Innovation Networks: Spatial Perspective*. Belhaven Press, London.

Casson, M. (1997), *Entrepreneurial Networks: A Theoretical Perspective*. The University of Reading. Discussion Paper in Economics and Management, no. 371.

Casson, M. and Cox, H. (1993), *Modelling Inter-Firm Network*. The University of Reading. Discussion Paper in Economics no. 278.

Casson, M. and Paniccia, I. (1995), *Business Networks and Industrial Districts: A Comparison of Northern Italy and South Wales*. The University of Reading. Discussion Paper in Economics, no. 301.

Coase, R. (1937), "The Nature of the Firm", *Economica*, vol. 4, pp. 386-405.

Dicken, P. (1998), *Global Shift*. Paul Chapman Publishing, London.

Dunning, J. (1998), "Globalization, Technological Change and the Spatial Organization of Economic Activity" in Chandler A., Hagstrom P., Solvell O. (eds), *The Dynamic Firm: The Role of Technology, Strategy and Regions*. Oxford University Press, Oxford.

Edquist, C. and Johnson, B. (1997), "Institutions and Organization in Systems of Innovation" in Ecquist C. (ed.), *Systems of Innovation. Technologies, Institutions and Organizatione,* Pinter Publisher, London.

Fujita, M., Krugman P., Mori, T. (1999), "On the evolution of hierarchical urban systems" *European Economic Review*, vol. 43, no. 2, pp. 209-251.

Gelsin, L. (1992), "Innovation and the Development of Industrial Networks" in Lundvall B-Å (ed.) *National Systems of Innovation. Towards a Theory of Innovation and Interactive Learning*. Pinter Publisher, London.

Gertler, M. (1995), "Being There: Proximity, Organization, and Culture in the Development and Adoption of Advanced Manufacturing Technologies", *Economic Geography*, vol. 71, no. 1, pp. 1-26.

Goodman, E., Bamford, J., Saynor, P. (1990) (eds), *Small Firms and Industrial Districts in Italy*. Routledge, London.

Granovetter, M. (1985), "Economic Action and Social Structure: The Problem of Embeddedness", *American Journal of Sociology*, vol. 19, pp. 481-510.

Granovetter, M. (1994), "Business Groups" in Smelser N., Swedberg R. (eds) *The Handbook of Economic Sociology*. Princeton University Press, Princeton.

Harrison, B. (1992), "Industrial Districts: Old Wine in New Bottles", *Regional Studies*, vol. 26, no. 5, pp. 469-483.

Helpman, E. (1997), "The Size of Regions", in D. Pines, E. Sadka and I. Zilcha, (eds), *Topics in Public Economics. Theoretical and Applied Analysis*. Cambridge University Press, Cambridge.

Helpman, E. and Krugman, P. (1985), *Market Structure and Foreign Trade: Increasing Returns, Imperfect Competition and International Economics*, MIT Press, Cambridge.

Hilhorst, J. (1998), "Industrialization and local/regional development revisited", *Development and Change*, vol. 29, no. 1, pp. 1-26.

Hodgson, G. (1998), "The Approach of Institutional Economics", *Journal of Economic Literature*, vol. 36, no. 1, pp. 166-192.

Hoover, M. (1948), *The Location of Economic Activity*. McGraw-Hill, New York.

Howells, J. (1995), "Tacit Knowledge, Innovation and Technology Transfer", *Technology Analysis and Strategic Management*, vol. 8, no. 2, pp. 91-106.

Krugman, P. (1991), *Geography and Trade*. MIT Press, Cambridge.

Krugman, P. (1995), *Development, Geography and Economic Theory*. MIT Press, Cambridge.

Krugman, P. (1996), *The Self-Organizing Economy*, Basil Blackwell, Oxford.

Krugman, P. and Venables, A. (1990), "Integration and the Competitiveness of Peripheral Industry" in Bliss C., Braza de Macedo J. (eds), *Unity with Diversity in the European Community*. Cambridge University Press, Cambridge.

Krugman, P. and Venables, A. (1994), *The Location of Economic Activity: New Theories and Evidence*. Centre of Economic Policy Research, London.

Krugman, P. and Venables, A. (1995), "Globalization and the Inequality of Nations", *Quarterly Journal of Economics*, vol. 110, no. 4, pp. 857-880.

Li, H., McDonald, F., Vertova, G. (2001), "Clusters, Industrial Districts and the Competitiveness of Chinese Industries" in Little S. and Thorpe R. (eds) *Global Change: The Impact of Asia in the 21st Century*. Palgrave, London.

Lundvall, B.Å. (1992), "User-Producer Relationships, National Systems of Innovation and Internationalisation" in Lundvall B-Å (ed.) *National Systems of Innovation. Towards a Theory of Innovation and Interactive Learning*. Pinter Publisher, London.

Lundvall, B.Å and Johnson, B. (1994), "The Learning Economy", *Journal of Industry Studies*, vol. 1, no. 2, pp. 23-42.

Maillat, D. (1995), "Territorial Dynamic, Innovative Milieu and Regional Policy", *Entrepreneurship and Regional Development*, vol. 7, no. 2, pp. 157-165.

Markusen, A. (1996), "Sticky Places in Slippery Space: a Typology of Industrial Districts", *Economic Geography*, vol. 72, no. 3, pp. 293-313.

Markusen, J. and Venables, A. (1999), "Foreign direct investment as a catalyst for industrial development" *European Economic Review*, vol. 43, no. 2, pp. 335-356.

Marshall, A. (1890), *Principles of Economics*. Macmillan, London.

Martin, R. and Sunley, P. (1996), "Paul Krugman's Geographical Economics and Its Implications for Regional Development Theory: A Critical Assessment", *Economic Geography*, vol. 72, no. 3, pp. 259-292.

McDonald, F., Sanchez, A. and Vertova, G. (2000), "Regional Economic Integration and the Development of Clusters and Industrial Districts: Lessons from the European Union" in Didier J. (ed.) *Integración Económica y Desarollo Empresarial: Europa y América Latina.* Eska Edition, Paris.

Nadvi, K. and Schimtz, H. (1994), *Industrial Clusters in Less Developed Countries: Review of Experiences and Research Agenda.* The University of Sussex. Institute of Development Studies. Discussion Paper no. 339.

Nelson, R. and Winter, S. (1982), *An Evolutionary Theory of Economic Change.* Harvard University Press, Cambridge.

North, D. (1990), *Institutions, Institutional Change and Economic Development.* Cambridge University Press, Cambridge.

North, D. (1999), *Understanding The Process Of Economic Change*, London. Institute of Economic Affairs. Occasional Paper no. 106.

Ottaviano, G. and Puga, D. (1998), "Agglomeration in the Global Economy: A Survey of the New Economic Geography", *World Economy*, vol. 21, no. 6, pp. 707-731.

Ouchi, W. (1981), *Theory Z*, Addison-Wesley, Reading, MA.

Park, S. (1996), "Networks and Embeddedness in the Dynamics of the New Industrial Districts", *Progress in Human Geography*, vol. 20, no. 4, pp. 476-493.

Perroux, F. (1955), "Note sur le notion de «pôle de croissance»", *Économie Appliquée*, vol. 8, no. 1-2, pp. 307-320.

Pessali, H. and Fernández, R. (1999), "Institutional Economics at the Micro Level? What Transaction Cost Theory Could Learn from Original Institutionalism (In the Spirit of Building Bridges)", *Journal of Economic Issues*, vol. 33, no.2, pp. 265-275.

Ping, H. (1997), "New Private Entrepreneurs in China: Family Relations and Social Connections" in Rutten M., Updhya C. (eds) *Small Business Entrepreneurs in Asia and Europe: Towards a Comparative Perspective.* Sage Publication, New Delhi.

Piore, M. and Sabel, C. (1982), *The Second Industrial Divide: Possibilities for Prosperity.* Basic Books, New York.

Pitelis, C. (1998), "Transaction Costs and the Historical Evolution of the Capitalist Firm", *Journal of Economic Issues*, vol. 32, no. 4, pp. 999-1017.

Porter, M. (1990), *The Competitive Advantage of Nations.* Macmillan, London.

Porter, M. (1994), "The Role of Location in Competition", *Journal of the Economics of Business*, vol. 1, no. 1, pp. 35-39.

Porter, M. and Solvell, O. (1998), "The Role of Geography in the Process of Innovation and the Sustainable Competitive Advantage of Firms" in Chandler A., Hagstrom P., Solvell O. (eds), *The Dynamic Firm: The Role of Technology, Strategy and Regions.* Oxford University Press, Oxford.

Powell, W. and Smith-Doerr, L. (1994), "Networks and Economic Life" in Smelser N., Swedberg R. (eds) *The Handbook of Economic Sociology.* Princeton University Press, Princeton.

Pyke, F., Becattini, G., Sengenberger, W. (1990) (eds), *Industrial Districts and Inter-firm Co-operation in Italy.* International Institute for Labour Studies, Geneva.

Pyke, F. and Sengerberger, W. (1990), "Introduction" in Pyke F., Becattini G., Sengenberger W. (eds), *Industrial Districts and Inter-firm Co-operation in Italy*. International Institute for Labour Studies, Geneva.

Redding, G. (1998), "The Changing Business Scene in Pacific Asia" in McDonald F., Thorpe R. (eds) *Organizational Strategy and Technological Adaptation to Global Change*. Macmillan, London.

Ricci, L. (1999), "Economic Geography and Comparative Advantage: Agglomeration versus Specialisation", *European Economic Review*, vol. 43, no. 2, pp. 357-377.

Russo, M. (1985), "Technical Change and the Italian Industrial District: The Role of Intrafirm Relations in the Growth and Transformation of Ceramic Tile Production in Italy" *Research Policy*, vol. 14, pp. 328-343.

Rutherford, M. (1996), *Institutions in Economics. The Old and the New Institutionalism*. Cambridge. University Press, Cambridge.

Samuels, W.J. (1995), "The Present State of Institutional Economics", *Cambridge Journal of Economics*, vol. 19, no. 4, pp. 569-590.

Saxenian, A. (1985), "The Genesis of Silicon Valley" in Hall P., Markusen A. (eds), *Silicon Landscapes*. Allen and Unwin, Boston.

Saxenian, A. (1991), "The Origins and Dynamics of Production Networks in Silicon Valley", *Research Policy*, vol. 20, pp. 423-437.

Saxenian, A. (1994), *Regional Advantage. Culture and Competition in Silicon Valley and Route 128*. Harvard University Press, Cambridge.

Schmitz, H. (1992), "On the Clustering of Small Firms", *IDS Bulletin*, vol. 23, no. 1, pp. 64-69.

Schimtz, H. and Musyck, B. (1994), "Industrial Districts in Europe: Policy Lessons for Developing Countries?", *World Development*, vol. 22, no. 6, pp. 889-910.

Scott, A. (1995), "The Geography Foundations of Industrial Performance", *Competition and Change*, vol. 1, pp. 51-66.

Sengerberger, W. and Pyke, F. (1991), "Small Firm Industrial Districts and Local Economic Regeneration: Research and Policy Issue", *Labour and Society*, vol. 16, pp. 1-24.

Stanfield, J.R. (1999), "The Scope, Method, and Significance of Original Institutional Economics", *Journal of Economic Issues*, vol. 33, no. 2, pp. 231-255.

Stöhr, W. (1986), "Territorial Innovation Complexes" in Aydalot P. (ed.), *Milieux Innovateurs in Europe*. GREMI, Paris.

Storper, M. and Allen, S. (1989), "The Geographical Foundations and Social Regulation of Flexible Production Complexes" in Wolch J. And Dear M. (eds), *The Power of Geography*. Unwin Hyman, Boston.

Swann, P. (1993), "Clusters in High-Technology Industries", *The Business Economist*, vol. 25, pp. 27-36.

Vertova, G. (2002, forthcoming), "Industrial Districts in Italy: the Case of Sassuolo" in Harris P. and McDonald F. (eds), *European Business and Marketing*. London. Sage.

Williamson, O. (1975), *Markets and Hierarchies: Analysis and Antitrust Implications*. Free Press, New York.

Williamson, O. (1979), "Transaction-cost Economics: The Governance of Contractual Relations", *Journal of Law and Economics*, vol. 22, no. 2, pp. 233-261.

Williamson, O. (1985), *The Economic Institutions of Capitalism*. Macmillan, London.

3 Networks and Proximity: Theory and Empirical Evidence from the Car and Telecommunications Industries

ANASTASSIOS GENTZOGLANIS

A growing body of theoretical and empirical literature examines inter-firm agreements and the role they play in the development of firms' strategies (Hagerdoorn and Schakenraad 1990; Chesnais 1988). According to this literature, geographical proximity plays a dual role in network formation. On the one hand, it contributes to the formation of networks through the establishment of personal contacts and the built-up of social capital in local business districts. On the other hand, geographical proximity plays a dissuasive role in the formation of networks by erecting barriers to entry and inhibiting innovation. This may happen when networks are densely located in some closely related business communities. Firms located in distant geographical areas are, apparently, more prone to establish network relations.

Some researchers (Teece 1982; Antonelli 1988) relate the formation of networks to the process of innovation and technological change. *Externalities* and spillover effects are important in some industries (high-tech for example) and highly dependent on distance. High levels of communication affect the transmission of externalities. Geographical proximity is thus a strong necessary condition to take advantage of externalities generated by other firms. Networks emerge as a result of efforts to internalize selectively the variety of factors necessary to master the process of innovation. Regional clustering in industrial districts enhances complementary advantages and provides the skills and specialization necessary to achieve higher levels of productivity and competitiveness. Intra-regional exchange relations are thus seen as a way of strengthening a firm's market base increasing, thereby, the industry's competitive position internationally. The problem with the externalities approach is that it fails to take into account the dynamic nature of networks and does not provide any analytical framework explaining the durability of the agreements.

Another strand of research emphasizes the presence of *transaction costs* as a factor contributing to the formation of networks. According to this theory, networks are seen as long-term agreements located between market transactions and internal organization and are set in order to internalize the transaction costs incurred by firms in the market place (Williamson 1985). Transaction costs are minimized especially when asset specificity and uncertainty are located at an intermediate level. The problem with the transaction costs approach is that it considers trade-offs between institutional arrangements in a static way. It also fails to explain why networks are established even when transaction costs are minimal or even not existent. There is a growing theoretical and empirical literature (Ciborra 1990; Zanfei 1990) arguing that networks are becoming an important strategy for acquiring and managing *knowledge assets*. Networks are increasingly seen as primary mechanisms by which firms formalize their links to external sources of innovation and the creation of new knowledge assets. An increase in knowledge contributes to a firm's competitive advantage. To the extent that competition, technological changes and other environmental factors increase R&D costs and risks and shorten products' life cycles, sharing resources among different organizations reduces costs and favors the formation of networks. Networks are thus considered to be the outcome of two simultaneous failures; of markets in transferring knowledge and of internal organization in accumulating it.

Firms use networks as a temporary solution to the problem of acquiring knowledge assets. Networks as a "wait-and-see" strategy are very valuable especially in uncertain and dynamic information environments. In that way, networks can be considered as "options" with real underlying value. In this paper we use the *option value theory* (Arrow and Fisher 1974) to specify the value of the flexibility of the network. We analyze it as an option in an uncertain and dynamic information environment. Networks are unstable strategies and as such they do not minimize transaction costs. Their value lay therefore in *dynamic* aspects such as *flexibility and interactive learning,* which further generate a new specific asset. As this new asset is gradually appropriated by the partners and it is progressively embedded into their routine processes, the collaboration of partners increases and the network becomes more integrated and therefore more stable.

There are benefits and costs of interactive learning, which depend on the "knowledge" distance between the two entities (Lundvall 1991). I argue that *distance does not necessarily have a geographical dimension but it is mostly associated with culture and distance in knowledge.* The more distant (different) firms' knowledge base is, the greater their learning potential. Once the network is set up, interactive learning becomes possible through the establishment of procedures, which allow information channels to be shared, and codes of information to be exchanged. The process of mutual understanding is costly when the knowledge distances are far apart (Llerena and Wolff 1990).

My approach, by using the concept of *knowledge proximity* rather than of geographical distance, explains the formation of networks better (both vertical and horizontal).

Networks are situated some distance apart on the knowledge continuum by complementary technologies (i.e., vertical networks) or closer to that continuum with similar streams of production process but with different knowledge bases (horizontal networks). Case studies from the car and the telecommunications industries serve as examples in testing my approach.

The next section examines, in more detail, the arguments for network formation and reviews the literature. I then present the analytical framework and the testable hypothesis of my model. To validate the thesis, I examine the reasons for establishing networks in the car and telecommunications industries. It appears that the networks are the preferred strategy when the degree of sunkness of costs (risk) is high. The net benefits are maximized when firms "buy" the option of "wait-and-see" strategy.

Networks, Agreements and Transaction Costs

Flexibility is a market characteristic, the cornerstone of any market mechanism. Economists argue that flexibility, through price and quantity adjustments, inherent in unfettered (not regulated) market structures ensures an optimal allocation of resources (Pareto optimality). Networks, as opposed to integration are more flexible organizational structures than hierarchies (integration).

If integration and other centralized strategies reduce flexibility why do firms decide to go ahead with this strategy? Williamson (1975, 1989) argued that firms use hierarchies instead of markets because of the existence of transaction costs. The latter are loosely defined to include any costs associated with the use of markets instead of hierarchies. Transaction costs are exacerbated because economic agents act opportunistically, especially in environments characterized by asymmetric information and uncertainties. If we add to this bounded rationality, i.e., the natural limitations in the cognitive abilities of economic agents to resolve complex situations, and asset specificity, economic agents would incur substantial costs to make contracts between parties that try to take into account every possible outcome. This *ex ante* limitation in writing perfect contracts and the costs associated with *ex post* complying, monitoring and enforcing the contract's contingent clauses provides firms with sound incentives to use hierarchies instead of market transactions.

Asset specificity and uncertainty play a significant role in explaining a firm's decision to use hierarchies. Asset specificity arises from the specialization of a valuable resource. The higher the specificity of an asset, the lower its ability to find alternative uses without sacrificing valuable productive capacity. Investments in specific assets with limited alternative uses are considered to have high sunk costs, which give rise to a small number environment with possibilities of strategic bargaining and opportunistic behavior. Asset specificity can take various forms such as geographic specificity, physical asset specificity, and human resources specificity.

Uncertainty arises from changing market and technology conditions. The recent radical technological changes greatly transformed many markets. The institutional changes (deregulation, globalization, internationalization and atomization of production) that have followed the technological innovations increased transaction costs and with them the specificity (the sunkness) of assets used in the production process. In these cases, transaction costs would make the use of hierarchies more cost efficient than market transactions.

In the past decade or so the use of hierarchies did not preclude the use of other strategies like networks. Firms use multiple strategies at the same time. For example, the telecommunications, computers and computer programming, biotechnology, pharmaceutical and the car industries, to name a few, have been dramatically transformed lately through consolidations and outright purchases of rival firms (Niosi 2001). At the same time these industries have created many networks. Transaction costs theory has difficulties in explaining the simultaneous adoption of these strategies. According to the transaction costs theory, hierarchies (integration) should be the outcome whenever changes in asset specificity result in an increase in the transaction costs. It can then be argued that the transaction costs approach does not fully capture the dynamic features of technology and the formation of networks. I demonstrate, later in the chapter, that option theory gives a more reasonable explanation for the formation of networks.

To substantiate the main argument of transaction costs theory, Llerena and Wolff (1990) used a diagram (Figure 3.1) to show the links among asset specificity, transaction costs and the various forms of organizational structure. Networks are situated between markets and hierarchies and correspond to an intermediate level of asset specificity. The governance structure that emerges is the one that minimizes transactions costs. But when asset specificity is too high (such as in the telecommunications and the car industries), transaction costs theory is inadequate to explain the formation of networks.

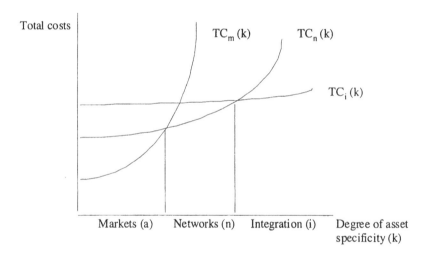

Figure 3.1   Asset Specificity and Choice of Organizational Form

It is my proposition that transaction costs are important but they are not the only factors considered by firms in their integration or network decisions. Other factors such as flexibility and the benefits arising out of it can be predominant factors. It can be the case that firms decide to use both strategies at the same time. If, for example, uncertainty is low, the benefits from using the market are much higher than for other strategies. At intermediary levels of uncertainty, integration is the more advantageous strategy, while when uncertainty is at a high level, networks provide a better choice. There is then a relationship between uncertainty (as measured by the amount of sunk costs) and net benefits of each alternative strategy.

The benefits from networks are valuable because they offer flexibility and interactive learning and contribute to the creation of knowledge (vertical and/or horizontal). Networks can thus be analyzed as a means of increasing flexibility. The nature of flexibility considered is a key to our analysis. Flexibility refers to the adaptation capability of the firm and its learning ability. Its adaptation capability protects itself from external shocks while its learning ability enables the network to create resources through a collective learning process (Favereau 1989; Aoki 1988).

Networks and Adaptability

Clusters and networks are becoming essential in the present context of globalization. Networks are not simply geographic concentrations of companies. It is a cooperation and interaction of learning through combinations of different kind of knowledge emanating from suppliers, customers, manufacturers of complementary products, government and other institutions such as universities, standards agencies and vocational training providers. Networks' growth is a self-reinforcing cycle. As a single firm's success brings other suppliers or inspires cooperation with other companies or institutions, other companies that can benefit from those resources are drawn closer to the network. Clustering and networking offer companies a favorable business environment that enables firms to get a competitive advantage they could not acquire in isolation (Porter 1998, p. 78).

The value of networks lies on their ability to create new specific assets. They are conducive to resource creation and innovation through information efficiency generated by cooperation among member firms. The creation of new specific resources increases the core competencies of member firms, their competitiveness and their profitability. Greater knowledge means a greater degree of adaptability and greater capacity to deal with changing economic and business environments. The degree of appropriation of the new knowledge determines the viability and the duration of the network. If spillover effects are low and the appropriation high then agreements tend to be more stable. Learning through interaction and confrontation increases the possibilities for combining diverse experiences and different kinds of knowledge. Such a way of learning brings more innovative approaches to resolve problems related to the management and innovation (R&D) within and among firms.

This interactive learning and the creation of new resources are not without costs. At the beginning of the formation of networks costs are particularly high. But as member firms learn from each other and share their newly created information, establish a common language of communication and reduce their cultural differences, the costs become less important. Once the initial stages of collaboration are set out and cooperation is smoothed out, the interactive learning process begins to bring about the benefits of collaboration. Complementarities in knowledge among member firms are more important in the interactive learning process rather than common knowledge already shared by firms. Accordingly, the benefits of interactive learning increase with greater knowledge distances of member firms. Lundvall (1991) examined the interactive learning in networks and illustrated graphically (Figure 3.2) the potential benefits and costs derived from knowledge distances among member firms. Obviously, the net benefits are maximized when these distances are at an intermediate (d*) level.

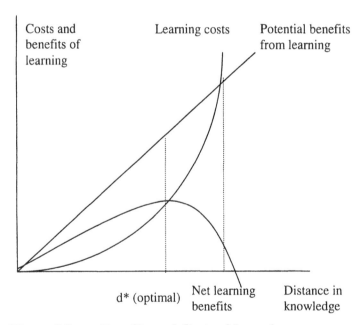

Figure 3.2   Benefits and Costs of Learning

The creation of new specific assets which are gradually incorporated into the networks become routine operations which contribute, in their turn, to the stability of the agreements. Networks become more stable as their capability to appropriate the creation of new specific assets is greater. The new information and communication technologies (ICT) play a pivotal role in shaping the appropriation of new specific assets. Broadband (high-speed data) and other ICT services have the ability to erase distances that have often been considered obstacles to the appropriation of spillovers and the establishment of networks. With ICT's help, many smaller communities and non-urban localities can now become part of a network and enjoy the benefits that used to be the sole province of concentrated activities around certain urban poles. New ICT infrastructure is within the reach of many far distant localities, giving distant firms the same digital opportunities as their urban counterparts. The building of wireless networks, the installation of coaxial cables, or the deployment of copper-based DSL lines and the decision of many high-tech companies to upgrade their own infrastructure and the expansion of the portfolio of services brings greater possibilities of network formation regardless of geographical distances.[1]

Uncertainties arising from technological diversification, market segmentation, changing economic and business environment and information asymmetries are increasing. Network-building strategies are flexible business decisions. They allow firms to wait until they accumulate more experience and information before choosing a definite organizational form. Networks are temporary strategies that give firms more time to cope with uncertainty and complexity of information (an intermediate solution between markets and hierarchies). In that sense networks is an "option" with a great underlying value. Viewed as such, the option theory can be used to analyze the formation of networks. The next section presents the option model.

Theoretical Elements of the Formation of Networks: The Option Theory Model

Option theory is concerned with the optimal timing of a strategic decision or when to exercise a strategic decision. The option of optimally acting in the future should be of value today. By undertaking a risky project (j) that is costly and difficult to reverse (sunk investment), the firm incurs costs and "kills" the option of investing if and when conditions are more favorable in the future. If the firm invests today, it would want the present value of expected benefits to equal or exceed the present value of expected costs plus the value of the option to wait. I argue that networks provide member firms the option to wait and see and act later when the firm has more information and knowledge especially in a complex and ever-changing dynamic environment where complexities and opportunistic behavior are more prevalent.

I begin with a simple two-period model to get a feel for these two important aspects of network building capacity. Consider a firm with the following project. Develop a new technology either internally (i.e., an integrated solution (i)) or through building a network (i.e., an agreement (a)). The outcome of this strategy is uncertain. The project (j) has (π) probability of success and ($1-\pi$) of failure.

Using the network entails more transaction costs than using the integrated approach. On static terms, the integrated approach will be favored instead of the establishment of networks. Nevertheless, the strategy to establish networks would be preferred over alternative strategies should we consider that the latter increases a firm's specter of choices in the future and allows it to get more timely information and elaborate more sound strategies. Because of the existence of an *"option value"* in the networks strategy, the latter would be preferred over alternative strategies. The network building process is more like a "buying time" strategy that allows firms to wait and see how the situation evolves before taking a more definite approach.

The value attached to this option strategy can be high enough to compensate for the higher transaction costs of network building ($c_a > c_i$), especially in a world characterized by ever-increasing information complexities. Flexibility is, however, synonymous to instability and the network building strategy is inherently unstable. Networks could become more stable when adaptation and learning are explicitly included into this framework. Suppose a firm decides to use the integrated approach and that the technology development provides T_0 revenues today and D_1 in the future. The present value of the firm choosing the integrated approach is

$$D = T_0 + \rho D_1 \text{ where } \rho = 1/(1+\delta) \text{ is the discount factor.} \qquad (3.1)$$

If the firm decides to use the "decisional flexibility" approach i.e., the strategy of building a network, its current value would be A_0. In the future, both this decision (A) and the revenues of the firm are uncertain. Suppose that there are two possibilities

- a positive state of nature (s=1) during which the network building is a success and the new technology is introduced
- a less positive state of nature (s=2) during which the network building is a failure and the technology is not introduced

In the first case, the net revenue $T_{1,1}$ is greater than the firm's current value $A_{1,1}$. In the second case (s=2) the net revenue $T_{1,2}$ is less than the value of the firm $A_{1,2}$. Thus, in the future state 1 $T_{1,1} > A_{1,1}$, and in future state 2, $A_{1,2} > T_{1,2}$.

Suppose we attach probabilities to these two strategies, π with state 1 (s=1) and (1-π) with state 2 (s=2), assuming that $T_0 > A_0 > 0$. If the integrated approach is not consummated today, it is optimal to use the integration strategy if state 1 occurs. By contrast, the network building strategy is more optimal if state 2 occurs. With this optimal, state-contingent decision rule, the expected present value of building a network is given by

$$P = A_0 + \rho[\pi T_{1,1} + (1-\pi) A_{1,2}] \qquad (3.2)$$

It is obvious from this equation that integration is a preferred strategy if D>P, while the network-building approach becomes more attractive if D<P because it gives the option to wait and see and adopt the most advantageous strategy depending on the prevailing state of nature in the time.

The point of indifference, where D = P, implies that

$$T_0 + \rho D_1 - A_0 = \rho[\pi T_{1,1} + (1-\pi)A_{1,2}] \qquad (3.3)$$

The left hand side of the equation represents the net value of adopting the integrated approach today while the option value in t = 0 has been deducted from $T_0 + \rho D_1$. On the right hand side the term $\rho[\pi T_{1,1} + (1-\pi)A_{1,2}]$ is the option value of not adopting the integrated approach today (t = 0). If the firm adopts the networking–building approach today instead of the integrated approach, it preserves the option of behaving optimally in the future (integrate in state 1 and use the network-building strategy in state 2). Option value in this case is the discounted expected net value of behaving optimally in the future. Option value is unambiguously positive with positive values for $T_{1,1}$ and $A_{1,2}$ and 1> ρ >0, 1 > π >0. The above results are presented in Table 3.1.

It is interesting making a comparative static analysis by examining the impact of changing certain values on the incentives to preserve the option of acting more freely in the future. First, an increase in $T_{1,1}$ or $A_{1,2}$ will increase option value and it will tend to increase the incentive to build a network instead of favoring the integration approach. In contrast, an increase in T_0, D_1 or a decrease in A_0 will increase the net value of integration (left hand side) and tend to increase the likelihood of the integrated approach. Finally, an increase in the discount rate δ, will reduce the option value of network formation (right hand side) more than it reduces the left hand side, thus integration becomes a more preferable solution than building a network today. Table 3.2 summarizes the comparative static results of alternative business strategies.

Table 3.1   Comparing Costs and Benefits of Various Business Strategies

Strategies	Transaction costs	Option value	Firm's present value	Decision rule
Network	High	high	$P = A_0 + \rho[\pi T_{1,1} + (1-\pi) A_{1,2}]$	If D<P Adopt the network strategy
Integration	Low	low	P = positive	If D>P Adopt the integration strategy

Table 3.2   Comparative Statics of Various Business Strategies

Factors	Value of the strategy	Decision rule
If $T_{1,1}\uparrow$ or if $A_{1,2}\uparrow$	↑ the network option value	↑ network formation
If $T_0, D_1 \uparrow$ or $A_0 \downarrow$	↑net value of integration today	↑integration adoption strategy
If $\delta \uparrow$	↓option value of network formation	Integration today (killing the option)

It is interesting enough to examine a relationship not so obvious *a priori* concerning the sign of $d\pi/d\delta$ and the optimal option offered to the firm of being indifferent between the integrated approach and the network building strategy. Multiplying both sides of the last equation by $(1+\delta)$ we get the following equation

$$(T_0 - A_0) \, d\delta = (T_{1,1} - A_{1,2}) \, d\pi, \quad \text{or} \tag{3.4}$$

$$d\pi/d\delta = (T_0 - A_0)/(T_{1,1} - A_{1,2}) \tag{3.5}$$

The latter takes into account the changes in π which must counter an increase in δ in order to preserve the indifference. I have assumed that $T_0 > A_0$. If $T_{1,1} > A_{1,2}$, it will be the case that $d\pi/d\delta > 0$, On the contrary, if $A_{1,2} > T_{1,1}$, then $d\pi/d\delta < 0$. Such an outcome is perfectly justified since an increase in the discount rate reduces option value and we would need to increase the probability of the higher-valued future state in order to maintain indifference. If $T_{1,1} > A_{1,2}$, then π must go up, whereas if $A_{1,2} > T_{1,1}$, π must go down in order for $(1-\pi)$ to go up.

Although the value of both strategies is quite high today, it is the network strategy that brings more value in the future because of the option it provides to the firm to act later when it possesses more information. This is illustrated graphically (Figure 3.3).

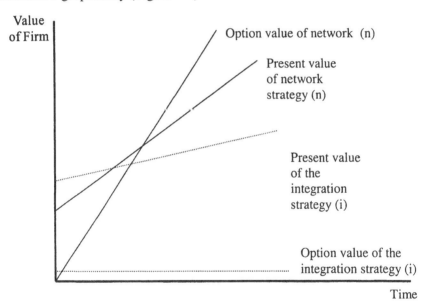

Figure 3.3   Comparing the Value of Network-building and Integration Strategies

Firms value the short and long term costs and benefits before they adopt a specific strategy. The present value of both integration and network building strategies is quite high but unequal. The integration strategy has a higher value today than the network strategy but its option value is quite low. In contrast, the network strategy has a lower value today but combined with its much higher option value, it has a total present value much higher than the integration strategy because of the flexibility it provides.[2] Firms will use the network strategy whenever uncertainty and other business factors are unstable. The analysis of the establishment of networks in the telecommunications and the car industries provides a heuristic proof of our arguments. Next section deals with this.

Networks and Risk in the Car and Telecommunications Industries

To illustrate our argument we take as an example the car and telecommunications industries. The first one is a more traditional industry although knowledge-intensive one, especially now with the integration of many new technologies in building and running the cars. Although cars seem to be standardized products their components are not. They are completely different from what they were in the past and they depend on a great number of new technologies and knowledge inputs. As Loasby (1998) has argued, firms are becoming increasingly multi-technology in their production processes. They are increasingly relying on a growing range of networks to get access to external capabilities.

The telecommunications industry has always been viewed as highly dynamic, especially after it has been deregulated and converged with information and media industries. It has a high-tech component and it is knowledge-intensive. Both car and telecommunication industries face major technological breakthroughs and a change in their competitive environment. Both have become more global and face market segmentation (micro-market phenomenon). Their degree of asset specificity and uncertainty is quite high, leading one to argue that transaction costs are potentially important to explain their integration strategies. It is true that both industries have used integration in the past few years, but the number of alliances and knowledge networks they have created has increased dramatically as well. The option theory can better explain this strategy.

In the past decade or so, car and telecommunications industries began forming alliances and networks beyond their national boundaries with the goals of rationalizing production through joint research, development, design, production, and engineering, component sharing and enhancing competitive positions in the markets. Ballard Power Systems, a Canadian firm with its new fuel-cell technology, has entered into agreements with all major car producers in Canada, the United States, Europe and Asia. The networks were established because of the knowledge proximity rather than the geographical distance of the partners. Geographical distance among partners was not an important factor in the creation of these networks. Rather the goal to increase their competitive edge through tapping into localized sources of specialized expertise (gaining a location advantage), complementary technologies and the knowledge proximity were the main incentives to form the networks.

Indeed, the car industry is a truly global one. It uses geographical spread in order to achieve technological diversification by using agreements and/or outright purchases of rival firms. This strategy gives firms a competitive edge and allows them to get into markets and territories entirely out of reach only few years ago. These strategies reduce uncertainties and risks and provide incentives to increase investment and innovations. There are a number of factors that make the car industry business environment more complex and risky. For example, there are tougher environmental regulations[3] worldwide, chiefly in California[4] that obliges car manufacturers to reduce the gases from emissions. Pollution cannot be reduced to predetermined levels without the use of new, more efficient technologies.

Ballard Power Systems is the inventor of the Ballard fuel cell, a proprietary zero-emission engine that combines hydrogen (which can be obtained from natural gas, methanol, petroleum or renewable sources) and oxygen (from air) to generate electricity without combustion. It is a promising technology that could revolutionize the world if it becomes economically viable. It could supplant existing technologies but as yet it is simply an interesting and promising technology. There are a multitude of similar technologies (e.g., Fuelcell Energy Inc., Global Thermoeletric Inc., Plug Power, Active power, Capstone Turbine Corporation), but at the moment, none of them has managed to establish itself as the standard of the industry. Car manufacturers could use this technology to make their cars cleaner and environmentally friendly. But there are many unknown factors. First of all, the new rules of the game are not clear yet. Environmental regulation differs from country to country and the introduction of clean cars is at the far bottom of the agenda of many countries especially the less developed ones. Carmakers have worried that investments made before these more stringent environmental regulations might become "stranded assets" and they are reluctant to go ahead with more investments if regulations are not clear.

The uncertainty arising from cleaner technologies and government regulations is compounded by a new market trend, which also affects the telecommunications industry. Carmakers have to face a micro-market phenomenon. They must provide a range of "quasi-customized" goods and services. Acquiring knowledge of market and demand changes is costly as market research is done for ever-thinner segments of the market. As a result, relative R&D costs increase and car manufacturers have to acquire a deep knowledge of their clients' future needs in order to integrate them early in the innovation process.

It is clear that, in the car industry, the degree of environmental uncertainty and the risks associated with the internal dynamics of technical progress are quite high.[5] According to my argument, the car industry can mitigate some of these uncertainties, especially the ones arising from market segmentation and changing customer preferences by acquiring competitors. Horizontal consolidation allows the industry to get the knowledge and know-how it needs in order to reduce marketing and production costs arising from market uncertainties. The desire to acquire *horizontal knowledge* favors consolidation as the recent examples from the car industry demonstrate (Daimler Benz buying Chrysler, Renault buying Nissan, etc.). Thus the acquisition of core competencies and strategic assets has many justifications, but transaction costs are an important motive. The formation of networks is a more appropriate strategy, however, should companies desire to acquire *vertical (upstream/downstream) knowledge.* Given that environmentally friendly technologies are quite new and not standardized yet, the wait-and-see strategy, as it was explained above, is the least expensive one and the most valuable. Thus, General Motors, Ford Motors, DaimlerChrysler, Honda, Nissan, Volkswagen, ALSTHOM and other major carmakers have created networks with the main provider of the clean environment technology, the Canadian firm, Ballard Power Systems.

By choosing major players in every continent, Ballard tries to get extensive expertise in engineering, management solutions and design of its fuel cell engine. Since it is a late R&D company there are many roadblocks to successful implementation of proton exchange membrane (PEM) fuel cells. There are costs challenges, competition and the uncertainty of the technology. Fuel cells are expensive to manufacture and economies of scale have not yet been mastered. The problem of competing technologies amplifies the uncertainties in this area. The primary rivals to fuel cells are hybrid engines – internal combustion plus an electric motor – and battery-powered cars. Next there is the problem of building a whole network of fueling stations. Putting into place an infrastructure for the entire country is a daunting task. But given that Ballard has a superior fuel cell why would car companies do their own? It is more advantageous to them to establish networks with Ballard and develop together this new technology. It is the least expensive and more profitable strategy for the car industry.

The same story can be said for the telecommunications industry. In the past decade or so, Bell Canada and other major telecommunication firms have made a number of agreements and established networks with other telephone firms and equipment manufacturers worldwide. When uncertainty is at an intermediate level, *upstream* and *downstream knowledge* is acquired by mergers and acquisitions. When uncertainty (as measured by the degree of sunkness of costs) is high, a networks strategy is used to acquire vertical knowledge.

After a decade of drastic regulatory and technological changes the telecommunications industry is still under the shock of convergence. New technologies and new services are continuously introduced while prices are dropping drastically making these services accessible to a great number of users. Like the car industry, the telecommunications industry faces a customization of its demand. New services or packages of services are offered in a variety of forms in order to satisfy the particular needs of almost every group of customers. Acquiring the necessary knowledge for evaluating the needs of its customers increases market research costs and relative R&D costs. Information, communications and the media (print and electronic) industries converge as new broadband, IP and DSL technologies expand the capacity of the network and transmission costs are reduced.

Regulatory risk is less important to the telecommunications industry than to the car industry. Telecommunications have been deregulated and the new regulatory rules are clear and well known to the parties concerned.[6] The uncertainties arise from technological changes and the absence of technological standards in the mobile and cellular telephony. Furthermore, it is not clear yet whether the new technologies will really allow various industries with such diverse line of services like basic telephony, data, multimedia (image, sound, etc.), Internet, television, PCS, print and electronic news, 3G technology, etc., to converge.

As may be expected, the telecommunications industry uses both integration and networks strategies at the same time. When uncertainties are at an intermediate level downstream or upstream knowledge is acquired by outright acquisition of suppliers and/or customers. At low uncertainty levels the benefits of using the market are much higher than the benefits of other strategies. Lastly, when the uncertainty is quite high, the network formation strategy is much more beneficial than the other strategies as illustrated in the graph below (Figure 3.4). The higher the uncertainty the higher the option value attached to the network formation strategy.

To illustrate my argument, (i.e., when risk is high network formation is the appropriate strategy), I report some historical statistical evidence from the telecommunications industry. When modern digital switches were introduced with storage-controlled programs, switch development changed from a hardware- to a software-based project. The development of a modern switch is a very lengthy process with high fixed (sunk) costs, switch software accounts for about 75 percent of its total cost (which in

1990 figures was about $US 1.5 billion). The next generation switches (optical switches designed to respond to the increased use of fiber optics or digital switches designed to handle broadband transmissions) are even more expensive to develop ($US 2 billion per switch). The risks arising from the introduction of these new technologies are quite high especially when markets are competitive and the costs are rising. To reduce risk, major telecommunication carriers forged network agreements. Their goal was to reduce the number of models from twelve to three or five switches. Table 3.3 lists some of the networks for this technology.

The same argument holds with the personal communications networks (PCN). In the 1990s the exact form of PCN technology was not clear. The cost of developing each of the three networks was estimated to be in the range of $US 1 billion to $US 2 billion each. Table 3.4 lists the three groups of companies that have established networks for developing these new technologies.

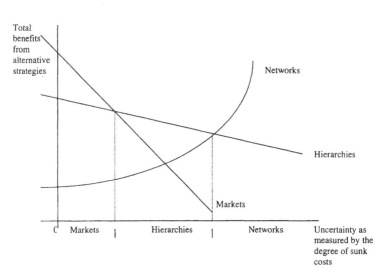

Figure 3.4   Benefits and Cost of Alternative Strategies

The striking characteristic of these networks is that they are international in nature. They are set regardless of geographical distances. What matters is the knowledge distances among the partners and the interaction of learning and the capacity of the new entity to create new resources.

Table 3.3   Networks in Central Office Switches

Companies	Country	Year
CGE (Alcatel) and ITT	France	1987
Ericsson and CGT	France	1987
AT&T and Philips	Netherlands	1986
AT&T and Italatel	Italy	1989
AT&T and GTE	United States	1989
Siemens and EC-Plessy (GTP)	United Kingdom	1989

Source: Hausman (1991)

Table 3.4   Networks in Personal Communications Technologies in the UK

Group 1	Group 2	Group 3
BAE (UK)	Cable & Wireless (UK)	STC (UK)
Pacific Telesis(USA)	Motorola (US)	Thorn-EMI (UK)
Matra (France)	Telefonica (Spain)	US WEST (USA)
Millecom (UK & US)		Deutsche Bundespost (Germany)
Sony (Japan)		

Source: Hausman (1991)

Conclusions

Networks and clusters have traditionally been thought of as being agreements among firms in specific localized geographic areas (e.g., biotechnology and pharmaceuticals in Montreal, or biotechnology and computer technologies in Texas, Massachusetts, California). Transaction costs theory has been advanced as one of the most prominent candidates in explaining their formation. In an ever-changing environment with great uncertainties arising from globalization, deregulation and above all technological changes and innovations, the use of markets entails substantial transaction costs. The latter are compounded by limited rationality, asset specificity and asymmetric information (the free-riding problem). Contracts are necessarily incomplete and their enforcement and monitoring is quite costly. The use of in-house approaches, such as integration, is a strategy, which allows firms to reduce transaction costs.

The transactions costs theory being static in nature fails to account for the ever-increasing use of agreements (networks, clusters, etc.,) among firms. It is argued in this paper that networks can be viewed as a wait-and-see strategy, which allow firms to get more information and knowledge and act accordingly in the future. Networks have an intrinsic value, which lies in the option offered to firms to have the choice to decide in the future. As an option, networks can be evaluated using the traditional finance and environmental option theory.

It is undeniable that integration may fetch certain advantages that cannot be realized by the use of networks. There may be *first-mover advantages* and integration may be the most appropriate strategy to get them. I argue that hierarchies are used in order to get core competencies and strategic assets immediately. This may be dictated by the degree of openness of the market, the change in policies of a country or a major technological breakthrough. Firms may proceed to horizontal (competitors markets) or vertical (highly complementary products or services) relations in order to reduce risk and uncertainties resulted from major changes (institutional, regulatory, competitive, political, etc.,), which dramatically affected the business environment.

There may be *second-mover advantages*, especially when the uncertainties arise from the introduction of new and expensive technologies and there is no standard in the industry. The risks are high and the business environment very uncertain. Integration can be a costly strategy. In such circumstances network formation and clusters have a value because they allow firms to elaborate clearer strategies in the future. This may be the case when products, services, or technologies of some firms are potentially related but at the current stage of knowledge and technological advances the outcomes are unclear. It is therefore more advantageous to adopt the wait-and-see approach. Option theory is a more robust one, capable of explaining networks and clusters in a dynamic environment.

The car and telecommunications industries have been used as a case study to illustrate these arguments. In effect, both industries work in a business environment, which is characterized by rapid technological changes and micro-segmentation of their market demand. Costs in developing new products or new techniques of production are quite onerous. Yet, there is no agreement as far as the technological standards are concerned. There are many competing technologies to be used for cleaner cars and there are many technologies (none of them quite well established) in the telecommunications (including cellular, PCS, 3G, etc.). Given that the business environment is quite uncertain and risky, networks provide a sound alternative to integration.[7]

Notes

1 Obviously, not all firms use the latest ICT services. In countries of digital "haves and have nots" the traditional reasons for network creation are still valid. The digital divide is a reality and the currently available technologies are not well suited to serving small numbers of customers spread over a wide area. Even in the USA, broadband reaches only 20 percent of zip codes in less urban areas (it is 57 percent in urban areas).

2 As with any other option, the network strategy will get a zero value in the future if the firm waits to long before acting (exercising it). But such an outcome is consistent with the option theory. It is not because your house did not pass on fire that your insurance is worthless.

3 The Kyoto accord specifies that 37 industrialized countries must reduce, by year 2012, their pollution emissions (greenhouse gases) by 6 percent from 1990 levels (Gentzoglanis 2000a).

4 By 2003 some 6 percent of all new vehicles sold in California have to be so-called "partial emission" cars, while 4 percent must be zero-emission standards. California has the strictest environmental regulations because it has the worst air pollution problems.

5 Although Ballard has not turned a profit – after 17 years of developing its fuel cell – and it is not expected to reach profitability until the middle of the decade, the company's future could potentially be huge.

6 There are still uncertainties concerning competition at the local level and in the new services (Internet, cellular, etc).

7 This is not to say that firms could use exclusively the network strategy. Integration may be used simultaneously especially when the firm wants to acquire rapidly core competencies or strategic assets, as we mentioned above.

References

Antonelli, C. (1988), The Emergence of the Network Firm, in C. Antonelli (ed.) *New Information Technology and Industrial Change*, Kluwer Academic Publishers.

Aoki, M. (1988), *Information, Incentives and Bargaining in the Japanese Economy*, Cambridge University Press, Cambridge.

Arrow, K.J and Fischer, A.C. (1974), Environmental Preservation, Uncertainty and Irreversibility, *Quarterly Journal of Economics*, vol. 88, May, pp. 312-319.

Ciborra, U. C. (1990), "Innovation, Networks and Organizational Learning" in *Perspectives in Industrial Organization*, B. Dankbaar, J. Groenewegen and H. Schenk (eds), Kluwer Academic Publishers, Dordrecht.

Chesnais, F. (1988), Les accords de coopération technique entre firmes indépendantes, STI Revue, no. 4, December, pp. 55-131.

Favereau, O. (1989), "Organisation et marché, *Revue Française d'Économie*, vol. 4, no. 1, pp. 65-96.

Gentzoglanis, A. (2000a), "Alliances stratégiques...." http://www.actq.qc.ca, Paper presented at the ACTQ Annual Conference, Vaudreuil, Canada, October 4.

Gentzoglanis, A. (2000b), "Greenhouse Gas Emission Caps and Sustainable Development" http://members.hme.net/gdufour99/Gentzoglanis.html.

Hagerdoorn, J. and J. Schakenraad (1990), "Strategic Partnering and Technological Co-operation", in *Perspectives in Industrial Organization,* B. Dankbaar, J. Groenewegen and H. Schenk (eds), Kluwer Academic Publishers, Dordrecht.

Hausman, J. (1991), "Joint Ventures in Telecommunications", *Regulation,* Winter, pp. 69-76.

Llerena, P. and Wolff, S. (1990), "R&D in Telecommunication and the New Economic Paradigm, *Eurotelecom Conference,* 5-7 June, Madrid.

Llerena, P. and Wolff, S. (1994), "Inter-firm Agreements in Telecommunications: Elements of an Analytical Framework, in Pogorel, G. (ed.), *Global Telecommunications Strategies and Technological Changes,* Elsevier, Amsterdam.

Loasby, B., J. (1998), "The Organization of Capabilities", *Journal of Economic Behaviour and Organisation,* vol 35, pp. 139-160.

Lundvall, B. A. (1991), *Closing the Institutional Gap,* unpublished.

Niossi, J. (2001), "Les « Cluster » de haut technologie" CIRST (centre interuniversitaire de recherche sur la science et la technologie (not published).

Porter, M. (1998), "Clusters and the New Economics of Competition", *Harvard Business Review,* November/December, p. 78.

Teece, D.J. (1982), "Towards an Economic Theory of the Multiproduct Firm, *Journal of Economic Behaviour and Organization,* vol. 3, March, pp. 39-64.

Williamson, O.E. (1975), *Markets and Hierarchies: Analysis and Antitrust Implications,* Free Press, New York.

Williamson, O.E. (1985), *The Economic Institutions of Capitalism,* Free Press, New York.

Williamson, O.E. (1989), "Transaction Costs Economics" in Schmalensee and Willig (eds), *Handbook of Industrial Organization,* vol. 1, pp.135-182, Elsevier, Amsterdam.

Zanfei, A. (1990), "Collaborative Agreements and Innovation in the US Telephony Industry", in *Perspectives in Industrial Organization,* B. Dankbaar, J. Groenewegen and H. Schenk (eds.), Kluwer Academic Publishers, Dordrecht.

4 Region, Knowledge, and Competitiveness

SEAN B. O'HAGAN AND MILFORD B. GREEN

Over the past ten years, two important lessons have emerged from research focusing on globalization and its influence on the distribution of economic activity. First, in the shift from an industrial to a knowledge-based economy, knowledge has become the most important resource. Drucker (1993) argues that knowledge is the only meaningful resource in achieving sustainable competitive advantage. Second, regional economies foster the creation of knowledge because they possess the fundamental attributes that are necessary to initiate the knowledge creation process. A shorter distance provides the basis for inter-firm relationships and thus, the transfer of knowledge between these firms. The purpose of this chapter is to review the concepts of region and knowledge and the relationship that exists between them.

To accomplish this, the chapter is broken down into five parts. First, we discuss the notion of region. Second, we examine the transition from a resource to a knowledge-based view of the firm. In the subsequent section we review the relationship between knowledge and the region. We then look at knowledge transfer and why the region is the most efficient scale to do this. In the penultimate section we review literature that questions the integrity of the region as the sole unit of analysis. Finally, we devote a section to revealing that tacit and explicit knowledge are not discrete concepts, rather they overlap to produce a continuum.

The Concept of the Region

Over the last twenty-five years the buzzword for economic activity has been globalization. With the expansion to global trade and investment it seems logical for this to occur. But as pointed out by Storper (1997, p. 3) a pocket of research in the 1980s turned its attention in the opposite direction. The region, always considered important by geographers, received increased attention by academics outside the discipline. Storper attributed this new found interest to the structure of the global economy. He suggests that new successful forms of production - different from mass production systems of the postwar period - were emerging in some regions and not others, and since they seemed to involve both localization and regional differences, it followed that there may be something fundamental that linked late 20th century capitalism to the region.

Before proceeding with the rest of this chapter, defining region is a necessary first step. Getis, Getis and Fellmann (2000, p. 477) define a region as a device of area generalization in order to separate the earth's surface into recognizable component parts. This broad definition corresponds with Hartshorne (1977) who suggests that there is no generally accepted boundary for a region. The boundary depends upon the economic phenomenon under investigation. In some instances the region may include a local neighborhood while in others an entire nation makes up the region. These encompassing explanations make a subset of definitions necessary. Here the concept of region is divided into two parts, formal or functional.

A formal region is an area of similarity throughout, be it in terms of physical or cultural features. This is a useful concept because it allows researchers to identify parts of the world that are comparable by certain features. In relation to knowledge, a formal region is defined by its knowledge content in a particular industry For example, Silicon Valley possesses a great deal of knowledge in software and hardware development for the computer industry.

For the most part, however, we are interested in knowledge as it relates to a functional region. Functional regions represent levels of integration between phenomena that make up one system - the world. Smith (1976, p. 4) suggests defining regions functionally because this allows researchers to describe firms of any scale as systemic entities that interact with one another and the environment in patterned ways. These systemic entities supply the analytical units needed for describing and comprehending the levels and linkages between regions and the world.

A phenomenon's boundaries remain the same until the spatial dimensions of the interaction change. Interaction between two firms yields some form of knowledge transfer between them. As resource dependency theory suggests, this interaction is necessary because firms are unable to internally generate all the necessary inputs for production. Firms respond with relationships to external elements of the environment to ensure a supply of the required resources, of which knowledge is the most important. Over time, the quality and quantity of relationships increase.

The result is a socially embedded culture where a knowledge threshold develops. This knowledge threshold retains the same boundaries until new lines of communication create a new knowledge threshold and thus a new region.

Research on the region has resulted in even more descriptive terms than formal and functional. The concept of agglomeration has been used extensively in the literature to describe the region as it relates to economic activity. For example, agglomeration is used to describe the advantages accrued through the collective use of infrastructure in the form of transportation, communications, and other services (Johnston, Gregory, and Smith, 1994). But terms such as clusters, industrial districts, and milieus that build upon the concept of agglomeration have become more fashionable.

Akoorie (2000, p. 143) describes a cluster as a system, where companies have achieved high rates of cooperation. They are usually based on local/historical/sectoral agglomerations of firms in which the different elements of the system are present in a relatively restricted geographic area. The institutional, cultural and historical thickness of a cluster is reinforced by the physical, cultural, and social infrastructure in which the cluster is embedded.

Similar to a cluster is an industrial district. These are defined as local clusters of a number of mostly small enterprises that compete with but also support each other. Clusters generally occur when functional linkages and geographic space join companies. A supply chain of firms in close proximity to each other describes an industrial district. Perhaps the best example of an industrial district is Third Italy. After World War II, regional production clusters of small and medium sized firms developed in Central and Northeast Italy. By specializing in ceramic tiles, textiles, and so on, cooperation between suppliers and buyers of this region has enabled firms to compete successfully against foreign competition.

Capello (1999, p. 357) suggests when cooperation and tacit knowledge is transformed into innovative synergy and capacity, rather than simply social solidarity and interaction, a local district becomes an innovative milieu. The concept of innovative milieu was first developed in the 1980s by the Groupe de Recherche Europeen sur les Milieux Innovateurs (GREMI). They argue that innovation is a dynamic process that involves an enterprise procuring resources and knowledge from the outside. If these dynamic relationships do not exist, the region remains an industrial district where the reduction of transaction costs leads to advantages.

From a Resource to a Knowledge-Based View of the Firm: the New Path to Sustained Competitive Advantage

Today, a firm's competitiveness relies on its technology, innovation, know-how, and ability to learn. In other words, prosperity for the firm is based on its knowledge. Firms succeed by creating, protecting, and refining knowledge to create superior products to their rivals. Or as Prusak (1997, p. ix) suggests, a firm's success depends upon what it knows, how it uses what it knows, and how fast it can know something new.

Today, the two major forces increasing the importance of knowledge are competition and technology. They have nullified the concept of the classic corporation. Huseman and Goodman (1999, p. 70) explain how the classic corporation was an island among its competitors, customers, and suppliers. This strategy allowed the company to protect its knowledge and thus its competitive advantage. Conversely, the learning company of today prospers by associating with its competitors, customers, and suppliers. These connections yield additional knowledge of the business environment that allows the firm to make superior business decisions than they would have otherwise.

Researchers have long known about the importance of knowledge to firms. Until recently though, the subject has been deemed too difficult to handle. Most importantly, mainstream researchers had a problem measuring knowledge; making verification of knowledge as a key ingredient for firm success difficult. Leading economist Paul Krugman provides an excellent example. Krugman (1997) follows Marshall's three rationales for regionalization: (1) labor market pooling; (2) the creation of specialist suppliers; and (3) the development of technological knowledge spillovers. However Krugman concentrates upon the first two types of factor arguing that knowledge spillovers are difficult to model quantitatively (Pinch and Henry, 1999, p. 818). Research such as this has prolonged mainstream explanations of competitive advantage of the firm by its possession of the traditional resources of land, labor, and capital.

In recent years though, a new group of researchers has recognized that the importance of knowledge cannot be ignored if firms want to remain competitive. In response, the quantity and quality of research has been enhanced. Perhaps the most significant contribution of this research is to delineate knowledge into distinct categories, explicit and tacit. Explicit knowledge comes in the form of words or numbers and therefore can be expressed formally via hard data, blue prints, computer code, and scientific formulas. Explicit knowledge transfer is often carried out from one individual to another by impersonal means, such as through a computer or a technical manual. For example, a repairman who determines what is wrong with a dishwasher after examining the manual is using explicit knowledge.

Tacit knowledge on the other hand is highly subjective and personal. Therefore, tacit knowledge is difficult to put into words. It is acquired through experience, which allows the individual to learn how to successfully execute an activity. Tacit knowledge is revealed only in its application and therefore, is most often learned through face-to-face communication. An example of tacit knowledge is the same repairman who determines what is wrong with the dishwasher based on its noise.

The definitions suggest important differences between the two types of knowledge. Explicit knowledge is more formalized and tacit knowledge is more socially embedded. This implies that explicit knowledge can move easily and quickly but barriers to tacit knowledge transfer are for the most part still intact. As revealed by Teece (1998), the more knowledge has been codified, the more easily it can be imitated and transferred. The more a firm's knowledge is tacit, the more difficult it is to reproduce and transport to its competitors. Since global competition has increased many firms' exposure to imitation, tacit knowledge, knowledge that is not easily imitated, is necessary to sustain competitive advantage.

Since explicit and tacit knowledge maintains distinct transfer capacities, they maintain vastly different spatial thresholds as well. Today, explicit knowledge is not a rare commodity because it can be mass produced and mass distributed. The ability to transfer tacit knowledge however is much more limited. Therefore the spatiality of tacit knowledge is much smaller than the spatiality of explicit knowledge. Competition and information technology transport explicit knowledge around the globe quickly. But tacit knowledge cannot be circulated so easily. It remains much more efficient at the regional level.

Sustained competitive advantage occurs when a firm possesses a value creating strategy not possessed by its competitors. Foss (1996) builds on this argument by suggesting that possessions of the firm must satisfy two conditions for sustained competitiveness to occur. It cannot be freely imitated and it cannot be freely transferred. Spatially constricted tacit knowledge is especially valuable because it satisfies both of these conditions. On the other hand, explicit knowledge can be easily imitated and transferred. Explicit knowledge may make the firm more competitive in the short run. Unless it is combined with other forms of knowledge, explicit knowledge does not create long-term competitiveness of the firm.

Therefore, tacit knowledge is a much more significant possession for a firm struggling for competitive advantage.

Grant (1997) reveals a firm's predicament with respect to imitation. On the one hand, competitive advantage for the firm requires possession of knowledge that is not easily imitated by its competition. On the other hand, to fully exploit this knowledge, the firm must be able to imitate it throughout the company for the benefit of its employees. It is one thing for a firm to create knowledge but it is another to be able to distribute this knowledge throughout the rest of the firm. This argument is significant for the region as well. Sustaining competitive advantage for the region requires knowledge to be transferred and replicated throughout. However, this same knowledge should not be accessible to external competitors if the region is to maintain competitive advantage. How is this accomplished? The answer lies in the characteristics of tacit knowledge, which are discussed in more detail in the next section.

Knowledge and the Region: A Symbiotic Relationship

The concepts of knowledge and region have been introduced, and it has been established that the two are vital for competitive advantage. But for the most part, we have treated them individually. The two are considerably more valuable when combined. In this section knowledge and region are discussed in greater detail as well as their relationship with each other.

Nonaka and Takeuchi (1995) argue that a relationship exists between explicit and tacit knowledge. In fact, they reveal how the interaction of the two types of knowledge actually converts old knowledge into new knowledge. To illustrate this relationship, Nonaka and Takeuchi (1995) present a dynamic model of knowledge creation, called the knowledge spiral (Figure 4.1). They suggest that the basis for knowledge creation is the conversion of tacit knowledge into explicit knowledge and back to tacit knowledge again.

Four modes of knowledge conversion essentially make up this knowledge creation process:

- Socialization - Transfer of tacit into a new form of tacit knowledge.
- Externalization - Procedure where tacit knowledge is converted into explicit knowledge. It is vital for knowledge creation to take place because personal knowledge is transformed in a way to be

accessed by other employees of the company.

- Combination - Linking of different bodies of explicit knowledge into to a new form of explicit knowledge. Nonaka and Takeuchi (1995, p. 67) suggest it is a process of systemizing concepts into a knowledge system. Documents, meetings, telephone conversations, and e-mail are just a few examples where individuals exchange explicit knowledge.

- Internalization - Occurs when explicit knowledge is converted back into tacit. When knowledge is spelled out in explicit form, it is easier for workers to convert this to tacit knowledge. Documents and manuals help workers internalize their experiences and therefore increase their tacit knowledge base.

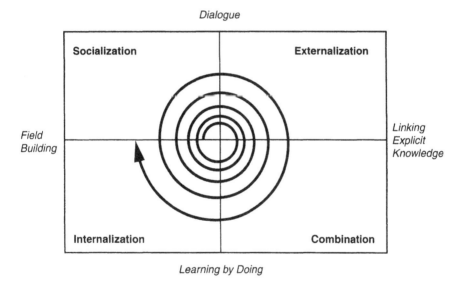

Source: Figure 3.3: *The Knowledge-Creating Company: How Japanese Companies Create the Dynamics of Innovation* by I. Nonaka and H. Takeuchi, copyright 1995 by Oxford University Press, Inc. Used by permission of Oxford University Press.

Figure 4.1   The Knowledge Spiral

In this chapter we are primarily interested in examining the first mode of Nonaka and Takeuchi's knowledge spiral, socialization. This mode is the transfer of tacit knowledge into to a new form of tacit knowledge. It is a method by which experiences are shared through observation, imitation, and practice. Eventually experience allows the knowledge to become part of the receiver's tacit knowledge base. If we return to the example of the dishwasher repairman, he/she can transfer their tacit knowledge on the condition of the dishwasher. But for this tacit knowledge to be transferred, the receiver must be in the same location.

Nonaka and Takeuchi (1995, p. 72) term the interaction between the four modes of knowledge a spiral of organizational knowledge creation (Figure 4.2). Here the interaction between tacit knowledge and explicit knowledge will become larger in scale as it moves up the ontological levels. Thus, organizational knowledge creation is a spiral process, starting at the individual level and moving up through expanding communities of interaction, that crosses sectional, departmental, divisional, and organizational boundaries.

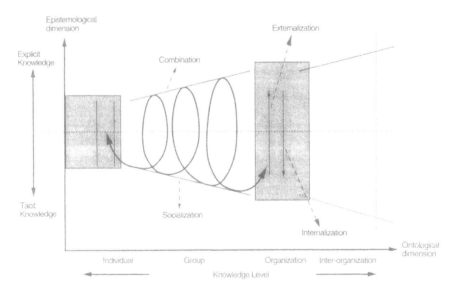

Source: Figure 3.5: *The Knowledge-Creating Company: How Japanese Companies Create the Dynamics of Innovation* by I. Nonaka and H. Takeuchi, copyright1995 by Oxford University Press, Inc. Used by permission of Oxford University Press, Inc.

Figure 4.2   Spiral of Organizational Knowledge Creation

We are only interested in one aspect of the spiral of organizational knowledge creation, inter-organizational knowledge transfer. This is a removal from the concept of the classic corporation where internal learning was the considered a superior means for achieving competitive advantage. In the classic corporation, knowledge is obtained through internal research and development while manual labor is separated from the learning process.

Hudson (1999) points out that it is important to move away from the concept of the classic corporation where emphasis is placed on achieving scale economies and increasing productivity growth. The primary shortcoming of this approach is the inability of customers to provide feedback to the innovator. Accordingly, goods produced by the firm could be out of line with customer needs and the chance for new product development could be neglected. He argues that as the production process becomes more complicated, the need for inter-organizational knowledge transfer increases. As a result, know-who is becoming important in the generation of know-how.

When the external and internal knowledges are combined new ideas and concepts translate into new processes and innovative products. Bierly and Chakrabarti (1996, p. 124) argue that internal and external learning are mutually dependent. They suggest:

> Firms must excel at internal learning and develop absorptive capacity before they can learn from external sources. Internal R&D can increase absorptive capacity in the specific area production experience, and advanced technical learning. On the other hand, the internal learning process can be substantially improved by effective external learning, since there will obviously be many new ideas generated outside the firm. In addition, external learning will enable firms to view some issues from different perspectives, which may be difficult to do with only internal learning due to established organizational routines and biases. Thus, internal and external learning are both vital to the success of the firm.

It should now be evident that knowledge cannot be entirely created from within the firm. To continually innovate, new knowledge must be acquired. External sources are ideal for procuring such new knowledge. External learning is necessary for the firm to remain familiar with new products and processes. It increases the flexibility of the firm, which is vital in today's competitive global economy. It could be argued that inter-organizational relationships are the most important for knowledge transfer because they introduce radically different knowledge to the firm. External knowledge allows a firm to solve problems more efficiently. This is important to the knowledge creation process and thus competitive advantage to the firm.

Japanese firms are well known for using this process. There are a number of examples where a basic idea developed by another company has been used to perfect an existing product or to create a new one. For example, Mitsubishi reverse engineered a high intensity lamp product introduced by the American firm Fusion Systems to create an almost identical product. But DiBella and Nevis (1998, p. 43) show how American firms do this as well. One need only look at how IBM used reflective imitation some fifty years ago to take what Univac had innovated - a computer's central processing unit - and gained domination of the field by better implementation of the concept.

Where does this external knowledge come from? Since tacit knowledge leads to competitive advantage and it can initially only be procured through face-to-face contact, generally external knowledge that leads to competitive advantage comes from the region. As a result, key regions where place-specific tacit knowledge exists have become vital for competitive advantage. The next section reviews literature that discusses knowledge transfer.

Knowledge Transfer

Historically, the study of knowledge transfer begins with Marshall's (1920) three rationales for regionalization revealed earlier in this chapter: (1) labor market pooling; (2) the creation of specialist suppliers; and (3) the development of technological knowledge spillovers. Over time, authors have built upon his third rationale to contribute important findings to the study of knowledge transfer. The initial contributions to this field rarely distinguish between information and knowledge. In fact, information, as it is defined in past literature, possesses many of the same characteristics as explicit knowledge, while knowledge in past literature takes on a form similar to tacit knowledge.

The distinguished list of contributions to information/knowledge transfer starts with Hägerstrand (1967). He wanted to answer the question how does a piece of information diffuse through space. All other things being equal the chance of one person getting to know the information from someone already possessing it depends entirely on the distance separating them. Although, today's technology has advanced well beyond Hägerstrand's highly simplified assumptions, the fact of the matter is that he suggested that a piece of information could only be advanced through face-to-face contact. This assumption still holds true for initial tacit knowledge transfer.

Hägerstrand also suggested that certain types of information appear to be spread through the system of urban centers. Thus, we would expect some information to spread over space by hierarchical diffusion. Hierarchical diffusion rests on the notion that connections between large urban centers may be closer than connections between proximal locations. As Szulanski (1996) points out the term transfer is used today instead of diffusion to highlight the movement of knowledge as a discrete experience, not a gradual one.

The pioneering study by Hagerstrand spurred additional important research on information and the region by Tornqvist (1968), and Thorngren (1970), and Taylor (1975). But it was not until Pred (1977) that a dynamic model of information transfer and its advantages were introduced. Pred's (1977) principle of circular cumulative causation argues that a region possessing knowledge in a certain industry is likely to grow because it possesses the necessary condition for growth. Firms want to have access to the knowledge that exists in this region. This brings in more actors, and thus more knowledge. When new people come to the region, they bring with them new ideas. The converging of the different knowledges dovetails into inventions and innovations through new and improved products. Multiplier effects promote the fulfillment of successive industrial thresholds. Today this is occurring in regions where superior tacit knowledge is transferred from one firm to another. Firms in this region continually maintain up-to-date knowledge that provides a competitive advantage to make superior products sooner.

While Pred's (1977) theoretical contributions were ingenious, he discussed a different knowledge than exists today. By exclusively considering knowledge in its explicit state, Pred was unable to fully explain how knowledge and the region currently lead to competitive advantage. Theoretical developments in knowledge transfer research over the last decade have accomplished this by differentiating between tacit and explicit knowledge. Therefore ramifications for knowledge transfer within a region take on a more important meaning.

Perhaps Malmberg and Maskell (Malmberg 2000; Malmberg 1996; Malmberg, Solvell, and Zander 1996; Maskell 1999; Maskell and Malmberg 1999a; Maskell and Malmberg 1999b; Maskell, Eskelinin, Hannibalsson, Malmberg, and Vatne 1998) have explored the spatiality of knowledge transfer more than any other researchers. They suggest that transfer of knowledge is dependent on the quality of social interaction between individuals. These are strengthened when the two individuals transferring knowledge share a similar social and cultural environment, both of which are enhanced when the two individuals live in the same region. Malmberg and Maskell argue that direct face-to-face relations allow individuals to build a basis for sustained trust that is conducive to the diffusion of technical knowledge and skills. Feldman and Florida (1994, p.214) agree with this argument by suggesting this trust allows for the cross fertilization of ideas between firms in the region.

While explicit knowledge can move directly from a source to destination across the globe, the transfer of tacit knowledge would likely require a number of individual exchanges for the same distance. Szulanski (1996, p. 32) suggests the success of such exchanges depends to some extent on the ease of communication and on the intimacy of the overall relationship between the source unit and the recipient unit. It seems obvious that if the source and destination exist in the same area, they will more likely share the same social qualities. Thus, the intimacy and ease of communication should be heightened at the regional level.

Morgan (1997) claims that dynamic regions are important centers of new knowledge in their industries of specialization. In particular, he suggests that feedback loops are an important source of knowledge. A lack of feedback indicates activities like research and development have little chance to learn from the past. For example, customers can contribute knowledge on product deficiency. The lines of communication for these feedback loops are heightened the closer the suppliers and buyers are.

Obtaining external tacit knowledge: Why is the region the most efficient scale?

As pointed out earlier, we are primarily concerned with obtaining external knowledge through inter-organizational relationships. There are a number of ways for a firm to procure this external knowledge. Alliances, foreign direct investment, acquisitions, and mergers are a few of the more permanent relations. Links to suppliers and buyers, interlocking directorates, start-ups by individuals belonging to another local firm, staff movement, and rumors are a few examples of less abiding but very important knowledge networks. For instance, Henry and Pinch (2000, p. 198) provide an example of the motor sport industry where the end of a racing season brings the transfer of workers between firms. As designers, engineers, managers, and drivers move between teams they take knowledge and ideas from their previous firms. They provide an example from an interview:

Then he moves to another team and he takes ways of one team into another. And you go from [leading F1 constructor] to McLaren and say 'at [leading F1 constructor] we did it this way' and they say 'oh really, let's try it'. And then visa versa, someone comes from McLaren to here and someone goes to Williams and you get all these exchanges of people and then we learn from each other all the time. Not trade secrets, obviously, but ways of doing things. If someone use to draw wings a McLaren or Williams and he comes to draw wings here, he is not going to bring the drawings from McLaren under his arm, but he is going to bring ways of doing it in here, so he is allowed to explain. He may improve because he is going to see what we have got here, he is going to see the way he did it before and he will say 'ah, I can mix these two and get something even better', and you improve that little bit, and it keeps happening.

Another example is Saxenian's (1994, p.147) comparison of Silicon Valley's network based system to Route 128's firm based system. She argues that the firm based system of Route 128 isolates producers from external sources of knowledge. On the other hand, the inter-organizational relationships foster learning that leads to competitive advantage for firms in Silicon Valley. The promotion of collective learning produces superior knowledge for the entire region:

In the words of Hewlett Packard manufacturing VP Harold Edmonson: 'we share our new product aspirations with them and they tell us the technological direction in which they are heading'. Another Hewlett Packard executive reported sharing proprietary product designs with suppliers as much as five years in advance in order to ensure access to state of the art components: 'A lot of our products are pushing the edge of technological barriers: we need the fastest, highest density SRAMS or the most powerful disk drives, and we need them early. If we collaborate, we share the risk of development'.

Cecil and Green (2000) suggest that firms are attracted to a region because they want to connect to flagship firms, or large firms that have a market presence. Since they play central roles in a network of firms, flagship firms are important to understand the industrial organizational structure. Dyer and Nobeoka (2000) support this argument by revealing the network Toyota maintains with its suppliers. The authors indicate that firms can be unwilling to share their knowledge because this is exactly what provides them a competitive advantage. Unfortunately, the knowledge that is most valuable to other firms is often this same knowledge.

Of course there are winners and losers, or firms that are able to gain more from cooperation. But the trick is to show suppliers that being a part of the knowledge network is advantageous for all. Shared learning creates more knowledge when compared to isolating themselves. Knowledge creation takes place because individual firms access a greater amount of external tacit knowledge. After this tacit knowledge is internalized, new higher ordered knowledge is created. This new knowledge is then shared with other firms in the network. This process leads to the sustained creation of superior knowledge, and thus competitive advantage for firms within the network.

For this process to work though, knowledge must continually be shared with other firms in the network, even if some of this knowledge spills over to competitors. As Dyer and Nobeoka (2000, p. 365) note:

> One Toyota executive observed, 'We are not so concerned that our knowledge will spill over to competitors. Some of it will. But by the time it does, we will be somewhere else. We are a moving target'. This executive is expressing the idea that Toyota's advantage is sustainable because Toyota and its suppliers have a dynamic learning capability and learn at a faster rate than competitors.

All three examples resemble Pred's theory of cumulative causation over twenty years after he first introduced his theory. They do this by asserting the importance of continual knowledge creation. In a business environment where product life cycles are becoming ever shorter, successful companies are those that consistently access new knowledge, and quickly apply it to new technologies and products. These are the companies that continually innovate and prosper. What is not instantly obvious in these examples is the importance of close geographic space. All three examples of tacit knowledge transfer occur in a region.

Region! The Be All and End All?

A counter argument to regional tacit knowledge transfer has been introduced. While Amin and Robins (1990) denote the importance of the region, they suggest it is overemphasized in the literature. Changes to the global economy and the structural changes that go along with it produce a number of diverse processes. Inter-organizational relationships at the local scale answer cannot explain all these processes.

There is little doubt that regional interaction is important for the transfer of tacit knowledge. But to consider local interdependencies as always superior is inadequate. For example, even in the entertainment business, not all relevant firms and holders of knowledge are located in Hollywood. To avoid this problem firms join a network of firms. These are cooperative but not necessarily in the same location. Oinas and Malecki (1999) point out that relationships with firms in other regions contribute new ideas. These ideas are a basis to contrast local concepts. They call the combination of regional innovation systems plus their connections a spatial innovation system.

Relationships beyond the immediate area are less apparent as sources for knowledge. Amin and Cohendet (1999) propose a number of questions for the concept of the region. Are imitation and adaptation suitable for innovation? Are regions flexible enough to adjust to radical changes in product or process technology if these changes take place outside the region? Can they continually establish global standards in their industries if they simply imitate and adapt to other firms in the region? If so can they retain these global standards? Even worse, when a region declines can it regain its' competitive advantage?

Pouder and St. John (1996, p. 1193) reiterate this argument by suggesting that firms in a region may initially be highly competitive. But over time these firms are inclined to be less innovative because they limit their competition to their region and not the entire global industry. This gives rise to restrictive blind spots which limit innovative potential and adversely affect their performance. These blind spots may have a negative impact on innovation as the region evolves.

As pointed out in the previous section, long-term associations are built up through suppliers and customers. But the previous section argued that loyalty and trust is heightened when suppliers and customers are located in the same region. Using the mechanical engineering industry of the Neckar-Alb region of South West Germany, Grotz and Braun (1993) suggest that innovation oriented relationships are far less spatially restrictive than generally assumed.

Tacit and Explicit Knowledge along a Continuum

The concept of region in the past has taken on a number of different geographic scales. Returning to Hartshorne (1977), this occurs because scale is determined by the economic phenomenon one is dealing with.

Different economic phenomena require a different scale, and thus a different geographical definition for a region. For example, custom software development maybe very local, while, the region for the auto industry is much larger. The same argument can be made for the region as it pertains to knowledge. Scale is different because different types of knowledge require different scales to be transferred.

In this chapter we introduced two separate schools of thought with regards to tacit knowledge transfer. One viewpoint suggests the region is important and the other suggests it is not. Both perspectives provide valid points. But both perspectives regard tacit and explicit knowledge as discrete concepts. We disagree. As revealed in Figure 4.3, knowledge should be arranged along a continuum where extreme tacit knowledge transfer lies at the far right. As one proceeds further to the left, the ease of knowledge transfer increases until extreme explicit knowledge is reached. French (2000) who argues that present explicit/tacit knowledge research has taken on restrictive global/local dimensions highlights the importance of examining knowledge along a continuum.

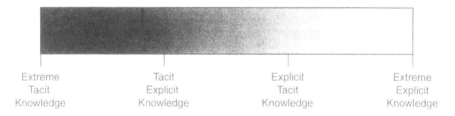

| Extreme Tacit Knowledge | Tacit Explicit Knowledge | Explicit Tacit Knowledge | Extreme Explicit Knowledge |

Figure 4.3 Knowledge Continuum

In the case of extreme tacit knowledge transfer, local relationships are necessary since this form of knowledge can only be transferred through face-to-face contact. Nonaka and Takeuchi (1995) provide the example of a bread-making machine developed by Matsushita Electric Company. Initially, the machine produced inferior bread. In response, the development team and engineers trained with the head baker at Osaka International Hotel to make superior tasting bread. To capture the tacit knowledge of the head baker, face-to-face contact was necessary to understand how to knead and bake bread. In the end, tacit knowledge transfer created a superior product through imitation and practice.

Further along the continuum in Figure 4.3 is tacit-explicit knowledge, a less localized form of tacit knowledge transfer. In this case, initial face-to-face contact is necessary to build up trust. Therefore, the region is initially important. But after the introductory bond is formed, continual face-to-face contact is not vital for this tacit knowledge to be transferred. Higher ordered tacit-explicit knowledge only needs periodic reaffirmation for the trust to remain. Corporate strategy is an example of tacit-explicit knowledge. Interlocking directorates (when a director of one company sits on the board of another company) is an example of this type of knowledge. Initial trust can be built up between directors when they come together for board meetings. But board meetings only occur periodically. Between meetings, when directors do not come into face-to-face contact with each other, we argue that corporate strategy can still be transferred over such things as the telephone. Of course, the ability to transfer this type of tacit knowledge is still superior at the regional level.

As revealed in the figure, the subsequent stage is explicit-tacit knowledge. Even less face-to-face contact is necessary for its transfer. An example is a university course via correspondence. The course manual inevitably leads to students interpreting the material differently. To overcome this shortcoming, the teacher must meet with students to clear any ambiguity.

Finally, extreme explicit knowledge can be transferred across the globe instantaneously. This type of knowledge transfer has increased exponentially over the past decade with the advent of the personal computer and the Internet. Files containing knowledge can be transferred from an individual in Toronto to another individual in Bombay without the two ever knowing each other.

Conclusion

Historically, classical location theory defines the sources of wealth as land, labor, and capital. For most of the last century, researchers have explained the competitive advantage by these factors and their spatial distribution. But today, the sources of wealth have changed. In this chapter we show how competitive advantage has shifted rapidly from tangible to intangible resources. Knowledge now leads to the prosperity of firms. The most successful firms have flourished in a global competitive business environment by either developing or acquiring these new sources of wealth. However, as argued by French (2000), our understanding of the spatiality of knowledge is still very much in its infancy.

Also in this chapter we introduced an interesting paradox. As economic activity becomes increasingly global, individual regions play a more critical role for competitive advantage. Competition and technology are likely to increase the value of proximity as it relates to tacit knowledge because codified knowledge can be transferred more easily. Therein lies a paradox: sustaining competitive advantages in a global economy lies at the regional level because tacit knowledge remains at the regional level. Thus as pointed out by Amin and Cohendet (1999, p. 90) "as long as institutional sclerosis can be avoided, the assets of regions can be seen as unique sources of success in a global economy."

Finally, in this chapter we introduced the concept of a knowledge transfer continuum. Here we argue that explicit and tacit knowledge are not discrete concepts. Rather they overlap. Previous research has focussed on extreme tacit knowledge and extreme explicit knowledge. Therefore, it seems logical that the next step is to examine knowledge transfer at different stages along the continuum. This will allow researchers to more completely determine the relationship between knowledge, region, and competitiveness.

References

Akoorie, M. (2000), "Organizational Clusters in a Resource Based Industry: Empirical Evidence from New Zealand", in M. Green and R. McNaughton (eds), *Industrial Networks and Proximity*, Ashgate, Aldershot, pp. 133-164.

Amin, A. and Cohendet, P. (1999), "Learning and Adaptation in Decentralized Business Networks", *Environment and Planning D: Society and Space*, vol. 17, pp. 87-104.

Amin, A. and Robins, K. (1990), "The Re-emergence of Regional Economies? The Mythical Geography of Flexible Accumulation", *Environment and Planning D: Society and Space*, vol. 8, pp. 7-34.

Bierly, P. and Chakrabarti, A. (1996), "Generic Knowledge Strategies in the U.S. Pharmaceutical Industry", *Strategic Management Journal*, vol. 17, Winter Special Issue, pp. 123-136.

Capello, R. (1999), "Spatial Transfer of Knowledge in High Technology Milieux: Learning Versus Collective Learning Processes", *Regional Studies*, vol. 33, pp. 353-365.

Cecil, B. and Green, M. (2000), "In the Flagships' Wake: Relations, Motivations, and Observations of Strategic Alliance Activity Among IT Sector Flagship Firms and their Partners", in M. Green and R. McNaughton (eds.), *Industrial Networks and Proximity*, Ashgate, Aldershot, pp. 165-187.

DiBella, A. and Nevis, E. (1998), *How Organizations Learn: An Integrated Strategy for Building Learning Capability*, Jossey-Bass Publishers, San Francisco.

Drucker, P. (1993), *Post-Capitalist Society*, Butterworth-Heinemann, Oxford, England.

Dyer, J. and Nobeoka, K. (2000), "Creating and Managing a High-Performance Knowledge-Sharing Network: the Toyota Case", *Strategic Management Journal*, vol. 21, pp. 345-367.

Feldman, M. and Florida, R. (1994), "The Geographic Sources of Innovation: Technological Infrastructure and Product Innovation in the United States", *Annals of the Association of American Geographers*, vol. 84, pp. 210-229.

Foss, N. (1996), "Knowledge Based Approaches to the Theory of the firm, Some Critical Comments", *Organization Science*, vol. 7, pp. 470-476.

French, S. (2000), "Re-scaling the economic geography of knowledge and information: constructing life assurance markets", *Geoforum*, vol. 31, pp. 101-119.

Getis, A., Getis, J. and Fellmann, J. (2000), *Introduction to Geography*, 7th Edition, McGraw Hill, New York.

Grant, R. (1997), "The Knowledge-based View of the Firm: Implications for Management Practice", *Long Range Planning*, vol. 30, pp. 450-454.

Grotz, R. and Braun, B. (1993), "Networks, Milieux and Individual Firm Strategies: Empirical Evidence of an Innovative SME Environment", *Geografiska Annaler B*, vol. 75, pp. 149-162.

Hägerstrand, T. (1967), *Innovation Diffusion as a Spatial Process*, Chicago University Press, Chicago.

Hartshorne, R. (1977), *The Nature of Geography*, Greenwood Press, Westport, CT.

Henry, N. and Pinch, S. (2000), "Spatialising knowledge: Placing the Knowledge Community of Motor Sport Valley", *Geoforum*, vol. 31, pp. 191-208.

Hudson, R. (1999), "The Learning Economy, the Learning Firm and the Learning Region: A Sympathetic Critique of the Limits to Learning", *European Urban and Regional Studies*, vol. 6, pp. 59-71.

Huseman, R. and Goodman, J. (1999), *Leading With Knowledge: The Nature of Competition in the 21st Century*, Sage Publications, London.

Johnston, R., Gregory, D. and Smith, D. (1994), *The Dictionary of Human Geography*, Blackwell, Cambridge, Mass.

Krugman, P. (1997), *Development, Geography, and Economic Theory*, MIT Press, Cambridge, Mass.

Malmberg, A. (1996), "Industrial Geography: Agglomeration and Local Milieu", *Progress in Human Geography*, vol. 20, pp. 392-403.

Malmberg, A. (2000), *The Elusive Concept of Agglomeration Economies: Theoretical Principles and Empirical Paradoxes*, Paper prepared for a seminar at the Swedish Collegium for Advanced Study in the Social Sciences (SCASSS), March.

Malmberg, A., Solvell, O. and Zander, I. (1996), "Spatial Clustering, Local Accumulation of Knowledge and Firm Competitiveness", *Geografiska Annaler*, vol. 78, pp. 85-97.

Marshall, A. (1920), *Principles of Economics*, Macmillan Company, New York.

Maskell, P. (1999), "Globalization and Industrial Competitiveness: the Process and Consequences of Ubiquification", in E. Malecki and P. Oinas, *Making Connections: Technological Learning and Regional Economic Change*, Ashgate, Aldershot.

Maskell, P. and Malmberg, A. (1999a), "The Competitiveness of Firms and Regions", *European Urban and Regional Studies*, vol. 6, pp. 9-25.

Maskell, P. and Malmberg, A. (1999b), "Localized Learning and Industrial Competitiveness" *Cambridge Journal of Economics*, vol. 23, pp. 167-185.

Maskell, P., Eskelinin, H., Hannibalsson, I., Malmberg, A. and Vatne, E. (1998), *Competitiveness, Localized Learning and Regional Development*, Routledge, London.

Morgan, K. (1997), "The Learning Region: Institutions, Innovation and Regional Renewal", *Regional Studies*, vol. 31, pp. 491-503.

Nonaka, I. and Takeuchi, H. (1995), *The Knowledge Creating Company*, Oxford University Press, New York.

Oinas, P. and Malecki, E. (1999), "Spatial Innovation Systems", in E. Malecki and P. Oinas, *Making Connections: Technological Learning and Regional Economic Change*, Ashgate, Aldershot.

Pinch, S. and Henry, N. (1999), "Paul Krugman's Geographical Economics, Industrial Clustering and the British Motor Sport Industry", *Regional Studies*, vol. 33, pp. 815-827.

Pouder, R. and St. John, C. (1996), "Hot Spots and Blind Spots: Geographical Clusters of Firms and Innovation", *Academy of Management*, vol. 21, pp. 1192-1215.

Pred, A. (1977), *City-systems in advanced economies: past growth, present processes and future development options*, Hutchinson, London.

Prusak, L. (1997), *Knowledge in Organizations*, Butterworth-Heinemann, Boston.

Saxenian, A. (1994), *Regional Advantage: Culture and Competition in Silicon Valley and Route 128*, Harvard University Press, Cambridge, Massachusetts.

Smith, C. (1976), "Analyzing Regional Social Systems", in Carol Smith (ed.), *Regional Analysis*, Academic Press Inc, New York.

Storper, M. (1997), *The Regional World: Territorial Development in a Global Economy*, Guilford Press, New York.

Szulanski, G. (1996), "Exploring Internal Stickiness: Impediments to the Transfer of Best Practice Within the Firm", *Strategic Management Journal*, vol. 17, Winter Special Issue, pp. 27-44.

Taylor, M. (1975), "Organizational Growth, Spatial Interaction and Location Decision-Making", *Regional Studies*, vol. 9, pp. 313-323.

Teece, D. (1998), "Capturing value from knowledge assets: The new economy, markets for know-how, and intangible assets", *California Management Review*, vol. 40, pp. 55-79.

Thorngren, B. (1970), "How do Contact Systems Affect Regional Development", *Environment and Planning*, vol. 2, pp. 409-427.

Tornqvist, G. (1968), *Flows of information and the location of economic activities*, Gleerup, Lund.

PART II:
INNOVATION IN LOCAL
NETWORKS

5 Spatially Binding Linkages in Manufacturing Product Chains

EDWARD J. FESER AND STUART H. SWEENEY

Industry clusters are typically defined as significant geographic concentrations of major end-market industries, their extended supply chains, other sectors that share close technological or human capital affinities, and various specialized supporting institutions (e.g., universities with specialized training or R&D activities, technical colleges offering relevant vocational training, technology assistance agencies, and the like). Firms in clusters are said to benefit from spillovers in formal and informal networks, basic economies of agglomeration, and a type of head-to-head competition that favors a degree of collaboration along with old-fashioned rivalry (Best 1990; Porter 1990, 1998, 2000a). To the extent that the productivity, cost, or innovation advantages that cluster firms enjoy arise from non-pecuniary sources, one can build a case for public sector activities that nurture the emergence and expansion of clusters.

But firms enjoy positive externalities that are both local and non-local in scope. A manufacturer of automotive wire harnesses in Juarez, Mexico might take advantage of a technological breakthrough made by a similar producer in Tokyo if enough information about the innovation was disseminated via some mechanism (e.g., simple word of mouth, trade journals, industry associations, conferences, etc.). The Japanese and Mexican wire harness firms are essentially members of a "global industry cluster", a large, diverse group of closely related industries and institutions that is far-flung in geographical extent. As the global cluster increases in size and diversity, the potential for such non-market, non-local spillovers increases. This notion is not new. The concept of localized versus non-localized spillovers is closely akin to Robinson's (1931) distinction between mobile and immobile external economies.

It is clear that enterprises with key economic linkages do not always cluster in space. But an interesting question is whether linked firms are likely to exhibit a greater or lesser degree of spatial clustering depending on the specific nature of the linkage. Recent studies of industrial districts, flexible production regimes, local firm networks, and regional innovation systems provide some clues as to the kinds of relationships that either encourage businesses to seek proximate locations or influence them to remain in existing agglomerations despite the proliferation of new information technologies that make peripheral sites less remote. Unfortunately, most direct studies of the link between inter-firm ties and co-location have viewed space only in discrete terms. Most often, well-known industrial regions or districts (e.g., Third Italy, the Silicon Valley) are studied to characterize localized business transactions, identify firm networks, and describe social and cultural factors contributing to the competitive success of the given agglomeration or district (Saxenian 1994; Rabellotti 1995; Schmitz 1995; Markusen 1996). Indeed, Porter's (1990) definitive study of industry competitiveness in ten industrialized countries takes this approach.

In this chapter, we seek to investigate the direct relationship between the types of linkages between firms and industries and observed patterns of spatial industrial concentration. We do this by combining information about business locations with data on industry linkages to characterize the "spatially binding ties" within identified economic clusters. Specifically, we use a point process model and enterprise-level data to isolate the sectors that drive observed spatial clustering of the US printing and publishing value chain. Our effort is purposely exploratory, with our goal as much to develop a workable methodological approach as it is to understand the spatial dynamics of the printing and publishing industry. We do not claim that our input-output based method of characterizing linkages between industries and firms is ideal. But we do argue that meshing a pre-defined specification of the economic relationship between firms in a given region with systematic empirical analysis of observed co-location can contribute important insights to the analysis of agglomeration, firm networks, and regional growth.

The paper proceeds as follows. The next section briefly notes pertinent literature and lays out our study questions and basic empirical approach. We then provide detail of method and results. A final section summarizes our approach and suggests areas of further research.

Do Clusters Cluster and Why?

Plenty of attention has been paid to the concept of industry clusters of late. Much of it has focused on defining what clusters are, how they can be identified in specific places, and what governments in those places can do to nurture their growth (Lazonick 1993; Doeringer and Terkla 1995; Held 1996; Jacobs and de Man 1996; Rosenfeld 1997; Meyer-Stamer 1998; Hill and Brennan 2000). Porter (1990, 1998, 2000a) makes a persuasive case that environmental factors – including a nation or locality's legal and regulatory framework, localized relationships between firms, the competitive structure of local industry, the local business climate, and the like – contribute importantly to industries' competitiveness. His ideas, presented from the point of view of strategic management theory, echo those of a variety of other perspectives, including classical agglomeration theory, the theory of new industrial districts, post-Fordism and flexible specialization, networks and regional milieu, and neoclassical spatial economics.

In an earlier paper, we examined the relatively straightforward conjecture that enterprises in the same nominal product value chain have a tendency to co-locate geographically (Feser and Sweeney 2000). This hypothesis was the subject of considerable research in regional science in the 1960s and 1970s (Streit 1969; Townroe 1970; Lever 1972; Taylor 1973; Roepke 1974; Bergsman, et al. 1975; Bopp and Gordon 1977; Streit 1977; Czamanski and de Ablas 1979). It attracted less and less attention as dissatisfaction with static input-output techniques, prevailing methods of testing for spatial association, and the often assumption-laden and contextually sterile approach of regional science, mounted (although see Howe 1991, and Ó hUallacháin 1984). Thus today one finds little reference to "industrial complexes"– essentially localized product value chains – in the urban and regional literature, despite their striking affinity with modern cluster concepts.

Despite its fundamental limitations, what research on industrial complexes had going for it was a very clear distinction between spatial and functional industry clustering, and, by extension, a certain basic consistency with concepts like mobile and immobile external economies. Industries may be linked in input-output product chains or in other ways (functional clusters), but given the myriad factors affecting the location calculus of individual enterprises, linked sectors and businesses may not concentrate in specific regions (spatial clusters or complexes). It is fair enough to question the means by which inter-industry ties or linkages are identified, i.e. input-output techniques. Certainly a strong case can be made that physical product flows and associated transportation costs are no longer as critical to the competitive bottom-line of the modern industrial enterprise as they once were. But the value of the basic research approach remains: if we believe that a specific kind of relationship between firms and industries has a spatial component or in some fashion depends on spatial co-location, then we should test that belief through direct observation of revealed location behavior. Input-output linkage is simply one type of relationship, as worthy of empirical investigation, a priori, as any other.

In Feser and Sweeney (2000), we outlined and illustrated an approach to testing whether establishments in nine different key product value chains in North Carolina are spatially clustered, controlling for the general pattern of enterprise locations in major urban areas and industrial districts of the state. In other words, we aimed to isolate that degree of spatial clustering that could be attributed specifically to presence in a nominal product value chain, as opposed to that driven by the more general advantages of urban agglomeration that might be enjoyed by any manufacturer. We found that among highly clustered value chains were computers and electronics and printing and publishing. Also clustered, but to a relatively lesser degree, were metalworking, vehicle manufacturing, chemicals and rubber, and packaged food products. Three value chains exhibited very modest clustering or even significant geographic dispersion at various spatial scales: fabricated textiles, knitted goods, and wood products and furniture. In general, more technology-intensive value chains tended to exhibit higher degrees of geographic co-location.

Our methodology permits us to test whether specific elements of a given value chain are more or less responsible for the overall spatial result. For example, do the high technology components of vehicle manufacturing (electronics, engines, etc.) account for observed clustering of the chain while lower technology elements (metals, automotive textiles) exhibit a countervailing tendency toward dispersal? Are end-market components of the chain more spatially clustered than intermediate market components or natural resource based elements? In effect, we can look for the "spatially-binding" segments of the chain and thereby better characterize the unique overall location pattern of a given set of related industries. Here again it is worth emphasizing that the notion of a product value chain, as operationalized with input-output analysis, is simply one possible means of characterizing ties between sectors and the enterprises that make them up. Through firm surveys and other techniques, we could characterize other types of linkages (e.g., labor or technology flows) and test for spatial association in a like manner.

In the following section, we outline the methodology in detail. But summarizing briefly, we take as a point of departure the analysis of value chains utilized in Feser and Sweeney (2000) and reported initially in Feser and Bergman (2000). We focus on one chain specifically, printing and publishing, breaking it into its major components and leading sectors. Using point process techniques and case-control methods, we then use establishment-level data geocoded to street address to test for spatial clustering of each component and key sector in a predefined study area, isolating parts of the chain that exhibit co-location versus dispersal. We interpret the results in the context of prevailing theories of agglomeration, industry clustering, location, and firm networks.

Methodology

Feser and Bergman (2000) used a slightly modified version of Czamanski's (1974) methodology for detecting groups of American industries linked through primary, secondary, and tertiary input-output linkages. Their analysis was conducted at the national level using highly detailed US benchmark input-output data for 1987, the objective being to identify a set of benchmark manufacturing value chains for use in regional economic analyses. One advantage of the benchmark value chains is that they characterize linkages between sectors irrespective of location and can therefore help summarize regional economic specialization using a product chain, rather than sector-based, logic (see Bergman and Feser, 2000, for a more extensive discussion). Another advantage of the benchmark chains is that they provide a reasonable first approximation of the groups of sectors that might comprise spatial industry clusters of the Porter (1990) variety. Indeed, in a recent study of information technology in Mississippi, Porter and his research team used informal value-chain logic to separate Standard Industrial Classification (SIC) sectors into information technology and communications clusters before documenting Mississippi-specific linkages and relationships (Porter 2000a, 2000b). The aspatial approach in Feser and Bergman (2000) is essentially analogous, though much more formalized through a statistical factor analysis of input-output flows.

Among the benchmark clusters identified was printing and publishing, a key value chain nationwide and in many states. Table 5.1 presents the chain's basic makeup. Individual sectors are separated into major components (lumber, paper, publishing, printing, and other). The loading for each detailed industry derives from a factor analysis of input-output relationships; the higher the loading, the tighter the degree of linkage between the sector and overall chain. Book printing (SIC 2732, with a loading of 0.98) loaded very tightly on the group, for example, while platemaking and related services (SIC 2796, loading of 0.43) loaded comparatively weakly. Indeed, the platemaking and related services sector is more closely linked to industries in the metalworking value chain than it is to sectors in printing and publishing.

The interpretation of the loadings and criteria for separating sectors into chains are discussed thoroughly in Feser and Bergman (2000) and Bergman and Feser (2000) and need not be reiterated in detail here. However, two points should help clarify the origin and meaning of the printing and publishing chain.

Table 5.1   Printing and Publishing Value Chain

Linkage	SIC	I-O Code	Description	Load	Establish-ments
Lumber components (n=42)					
Secondary	2421	I200200	Sawmills and planing mills, general	0.50	32
Secondary	2448	I200901	Wood pallets and skids	0.47	10
Paper components (n=78)					
Primary	261	I240100	Pulp mills	0.76	2
Secondary	2677	I240400	Envelopes	0.68	1
Primary	2676	I240500	Sanitary paper products	0.77	0
Primary	2671-2	I240701	Paper coating and glazing	0.91	8
Primary	2673-4	I240702	Bags, except textile	0.69	7
Primary	2675	I240703	Die-cut paper and paperboard and cardboard	0.85	5
Primary	2678	I240705	Stationery, tablets, and related products	0.90	1
Primary	2679	I240706	Converted paper products, nec	0.87	10
Secondary	262-3	I240800	Paper and paperboard mills	0.42	1
Primary	265	I250000	Paperboard containers and boxes	0.90	43
Publishing components (n=87)					
Primary	271	I260100	Newspapers	0.79	42
Primary	272	I260200	Periodicals	0.67	18
Primary	2731	I260301	Book publishing	0.87	7
Primary	274	I260400	Miscellaneous publishing	0.63	20
Printing components (n=294)					
Primary	2732	I260302	Book printing	0.98	1
Primary	275	I260501	Commercial printing	0.96	254
Primary	276	I260601	Manifold business forms	0.87	2
Primary	2782	I260602	Blankbooks, looseleaf binders and devices	0.97	3
Primary	277	I260700	Greeting cards	0.90	0
Primary	2789	I260802	Bookbinding and related work	0.93	14
Secondary	2791	I260803	Typesetting	0.64	7
Secondary	2796	I260806	Platemaking and related services	0.43	13
Other (n=13)					
Secondary	2843	I290203	Surface active agents	0.41	7
Secondary	3274	I361300	Lime	0.53	0
Primary	3275	I361400	Gypsum products	0.63	2

Table 5.1   Printing and Publishing Value Chain (continued)

Linkage	SIC	I-O Code	Description	Load	Establish-ments
Secondary	3652	I560200	Prerecorded records and tapes	0.54	1
Secondary	386	I630300	Photographic equip. and supplies	0.39	1
Secondary	3944	I640301	Games, toys, and children's vehicles	0.35	1
Primary	3955	I640504	Carbon paper and inked ribbons	0.83	0

First, the benchmark value chains are not mutually exclusive, given that many sectors are suppliers to (and/or buyers from) many divergent industries. Thus some sectors in the printing and publishing chain are also members of the metalworking, computers and electronics, and wood products value chains. Second, the loading serves as a useful measure of strength of linkage to identify "primary" versus "secondary" members of each chain, where the latter are defined as members/sectors that are more closely tied to other chains on the basis of the statistical analysis. In Feser and Sweeney (2000), as well as below, we test whether tightly-linked members/sectors are also more commonly clustered geographically than weaker members/sectors.

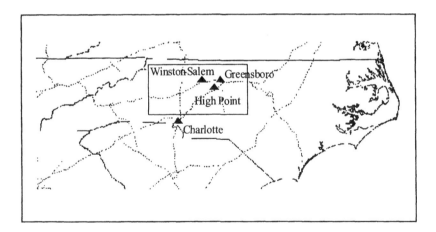

Figure 5.1   Study Region Boundary

Given the definition of the printing and publishing value chain, we defined a study region for the spatial analysis (see Figure 5.1). The region encompasses the industrial heart of North Carolina, including the manufacturing-oriented cities of Greensboro, Winston-Salem, High Point, and Hickory. Interstate 40 bisects it east to west, and Interstates 85 and 77 bisect it north to south. Using confidential establishment-level data from the North Carolina Employment Security Commission, we geo-coded manufacturing establishments in the state, revealing the point pattern of printing and publishing enterprises as well as all other manufacturing plants.[1] The selection of the region was more or less arbitrary within the methodological bounds of the spatial analysis (we avoided splitting major metro areas or concentrations of manufacturing activity). The numbers of printing and publishing establishments in the region are reported by sector in Table 5.1.

Figure 5.2 maps the location of manufacturing enterprises in the region (printing and publishing establishments are in light gray). Printing and publishing plants are clearly "clustered" in the region's primary metropolitan centers. However, that may simply be a function of the general tendency of plants to seek locations in agglomerated areas where infrastructure, plentiful workers, and other general advantages of urban locations are present. In effect, we need to control for this large-scale variation in the point pattern of human settlement, thereby isolating the relationship between membership in the value chain and spatial concentration. We can do that by setting up a case-control framework where the cases (printing and publishing enterprises) are hypothesized to cluster and the controls (all other manufacturers) capture the general tendency of businesses to concentrate in urbanized areas or in specific districts within those areas.

More precisely, the spatial distribution of manufacturing plants is modeled as the outcome of a isotropic, stationary bivariate point process with intensity function, $\lambda_i(x) = \lambda_i$, where i=1 (cases), 2 (controls). The bivariate K-function,

$$K_{ij}(s) = \frac{2\pi}{\lambda_i \lambda_j} \int_0^s \lambda_{ij}(u)u \ du$$

is interpreted as the number of additional type j plants within distance s of a type i plant.[2] When i=j, the bivariate K represents the K-function for either cases (i = j = 1) or controls (i = j =2). If the case-control labels are randomly assigned to establishments, then the K-function for cases, K_{11}, should equal the K-function for controls, K_{22}. In contrast, if the hypothesis of clustering among printing and publishing enterprises is true, then K_{11} should exceed K_{22}. The difference between the two estimated K-functions is the D-function:

$$\hat{D}(s) = \hat{K}_{11}(s) - \hat{K}_{22}(s)$$

which takes positive values when cases are more clustered than the controls. Estimators for D and the covariance of D are provided in Diggle and Chetwynd (1991).

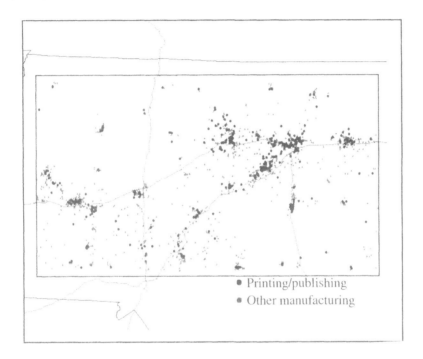

Figure 5.2   Distribution of Regional Manufacturing Establishments

The economic meaning of the test is straightforward: if printing and publishing plants mimic the general spatial pattern exhibited by the manufacturing sector as a whole (D tends to zero), then we have no basis for asserting a direct association between membership in the printing and publishing chain and co-location in the region. In such a case, any observed absolute clustering of printing and publishing businesses is a function of the general pattern of industrial locations (perhaps driven by urbanization economies) and not dynamics unique to the value chain itself (e.g. localization economies, chain-specific spillover effects, etc.). Defining the cases more finely (i.e., specific components of the overall value chain) allows us to further explore which sectors are driving any aggregate finding of clustering (or dispersion).

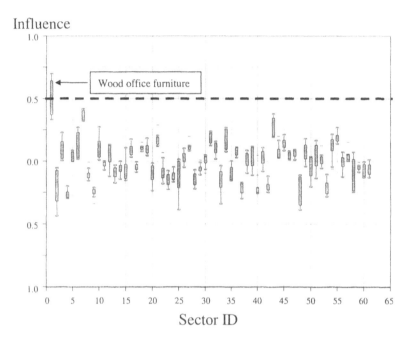

Figure 5.3   Industry Influence Visual

It should be evident that the robustness of the test depends heavily on an appropriate specification of the properties of the spatial process represented by the control group. Two fundamental issues concern the selection of controls. First, as in any case-control design, the controls should closely conform to the cases on all theoretically important dimensions save the dimension of interest. For example, if small firms have a tendency to cluster more than large firms, and the printing and publishing chain is disproportionately populated by small enterprises compared to the manufacturing sector as a whole, a finding of statistically significant spatial clustering could easily be a result of firm size effects rather than value chain effects. Indeed, in Sweeney and Feser (1998), we found a clear relationship between firm size and clustering. Using that study as a guide, our controls are proportionally matched samples that follow the same size distribution as the cases.

Second, the controls are effectively a benchmark, or referent, against which the spatial pattern of cases is evaluated. The K function for controls should capture the average spatial covariance structure of revealed location choices for establishments with a comparable size distribution to the cases. In economic terms, those revealed location choices should reflect the average spatial profit surface faced by a randomly selected establishment choosing a location in the study area. If the control group manufacturing sectors in a region is dominated by one or more sectors with aberrantly clustered facility locations, our test will be biased against a finding of clustering among the cases. In essence the hyperclustering of a given sector should be regarded as an outlier since it is not reflective of general profit surface faced by the average establishment.

Figure 5.4   Distribution of Wood Office Furniture Locations

The control group for the North Carolina study region has that exact problem. North Carolina is a world-renowned center of furniture production, and much of that activity is located in the central or Piedmont region of the state, where our study region is drawn. The High Point area resembles, in many respects, a Marshallian-type industrial district of furniture design, production, marketing, and sales. To the extent that the furniture district influences the spatial pattern of the controls, the control group sample of "background variation" is biased.

To address this issue, we devised a means of testing the influence of individual manufacturing sectors on the resulting D statistic. Essentially, the test works by systematically removing significant (in terms of sample size) sectors and re-calculating D. The absolute difference between the D with the sector included in the controls and D with the sector excluded from the controls provides a measure of the influence of the individual industry on the final result. Since D is a function over multiple distances s, we end up with a distribution of differences for each control sector. Box plots, with the interquartile range of values in the box and the maximum and minimum values defining the outer stems, can represent those distributions. To facilitate comparisons across control sectors, we standardize the D (and thus the difference) as z-scores. We can then array the box plots in a single graphic, permitting a convenient visual inspection of the influence of individual sectors.

The results of our influence examination are displayed in Figure 5.3. Sixty-five manufacturing sectors were of sufficient size to possibly influence the background distribution. The box plots for each of those sectors are arranged along the x-axis, left to right, according to sample size. We see that most of the differences hover around zero and there is a faintly discernable tendency for influences to lessen as the sectors become smaller, as we would expect. One sector, wood office furniture, appears to be an outlier. Excluding the sector significantly increases D at all distances. Conversely, including the sector in the background appears to bias D downward, leading us to falsely reject a finding of clustering in printing and publishing. Figure 5.4 shows why. The wood office furniture industry in the region is very tightly clustered in two cities: High Point and Hickory, a significantly different pattern than either the printing and publishing chain or the manufacturing sector as a whole (compare to Figure 5.2). On the basis of that finding, and given its consistency with what we know about the concentration of furniture production in the region, we excluded the wood office furniture sector from the controls in our subsequent calculations.

To test for spatially binding ties in printing publishing, we partitioned the value chain by degree of functional linkage within the chain, by functional component or broad industry, and by individual sector. D-functions were estimated for each of these partitions, or "case" definitions. Our findings are summarized in Figures 5.5-5.8, which plot the standardized D at distances out to 30 kilometers. A value of D greater than 2.0 indicates significant clustering at the 95 percent confidence level at the given distance. Similarly, any value of

D less than -2.0 indicates statistically significant dispersion at the given distance.

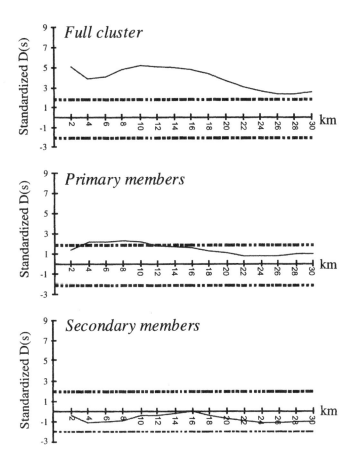

Figure 5.5   Spatial Clustering: Strength of I-O Linkages

To interpret D at different distances, it is important to remember that the K functions from which D is derived are not calculated from fixed points but rather are evaluated at every sample point. For example, the top panel of Figure 5.5 reports D(*s*) for the full sample of printing and publishing enterprises. We

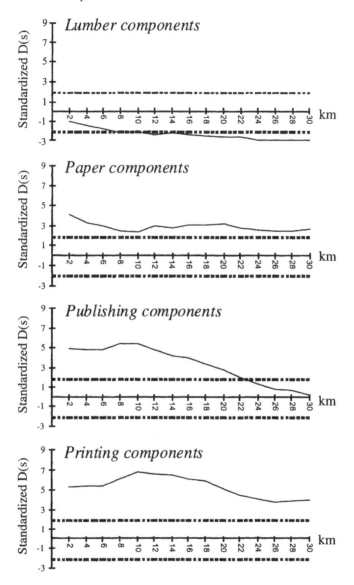

Figure 5.6   Spatial Clustering: Functional Components

see that the printing and publishing value chain is significantly clustered at all distances, controlling for the general concentration of manufacturing in the urban centers of the study region. Clustering is stronger the smaller the distance (i.e., D is highest at a distance of 2 kilometers, decreases slightly from 4-6 kilometers, then rises and falls gradually from 8 kilometers on). What that means is that the spatial distribution of printing and publishing firms deviates most significantly from the general manufacturing distribution at smaller geographical scales; printing and publishing is not necessarily concentrated in one city or sub-area in the region but rather in multiple smaller concentrations or districts.

The remaining panels of Figure 5.5, as well as Figures 5.6-5.8, report the results for specific sub-samples of the printing and publishing value chain. The bottom two panels of Figure 5.5 test whether establishments in primary sectors of the chain (i.e. those sectors most tightly linked to the chain on the basis of the statistical factor analysis) are more tightly clustered than secondary members of the chain. Primary and secondary members are listed in the first column of Table 5.1. Core primary sectors include commercial and book printing, paper coating and glazing, paperboard containers, book publishing, and blankbooks and binders. Key secondary sectors include sawmills, wood pallets, typesetting, platemaking, and surface-active agents. Indeed, we find evidence of clustering of enterprises in the primary sectors at scales of 4-10 kilometers while enterprises in weakly linked secondary sectors show no clustering at all. The result, which is consistent with findings in Feser and Sweeney (2000), is modest evidence that the stronger the functional linkage within the chain, the tighter the spatial clustering of production chain enterprises.

Breaking the production chain into its various components, we might expect to observe a high degree of clustering of its knowledge-intensive segments (e.g., publishing) and little to no clustering, or perhaps even dispersion, in resource-intensive segments such as wood and paper supplies. The printing segment of the chain, which includes standardized printing activities as well as typesetting and platemaking, is more difficult to predict. In our study region, the printing segment of the chain is heavily dominated by commercial printing. This includes a great many small job print shops that serve publishing companies as well as other corporate and government clients. Thus while we might expect some commercial printing firms to seek peripheral locations attractive to any cost-sensitive, standardized producer, there are also clear advantages to concentrating nearby publishing firms, other corporate customers, and government centers. Commercial printers often provide limited editing, layout, and design services and specialize in quick turnaround times, activities that benefit from close proximity to customers, especially publishing companies.

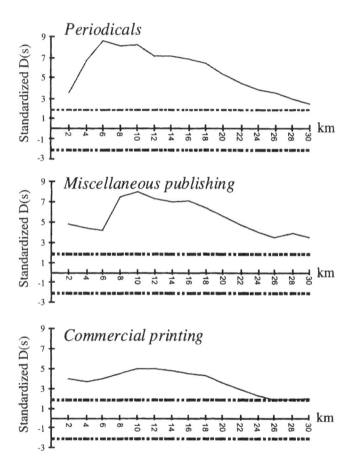

Figure 5.7   By Sector: High Degree of Clustering

The results in Figure 5.6 are consistent with some of our pre-conceptions and challenge others. Lumber components of the chain (essentially sawmills and wood pallets) are significantly dispersed at scales in excess of eight kilometers while publishing enterprises are highly clustered. Somewhat surprising is the clustering of paper enterprises, which in our study region are mainly paperboard containers and boxes, converted paper products, paper coating and glazing, and paper bags. There is certainly much inter industry trade within the paper segments of the chain, with pulp mills supplying paper and paperboard plants which are, in turn, suppliers to end-market producers such as greeting cards and miscellaneous converted paper products. The printing components also show a high degree of clustering at all spatial scales, suggesting that advantages of proximity out-weigh any cost-savings that might be had by choosing more peripheral locations.

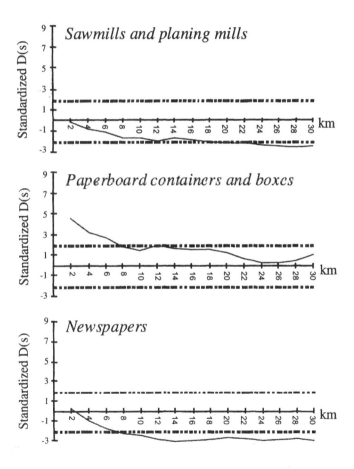

Figure 5.8 **By Sector: Dispersion or Little Clustering**

We can derive an even finer-grained look at location patterns in the chain by calculating results by specific sector (see Figure 5.7). Highly clustered are periodicals (SIC 272), miscellaneous publishing (SIC 274), and commercial printing (SIC 275). By contrast, we observe modest clustering or even dispersion in sawmills and planning mills (SIC 2421), paperboard containers and boxes (SIC 265), and newspapers (SIC 271). Therefore, with respect to the highly clustered publishing segment of the chain, we add the caveat that, taken singly, the newspaper industry actually demonstrates a high degree of dispersion. That is unsurprising given that many even modestly sized towns have their own hometown newspapers while larger newspaper companies scatter printing facilities in order to minimize the costs of transporting their finished product. Yet despite the "pull" of dispersed newspaper establishments, the publishing segment of the chain remains clustered as a whole, a finding that suggests a geographic pattern of multiple, small clusters of publishing enterprises across the study region.

Summary and Discussion

In this chapter, we outlined and illustrated an approach for examining the relationship between firm linkages and spatial concentration or clustering. Our objective was to decompose one manufacturing value chain, printing and publishing, and determine which of its components are driving spatial concentration observed in a broad multi-city region in one southern state, North Carolina. Of principal concern in such an exercise is controlling for the general tendency of firms to seek locations in concentrated agglomerations. We were able to do this by joining establishment-level data with point process techniques and a case-control research design.

We found that much of the clustering of printing and publishing firms in the study region is due to clustering of periodicals and miscellaneous publishing houses, along with commercial print shops. We also found evidence of clustering of the paper components of the value chain and significant dispersion of the resource-intensive wood components. Examining clustering according to the strength of the production linkage as revealed in the US input-output table showed that the sectors most tightly integrated in the value chain were spatially clustered while those only weakly linked were not. While clearly more research must be conducted for additional regions to determine whether our findings can be generalized, it is comforting that they are broadly consistent with prevailing theories of industry clusters and agglomeration, which postulate advantages to co-location for linked and related industries.

Notes

1   Using standard GIS software and proprietary base streets files, we were able to address
     match about 70 percent of the manufacturing establishments in the study area.
2   Estimators for the K-function and bivariate K-function include corrections for edge
     effects.

References

Bergman, E. M. and Feser, E. J. (2000), "Industrial and Regional Clusters: Concepts and
    Comparative Applications", in S. Loveridge (ed), *Web Book in Regional Science*,
    Regional Research Institute, West Virginia University, Morganton, WV, online at
    www.rri.wvu.edu/regscweb.htm.
Bergsman, J., Greenston, P. and Healy, R. (1975), "A Classification of Economic Activities
    Based on Location Patterns", *Journal of Urban Economics*, vol. 2, pp. 1-28.
Best, M. (1990), *The New Competition: Institutions of Industrial Restructuring*, Polity Press,
    Cambridge.
Bopp, R. and Gordon, P. (1977), "Agglomeration Economies and Industrial Economic
    Linkages: Comment", *Journal of Regional Science*, vol. 17, pp. 125-27.
Czamanski, S. (1974), *Study of Clustering of Industries*, Institute of Public Affairs, Dalhousie
    University, Halifax, Canada.
Czamanski, S. and Ablas, L. A. (1979), "Identification of Industrial Clusters and Complexes:
    A Comparison of Methods and Findings", *Urban Studies*, vol. 16, pp. 61-80.
Diggle, P. and Chetwynd, A. (1991), "Second-order Analysis of Spatial Clustering for
    Inhomogeneous Populations", *Biometrics*, vol. 47, pp. 1155-63.
Doeringer, P. B. and Terkla, D. G. (1995), "Business Strategy and Cross-Industry Clusters",
    Economic Development Quarterly, vol. 9, pp. 225-37.
Feser, E. J. and Bergman, E. M. (2000), "National Industry Cluster Templates: A Framework
    for Applied Regional Cluster Analysis", *Regional Studies*, vol. 34, pp. 1-19.
Feser, E. J. and Sweeney, S. H. (2000), "A Test for the Coincident Economic and Spatial
    Clustering of Business Enterprises", *Journal of Geographical Systems*, vol. 2, 349-73.
Held, J. R. (1996), "Clusters as an Economic Development Tool: Beyond the Pitfalls",
    Economic Development Quarterly, vol. 10, pp. 249-61.
Hill, E. W. and Brennan, J. F. (2000), "A Methodology for Identifying Drivers of Industrial
    Clusters: The Foundation of Regional Competitive Advantage", *Economic Development
    Quarterly*, vol. 14, pp. 65-96.
Howe, E. (1991), "Simple Industrial Complexes", *Papers in Regional Science*, vol. 70,
    pp. 71-80.
Jacobs, D. and de Man, A. P. (1996), "Clusters, Industrial Policy and Firm Strategy: A Menu
    Approach", *Technology Analysis and Strategic Management*, vol. 8, pp. 425-37.
Lazonick, W. (1993), "Industry Clusters versus Global Webs: Organizational Capabilities in
    the American Economy", *Structural Change and Economic Dynamics*, vol. 4, pp. 1-24.

Lever, W. F. (1972), "Industrial Movement, Spatial Association and Functional Linkages", *Regional Studies*, vol. 6, pp. 371-84.

Markusen, A. (1996), "Sticky Places in Slippery Space: A Typology of Industrial Districts", *Economic Geography*, vol. 72, pp. 293-313.

Meyer-Stamer, J. (1998), "Path Dependence in Regional Development: Persistence and Change in Three Industrial Clusters in Santa Catarina, Brazil", *World Development*, vol. 8, pp. 1495-1511.

Ó hUallacháin, B. (1984), "The Identification of Industrial Complexes", *Annals of the Association of American Geographers*, vol. 74, pp. 420-36.

Porter, M. E. (1990), *The Competitive Advantage of Nations*, Free Press, New York.

Porter, M. E. (1998), "Clusters and the New Economics of Competition", *Harvard Business Review* (November/December), pp. 77-90.

Porter, M. E. (2000a), "Locations, Clusters, and Company Strategy" in G. L. Clark, M. P. Feldman and M. S. Gertler (eds), *Oxford Handbook of Economic Geography*, Oxford University Press, Oxford, pp. 253-74.

Porter, M. E. (2000b), "Enhancing the Competitiveness of the Central Mississippi Region: The Communications and Information Technology Cluster (CIT)", presentation slides, mimeo.

Rabellotti, R. (1995), "Is There an "Industrial District Model"? Footwear Districts in Italy and Mexico Compared", *World Development*, vol. 23, pp. 29-41.

Robinson, E. A. G. (1931), *The Structure of Competitive Industry*. Cambridge University Press, Cambridge.

Roepke, H. (1974), "A New Approach to the Identification of Industrial Complexes Using Input-Output Data", *Journal of Regional Science*, vol. 14, pp. 15-29.

Rosenfeld, S. A. (1997), "Bringing Business Clusters into the Mainstream of Economic Development", *European Planning Studies*, vol. 5, pp. 3-23.

Saxenian, A. (1994), *Regional Advantage: Culture and Competition in Silicon Valley and Route 128*, Harvard University Press, Cambridge, MA.

Schmitz, H. (1995), "Small Shoemakers and Fordist Giants: Tale of Supercluster", *World Development*, vol. 23, pp. 9-28.

Streit, M. E. (1969), "Spatial Associations and Economic Linkages between Industries", *Journal of Regional Science*, vol. 9, pp. 177-88.

Streit, M. E. (1977), "Agglomeration Economies and Industrial Linkages: A Reply", *Journal of Regional Science*, vol. 17, pp. 129-30.

Sweeney, S. H. and Feser, E. J. (1998), "Plant Size and Clustering of Manufacturing Activity", *Geographical Analysis*, vol. 30, pp. 45-64.

Taylor, M. J. (1973), "Local Linkage, External Economies and the Iron foundry Industry of the West Midlands and East Lancashire", *Regional Studies*, vol. 7, pp. 387-400.

Townroe, P. M. (1970), "Industrial Linkage, Agglomeration and External Economies", *Journal of the Town Planning Institute*, vol. 56, pp. 18-20.

6 Skills Networks and Local Dynamics

PATRICK BURLAT AND SOPHIE PEILLON

For several years, while reorganizing their internal activities, firms have launched vertical disintegration strategies in order to concentrate on their core competencies. In this context of deep transformation of the relations between firms, a new organizational form emerged: the network. Our research addresses the way in which proximity influences the formation and the performance of networks. We assume that the benefits of dynamic networks of firms lie mainly in the fact that they constitute a preferential way to acquire external skills while preserving each partner's independence.

Furthermore, co-operation between firms shows particular characteristics in areas like the Rhône-Alpes region in France. In this area, a multitude of small subcontractors accounts for the most significant industrial activity. In this region we observe the emergence of dynamic networks intended to mobilize distributed skills and know-how. However, unlike information, which forwards instantaneously, skills sharing, within a non-hierarchical framework of co-operation, is not easily freed from cultural barriers and linguistic borders. The process of constitution of non-hierarchical networks, founded on the exchanges of skills and on the establishment of trust, is thus fully carried out only in a context of proximity.

Starting from investigations into corporate networks behavior in France, as well as more extensive observations of two networks of the Rhône-Alpes region, we attempt to show that the sharing of skills is the driving element of the constitution of networks, and to what extent it requires geographical, technological, organizational or institutional proximity of their members.

To do so, we first present an analytic framework to describe links between proximity and learning processes. Next, we decompose SME networks into strategic and non-strategic networks. Then we show to what extent strategic networks need organizational and institutional proximity to enable organizational learning, whereas non-strategic networks require technological and geographical proximity to promote technological learning. Two case studies from the mechanical sector and the building sector contribute examples to illustrate our approach.

Competence-based Theories Applied to SME Networks

Network of Firms

We are interested here in the "network of firms", i.e., in industrial structures linked with horizontal agreements (unlike the "firm network" made of vertical agreements and managed by a focal firm). Those networks are made of independent firms virtually linked together to achieve a goal. Different types of network can be identified according to the nature of the relations that federate their members, for example:

- Purchasing network - economies of scale for purchases and supplies,
- Production network - joint production,
- New market oriented network - sharing new business services to increase turn over,
- Quality certification network - sharing quality experts to obtain ISO 9000 certification,
- Data exchange standardization network - constructing and adopting common norms to exchange data,

It is noted that these types of network are not mutually exclusive. For example, a group may correspond at the same time to a production network and a purchasing network. In that context, our research specially addresses SME networks. SME networks are particular because the shareholder and the manager of a SME is often the same person. For this reason, each partner of a SME's network usually acts so as to preserve strongly its independence within the group.

Reasons for Networking

An investigation funded by the Ministry of Industry in France has revealed that within a panel of 1600 enterprises, 80 percent have co-operation links with other firms.[1] According to this survey, manufacturers co-operate in a large majority (64 percent) with others enterprises having complementary activities. Furthermore, this investigation shows that acquisition of know-how and experimentation constitutes the first goal (60 percent) of co-operation between manufacturers, before economies of scale. Our own observations and investigations about networking in the Rhône-Alpes region also led us to presume that knowledge exchanging is the main reason why independent firms join networks. So, assuming that skills sharing are the principal *raison d'être* of networking, we will now use competence-based theories to analyze SME networks.

Using Competence-based Theories

The competence-based theories of the firm consider that the firm's essential attribute is its "competencies" or "organizational capacities". From this point of view, the creation of new knowledge and the learning processes are at the heart of the firm's composition. These competence-based theories of the firm cover many theoretical approaches, among which is the evolutionary theory of the firm (Hodgson 1996; Teece and Pisano 1994).

This point of view emphasizes the essential role of cognitive mechanisms: in the face of environmental constraints, the network organization allows generation of learning effects and accumulation of joint information, led by lasting relations between the partners. The network thus permits the construction of a "collective asset" made up of joint knowledge and competencies.

But this requires the development of a collective base of knowledge, and the definition of a set of rules, codes and joint languages among the actors of the network.

Developing such a collective set of knowledge requires proximity between the members of the network. But this does not necessarily mean geographical proximity. Because of the process of disintegration of firms' activities and their coherent recombining within networks, the traditional borders, which defined the firm as a place of production, are not relevant any more. Using competence-based theories leads to accepting that boundaries delimiting networks are cognitive rather than physical. The main question is then to determine which new "proximity factors" affect success and performance within networks. Adopting a competence-based point of view, we will try to answer this question by proposing an analytic framework describing links between proximity and learning processes. To do so, we will first define the terms knowledge, learning and proximity.

Towards an Analytic Framework to Link Proximity and Learning Processes

Knowledge and Rationality

This section reviews definitions for knowledge and rationality within organizations. We will consider here "knowledge" as a set of known facts in an organization and rationality as a guide for decision. We will first decompose knowledge into two parts: the knowledge of facts and the knowledge of rules (Crémer 1990).

The knowledge of facts   This deals with the environment in which the organization is functioning: location of plants, physical processes of production, description of products, and any fact about society at large.

The knowledge of rules   This is a collection of principles, standards and routines that agents usually follow inside an organization. The knowledge of facts and the knowledge of rules can be considered as a common and collective knowledge that facilitates co-ordination between agents. The shared knowledge of facts improves collective decision making processes by constituting a common representation of an organization, and the shared knowledge of rules favors conjoint actions in the way agents can predict others agents actions.

Rationality   We will use here the term "rationality" as synonymous with reason, argument, motive, cause or justification for a particular behavior. Behavior and decision-making are considered *rational* if they are consistent and are justified by the precepts, norms and guidelines of rationality. We will also decompose rationality into two parts: the structural rationality and the evaluative rationality (Van Gigch 1991).

The structural rationality   This guides the establishment of the structure of the decision making process (who decides and when within an organization). It consists of instructions on how to organize the decision structure.

The evaluative rationality   This refers to either the goals towards which decision makers appear to strive, and/or the criteria by which goal attainment is defined and evaluated. At a strategic level, the evaluative rationality designates the way performance is evaluated (e.g., profitability, or return on investment). At a tactical level within a manufacturing organization, the evaluative rationality is made of the criteria by which operational objectives (such as cost, output, quality and time objectives) are determined. At a more operational level, the evaluative rationality describes the indicators of efficient allocation for available resources (raw material, tools, equipment and personal).

We will now precis the effects of learning processes onto knowledge and rationality within organizations.

Technological Learning and Organizational Learning

Learning is considered here as a permanent change of behavior resulting from experiment. Classical ways of learning are well known especially learning by doing (which is the base of classical learning curves in economics) and learning by using. But in the context of SME networks, we are much more interested here in the concept of learning by interacting (learning by interacting means exchanging knowledge and skills between agents acting together) (Lundvall 1992).

Indeed, some particular skills are tacit and not codified (Polanyi 1967). These skills cannot be transmitted like information, and it usually takes time for agents to assimilate and to appropriate them. So we assume that networking enables firms to acquire these particular external skills that they could not get by economic intelligence processes. We also assume that these skills are exchanged inside networks by a way of learning by interacting.

To go further, learning will be decomposed into two forms, the technological learning and the organizational learning.

Technological learning We will use "technological learning" to identify a learning process modifying the knowledge of facts and the knowledge of rules we defined before. In that way, technological learning improves the efficiency of technical tasks inside an organization. For instance, technological learning by interacting inside a network will facilitate the transfer of a specific savoir-faire in a physical process from one firm to another (knowledge of fact), or it will help to put into action an efficient routine (knowledge of rule).

Organizational learning We will use "organizational learning" to identify a learning process modifying the structural or the evaluative rationality within an organization. Organizational learning adjusts the structure of the decision making process (who decides and when), the goals towards which decision-makers appear to strive, or the criteria by which goal attainment is defined and evaluated. Organizational learning does not directly modify the knowledge of facts and the knowledge of rules, but modifies the way facts are used within the decision making process and the way rules are selected to meet the goals.

Either technological or organizational learning will be activated within networks, according to the proximity of their members.

Geographical, Technological, Organizational and Institutional Proximity

Before connecting learning processes with proximity, we have to be more precise about the concept of proximity. To do so, we will detail this concept according to the following typology: geographical, technological, organizational and institutional proximity (Kirat and Lung 1995).

- Geographical proximity refers to the localization of agents in the same place. This proximity is not exactly synonymous with physical distance between agents in the way it depends on the transport infrastructures. For this reason, geographical proximity may be considered as a social construct resulting from the edification of transport and communication structures, and is limited by technical constraints.
- Technological proximity designates closeness between activities. This proximity exists among firms having complementary technologies (e.g., vertical networks) or among firms having complementary or similarly activities in the same stream of the production process (e.g., horizontal networks). Technological proximity is to be connected with core competencies, skills and know-how.
- Organizational proximity links agents contributing together to a finalized activity inside a particular structure. This proximity is the result of organized relations between partners. Agents will be close if they accept a common framework to structure their exchanges. It exists inside firms, and also among firms linked by economical or financial interdependencies. In that way, organizational proximity is a strong characteristic of structured networks.
- Institutional proximity refers to independent agents accepting common laws, common mental models, common values and common ways of thinking. This proximity results from an adhesion

to social conventions and behavior norms. It differs from the organizational proximity in the way it does not require organized and coordinated actions. A mental adhesion to institutional values is enough to ensure institutional proximity.

Proximity and Learning

Now we need to connect proximity and learning processes, by the way of knowledge and rationality. We first consider that networks can only emerge through the construction of a common knowledge framework. But this construction will be decomposed into three different steps, data exchange, knowledge sharing, and shared knowledge structuring (Figure 6.1). Data exchange is the first step when creating a network. It modifies the knowledge of facts and the knowledge of rules. Then, knowledge sharing is the second step towards the construction of a collective asset made up of joint knowledge and skills. The knowledge sharing process affects the knowledge of facts and the knowledge of rules, but also in a lesser way structural rationality and evaluative rationality. At the highest level, agents will structure together their shared knowledge. To do so, they will co-ordinate their decision making process. They will also modify the criteria by which goal attainment is defined and evaluated, and even the goals that guide decision-making processes, to make them consistent with the network project.

According to the definitions we used before for technological and organizational learning, the figure is fractionated into two zones: a technological learning area where the knowledge of facts and the knowledge of rules are modified via data exchange and knowledge sharing processes, and an organizational learning area where the structural rationality and the evaluative rationality are modified via the knowledge sharing and the shared knowledge structuring processes.

Now we consider that geographical proximity and technological proximity further data exchanges and knowledge sharing (we keep in mind that geographical proximity is not here synonymous with physical distance, but depends on the transport infrastructures for people and data). At a higher level, organizational proximity and institutional proximity further knowledge sharing and shared knowledge structuring. The geographical proximity and technological proximity have an influence in the technological learning area, whereas organizational proximity and institutional proximity are located in the organizational learning area.

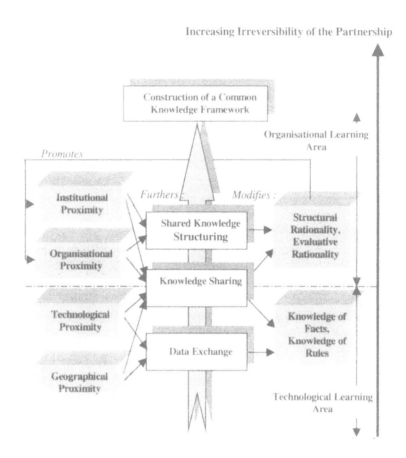

Figure 6.1   Proximity and Learning

Finally, a feedback loop connects both structural and evaluative rationality with organizational and institutional proximity. Indeed, we consider that building up a coherent set of goals and a common decision making structure promotes organizational proximity and institutional proximity, in the way it links agents acting together within a finalized activity inside a particular structure, and in the way it contributes to the acceptation by agents of common mental models, common values and common ways of thinking.

SME networks can be observed at the three different steps of this model, and we noticed that the higher the step, the more irreversible the partnership is. To be more precise about this, we will now decompose networks into strategic and non-strategic and describe some case studies using this model.

Networks and Proximity

A Typology of Networks: Strategic and Non-Strategic Networks

In spite of diversity in the motives leading to the formation of networks by SMEs, we think it possible to conceive a simple typology distinguishing two main types of networks.

Indeed, there are two main categories of motives for networking: either a reduction of costs, or a pursuit of new opportunities. These two types of objectives reveal rather different strategies: one remains passive (non-strategic networks which aim at reaching an optimal size) and consists of adaptation to the environment; the other is more active and aims to have an effect on the environment (strategic networks directed towards a commercial or technological activity).

Non-strategic networks, which do not imply the development of collective competencies, are reversible and rest primarily on the geographical and technological proximity of the partners. On the other hand, strategic networks result in the creation of a common knowledge framework and network-specific routines and competencies, which make networking increasingly irreversible. This second type of network requires not only geographical and technological proximity of the partners, but also organizational and institutional proximity.

Geographical and Technological Proximity in Non-Strategic Networks

Non-strategic networks In non-strategic networks, co-operation is focused on human or material resource sharing, or on the centralization of particular functions, in order to gain economies of scale. Networking then allows firms either to reduce their costs of operation, or to have access to resources for which they do not have full-time needs but which endow their activity with an unquestionable advantage.

For instance, several firms can share the cost of a common sales department in order to promote their products, pool their productive capacities so as to meet larger orders from their customers, join their purchasing power in order to get better supply terms, make use of a common training agenda for their employees, share the purchasing and use of expensive production facilities, etc.

Such networks are called non-strategic because they do not involve strong interdependencies between the partners. Within these networks, partners exchange data and share knowledge; but networking does not mean structuring shared knowledge.

Learning in non-strategic networks Within non-strategic networks, the description of the purpose (which is usually limited to a single task) and of the means to reach it is clear. Even though learning opportunities exist, learning processes remain essentially individual. Indeed, each firm can learn about the practices used by the others (benchmarking). But, insofar as firms do not really share a common activity, learning remains individual within each single firm, and does not lead to network-specific collective and organizational routines.

Learning in non-strategic networks is essentially technological, and enhances the effectiveness of firms in achieving tasks. Hence, learning is not organizational, since it does not generate modifications in the network decision structure, goals or assessment criteria.

Non-strategic networking can be altered Non-strategic networks are characterized by a low level of irreversibility insofar as they do not need the creation of a common knowledge framework: data exchanges do not imply the construction of a common culture among the partners.

The life of non-strategic networks seems to equal the time necessary to achieve the projected mission. Deadlines and goals are defined previously, allowing the firms to lay down concrete and accurate objectives. The roles, the remuneration rules and the organization of work are defined ex ante. Non-strategic networks are stable during the mission, that is, they go on until their goal is reached, and then are dissolved.[2]

Geographical and technological proximity in non-strategic networks In non-strategic networks, only geographical and technological proximity seem to play a role. The geographical proximity of the partners facilitates data exchanges within the network. The technological proximity, which is related to the nature of the partners activity and thus to the existence of a "business culture", makes the understanding of exchanged data and the knowledge sharing easier.

However, organizational proximity and institutional proximity are not really necessary: work remains above all individual, and co-operation does not need the construction of a common culture among the partners.

The Need for Organizational and Institutional Proximity in Strategic Networks

Strategic networks are generally set up around a common commercial or productive approach. They bring together competing or complementary firms, and aim at increasing sales and gaining new customers. The partners relate them to a joint achievement of resources production.

More specifically, strategic networking refers to the development and use of a market, product or resource mutual complementarity, at once in the same industry and among industries. Co-operation may concern for instance specialist firms, each of which bringing a component of a product which is then sold on behalf of the network, acting therefore as a single entity. Each firm alone would have not been able to produce this end product, which can only be the outcome of a co-operative process.

Such co-operation can lead to economies of scale: because of the increased total orders, each firm in the network can make a full use of its production facilities, and by the means of increased specialization, duplication is avoided and existing facilities can be used with more effectiveness. Moreover, co-operation can also provide economies of scope, since specialist firms acting as a collective entity can offer their customers a larger range of products than each firm alone could do. So within a strategic network, actors try to exploit joint complementarities among tangible or intangible assets (e.g., facilities, or knowledge) by coordinating their activities and decisions so as to solve specific problems. Firms join together in order to achieve a specific project, involving a pool of resources and competencies.

Therefore, strategic network efficiency must be assessed on the long run: the construction of collective competencies can endow the network with a competitive advantage. The "core competence" of a network refers to all the learning processes generated within the network, especially learning relating to the co-ordination of production capabilities. These core competencies are enhanced by use, they can be saved (their value improves with time) and above all, they allow the network to reach new markets and to become differentiated from its competitors (thanks to the competitive advantage these core competencies provide).

Strategic networks are much more complicated than non-strategic ones: they refer to a kind of co-production of new resources or new knowledge. Therefore, the question is how to favor learning processes throughout the co-operation.

Learning in strategic networks: the role of a common culture and of collective competencies Independent firms have their own corporate culture and their own production organization. A major difficulty for them is therefore to work jointly in an efficient way and to develop quickly some synergy. Indeed, the firms must co-ordinate their actions in an efficient way. But, collaborative work will only be possible if the firms own a basic amount of common tools. Hence, co-operating needs harmonization of procedures and communication tools. This is all the more important, since we are concerned with strategic networks implying joint production.

Moreover, collaborative work necessitates pooling different competencies. Thus, for the project to be successful, partners must develop learning effects in the joint work, leading to the creation of collective competencies. These learning processes are collective since partners learn to work together. Learning is first interactive: the partners get to know each other. This learning by interacting allows the development of a common culture, a common knowledge framework, and leads to network-specific organizational routines.

Strategic networks are not easily altered Strategic networking refers to the pool of competencies, but the partners' interrelations themselves create network-specific competencies through the learning processes. In fact, the creation of competencies is not only the result of pooling resources, but also the result of the implementation of a particular co-ordination mechanism between different firms. This co-ordination mechanism must be supported by the repetition of interactions between the firms and the definition of network-specific routines. This idea is closely akin to that of Nelson and Winter (1982) applied to network analysis: beyond the pooling of resources or competencies, networks generate co-ordination routines on which the creation of network-specific competencies is based.

As a result of the importance of learning processes that might rise out of strategic networks, the partners face an important risk, that of being locked in their relationship. Collective learning gives rise to irreversibility. As the relationship progresses, stopping co-operation is less and less conceivable (since sunk costs are very high) and simultaneously its continuation is more and more valued. Generally, when there is joint production, firms become more and more dependent on each other and the network. Thus, the network becomes an organizational form that cannot be easily altered, and might lead to a merger.

So, if strategic networks seem to present more opportunities for firms than non-strategic ones, they also entail higher risks for their members.

Organizational and institutional proximity in strategic networks In strategic networks, the four forms of proximity play a role, but organizational proximity and institutional proximity are the most important.

Indeed, the basic objective of learning processes is there to develop a common knowledge framework. Learning by interacting processes will be mobilized since part of knowledge is tacit and not codified. Now organizational proximity and institutional proximity constitute an essential medium for cognitive interactions. Organizational proximity and institutional proximity help to build a common structural and evaluative rationality within strategic networks. Organizational proximity provides a common goal and a common decision structure to the network members, and helps to direct the learning processes by promoting knowledge sharing and structuring. Institutional proximity is closely akin with interactions between agents, and thus makes learning by interacting easier. Among the partners, interactions promote knowledge sharing, and shared representations further knowledge structuring.

Case Studies

An Example of a Non-Strategic Network: EDI-BTP Rhône

EDI BTP Rhône is a non-profit-making association intended to promote computer-based data exchanges. This network federates firms from all the building trades: owners, project managers, architects, economists, and suppliers. The goal of this network is to implement a common data processing infrastructure and common systems for information sharing. Within EDI-BTP Rhône, all the partners have adopted the same software package, which allows computer-based data exchanges between them.

To us, EDI-BTP Rhône is a non-strategic network involving only data exchanges and knowledge sharing, but no collective competencies are created. Learning inside the network is essentially technological, related to technical information and knowledge, processes and rules.

Furthermore, this network is characterized by a high degree of reversibility, since it does not involve a real structuring of shared knowledge that could result in a modification of the decision structure or the assessment criteria within the network.

Finally, there seems to be neither organizational nor institutional proximity between the partners. Indeed, firms have very different modes of operation and sizes, do not really belong to a coherent economic territory and do not share the same values or representations. Only geographical proximity and technological proximity seem to have played a role in its formation and operation by making encounters and information exchanges easier.

An Example of a Strategic Network: Mécanergie

Further to a modification in the purchasing policy of their main contractors and following cuts in the number of suppliers, seven subcontractors from the mechanical engineering industries set up, in 1995, a network named Mécanergie. The Mécanergie group federates a boilermaker, a sheet-metal worker and five mechanics firms.

Here, the basic goal leading the firms to networking is commercial: each firm aims to increase its sales by reaching new customers. The network then recruits a sales manager, the quest for clientele becomes national and is directed towards the manufacturing of components and subcomponents.[3]

To us, the Mécanergie group is a strategic network, because it needs strong interdependencies between firms. Moreover, these interdependencies are increasingly strong as the network goes on, and networking is less and less reversible. For instance, the partners are currently considering a centralization of their purchasing and inventory management functions and several network members are re-locating their manufacturing facilities to the same place of production. Thus, they are increasingly deeply tied within the network.

Furthermore, networking involves numerous data exchanges and knowledge sharing (about products, production processes, markets, or customers). But what seems the most important is that it results in a real structuring of shared knowledge. Indeed, as the network aims to produce entire sub-components, the different firms must structure their knowledge and competencies in order to co-ordinate their production. Thus, learning within the network is really organizational, because it leads to deep modifications in the decision structure, the goals and the assessment criteria of each firm and of the network as a whole.

Finally, the four types of proximity seem to have played an important role in the creation and the operation of the Mécanergie network, but organizational proximity and institutional proximity were the most important.

- The geographical proximity of the members favored personal contacts and data exchanges.
- The technological proximity between firms coming from the same business, facing the same type of clientele (big contractors) and meeting similar technical problems favors a certain coherence in the information and the knowledge shared within the network, and thus makes technological learning easier.
- The organizational proximity between small-sized firms with similar processes and modes of operation, with the same goal facilitates the structuring of knowledge and competencies within the network.[4] This organizational proximity guides learning processes towards the "right" direction.
- The institutional proximity between firms belonging to the same little economic area (the Roannais area), sharing the same values and representations and facing the same structural difficulties, makes the creation of a common knowledge framework easier. Institutional proximity combined with organizational proximity favors organizational learning within the network.

These four types of proximity have favored the construction of a Mécanergie-specific common culture at once in terms of product, process, business and projects. Besides, according to the firms' managers, a common culture is a necessary condition for the network to succeed. This common culture, which is of paramount importance in strategic networks, is a result of the geographical, technological, organizational and institutional proximity of the partners.

For instance, Mécanergie has experienced a long organizational learning stage, which allowed an improvement of the coordinating modes within the network. The first deals led to technical and financial information sharing. Then the need for a better organization emerged: as orders arrived Mécanergie network operational routines (work sharing out, expenditure and profit distribution) that had been planned when the network was created, soon appeared ill adapted. So, learning resulted in the definition of new rules, goals and assessment criterions and finally in a better co-ordination of the partners.

In that case, proximity favors learning processes, especially organizational ones, and the resulting common culture is strengthened as the network goes on.

Conclusion

The analytic framework described in this chapter may also guide a policy to promote the building up of networks within a particular district. Extending geographical and technological proximity (for example by the way of information and communication technology such as Web sites) will facilitate the creation of non-strategic networks, whereas increasing institutional and organizational proximity (for instance through clubs, or by the way of funded projects) will encourage the creation of strategic networks.

These two policies are different and complementary. The first one favors virtual enterprises about well defined short-term projects. The second one will promote the development of local dynamics based on the creation of long-term valuable skills.

Notes

1   *Cf.* Hannoun, M. and Guerrier, G. (1996), *Le partenariat industriel*, Paris, Ministère de l'Industrie, de la Poste et des Télécomunications, SESSI, Paris.

2   We must not confuse stability and duration of the network. Here the notion of stability refers to the fact that the mode of co-operation remains the same until the goal is reached.

3   This is partly due to the importance of the total number of machines within the network.

4   The goal of the firms is here to survive, on account of the drastic reduction made by contractors in the number of their suppliers.

References

Crémer, J. (1990), "Common Knowledge and the Co-Ordination of Economic Activities", in M. Aoki, B. Gustafsson and O.E. Williamson (eds), *The Firm as a Nexus of Treaties*, Sage Publications, London, pp. 53-76.

Hannoun, M. and Guerrier, G. (1996), *Le partenariat industriel*, Ministère de l'Industrie, de la Poste et des Télécommunications, Direction Générale des Statistiques Industrielles, Service des Etudes et Statistiques Industrielles, Paris.

Hodgson, G.M. (1996), "Evolutionary and Competence-Based Theories of the Firm", in C. Piletis (ed.), *The Economics of Industrial and Business Strategy*, Basil Blackwell, Oxford, pp. 1-38.

Kirat, T. and Lung, Y. (1995), "Innovations et proximités : le territoire, lieu de déploiement des processus d'apprentissage", in N. Lazaric and J.M. Monnier (eds), *Coordination économique et apprentissage des firmes,* Economica, Paris, pp. 206-27.

Lundvall, B.A. (1992), *National Systems of Innovation. Towards a Theory of Innovation and Interactive Learning*, Pinter Publishers, London.

Nelson, R.R. and Winter, S.G. (1982), *An Evolutionary Theory of Economic Change*, Harvard University Press, Cambridge, Mass.

Polanyi, M. (1967), *The Tacit Dimension*, Doubleday, New York.

Teece, D.J. and Pisano, G. (1994), "The Dynamic Capabilities of Firms: An Introduction", *Industrial and Corporate Change*, vol. 3, pp. 537-56.

Van Gigch, J.P. (1991), *System Design Modeling and Metamodeling*, Plenum Press, New York.

7 Birthing Biotech: Agglomerations in San Diego and Atlanta

SUSAN M. WALCOTT

Companies associated with the highly profitable life sciences industry[1] are courted and cultivated in cities around the world (Feldman 1985; Aydalot and Hall 1994). A growing literature in economics (Audretsch and Stephan 1996; Stephan, et. al. 2000) and regional development (Blakely and Nishikawa 1992; Haug and Ness 1993; Lyons 1995; Willoughby 1995) examines case studies of successful life science clusters, but fails to adequately address issues embedded in human elements of the spatial context. This research focuses on the role of place characteristics and spatial proximity in creating networks that convert a cluster of innovative life sciences companies to a spawning ground of corporate growth - and the impediments to such a development. The presence of any one element, such as a prominent research university with acknowledged strengths in the life sciences, does not necessarily lead to successful businesses (Feldman 1994). A nationally recognized cluster of high technology companies in a field such as Atlanta's telecommunications node, however, does not necessarily mean the region is ripe for other high tech clusters.

Firms and employees drawn to or created by their predecessors in a particular place generate a self-sustaining critical mass of companies if they occur in large enough numbers to keep adding others. Elements necessary to nurture the growing cluster also must increase: suitable facilities for each of three growth stages, large infusions of capital over several years of development, highly educated employees, and a research institution (university or corporate) with applications transferable to the marketplace. The particular location of a life science industry agglomeration is usually based on a real estate configuration. Examples include a deliberately constructed incubator or industrial-science park close by the site where relevant research is being conducted, or second stage facilities for the incubator's fledgling graduates, followed by an amenity-equipped customized office/lab space. But the process of transforming a built environment to an innovative environment also needs to be designed and this part is less well understood.

The hypothesis of this examination proposes that based on an understanding of what is needed to construct a cluster, participants can create an appropriate business and living environment by attracting missing components like kindling, then hope a spark emerges to light the local fire. San Diego and Atlanta were chosen for a comparative case study to test these assertions due to their similar metropolitan size of around four million residents, temperate weather, overall dynamism of their local economy (SANDAG 1997), and the difference in their life science industry cluster construction to date. San Diego's strength lies in biotech companies, firms using "a collection of technologies [to]... develop products from living cells" (USGAO 1995). Atlanta's agglomeration is primarily composed of small pharmaceutical and medical device components. Both cities evidence minimal but increasing government intervention in the process. San Diego is clearly the most successful biotechnology site, with a third more employees and firms. Atlanta leads in technology fields other than the life sciences, particularly telecommunications (Table 7.1).

Two elements seem to account for the success of particular places in breeding innovation-based life science companies. First, place characteristics include a business environment that encourages risk-taking and communication, increasing synergies of information sharing and network building. Financing needs of start-up and high-risk innovative companies demand access to a supply of deep-pocket investors. These venture capitalists tend to fund promising companies in their own metropolitan region. Financial risks are reduced by familiarity with local conditions and ready access to companies in their investment portfolio. Places therefore must be attractive for capitalists to live or at least visit manageably. The living environment should include affordable amenities for high demand employees: luxury housing, good schools, and recreation/entertainment options.

The final critical component is spatial proximity, both in business locations reflecting or building networks, and residence locations conducive to building familiarity. A group of key individuals then hopefully emerges to compel connections by forcefully networking with others, generating needed political-economic synergies to make their company, industry, and region prosper. These actors could come from businesses involved in the industry, or mediating organizations set up to bridge laboratory and marketplace, assisting in bringing ideas to a profitable conclusion.

Table 7.1   Life Science Industry, Atlanta and San Diego, 1997

SIC	Business	Firms: Atlanta	Firms: San Diego	Labor: Atlanta	Labor: San Diego
2833	BioPharm	26	100	5,547	15,931
3841	Medical Devices	25	35	1,660	1,729
8071	Medical Labs	88	105	3,660	392
8731	Research and Development	32	15	1,250	868
	Total Life Sciences	171	250	12,117	18,928
366, and 481-489	Telecommuni- cations Cluster			72,368	
737	Computer Cluster			68,725	

Source: American Business Directory (1997), CONNECT (1997), ES202 data

This research first examines innovative milieu theory as it applies to the interactive effect of the life science industry on the growth of a metropolitan region. The next section reviews the development of this industry, particularly the highly innovative biotech sector. Contrasts between San Diego and Atlanta as general sites for life science agglomeration development precedes a more detailed examination of key aspects in each place. The conclusion summarizes extensions to theory provided by these case study contrasts.

Theoretical Implications

Innovative milieu theory (Aydalot and Keeble 1988; Hall 1990) generally focuses on structural regional attributes. This shortchanges examining networks constructed by individuals through their associations with mediating institutions or by virtue of personal dynamism (Sternberg 1996). The concept of innovative milieu refers to a local atmosphere encouraging and supporting innovation, including production but not limited to industry. Signature elements are entrepreneurs, close interaction among firms, externalities such as a pool of labor to supply the needed range of managerial, technically skilled, and basic support personnel, and a flexible specialization component capable of responding to small batch, highly customized requirements (Camagni 1995). Theorists divide innovative seedbeds into either growth pole type spatial diffusion mechanisms or aspatial attributes of individuals rather than industry characteristics (Goldstein and Luger 1993).

Structural elements of the life science industry fit well within a general innovative milieu framework. Different sectors and sizes of firms illustrate three types of innovation (Aydalot and Keeble 1988; Hall 1990). Large research-focused pharmaceutical companies, referred to within the industry as "Big Pharma", foster in-house creative activity. Synthesis of new technology to revitalize an old production form occurs in medical device manufacturing. Production of knowledge and translation to commercial application characterizes the dynamic biotechnology sector. Studies comparing the participation of "star" scientists in a biotech firm's initial public stock offering with the growth of biotech companies in a particular area (Zucker, et. al. 1998; Audretsch and Stephan 1996) highlight institutional factors in regional synergy, such as the limited spread of knowledge spillovers, without accounting for the impact of individuals. Yet scientific discoveries, like corporate founding, are strongly affected by a particular person. The driven entrepreneur linking the laboratory and business worlds (Kenney 1986) often fails to feature prominently enough in innovative milieu theory.

The place context of economic activity - the embedded culture that blurs the essentially economic with less economic features (Barnes 1998) - is also not dealt with sufficiently by innovative milieu theory. Production of innovation goes beyond lab space and trained labor, extending into surrounding social and institutional conditions - the spatial relations of social processes involved in weaving information networks (Sunley 1996). When research focuses on a broad picture of "the economic", defined as how businesses go about trying to make money in the name of "survival," cultural elements clearly intrude on and blur considerations based on economic rationality (Schoenberger 1997). Site characteristics strongly impact situations, providing economic links with innovative industries such as the life sciences, in the social construction of production space (Sheppard 1996). The intersection of science, business, networking and individual activity is crucial, and strategies to capture it must include multiple approaches.

Data and Methodology

Geographic clusters of industries served to distinguish locational targets for interviews. A list of the relative number of companies and employees in each sector, for each city (Table 7.1) demonstrates that San Diego's cluster is heavily weighted toward pharmaceutical and biotech firms, while the headquarters of a large medical laboratory skews Atlanta's distribution. Overall, San Diego has more large firms in the life sciences. Atlanta's strength in high technology clearly lies elsewhere, in both telecommunications and computer clusters.

In Atlanta, interview results were combined with a survey for a total of 70 responses (a 40 percent return rate), composed of 43 questionnaires in usable form and 25 interviews conducted with corporations, government professional planners, and real estate developers. Types of questions covered 1) why the company was in that particular location, 2) the major advantages and disadvantages of being in that location and city, 3) particular unaddressed needs such as labor availability (managerial, skilled, routine labor), financing, transportation connections, and 4) networks and leadership enhancing success in that place. Interviews served to amplify otherwise elusive insights as to the underlying dynamics of this industry (Schoenberger 1991; Creswell 1997). Survey results were very similar to but less detailed than interview information. Results are discussed in the analysis section.

Names, addresses, and SIC codes of companies in both Atlanta and San Diego's life science industries (SIC 283 pharmaceutical manufacturers, SIC 384 medical device manufacturers, SIC 873 testing laboratories) were obtained from several sources. Although manufacturing sectors such as custom plastic extruders, and service components such as lawyers, industry consultants, and universities are important, it is not possible in every case to distinguish those affiliated to the life science industry by SIC code alone. Interviews were, however, conducted with those identified by informants. In Atlanta, additional information came from the American Business Directory for Georgia (1997), Georgia Biomedical Partnership lists (including non-members), and interview leads. For San Diego, lists from major industry organizations such as CONNECT, BIOCOM and the San Diego Association of Governments (BIOCOM 1997; Ekstrom 1997; SANDAG 1998) augmented the American Business Directory corporate listings. A set of balanced nonrandom interviews targeted business and development leaders in major life science industry groups and different locations within the two cities (Table 7.2).

Table 7.2   Life Science Industry Interview Sectors

	Bio/ Pharm	Medical Device	Developer Financier	University Connected	Service Industry	Total
San Diego	13	1	2	3	9	28
Atlanta	9	6	5	2	4	26
Total	22	7	7	5	13	54

Source: Author

Table 7.3   Biotech Timeline

1953	Discovery: Watson & Crick unravel DNA's double helix
1970	1st synthesis of a gene
1971	*Cetus* founded (San Francisco Bay area-SFB)
1976	DNA sequencing, 1st working synthetic gene; *Genentech* (SFB)
1977	*Biogen* and *Hybritech* (San Diego–SD) founded
1978	Human growth hormone synthesized
1980	Lifeforms patentable; *Amgen* (SD), *Calgene, Genetic Systems* founded
1981	Gene synthesizing machines and monoclonal antibody kit
1982	1st synthetic DNA product approved for human use (Humulin – Lilly) and synthesized vaccine; *Chiron* (SD) founded
1983	1st artificial chromosome and sales of Humulin
1984	1st genetically engineered vaccine
1985	2nd genetically engineered product approved; Bristol and Lubrizol buy biotechs
1986	1st genetically engineered vaccine approved; Lilly buys *Hybritech* (SD)
1987	Stock market drops
1988	FDA accelerates approval process for drugs against terminal diseases
1996	Monsanto & Incyte plant genomics project; Cloning of Dolly
1998	Record twenty biotech projects approved by FDA; IPO market dries up; new global venture groups; pharmacogenomics path for drug discovery
1999	Record amount of money raised in biotech deals
2000	Biotech companies increasingly move into market, pharmaceuticals increase R&D capability
2001	Human Genome Project and Celera Genomics announce mapping of human gene sequence; bioinformatics and proteomics new areas of interest for future development

Source: Burrill and Ernst and Young High Technology Group (1990), Morrison and Giovannetti (1999, 2000, 2001)

A Tale of Two Cities

Biotechnology as a commercial enterprise dates from 1971 with the formation of Cetus in the San Francisco Bay area (Hall, et al., 1988). The timetable shown in Table 7.3 tracks the annual rise and fall of an industry dependent on scientific breakthroughs and sensitive to the prevailing legal and economic climate, from a court ruling on the legitimacy of patenting a gene to a stock market dip. Cities with significant life science industry concentrations include, in order: Boston, the San Francisco Bay area, Los Angeles, San Diego, North Carolina's "Research Triangle", and the Philadelphia - New Jersey "Pharm Country" (Burrill and Ernet and Young high Technology Group 1997; CHI and KPMG 1998). While the northern California "Biotech Bay" area led with early company stock initial public offerings (IPOs), San Diego made the southern California BioBeach scene in 1977 with the establishment of Hybritech from an invention at the University of California, San Diego (UCSD). California's coastline remains fertile ground for spawning life science clusters (Figure 7.1). It should be noted that the source for the company count in Figure 7.1 does not include medical device establishments, which are otherwise included in this research.

The link between a commercially successful biotech community and a research-rich university with entrepreneurial tenured professors is well established (Kenney 1986; Audretsch and Stephan 1996). The exact model of technology transfer followed is important, since outside financiers are leery of placing private money in ventures where patent and personnel are also tied to a university with a corresponding encumbrance on any future revenue stream. There are obvious advantages in a university setting for initial development of an idea with commercial potential. These include the presence of expensive laboratory facilities, inexpensive and skilled labor from graduate students, a research leader who receives a guaranteed salary regardless of the research's outcome, and access to federal grant money through the university. Biotechnology companies often face a critical need for funds due to the lengthy federal approval process for untested medical products. They remain attractive acquisitions for pharmaceuticals that constantly require new products in their "pipeline". Major pharmaceutical companies negotiate the conversion of science to technology through a range of contract options: building in-house research and development groups, signing open-ended multi-year contracts for a particular project with a scientist (Gambardella 1995), and acquiring rights to a product or ultimately owning a biotech company. Acquisition or a contractual relationship can lead to company relocation to a more proximate place, where other elements vie to support the entrepreneur and the company in which they have an interest. The general production chain for life science companies (Table 7.4) emphasizes the role and needs of the principal players. City regions with these elements hold the best potential.

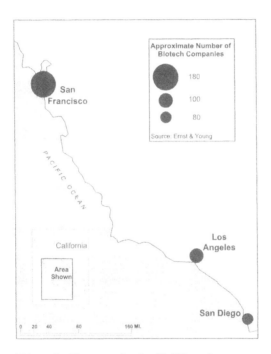

Figure 7.1   Biotech Companies in California

San Diego and Atlanta are economically dynamic Sunbelt cities, with rapidly growing high technology sectors that include a life science industry component. Both cities exhibit clusters of related companies within a few north metro areas (Figures 7.2 and 7.3), discussed more fully in each location section. Despite geographic similarities, the level of development and innovative dynamism varies widely. Industry attraction to an area operates on two levels: luring established firms from other locations and growing them locally. San Diego is further advanced on both fronts than Atlanta, which looks to the Californian as a role model and a potential source of employees or companies seeking opportunities and potentially more profit at an earlier stage of regional development. The two fast-growing cities watch each other, seeking to emulate respective strengths. Contrasts in specific areas follow a general introduction to the life science industry in each city.

Table 7.4   Life Science Industry Production Chain

Entity	Has	Needs	Relationships
Scientist	Ideas	Funds	Receives $US from entrepreneurs for research, royalties
University	Scientists	Funds	Receives $US from entrepreneurs/VC for scientists ideas, product royalties
Pharmaceutical Company	Funds	New products	Contracts with entrepreneur to buy company, contract scientist new ideas
Venture Capitalist (VC)	Funds	Companies & Profits	Contracts with entrepreneur for royalties, with developer for facilities
Economic Developer (ED)	Tax, land credits	Companies	Works with entrepreneur, VC, BA, developer to bring in jobs, companies
Business Association (BA)	Labor	Companies	Works with university, scientist, business, all players for synergy
Accountants	Business skills	Company/ Clients	Works with university, scientist, business, for profitable clients
Developer	Land, facilities	Companies	Works with entrepreneur, VC, ED, BA to construct marketable facilities
Entrepreneur	Product, Company	Facilities, $US, Employees	Works with all to obtain everything all need, including employee amenities.

Source: Author

San Diego: "Biotech Beach" as Innovative Milieu

The biopharmaceutical cluster in San Diego (Figure 7.2) is a picture-perfect poster child of a cutting edge region bubbling with inventive entrepreneurial energies. The size of the clusters generalized on this map does not reflect the number of companies but rather the spatial extent of the associated cluster. The largest by far in terms of associated businesses surrounds the University of California, San Diego at the intersection of routes 5 and 805. San Diego is California's fastest growing life science location, doubling in the mid-1990s to over 400 companies (CHI 1998). While the West Coast region is relatively open to new ideas and innovators, San Diego is particularly hungry for distinction in the shadow of its northern neighbors, Los Angeles and San Francisco. Nationally, San Diego forms a biotech triangle with Boston and the San Francisco Bay area. San Diego's life science agglomeration received an early boost due to the financial backing of successful computer-related companies who attracted venture capital to the area before biotech's debut.

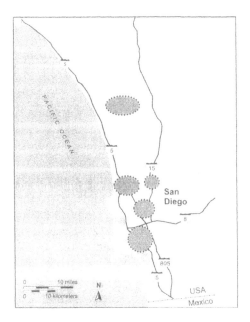

Figure 7.2   Location of Biotech Firms in San Diego

Individuals and their investments reportedly flowed fairly smoothly to biotech, while local military facilities (such as the Naval Ocean Systems Center) supply and train a labor base of engineering talent. The timing of San Diego's biotech birth coincided with the most optimistic early industry trajectory, when venture capitalists were relatively willing to take a risk on this new innovative investment opportunity.

The life story of the region's most successful early baby biotech illustrates a model with lingering reverberations. Starting as a technology transfer from the laboratory of two University of California San Diego (UCSD) scientists, Hybritech begot in turn many other firms. The initial corporate location was as close as possible to the UCSD campus, according to early founder and now major biotech venture capitalist Tom Wollaenger.

Former university employees and company scientists did not want their neighbors to know they had "sold out" to making money, so they continued to drive to work in the same direction as to their previous jobs. Salaries from corporate success quickly changed the mindset but not the setting, as the original canyon top location still produces numerous bio-related businesses.

Financing demands for supporting companies through the lengthy years of testing and ultimate FDA sanctioning often leads to absorption of biotechs by more deep-pocket pharmaceutical giants eager for new product ideas in their pipeline. Hybritech's recombinant DNA technology and potential application to its major diabetes focus attracted Indianapolis' Eli Lilly and Company, who acquired Hybritech for a promising colon cancer breakthrough. The biotech's founders made millions, though the technology ultimately did not live up to its promise and the company was resold to a diagnostics firm. The price tag attracted attention to biotech's possibilities, creating a core of local venture capitalists. The number of company failures in biotech is legion, and a major risk factor featured in numerous calculations. Economies of cluster size reflect this instability, from real estate sites (financing available only for the highest cost, highest demand areas) to labor pool considerations (lots of job possibilities needed to absorb a high turnover sector). A key characteristic of San Diego's innovation-supporting milieu is the lack of onus attached to failure - better to have tried, and learned something, with plenty of job opportunities available to former employees and would-be owners.

Atlanta: Growing a "Technology Forest" in the Peach State

Atlanta adopted this slogan to reflect the area's arboreal abundance, but in relation to the life sciences industry the city harks more to Hansel and Gretel, having ventured in but not yet found their way through. On the research side, Atlanta's triumvirate of area universities includes the University of Georgia (in Athens, with start-ups migrating to Atlanta), in-town Georgia State University and Georgia Institute of Technology. Seventeen successful Georgia Tech graduates pooled funds and expertise to establish the first technology park in the region in 1971.

Proximity increases the odds of interaction, but is far from a causative agent. Life science companies in Atlanta gravitate north of the city (Figure 7.3), particularly in an area known as the "Norcross Cluster". This area made the national news in 1999 when groups attracted by its affordable real estate in a hot market clashed. Led by a group of citizens seeking to preserve a new upscale image that transformed a derelict railroad station to a trendy restaurant, the city council (in a move later overturned) forbade signs not in English. Signs prominently displayed on establishments catering to Hispanics in an ethnic retail strip moving eastward from Atlanta were particularly targeted. Several firms in clusters on the northeast and northwest sides of town sublet space from potential business partners or mentors. On the other hand, some nearby complementary companies lack any business ties - in one case due to the close presence of a firm under similar ownership. Overall, Atlanta's life sciences CEOs see themselves as geographically isolated from each other, but well situated within the Southeast as a booming region.

Analysis: Spatial Proximity Effects

Charting responses to interviews and surveys in the two cities profiled yields a picture of the strengths and needs of the area and the companies in it (Table 7.5).

Atlanta's Hartsfield Airport is the world's busiest, while San Diego's Lindbergh has only one runway. The category of "transportation" thus unsurprisingly displays the greatest split between the two cities. The area of greatest strength in both cities was in knowledge spillovers from local research centers, a crucial consideration in innovation dependent life science. Atlanta's lowest points were in financing and critical mass. In a region nationally known for booming construction the availability of real estate was a major plus. Given its larger size, San Diego felt a labor pinch more especially in the highest level of trained scientists, while Atlanta respondents noted the need for more networking. The following subsections detail the situation in each city.

Technology Transfer

A key hypothesis of this research holds that an innovative milieu builds on a group of research universities that encourages applications of research into the business community, facilitates a free flow of ideas openly communicated and discussed, and is bridged by entrepreneurs who carry ideas into products. A frequent interview response to the initial query of "Why biotech in San Diego?" named the cluster of Nobel-rich research universities. Scripps Institute of Oceanography (the largest private biomedical research institute in the world), the Salk Institute (one of the largest private biological research centers), the University of California at San Diego (UCSD) and other research hospitals in the area such as the Scripps Clinic, furnish both innovative ideas and individuals (Stutz 1992). Scripps, Salk, and UCSD professors coordinate lectures as an example of the cross-fertilization prevalent in this cooperative setting. With an interest in applied technology along the MIT model, UCSD classes on legal and regulatory issues such as the FDA process drew large enrollments when offered in response to local business urging.

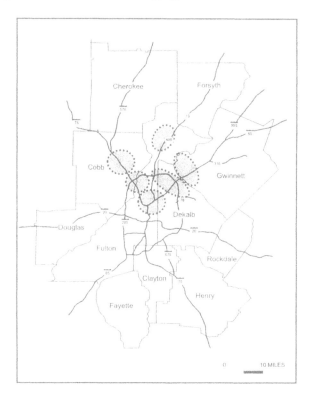

Figure 7.3   Location of Biotech Firms in Atlanta

Examples of physically collaborative information and instruction exchange embody San Diego's competitive edge, at both the business and university level. Another medium of integration between the two worlds is the availability of a schedule of lectures of interest to the local life science industry on a local web site. One CEO gave the example of a lecture at Scripps given by a noted Japanese scientist, who he questioned closely after the talk. The businessman then joined a group of four men, including two Nobel laureates, debating the presentation in the hall outside. They were all examining how to integrate findings with possible application for new drugs.

One measure of relative technology strength is provided by grants from the National Institute of Health for research and development in the life sciences (Table 7.6). For the earliest year available, Atlanta institutions captured about one third of metropolitan San Diego's share. Across the next five years, Atlanta's grants dropped to one quarter of San Diego's. The huge increase since 1995, it should be noted, marked the advent of one particular San Diego company, SAIC. Using another measure, the Association of University Technology Managers' figures show that Georgia's two major research universities launched two start-up firms and granted 25 licenses for biotech innovations in 1997. UCSD alone accounted for 20 licenses in the same year, but the most telling impact is the twelve start-ups using UCSD technology, of which half relied solely on that university for their inventions. Since the San Diego branch tech transfer office opened four years ago, an estimated $US87 million has been raised by new start-ups using only UCSD technology, resulting in over 230 new jobs. The total number of licenses for technology in those four years is 47, of which 80 percent were related to biomedicine.

Table 7.5   Interview Response Chart: Atlanta and San Diego

Reason for Location	Atlanta	San Diego
Knowledge spillovers	12	8
Dynamic individual	2	6
Available real estate	11	4
Banks forced	1	4
Critical mass	1	4
Transportation	10	0
Spin-off	3	6
Venture capital	3	6
Attractive place	8	6
Network organizations	4	8
Labor	4	3

Source: Author

Atlanta's major tech transfer institutions include the locally headquartered Centers for Disease Control, Yerkes Primate Center, and the

American Cancer Society, aside from the previously mentioned metropolitan area research universities. Specialization assists in creating a cluster focused - thus more easily identified and assembled - on a particular aspect. Academic and corporate strengths vary. One sign of a local Atlanta specialty concentration similar to San Diego's focus on genomics is a nuclear implant interest on the part of several companies. The Georgia Research Alliance's latest push funds a bioinformatics focus. A successful local business endowed an applied research building in construction on the Georgia Tech campus, and a new bio-focused facility called EmTech on the Emory campus draws attention to its partnership with the Institute of Technology on the other side of the city. Atlanta's life science cluster is more heavily composed of companies who migrated there from other states than from nearby university technology transfers. None of the universities possess a strong applied research focus in biomedicine, though companies have used several local patents as core technologies.

Table 7.6   National Institute of Health Grants (percent increase), 1993-1997

	1997	1996	1995	1994	1993
Atlanta	120,007	98,665	96,947	96,312	94,718
	(2.16)	(1.77)	(0.6)	(1.6)	
San Diego	472,329	427,950	411,943	280,634	270,326
	(10)	(3.8)	(46)	(3.8)	

Source: National Institute of Health web page (www.gov.nih)

Mediating Organizations

The first major network organization linking San Diego's life science industry companies, CEOs, and products with each other and the larger community was CONNECT. Assembled by San Diego's Economic Development Council (EDC), it was founded through UCSD in 1985 as an "incubator without walls" for nurturing high technology companies. BIOCOM/*san diego* came from the Biomedical Industry Council (BIC) and the San Diego Biocommerce Association (BIOCOM). Since 1991 BIOCOM raised biotech's profile with groups impacted by biotech's success from law and accounting firms to hospitality and real estate representatives. Representatives of both BIOCOM and CONNECT actively lobby on issues from local schools (affecting quality of the local labor base) to national industry policies.

Lobbying the San Diego Association of Governments (SANDAG) and the Economic Development Council (EDC) increased the impact of San Diego's life science industry by bringing their concerns to policy makers' attention. A classic example came into play with the controversy over re-zoning the now-defunct Marine Recruiting Depot. When originally allocated for homeless shelters and other populations difficult to locate within the city, the land became the object of a life science lobbying effort advocating its use for a potential second runway. A re-vote found in favor of the airport expansion. The head of UCSD's CONNECT was frequently characterized by respondents as "a bulldog for biotech in San Diego." A retired high tech entrepreneur, his confrontational style involves forcefully bringing together individuals whose interest, abilities, or companies can help each other to grow – and by extension their region and industry.

Atlanta's life science industry agglomeration, by contrast, needs both a dynamic leader and a more broadly networked advocacy organization. While the Georgia Research Alliance (GRA) provides attractive incentive packages to lure "Eminent Scholars" from out-of-state institutions, coordinated leadership from the disparate corporate and educational institutions is missing. The Georgia Biomedical Partnership (funded by the GRA under state legislative sponsorship) organizes monthly forums for industry discussions. But in the academic and business culture, little dynamic cross-fertilization exists. On a metropolitan scale, client organizations such as large accountancy-consulting firms and venture capitalists provide the major occasions for CEO conferring, but with little carry-over at present.

Funding Sources

The major fund-raising outlet other than selling parts of promising proprietary products to large pharmaceutical companies is to attract venture capital investment. The unprecedentedly large price tag paid by Lilly for San Diego's Hybritech caught the attention of investors who suddenly realized biotech could be a source of profit. Venture (less charitably termed "vulture") capital and "angel" financiers consolidate and solicit attention to their voraciously capital-consuming expanding brood of baby biotechs by reinvesting their locally earned millions and raising capital (often from other high tech companies and magnates) on a national scale. Not just a Silicon Valley phenomenon, these California-based investors solicit biotech funds from Bill Gates to Yale University, spurred by descendants of local hero Hybritech.

The venture capital link to nourish emerging start-ups draws on a more restricted, if expanding, pool in Atlanta. The absence of a successful corporate godfather, and the enormous number of wealthy computer companies in the Bay area, is keenly felt. A few "angel" financiers have been attracted from other cities, but a critical mass of corporate successes and deep wells to draw from are not yet established. Nor has a prominent multinational pharmaceutical begun to acquire companies, with the exception of Canadian Murex and Belgian Solvay pharmaceuticals. Investors enticed east to Atlanta from southern California have in some cases continued to look east for their investments, putting money in more established and rapidly developing targets around North Carolina's Research Triangle Park area of Raleigh-Durham.

Real Estate and Spatial Proximity

Geographic concentration in a critical mass does not occur simply because "proximity serves to amplify... productivity and innovative benefits of clustering" (Porter 1998, p. 11). Several life science clusters are clearly present in both San Diego and Atlanta (Figures 7.2 and 7.3). In each case, automobile-dependent north suburban metro area clusters occur strung along or between major highways. This pattern follows the suburban reshaping of metropolitan economics dispersing homes and jobs fanning out from the former and ever less central city (OTA 1995).

The setting of headquarters location varies by type of building and surrounding land use. In San Diego, the "Golden Triangle" of I-5, 805, Rte. 52 holds the vast majority of biotech companies. All claim around a ten minute commute from most employees' residences and the major university and research institution campuses - another sort of Golden Triangle. A glass high-rise office park in University Town Center is within ten freeway minutes of one-story warehouse conversions in Sorrento Valley housing a cluster of budding biotechs and their chief lobbying organization. Sorrento Valley and the Mesa in Torrey Pines hold a combined total of around 100 companies. Contemporary science parks overlook sports facilities, from tennis courts to a golf course on the PGA tour. Financial institutions favor loans for businesses in the most expensive real estate due to the potentially quick turnaround of space. When one company disappears, plenty more are seeking its lease space. Banks are more reluctant to loan money for quarters in the more affordable eastern section of the county.

At 20 freeway minutes away, northern suburbs bordering San Diego's La Jolla community offer lots carved out of "pueblo land" granted to the city for non-residential use and zoned for light industry. Connected to science and research centers by freeways, industrial and office parks cover the hillsides along Palomar Airport Road. Due to the relative isolation and non-urban setting, the labor market is geographically focused in surrounding subdivisions. Another cluster in the northeastern section close to I-215 is differentiated by whether or not residents need a high performing school district.

In Atlanta, the Advanced Technology Development Center provides the standard advice-and-overhead high technology incubator in a warehouse setting on the Georgia Tech campus. A second incubator, designed expressly for biotech start-ups, is under construction near Emory University on the opposite side of town. Emory's strength is its research hospital, while Tech concentrates on applied science and engineering. A shortage of affordable space in offices conducive to biotech's messy needs (from animals to blood and nuclear material) promotes clusters of companies who moved into spaces vacated or acquired by more established tenants in anticipation of expansion needs. Interaction within the life science cluster is greatest where the number of companies is highest. Assistance and advice comes from those located closest, which may be a reflection of the initial choice to locate in adjacent or sub-leased real estate.

The most prominent local biomedical-invested venture capitalist, lured to Atlanta from California by the GRA, supported the needs of his growing corporate progeny by teaming with state and regional officials to "educate" developers on the need for mid-size biotech facilities. An office park focused on life science industry tenants is now planned in a centrally located northern suburb of Atlanta, along Route 400 (Miller 1998). Current biomedical corporate clusters are northeast and northwest of the city of Atlanta. Technology Park to the northeast opened 27 years ago, designed specifically by wealthy Georgia Tech graduates to keep more alumni and their companies in the Atlanta area by providing a corporate campus. Northwest of Atlanta, the Cobb-Marietta Industrial Park off Route 75 attracts intermediate-size life science firms.

Successful firms expand out of the industrial parks to build their own footprint on cheaper land in a directional trajectory ever northward along the same interstate as previously, and now along the central corridor of Route 400. The key consideration is access, avoiding traffic snarls along the Perimeter/Rte. 285 connecting the northern routes out of the city, but bottling up much of the cross-county traffic. Centrally located Route 400 serves as a barricade, discouraging interaction between companies along the northwest and northeast interstates. As in San Diego, availability of amenity housing and high-scoring school systems anchor employees in the northern suburbs.

Innovative Milieu: Structural Context and the Leadership Factor

Creating places of concentrated innovative activity occurs as the result of deliberate leadership moving a region toward openness and united activities flowing from a shared purpose (Castells and Hall 1994), in the classic Rostow pre-takeoff to take-off model of development. Numerous national efforts to build biotech energy, from Washington, California, Utah, and Colorado, to Michigan, Ohio, North Carolina and Georgia, all seek to pour money into facilities and salaries (Blakeley and Nishikawa 1992; Haug and Ness 1993). As Malecki (1997) contends, however, "it is not at all clear that high tech ...can be 'created' in regions which lack agglomeration economies and other dynamics common to high tech centers" (p. 44). Along with pre-existing, constructed and promoted features, a region also has to get lucky with its individuals. The role of political entities is marginal, assisting or obstructing, but in response to initiatives of individuals.

Networks formed in the San Diego case study show integration of military, political (on municipal, county and state scales), educational, and business interests - echoing earlier theories incorporating individual, organizational, and structural aspects strengthened by spatial proximity of agglomeration (Malmberg 1996, 1997; Malmberg et. al. 1996). Innovation tends to be place-specific (Scott and Storper 1992). This is due not only to a particular structural setting within a supportive culture (Saxenian 1983, 1994; Scott and Storper 1987) but through the spark of leadership. Organizational networks can be easily constructed. A community of open inquiry and targeted advocacy is another matter. Even within a region supportive of one technology sector, another struggles to become established for lack of the same high profile attention, local successful landmark companies drawing others, and dynamic leadership from within the corporate ranks.

Conclusion

Spatial proximity of companies in a similar industry is not enough in itself for success. Nor is it necessarily a predictor of interaction. Cluster concentrations are often caused by real estate considerations, determined by bank loan policies that favor supporting businesses (particularly in the perceived risky line of life sciences) in locations with rapid resale potential. The main attribute of spatial proximity for a company is location within a metropolitan area that is convenient for visits by customers, suppliers, financiers, and networking with neighbors. In terms of the life science industry, Atlanta is an island, with all the implicit advantages of its nodal transportation hub linkages and disadvantages of regional exceptionalism. San Diego aggressively competes for capital, personnel, and attention with regional and national rivals. The initial scale of local clustering in a university-affiliated location (whether enclosed on a campus as in Atlanta, or along a nearby roadway as in San Diego) expanded in both cities to a regional scale, encompassing prime residential as well as customized office facilities.

The presence of categorical elements is not in itself sufficient. This explains why, for example, San Diego succeeded in establishing a lively life science cluster rather than did nearby Los Angeles. The level and type of activities found in the two case study cities clearly demonstrate the dynamic affect of individuals who fit the particular needs of an industry that in turn thrives on inherent regional attributes: e.g., energetic entrepreneurs in the high-risk, high-reward life science industry within an open, experimental region. The conservatism of Atlanta's banking community, for example, necessitates enticing scarce outside venture capital to invest in relatively risky - albeit promising and potentially fabulously profitable - local life science start-ups.

Spatial proximity assists in mentoring relationships of firms that may be initially driven together by real estate opportunity (Malmberg 1997). In a highly competitive world of proprietary innovative edges, such relationships must be seen as mutually advantageous. However, knowledge spillovers flow more from *regional* attributes to resident firms, in the form of access to lectures and organizations funneling ideas from labs into businesses. Companies located close to each other may not do business directly with each other, but interactions of researchers and CEOs bind them to industry concerns and facilitate a mutually beneficial stimulation of ideas through information interchange. Leadership provided by key individuals is crucial to this network.

Additional carefully constructed case study comparisons targeting interactions among industry components in similar or contrasting metropolitan regions would further test the hypotheses suggested in this research. Examination of high tech regions in different sections of the country, or in different industry sectors, would add empirical strength - or challenges - to innovative milieu theory extensions suggested in this examination of the life science industry in two booming Sunbelt metropolitan areas.

Note

1   Defined in this research as pharmaceutical and medical device manufacturers, biotechnology and testing laboratories, and universities engaged in related research.

References

American Business Directories (1997), *Georgia Business Directory.* American Business Directory, Omaha.

Audretsch, D. and Stephan, P. (1996), "Company-Scientist Locational Links: the Case of Biotechnology", *The American Economic Review*, vol. 86, pp. 641-52.

Aydalot, P. and Keeble, D. (1988), *High Technology Industry and Innovative Environments: The European Experience,* Routledge, London.

Aydalot, P. and Hall, P. (1994), *Technopoles of the World: The Making of 21st Century Industrial Complexes,* Routledge, London.

Barnes, T. (1998), "Confessions of a Political Economist", *Progress in Human Geography,* vol. 22, pp. 94-104.

BIOCOM/san diego (1997), San Diego County Life Sciences Facilities Guide, San Diego.

Blakely, E. and Nishikawa, N. (1992), "Incubating High-Technology Firms: State Economic Development Strategies for Biotechnology", *Economic Development Quarterly,* vol. 6, pp. 241-54.

Burrill, G. and Ernst and Young High Technology Group (1990), *Biotech 90: Into the Next Decade*, Ernst and Young, Palo Alto.

Burrill, G. and Ernst & Young High Technology Group (1997), *Biotech 97 Alignment.* Ernst & Young, Palo Alto

California Healthcare Institute and KPMG (1998), *The Biomedical Frontier: 1998 Report on California"s Biomedical R&D Industry.* KPMG, California.

Camagni, R. (1995), The Concept of Innovative Milieu and its Relevance for Public Policies in European Lagging Regions. *Papers in Regional Science: The Journal of the Regional Science Association,* vol. 74, pp. 317-40.

Castells, M. and Hall, P. (1994), *Technopoles of the World,* Routledge, London.

Creswell, J. (1997), *Qualitative Inquiry and Research Design: Choosing Among Five Traditions*, Sage Publications, Thousand Oaks, CA:

Ekstrom, C. (ed.) (1997), *UCSD CONNECT Directory*, CONNECT, San Diego.

Feldman, M. (1985), "Biotechnology and Local Economic Growth: The American Pattern", in P. Hall and A. Markusen, (eds), *Silicon Landscapes*, Allen & Unwin, Boston, pp. 65-79.

Feldman, M.P. (1994), "The University and Economic Development: The Case of Johns Hopkins University and Baltimore", *Economic Development Quarterly*, vol. 8, pp. 67-76.

Gambardella, A. (1995), *Science and Innovation*, Cambridge University Press, Cambridge.

Goldstein, H. and Luger, M. (1993), "Theory and Practice in High Tech Economic Development", in R. Bingham and R. Mier (eds), *Theories of Local Economic Development: Perspectives from the Disciplines*, Sage, Newbury Park, pp. 147-71.

Hall, P. (1990)," The Generation of Innovative Milieu: An Essay in Theoretical Synthesis", *Working Paper 505, Institute of Urban and Regional Development*. University of California Press, Berkeley.

Hall, P., Bornstein, L., Grier, R. and Webber, M. (1988), *Biotechnology: The Next Industrial Frontier*. Biotech Industry Research Group, University of California, Berkeley.

Haug, P. and Ness, P. (1993) "Industrial Location Decisions of Biotechnology Organizations", *Economic Development Quarterly*, vol. 7, pp. 390-402.

Kenney, M. (1986), *Biotechnology: The University-Industry Complex*, Yale University Press, New Haven, CT.

Lyons, D. (1995),"Agglomeration Economies Among High Technology Firms in Advanced Production Areas: The Case of Denver/Boulder", *Regional Studies*, vol. 29, pp. 265-78.

Maillat, D. (1998), "Innovative Milieux and New Generations of Regional Policies", *Entrepreneurship and Regional Development*, vol. 10, pp. 1-16.

Malecki, E. (1991), *Technology and Economic Development: The Dynamics of Local, Regional, and National Change*, Longman Scientific and Technical, New York.

Malecki, E. (1997), *Technology and Economic Development: The Dynamics of Local, Regional, and National Competitiveness*. Addison Wesley Longman, London.

Malmberg, A. (1996), Industrial Geography: Agglomeration and Local Milieu. *Progress in Human Geography*, vol. 20, pp. 392-403.

Malmberg, A. (1997), "Industrial Geography: Location and Learning", *Progress in Human Geography*, vol. 21, pp. 573-582.

Malmberg, A., Solvell, O. and Zander, I. (1996), "Spatial Clustering, Local Accumulation of Knowledge and Firm Competitiveness", *Geografiska Annaler*, vol. 78 B, pp. 85-97.

Miller, A. (8/14/98), "Biotech Facility Would Nurture Young Firms", *The Atlanta Journal-Constitution*, Atlanta, pp. F1-2.

Morrison, S. and Giovannetti, G. (1999), *New directions 98*, Ernst & Young, Palo Alto.

Morrison, S. and Giovannetti, G. (2000), *Bridging the Gap*, Ernst & Young, Palo Alto.

Morrison, S. and Giovannetti, G. (2001), *Convergence: The Biotechnology Industry* Report, Ernst & Young, Palo Alto.

Office of Technology Assessment, Congress of the United States (1995), "The Technological Reshaping of Metropolitan America", Washington, D.C.

Porter, M. (1998), "The Adam Smith Address: Location Clusters, and the "New" Microeconomics of Competition", *Business Economics*, vol. 33, pp. 7-13 .

San Diego Association of Governments (SANDAG) (January-February 1997), "Population and Income Characteristics of the San Diego Region", *Info*, SANDAG, San Diego.

Saxenian, A. (1983), "The Urban Contradictions of Silicon Valley: Regional Growth and the Restructuring of the Semiconductor Industry", *International Journal of Urban and Regional Research*, vol.7, pp. 237-62.

Saxenian, A. (1994), *Regional Advantage: Culture and Competition in Silicon Valley and Route 128*, Harvard University Press, Cambridge, MA .

Schoenberger, E. (1991), "The Corporate Interview as a Research Method in Economic Geography", *Professional Geographer*, vol. 43, pp. 180-189.

Schoenberger, E. (1997), *The Cultural Crisis of the Firm*, Blackwell Publishers, Cambridge, MA.

Scott, A. and Storper, M. (1987), "High Technology Industry and Regional Development: A Theoretical Critique and Reconstruction", *International Social Science Journal*, vol. 9, pp. 215-32.

Scott, A. and Storper, M. (1992), *Pathways to Industrialization and Regional Development*. Routledge, London.

Sheppard, E. (1996), "Site, Situation and Social Theory", *Environment and Planning A*, vol. 28, pp.1339-44.

Stephan, P., Hawkins, R. and Audretsch, D. (2000), "The Knowledge Production Function: Lessons From Biotechnology", *International Journal of Technology Management*. Special issue on "Intellectual Property Protection and Economic Development", E. Mansfield, (ed), vol. 19, pp. 165-78.

Sternberg, R. (1996), "Regional Growth Theories and High-Tech Regions", *International Journal of Urban and Regional Research*, vol.20, pp. 518-38.

Stutz, F. (1992), "Working the Cities: The Regional Economic Base", in P. Pryde (ed), *San Diego: An Introduction to the Region*, pp.155-64, Kendall/Hunt Publishing Co., Dubuque, Iowa.

Sunley, P. (1996), "Context in Economic Geography: The Relevance of Pragmatism", *Progress in Human Geography*, vol. 20, pp. 338-55.

United States General Accounting Office. Health, Education, and Human Services Division (1995), "Biotech R&D, Reform, and Market Change", The General Accounting Office, Washington, DC.

Willoughby, K. (1995), "The Local Milieux of Knowledge-Based Industries: What Can We Learn From a Regional Analysis of Commercial Biotechnology?" in J. Brotchie; E. Batty; P. Blakely; P. Hall and P. Newton (eds), *Cities in Competition*, Longman Australia, Melbourne, pp. 252-85.

Zucker, L., Darby, M. and Brewer, M. (1998) "Intellectual Human Capital and the Birth of US Biotechnology Enterprises', *American Economic Review*, vol. 88, pp. 290-306.

8 Innovation Networks in Reconversion Regions – The Case of Styria

FRANZ TÖDTLING, MICHAELA TRIPPL AND HUBERT BRATL

Concepts of innovation have changed in the recent years, the focus shifting from a company perspective to innovation networks and to systems of innovation. Old industrialized areas are generally considered as regions with considerable barriers for innovation and networking and with disadvantages in this respect. However, under certain conditions a renewal process may get started, improving the innovation performance of such regions (Cooke 1995; Heinze et al 1998). Such a renewal will only become effective and lasting, however, if innovation activities reach beyond single firms and become "systemic". This requires networking within the region and beyond. In the "old" industrial region of Styria in Austria such a renewal process has been taking place. It is strongly related with the regional innovation system, which we briefly describe in the third section. Using results from a European research project (REGIS) we investigate the extent Styrian firms are in fact innovating and engaged in innovation networks. A final section focuses specifically on the automotive industry, which has been a target of an official cluster policy in the region. Here, the process of network formation and the role of specific actors of the regional innovation system are looked at.

Conceptual Background

In recent years the linear innovation model has been successively replaced by a non-linear and interactive view of the innovation process (Kline and Rosenberg 1986; Dosi 1988; Dodgson and Rothwell 1994). Non-linearity implies that innovation is not exclusively driven by science and R&D departments but stimulated and influenced by many actors and sources of information both inside and outside the firm. In particular, there are interactions feeding back the experience of production, marketing, and of customers into earlier phases of the innovation process. Interactivity refers to the internal collaboration between several departments of a company (R&D, production, marketing, distribution, etc.) as well as to external relations with other firms (especially with customers and suppliers), knowledge providers (like universities and technology centers), finance, training, and public administration (Cooke and Morgan 1993, 1998).

Networks can be considered as institutions "between markets and hierarchies", facilitating interaction among firms and other organizations (De Bresson and Walker 1991; Grabher 1993; Genosko 1997). Since networks are more durable and trust-based relations than market links they ease knowledge exchange and access to complementary competences and resources (Hakanson 1987; Fritsch et al. 1998). Networks may be of different kinds and configurations (social/economic/political; formal /informal; hierarchical/egalitarian; strong/weak; local/distant). Here, we are mainly focusing on networks among firms and other actors in the innovation process, and in particular in the territorial and spatial aspect of networks (Storper and Harrison 1991; Malecki and Oinas 1999). Since local and regional networks are more often based on face-to-face contacts, and a shared culture and trust, they are said to ease, in particular, the exchange of tacit knowledge (Maillat 1991; Asheim 1996). Distant networks, on the other hand, open up new market and technology perspectives of firms and to access complementary competences. Therefore they are considered important for the long-term innovativeness of regional firms and the avoidance of "lock-in" (Camagni 1991; Lundvall and Borràs 1998; Sternberg 1998).

The territorial and institutional dimension of innovation has been stressed more recently in the concept of innovation systems (Lundvall 1992; Edquist 1997). Studies on national innovation systems (NIS) have shown that there are significant differences in the innovation pattern between countries, depending on their economic structure, knowledge base and institutional specifities (Nelson 1993). Autio (1998) argues in this context that NIS approaches have been stressing the links and flows between relevant institutional spheres (finance, research, education, business), but that they have not seen the actors generating these flows. Many of the more tacit elements have been left out. He argues that a focus on the regional innovation system (RIS) can better accomplish this. Autio (1998) conceives a RIS as being composed of two subsystems, a knowledge generation and diffusion subsystem and a knowledge application and exploitation subsystem. While the first consists of research institutions, educational institutions, as well as of technology- and workforce-mediation, the second refers to the industrial companies and their vertical and horizontal networks (customers, contractors, collaborators and competitors). Furthermore, the RIS is externally linked to the NIS, to other RISs as well as to international institutions and systems. Regional innovation systems have been analyzed recently in Braczyk et al. (1998), De la Mothe and Paquet (1998) and in Cooke et al. (2000). Questions raised include the extent to which innovation systems can be identified at the regional level, how they are functioning, and how they are linked with systems at higher spatial levels.

These and other studies have shown that under certain conditions the innovation process becomes "embedded" in the region (Aydalot and Keeble 1988; Camagni 1991; Grabher 1993; Tödtling 1994; Storper 1997; Malmberg and Maskell 1999). This may eventually lead to the development of a regional innovation system (Cooke 1998). The following factors and mechanisms have been identified in the literature in this respect:

- There are immobile factors for innovation such as the qualification of the labor force as well as knowledge externalities and spillovers emanating from research institutions (Jaffee et al. 1993; Castells and Hall 1994; Malecki 1997).
- Localized industrial clusters may give rise to vertical and horizontal innovation networks and to a process of collective learning (Enright 1995; Simmie 1997; Steiner 1998).
- Through these links, a common technical and organizational culture may develop in a region, leading to a specific innovative milieu (Camagni 1991; Maillat 1991; Saxenian 1994; Ratti et al. 1997).
- Regional policy has been taking a more active role regarding innovation recently and has provided innovation support often through independent institutions and agencies (Sternberg 1995; Hassink 1996; Malecki 1997). These see themselves as intermediaries and as stimulators of networks rather than as providers of direct support (Cooke and Morgan 1998; Morgan and Nauwelaers 1999).

It becomes clear that a RIS is more generic than a cluster. While clusters refer to the local concentration of specific industries, their vertical and horizontal relations, and their various support organizations, the RIS includes also elements that reach beyond specific clusters. This may be generic research, education, innovation support and other generic institutions. The RIS has the function to integrate these elements in a coherent way and to provide an institutional framework to link the more specific networks of industries and clusters. An effective RIS, thus, would also stimulate knowledge flows and relations between clusters.

The question arises whether innovation networks and innovation systems can be observed in regions with excellent preconditions (innovative milieux) only, or if they can be identified also in the less ideal situation of older industrial regions like Styria. In general, old industrial regions are not considered as being highly innovative due to the dominance of mature sectors, a large share of branch plants with little competence for innovation, and a lack of entrepreneurship (Tödtling 1992; Grabher 1993). Nevertheless, it is often a crisis situation that triggers processes of industrial, organizational and institutional renewal, leading to a re-enforcement of innovation (Friedman 1991). Renewal processes have been observed in the past years in several European and North American "rust belt regions" (Cooke 1995; Heinze et al. 1998).

This chapter investigates innovation activities and its systemic aspects for the industrial region of Styria in Austria. The results for Styria are put in perspective with other regions analyzed in the European REGIS project. The aim of REGIS was to identify key elements of regional innovation systems and their interaction through the comparative analysis of nine regions in Europe. In particular, the following questions are investigated:

- To what extent can we identify innovation activities and networks in an "old" industrial region like Styria?
- What is the role of the regional innovation system, i.e. firms and institutions from the region as partners in the innovation process, compared to those at higher spatial levels (national, European Union, global level)?
- Specifically for the automotive cluster, we are interested in the more detailed qualitative aspects of innovation networking as well as in the development of networks, starting from a situation where few such existed.

Economy and Innovation System of Styria

Styria is located in the South East of Austria, bordering the newly formed state of Slovenia. It is a peripheral and a border region from the Austrian as well as the EU perspective. It has the status of a *Bundesland* (province) with its own government and parliament, but the region is not endowed with sufficient financial means to have an autonomous economic policy.

Styria has a population of about 1.2 million and it contributes 12 percent to the Austrian GDP. Being a region of basic industries (steel, metal products, pulp and paper) its economy had been strong in the past but was declining since the 1970s. Intensive restructuring occurred in the 1980s in particular in the *Obersteiermark,* which has been the largest Objective 2 area in Austria in the EU-structural funds period 1994-1999. As a consequence, the Styrian rate of unemployment (8 percent in 1998) has been consistently above the Austrian average in the past years. The Styrian GDP per head is still below the Austrian level but it has been growing faster since 1994. More dynamic economic development can be observed in the 1990s in particular in the area of Graz, the economic and political center of Styria. Dynamic industries are mechanical engineering, machines, vehicles, and the service sector.

The successful restructuring of the economy seems to be strongly linked to a well developed regional innovation system. Applying Autios' (1998) categories we find that Styria has a strong knowledge generation and diffusion system (Figure 8.1). The Technical University of Graz has strengths in machinery, electrical engineering, construction engineering, and the University of Leoben has an international reputation for competences in mining and materials technologies. Joanneum Research is a large contract research institution (owned by the Land), with competences in environment/energy, informatics, sensorics and materials. All these research institutions actively develop interfaces with industry: the universities have liaison offices as well as cooperative R&D institutions attached. There are six "Christian Dopper (CD) Laboratories" engaged in cooperation with firms with the aim of developing new products and processes. Of more recent origin is the materials center Leoben, a cooperative institution among university institutes and firms with the task to engage in joint basic and applied research. A new element (since 1995) in the Austrian and Styrian innovation systems are the technical colleges ("Fachhochschulen") providing more applied education and training than the universities. In Styria there are currently colleges for design, automotive technologies, information management, industrial electronics and business administration. Student numbers are still small but strongly growing, since the firms have a high demand for these kinds of qualifications. Another important actor in the region is the Styrian Economic Development Agency (SFG). It was founded in 1991 as an independent semi-public agency, controlled and financed by the Land. The agency supports new and growing firms, innovation projects of firms and the setting up of incubators and technology centers. More recently it became more involved in the development of clusters such as the automotive cluster described further below. Regarding the knowledge application and exploitation subsystem, we find in Styria cluster structures of different degrees of development. They are best developed in the automotive sector with vertical and horizontal relations and efficient support organizations. Cluster structures exist but are weaker in railway technologies, metals and materials, as well as in the wood and paper products (Janger et al. 2000).

CONTRACT RESEARCH	SCIENCE/UNIVERSITY EDUCATION	TECHNICAL COLLEGES
Joanneum Research	Technical University Graz, Karl Franzens University Graz, University Leoben	Technikum Joanneum
> Environment/energy > Informatics > Sensorics > Materials > Economy/technology	> Architecture, construction engineering, machinery, electrical engineering, natural sciences > Law, social sciences/economics, medicine, humanities, natural sciences > Mining, materials	> Design > Automotive technologies > Information management > Industrial electronics > Business administration
CO-OPERATIVE R&D-INSTITUTIONS at universities	COMPANIES Emerging cluster structures!	VOCATIONAL TRAINING WIFI, BfI, HTL
> 6 Christian Doppler (CD) Laboratories > Competence center for materials Leoben (MCL)	> Automobiles > Railway technologies > Metals/materials > Wood/paper	> Very broad range of training programmes in business administration and technology
TECHNOLOGY TRANSFER/ CONSULTANCY	TECHNOLOGY CENTRES/ INCUBATION CENTRES	PUBLIC SUPPORT/FINANCE SFG, Innofinanz
> Liaison offices of the universities > TTZ Leoben >AGIPLAN and other consulting firms	> 3 Technology centres > 4 Incubation centres >"Wirtschaftspark Obersteiermark"	> Subsidies > Finance > Regional development policy > Technology policy

Figure 8.1   The Regional Innovation System in Styria

Innovation Activities and Networking

To which extent have Styrian firms been undertaking innovation activities and which kind of partners did they use in the innovation process? To answer these questions we rely on the database of the European REGIS project in which nine regions of Europe have been investigated in this respect (Cooke et al. 2000). There were high performing engineering regions such as Baden-Württemberg (Germany) and Brabant (The Netherlands), reconversion regions such as Styria (Austria), Tampere (Finland), Wales (UK), Wallonia (Belgium) and the Basque country (Spain), as well as industrial districts such as Friuli (Italy) and Centro (Portugal). Firm surveys and interviews were undertaken in a comparative setting. The response rates to the surveys varied from 15 percent (Styria) to 35 percent (Wales). They were lower in Styria due to broader industry coverage. In total 833 firms responded to the REGIS survey. In Styria 107 firms responded including manufacturing and business services.

Table 8.1   **Competitive Advantages of Firms (percent of firms indicating the following advantages)**

	All REGIS regions	Styria
	n=833	n=107
Competitive advantages		
Quality	75	82
Delivery time	57	66
Innovativeness	55	75
Services	40	63
Price	29	21
User friendliness	24	25
Ecological aspects	17	25
How do firms maintain competitive advantages?		
Skills/knowledge	63	68
Internal R&D	50	50
Patents/licences	12	12
Organization of production	48	38
Marketing	38	36
Cooperation – regional	19	18
Cooperation – national	17	18
Cooperation – European	17	28
Cooperation – global	10	14

Source: REGIS firm survey

In comparison with all REGIS regions the Styrian companies have been competing more often on advantages such as product quality (82 percent) and innovativeness (75 percent), whereas the price of the product has been less often stated as an advantage (Table 8.1). Moreover, it could be seen that the skills and knowledge of labor is for the Styrian companies the most important factor (stated by 68 percent) in order to maintain these advantages. Overall, this reflects the situation of a region with a good knowledge base and a well-qualified labor force but with relatively high labor costs. Regarding innovation activities Table 8.2 shows that Styrian firms have slightly less product and process innovations in general, but relatively more of those which can be considered as "new to the market" and not just "new to the firm". Basically this means that Styrian companies have more products or processes that are newly developed (similar to Baden-Württemberg firms) and less of which are simply adopted from other firms (such as in Centro/Portugal or in Wales). This finding is confirmed by the fact that the firms in Styria have relatively higher R&D inputs (budget and staff) than the REGIS average. This finding of good innovation performance by Styrian firms has to be qualified, however. Subsequent firm interviews have shown that the predominant innovation type is incremental innovation along existing technology paths. More radical innovations opening up new technology trajectories are a rare phenomenon.

Table 8.2   **Product and Process Innovation (percent of firms having introduced the following innovations)**

	all REGIS regions	Styria
	n=833	n=107
New products	67	65
Products new to the market	39	47
New processes	46	41
Processes new to the market	17	20

Source: REGIS firm survey

We found that the firms in all REGIS regions rely to a high degree on customers and suppliers (Table 8.3). Customers provide first ideas and guidance for product changes, and they may act as partner in the design and development process (Von Hippel 1988; Lundvall 1992). Suppliers provide required materials, components or services for new products, or they contribute to the process technology. Frequently, these links go beyond the market-type relation by becoming more durable and interactive (network-type). Geographically, networks to customers and suppliers as innovation partners, clearly reach beyond the region, and we find them at national, European and global levels. This is not surprising because it reflects the spatial distribution of the input/output markets of the companies. Still, customers and suppliers of the region are also relevant innovation partners for the firms, and in fact, they are at the regional level, still more important than any other type of partner.

Consultants also play a vital role in the innovation process. They provide know-how in various fields, from legal aspects of patenting and licensing to technology and innovation consulting (Moulaert and Tödtling, 1995). Due to the specialized nature of the required knowledge, they are not only drawn from the region but more frequently from the national and also the European levels. An important type of innovation partner to the firms is also universities. They have a multiple function as source and interface for new ideas, as partners in the R&D process, and as a source for highly qualified labor. Universities are relatively more important at the level of the region and the respective country. This is probably due to the limited geographical mobility of graduates and the often tacit nature of knowledge involved in those links. From the other potential partners, providers of subsidies, training and government institutions have been less often indicated in all the REGIS regions than could be expected. For these, the level of the region is relatively more important than the respective country. Rarely named as innovation partners are organizations for venture capital and for technology transfer. The low indication of support organizations may partly be due to the fact that some of these services (such as training) are regarded more as an "externality" rather than as a specific and identifiable contribution to the innovation process.

Table 8.3   Innovation Partners of Firms in All REGIS Regions (percent of firms with the following innovation partners, n = 833, missing 14 percent)

	Regional	National	European	Global
Customers	44	61	48	25
Suppliers	35	52	37	14
Consultants	16	20	10	4
Research organizations	13	17	6	3
Universities	24	22	8	3
Technology transfer	11	9	3	2
Venture capital	9	7	2	1
Subsidies	17	16	6	0
Government	14	10	3	0
Trade associations	12	17	4	0
Training institutions	17	14	3	0

Share of firms with partners 20-39 percent
Share of firms with partners 40 percent

Source: REGIS firm survey

For the investigated firms in Styria (Table 8.4) we find some differences to the more general picture of the REGIS regions. First, we can see that Styrian firms rely more often on innovation partners in general than the firms in most other REGIS regions (with the exception of those in Baden-Württemberg). This may be partly explained by the fact that among the responding firms in Styria there are relatively more medium sized and large firms which typically have more often innovation partners (Tödtling and Kaufmann 1999). Partly this finding probably has also to do with the relatively well-developed regional innovation system in Styria, which stimulates firms more to networking than in other regions. Second, looking at the pattern of innovation partners we can see that Styrian firms interact more often with suppliers and customers at European and global levels, with regional, national and European universities and research organizations, as well as with regional and Austrian support organizations. Regarding the customers and suppliers this pattern follows largely the spatial distribution of input and output markets of Styrian firms which are to a higher degree European and global (see Tödtling et al. 1998). The more frequent links to universities and research organizations partly reflect the respective strength of the regional innovation system as described above. These refer to the strengths in research fields relevant for industry and to an active engagement in collaborative activities from both sides. Since some of these collaborative activities (e.g., competence centers and Framework program activities) increasingly include partners from all of Austria and from Europe, it is not surprising to find that Austrian and European university/research links are also relatively prominent.

So far the survey results produce a rather positive picture of the Styrian innovation system. The subsequent interviews, which were carried out in the course of the REGIS project (15 with firms and 16 with support organizations), brought forward some weaknesses and caveats regarding the above results. The first refers to the dominance of incremental innovations in most of the firms. In this respect it appears that the full potential of universities and research organizations for more radical innovations is not really exploited. Firms often use university institutes for small tasks in the innovation process (such as testing and measurement, the contracting-out of certain development tasks and small research contracts) but not for more intensive interaction or more radical technology changes. This behavior might "lock" firms too much into existing technology paths. Second, companies often have indicated links to innovation partners, but many of those relations were not considered as highly important (Tödtling et al. 1998). From the interviews it appeared, in fact, that there are considerable barriers for cooperation, such as a strong inward orientation of firms and a fear of know-how loss. Such barriers existed in particular in the case of the small companies (below 50 employees).

Table 8.4   **Innovation Partners of Firms in Styria (percent of firms with the following innovation partners, n = 107, missing 13 percent)**

	Regional	National	European	Global
Customers	48	60	69	37
Suppliers	38	54	43	19
Consultants	20	22	15	7
Research organizations	21	23	16	4
Universities	33	31	26	9
Technology transfer	8	13	8	4
Venture capital	13	19	7	4
Subsidies	27	41	22	0
Government	14	14	5	0
Trade associations	25	25	9	0
Training institutions	24	19	5	0

     Share of firms with partners 20-39 percent
     Share of firms with partners 40 percent

Source: REGIS firm survey

Networking in the Styrian Automotive Cluster

The previous section presented general results concerning the main actors of the Styrian innovation system, as well as the interaction pattern of Styrian companies in the innovation process at regional, national and international levels. Here, we examine these and related questions for one of the most important industrial sectors of the Styrian economy, namely the automotive industry.

The findings presented below stem from the recently finished research project "Systemic Development of Regional Economies" conducted for the Austrian Federal Chancellery. The aim of this project was to gain new insights in the "inner life" of clusters and innovation systems and to deepen the understanding of the importance of their external connections. For different Styrian clusters patterns of communication, the degree of various sorts of internal linkages, as well as the importance of institutional arrangements for enhancing coordination capacity were examined.

Furthermore, the role of integration in non-local networks for staying competitive was analyzed and policy actions in the form of cluster development initiatives to strengthen regional and extra-regional ties of clusters were evaluated. For this purpose, more than 80 qualitative face-to-face interviews were carried out in 1999, 35 of which were conducted with actors from the automotive sector, mainly in companies, but also from universities, other research organizations, educational organizations, consultants, representatives from politics and the regional development agency.

In this section, the following questions and aspects will be dealt with:

- the development of networks and more binding forms of interaction within the Styrian automotive industry, putting a special focus on the dynamics of this process;
- then, the role of different actors in this process will be highlighted, especially the role of the state, and the signs of a redefinition of its role and its function;
- finally, the regional dimension of networks will be contrasted with its national and international dimension.

Before referring to our findings, some conceptual remarks need to be made. In the first section, networks were defined as all non-market types of interaction during the innovation process. Here, we want to contrast these innovation networks with social networks, i.e., personal, trust-based relationships of latent character, which often constitute an important precondition for the emergence of innovation networks (Granovetter 1994; Ebers 1997). Co-operations we regard here as a specific form of innovation networks. They can be understood as contract-based collaborations between two or more partners with clear rules concerning responsibilities and the sharing of risks and outcomes.

Now we want to focus on the results for the automotive cluster. We intent to show, how networks between hitherto unrelated actors and new institutional arrangements were built up with public support, leading to completely new forms of interaction and coordination, and allowing a collective response to new challenges.

The Styrian Automotive Cluster at the Beginning of the 1990s

The automotive industry is one of the most important industrial sectors of the Styrian economy. Twenty percent of the region's total exports are accounted for by this industry, which is - as some studies (Fabris et al. 1995; Adametz et al. 2000) have shown - characterized by vigorous growth. Several internationally known companies are located in Styria, some of which are domestic, local companies, which have a long tradition in the automotive field. Steyr Daimler Puch Fahrzeugtechnik (SFT) is developing and producing cars, auto-components, and auto-systems and has a special competence in four-wheel drive vehicles. AVL-List is engaged in research and development of combustion engines, and a specialist in control engineering and acoustics. The region has also attracted international companies. Eurostar belongs to Daimler-Chrysler and assembles the Chrysler Voyager. Magna is a global supplier to the automobile industry and has several factories in Styria. This core is surrounded by about 100 SMEs, mainly suppliers of components, parts, and basic materials as well as by some small engineering companies. Furthermore, a strong base of basic and applied research can be found in the region. There are two universities (Technical University of Graz, and the University of Leoben), some specialized smaller research institutes like Joanneum Research (Laser Center, Institute of Digital Image Processing), the Austrian Foundry Institute as well as the college for automotive engineering.

Until the mid 1990s very few linkages had existed between these actors. This holds true both for market and non-market relationships. Given the small size of the Styrian and Austrian markets and the fact that only very few clients exist within the region, the Styrian automotive suppliers mainly deliver their products and services to international markets, above all to large German car makers. As a consequence the clusters' export rate amounts to nearly 80 percent. But until recently, one could also hardly identify relationships beyond direct input-output links within the cluster. Indeed, one striking feature of the cluster was that firms had only little knowledge about each other's products and competences, showing a lack of willingness to co-operate and a lack of experience in working together. With few exceptions little interaction could be found between research institutions and the economic actors.

In recent years the Styrian automotive industry was confronted with a major change of external conditions, as the world automobile industry ("being one of the most global of all manufacturing industries" Dicken 1998), was undergoing a substantial restructuring process. A slowdown of overall market growth, the existence of a considerable excess capacity amounting to several million vehicles, tendencies of increasing market segmentation and fragmentation, and a dramatic shortening of product development and innovation cycles have resulted in fierce competition in the industry. The outcome of these processes is twofold: On the one hand there is a strong pressure to lower production and development costs. On the other hand, there is the need to compete via the innovativeness and the technological improvements of products and processes. As a consequence, activities have been increasingly outsourced and supply chains have been re-arranged. Different developments can be observed. For standardized parts, global sourcing and Internet platforms are used as tools to lower input costs. For more sophisticated components there is a trend towards systems suppliers which are required to have strengths not just in production but also in technological development and innovation (Graves 1994). All these trends herald a significant competitive threat and imply the need – both for individual suppliers as for whole clusters and regions – to develop a strong innovation competence and innovation capabilities in order to survive. How did the Styrian automobile cluster respond to these changing external circumstances?

The Emergence of Networks and Co-operative Relationships in the Styrian Automotive Cluster: A Collective Response to New Challenges?

Faced with these new realities the Styrian automotive cluster was undergoing a far-reaching transformation process. This resulted in more co-operative relationships at different levels of the cluster and a further differentiation and specialization of its innovation system. Thus, the problem solving capacity of the cluster as a whole was enhanced. The restructuring process of the cluster's internal linkages was to a large extent shaped by an integrated cluster development project, which was started in 1996. It covered a comprehensive set of actions, aiming at "more strength to Styria as a site of the automotive industry" (Holzschlag 1997). In the context of this project two substantial institutional innovations were realized which can be regarded as new elements in the institutional arrangement of the automotive cluster. They represented innovations for the whole cluster, enabling the formation of new patterns of interaction within the cluster with the outcome that coordination reached a higher level.

The first relates to the establishment of an advisory committee ("Clusterbeirat"), which brought together delegates from manufacturers, larger local companies and SMEs with representatives of the political, scientific and educational systems to regular meetings. The value of these meetings, which were organized and moderated by the Styrian Economic Development Agency (SFG), must not be underestimated, as the general pattern of interactions between the main elements of the cluster's innovation system, i.e. economy, politics, science, and education, was changed. A continuous communication between them was established, leading to a change of perspectives and the rise of the understanding of problems as well as the settlement of conflicts. Communication about the cluster as a whole started, collective reflections about its future developmental potential and transformation needs were taken, strategies for the cluster were worked out, the focus of work was fixed and activities from various interest groups were combined. All these activities enabled a high level of coordination in the Styrian automotive cluster.

The second institutional innovation of critical importance concerns the establishment of a management unit for the cluster, representing the central supportive input of the political system for the development of the cluster. A key person of the semi-public SFG, supported by a private consultancy firm, became responsible for a range of activities like the promotion of the cluster in international markets, the carrying-out of benchmarking projects with other European automobile clusters, and the organization of workshops and conferences to improve the informational basis of the firms. In order to bring them together, communication between the cluster firms was fostered and co-operative projects between them were initiated. One could argue that politics (in the form of its semi-public RDA) has played a critical role in the cluster development, but not in form of direct intervention (for example by giving financial support to individual enterprises). Instead, a new style of intervention was adopted, focusing on the development of new forms of relationships among firms and between firms and other organizations. This seems to be an important step towards a more systemic policy, which is characterized (1) by a focus on inter-organizational systems like clusters, networks, and university-industry partnerships instead of on individual companies; and (2) new forms of intervention and support by acting as a facilitator and as a moderator to foster such systems. This practice has become increasingly popular in economic, innovation and technology policy in Austria and other European countries, both on the regional and national level (Cooke and Morgan 1998; Lagendijk 1999; Bratl and Trippl 2000; Bratl et al. 2000).

In the case of the Styrian automotive cluster, one of the most important activities consisted of the strengthening of the social networks between formerly unrelated partners. A large number of workshops and conferences were organized by the cluster management unit to improve the informational base of the firms with respect to new challenges, the application of new technologies with relevance for the automotive industry and new forms of co-operation. Firms met on a regular basis, got access to relevant information and after a while a process of sharing information and experiences among a core group of firms set in. This emerging social network, which was becoming stronger, constituted a necessary precondition for the rise of more binding forms of interaction between local actors. After a while one could observe the start of several co-operative endeavors, ranging from outsourcing projects, collaboration in the entry of new markets and certification, to a range of projects in the field of qualification. Some of these projects were carried out with support of the cluster management unit, which became engaged in the matching of partners and the legal support for defining co-operation contracts. Beyond the development of networks and co-operation the cluster management unit also took considerable efforts in attracting new firms like a company offering measurement techniques and services to satisfy the needs of local firms in the cluster.

Of special interest are interactions that aid innovation and technology. Several types of more co-operative relationships in innovation and technology have arisen, both among companies and between companies and research organizations. These projects have demonstrated that it is possible to build up such innovation linkages. Some local SMEs, which are suppliers of parts for oil pumps, cooperated to develop and produce a new oil pump by bundling their resources and competences. They also have incorporated a larger local research and development company in order to tap into its specialized pool of know-how. This has secured access to technical competences, which turned out to be necessary to realize the development and production of the new product. Another example can be found in the field of digital image processing, where Styrian suppliers sought opportunities of an application for this technology in the automotive industry. Contacts were established to an institute of Joanneum Research, specialized in this technology, resulting in ongoing co-operative projects between the research institutes and some smaller companies and a larger leading company of the automobile cluster.

The most interesting case is the emergence of new forms of relationships between two leading companies, who possess an extended know-how in the development of complete cars and engines. Although they have been located many years in the same city, almost no co-operative linkages had existed between them, as they regarded each other as competitors. But things have changed, and this is - as both partner confirmed in the interviews taken with them - partly due to the cluster development project. They have intensified communication and are searching actively for synergy potentials. One outcome of this change in behavior is the establishment of a common acoustic center for applied research, where they share both costs and risks of the establishment and running of this R&D infrastructure.

Additionally, a large number of co-operative relationships between Styrian research institutions and the Styrian automotive industry can be identified. This pattern corresponds to those outlined above for the whole Styrian innovation system. The university-industry-partnerships found in the automotive cluster range from contract research making use of the technical infrastructure of the universities to joint research and development projects. Some of these co-operative endeavors are carried out between partners that have long lasting relations, as for example between AVL List and the Technical University of Graz. They are currently engaged in the joint running of two CD-Labs, pooling their competences in the field of engine acoustics and simulation. Another example includes the joint development of laser-welded gearbox parts between a research institute and a large leading company, enabling the company to produce new gearboxes, which were introduced in the market with a substantial success. This cooperation emerged independently from the cluster development actions and can thus not be set in direct relation to it. But they can be regarded as an outcome of a self-supporting process, which set in through the cluster project.

In spite of these "success stories" it must be pointed out that no large number of co-operative linkages in innovation and technology can be found between local firms. What can be observed is a strengthening of social networks between several core partners and the start and realization of some concrete cooperation aimed at the development of new products or the introduction of new processes.

But some other aspects should not be overlooked: Of special interest are projects like the common establishment of new technical infrastructure, as mentioned above, as well as the attraction of companies, offering specialized services (as in the case of the center for measurement techniques). They lead to a further differentiation and specialization of the cluster's innovation system. In the same light one could regard the establishment of the Material Center Leoben (see also above), where several research institutes, specialized in material technologies are co-operating with large Styrian suppliers of the automotive industry like Böhler Uddeholm and Voest Alpine and other firms to achieve new breakthroughs in materials technologies. By bundling their resources and know-how, they give an impetus to a further strengthening of one of the core competences of the region, which is also of relevance for the automotive industry.

To conclude, the Styrian automobile cluster has clearly demonstrated that global challenges can be met by taking actions at the regional level, mainly by animating the creation of networks and co-operations. One could observe the formation of new forms of interactions between cluster firms and other partners, which would have been unthinkable some years ago. A good indicator for its relative success and its value for the involved firms is the fact, that in 1999, when the public support for the cluster came to an end, the cluster management unit, its tasks and functions were taken over by private companies and other institutions. However, such regional responses to global challenges also have their limit, as many processes are better started at the national or international level.

National and International Networks – the Limits of the Region

Notwithstanding the importance regional innovation networks may have for securing competitiveness, the regions' or clusters' national and international linkages are becoming more important than ever today (Amin and Thrift 1994; Oinas and Malecki 1999). A lack of resources or competent partners within the region often forces companies to leave the limited space of the region and integrate themselves into national and international networks. Indeed, many challenges in innovation and technology can to an increasing extent only be met by collaborating with other national and international partners, which possess the necessary complementary competences and pools of know-how. This also holds true for the Styrian automotive industry.

As our research project has shown, Styrian firms from the automobile industry, especially the larger ones, are engaged in a considerable number of co-operative relationships in innovation and technology with partners from outside the region. To name but two: some larger Styrian companies are integrated in an Austrian wide research co-operation between leading national automotive suppliers where co-operative research is done in fields like car bodies and power train. Another example include the development and production of new materials and parts with reduced weight to meet the challenges stemming from the intention to develop the "3-Litre-Car", where Styrian firms like Böhler Uddeholm and Magna are working together with international partners. There are a lot of other examples that clearly demonstrate the importance of national and international networking in innovation. Space prevents the enumeration and description of all the relations and projects identified during our interviews. One very clear conclusion can be drawn from our findings: external relationships are the norm, not the exception. Thus, these results for the Styrian automotive cluster are in line with the finding that Styrian firms were rather strongly integrated in international innovation networks.

The insights mentioned above, namely the importance of extra regional networks in innovation and technology also has consequences for the "right" geographical scope in organizing networks and in fostering cooperative relationships. This was properly recognized in the case of the formation of an Austrian wide network for diesel technology, a technological field, where Austrian enterprises and public research institutes are among the leaders. To establish a network in diesel technology within a region would have been the false way, as the relevant partners are located in various Austrian regions. Consequently, an Austrian wide network - currently consisting of 80 partners - was created, comprising major industrial enterprises involved in engine production, engine components and production facilities, who intent to bundle their resources and to concentrate their industrial and research competences. Several partners of the Styrian automotive cluster (11 SMEs, 8 larger companies and 4 institutes of Styrian universities as well as the college for automotive engineering) are integrated into this national network. Once more we can observe the new style of public intervention: the ministry of economic affairs and the province of Upper Austria are financing specialists who try to support firms to search for synergy potentials and to carry out co-operation processes.

To summarize, one could argue, that the dynamics we can observe within the Styrian automotive cluster, rest on a combination of two sets of connections: local as well as extra-local innovation networks shape, its international competitiveness and adaptive capability in the long run. Both types of relations turned out to be of significance.

Conclusions

Old industrialized regions on the one hand and innovation activities and networking on the other hand are generally viewed as being two mutually excluding phenomena. However, this contribution has clearly demonstrated that innovation and networking need not to be for all times a mythos in reconversion areas. The research carried out in the context of the REGIS project has demonstrated that Styrian companies were quite innovative in comparison to the other European regions investigated. Many firms have introduced products "new to the market", although more detailed investigations have shown that many of these can be regarded just as incremental changes. Furthermore, Styrian firms were frequently engaging in innovation networks with customers, suppliers, and knowledge providers at regional, national and international levels. The companies are backed in this respect by a well-developed regional innovation system where in particular the universities, other knowledge providers and the regional development agency play an active role. This finding was supported by the qualitative research carried out for the Styrian automotive cluster where also a re-orientation towards innovation strategies as well as the formation of innovation networks was shown. Thus, it could be argued, that even in older industrialized regions, often characterized by considerable barriers for innovation activities and networking, the hostile climate for such processes can eventually be broken up.

To be sure, a focus on innovation strategies and the creation of co-operative relationships seldom emerge from alone in the regions in question. What seems to be needed is an intelligent form of public intervention. To build up and strengthen a dense system of innovation support institutions may be one important step. But, as exemplified for the Styrian automotive cluster, also required is the setting up of new institutional arrangements, which enhance the coordination power and collective efficiency of clusters and innovation systems.

It becomes increasingly accepted - and this was also confirmed in this contribution - that it is systems - clusters, innovation systems, and networks - and not individual companies that shape innovation processes and that compete in global markets. Firms are inserted in various types of networks during the innovation process. Given these constellations, public policy keeps its importance, but in ways that break with traditional forms of intervention, such as offering financial incentives to individual firms. We argue that policies should move from being firm-centered, towards becoming system-centered, addressing system failure, initiating communication between different actors and facilitating the creation of networks, clusters, and innovation systems. This requires new institutional arrangements for securing that coordination takes place in such systems, and it implies that policy must re-define its role and functions. The suggestion is, that public policy should focus on whole regional systems and become integrated in them as one actor among others, trying to enhance the innovation performance of the regional economy. This principle seems to be of special relevance for old industrialized regions, where innovation and regional networks rarely arise spontaneously. However, the strengthening of local ties, is not sufficient. Policy should also contribute to an opening up of regional systems and secure their integration and standing in national and international networks in order to avoid regional lock-in effects.

Due to an extended theoretical and empirical literature, we have gained in recent years a great deal on understanding of how innovation processes occur. It is widely acknowledged nowadays that innovation is an interactive process, taking place in networks, clusters and innovation systems. However, the specific nature of these interactions is not yet clear and the "inner life" of innovation systems and clusters remains little understood. Several aspects have to be further explored: How does communication flow within these systems and how are the different elements connected? How can institutional arrangements be created in order to enhance the collective efficiency of such systems? Can we learn from best-practice examples in this respect? Also, the relation between regional and extra-regional innovation networks for securing international competitiveness remains to be further explored. Finally, there is the question of how clusters and innovation systems can keep their capability to adjust to new conditions in the long run, in order to avoid that today's growing regions become the old industrialized areas of tomorrow. As highlighted in this contribution, many lessons can be learnt from reconversion regions. Nevertheless, more research, above all that of a qualitative nature, is needed to answer these questions.

Acknowledgement

The REGIS project ("Regional Innovation Systems: Designing for the Future") was funded by the European Union DGXII Targeted Socio-Economic Research in the period 1996-1998). The authors wish to express gratitude to the funding organization and the following TSER project leaders: Ph. Cooke (U.K., coordinator), G. Bechtle (Germany), P. Boekholt (Netherlands), E. de Castro (Portugal), G. Extebarria (Spain), M. Quevit (Belgium), M. Schenkel (Italy) and G. Schienstock (Finland).

References

Adametz, C., Fritz, O. and Hartmann, C. (2000), Cluster in der Steiermark. Lieferverflechtungen, Kooperationsbeziehungen und Entwicklungsdynamik, Joanneum Research, Graz.

Amin, A. and Thrift, N. (1994), "Living in the Global", in A. Amin and N. Thrift (eds), *Globalization, Institutions and Regional Development in Europe*, Oxford University Press, Oxford, pp. 1-22.

Asheim, B. T. (1996), "Industrial districts as 'learning regions': A condition for prosperity?" *European Planning Studies*, vol. 4, no. 4, pp. 379-400.

Autio, E. (1998), "Evaluation of RTD in regional systems of innovation", *European Planning Studies*, vol. 6, no. 2, pp. 131-40.

Aydalot, Ph. and Keeble, D. (eds) (1988), *High Technology Industry and Innovative Environments: The European Experience*, Routledge, London.

Braczyk, H., Cooke, P. and Heidenreich, R. (eds) (1998), *Regional Innovation Systems*, UCL Press, London.

Bratl, H. and Trippl, M. (2000), "Reflexions on the future role of the national government in the territorial development policy system of Austria", Background paper submitted to the OECD-high-level seminar *Spatial Development Policies and Territorial Governance in an Era of Globalization and Localization*, 10-11 April 2000, OECD, Paris.

Bratl, H., Miglbauer, E. and Trippl, M. (2000), Erhebung und vergleichende Analyse von neuartigen Förderungsaktionen zur Entwicklung von Regionen in Europa, unveröffentlichte Studie im Auftrag des Bundeskanzleramtes, Abteilung IV/4, invent, Wien.

Camagni, R. (ed.) (1991), *Innovation Networks – Spatial Perspectives*, Belhaven Press, London.

Castells, M. and Hall, P. (1994), *Technopoles of the World – The making of twenty-first-century industrial complexes*, Routledge, London/New York.

Cooke, P. (ed.) (1995), *The rise of the Rustbelt*, UCL Press, London.

Cooke, P. (1998), "Regional Innovation System - An Evolutionary Approach". In H. Braczyk, P. Cooke and R. Heidenreich (eds) *Regional Innovation Systems*, UCL Press, London, pp. 2-25.

Cooke, P., Boekholt, P. and Tödtling, F. (2000), *The Governance of Innovation in Europe – Regional Perspectives on Global Competitiveness*, Pinter, London and New York.

Cooke, P. and Morgan, K. (1993), "The network paradigm: new departures in corporate and regional development", *Environment and Planning D: Society and Space*, vol. 11, pp. 543-64.

Cooke, P. and Morgan, K. (1998), *The Associational Economy: Firms, Regions, and Innovation*, Oxford University Press, Oxford.

De Bresson, C. and Walker, R. (eds) (1991), "Network of Innovators", *Research Policy*, vol. 20, no. 5 (Special Issue).

De la Mothe, J. and Paquet, G. (eds) (1998), *Local and Regional Systems of Innovation*, Kluwer Academic Publishers, Norwell.

Dicken, P. (1998), *Global Shift*, Paul Chapman, London.

Dodgson, M. and Rothwell, R. (eds) (1994), *The Handbook of Industrial Innovation*, Edward Elgar, Aldershot.

Dosi, G. (1988), "The nature of the innovative process", in G. Dosi, Ch. Freeman, R. Nelson, G. Silverberg and L. Soete (eds) *Technical Change and Economic Theory*, Pinter, London/New York.

Ebers, M. (1997), "Explaining Inter-Organizational Network Formation", in M. Ebers (ed), *The Formation of Inter-Organizational Networks*, Oxford University Press, New York, pp. 3-40.

Edquist, C. (ed.) (1997), *Systems of Innovation - Technologies, Institutions and Organizations*, Pinter, London/Washington.

Enright, M. (1995), "Regional Clusters and Economic Development: A Research Agenda", Harvard Business School Working Paper, Cambridge, Massachusetts.

Fabris, W., Hohl, N., Mazdra, M. and Schick, M. (1995), *Wirtschaftsleitbild Steiermark*, IWI-Studien, Band XXV, Industriewissenschaftliches Institut, Wien.

Friedman, J. (1991), "The Industrial Transition: A Comprehensive Approach to Regional Development", in E. M. Bergman, G. Maier and F. Tödtling (eds) *Regions Reconsidered. Economic Networks, Innovation, and Local Development in Industrialized Countries*, Mansell, London, pp. 167-78.

Fritsch, M., Koschatzky, K., Schätzl, L. and Sternberg, R. (1998), Regionale Innovationspotentiale und innovative Netzwerke, *Raumforschung und Raumordnung*, vol. 4, No.56, pp. 243-52.

Genosko, J. (1997), "Networks, Innovative Milieux and Globalization: Some Comments on a Regional Economic Discussion", *European Planning Studies*, vol. 5, no. 3, pp. 283-97.

Grabher, G. (ed) (1993), *The embedded Firm: On the Socio-Economics of Industrial Networks*, Routledge, London.

Granovetter, M. (1994), "Business Groups", in N.J. Smelser and R. Swedberg (eds), *The Handbook of Economic Sociology*, Princeton University Press, Princeton, pp. 453-75.

Graves, A. (1994), "Innovation in a Globalizing Industry: The Case of Automobiles", in M. Dodgson and R. Rothwell (eds), *The Handbook of Industrial Innovation*, Edward Elgar, Aldershot, pp. 213-31.

Hakansson, H. (ed) (1987), *Industrial Technological Development: A Network Approach*, Croom Helm, London.

Hassink, R. (1996), "Technology Transfer Agencies and Regional Economic Development", *European Planning Studies*, vol. 4, no. 2, pp. 167-84.

Heinze, R.G., Hilpert, J., Nordhause-Janz, J. and Rehfeld, D. (1998), "Industrial clusters and the governance of change: lessons from North Rhine-Westphalia (NRW)", in H.J. Braczyk, P. Cooke and M. Heidenreich (eds), *Regional Innovation Systems – The Role of Governances in a Globalized World*, UCL Press, London, pp. 263-83.

Holzschlag, G. (1997), "The Styrian Automobile Cluster: Present state and Future Tasks", in Steiner, M. (ed.), Competence Clusters. Workshop Report, Leykam, Graz, pp. 32-37.

Jaffee, A.B., Trajtenberg, M. and Henderson, R. (1993), "Geographic Localization of Knowledge Spillovers as Evidence of Patent Citations", *Quarterly Journal of Economics*, vol 43, pp. 577-98.

Janger, J., Nagy, M., Markowitsch, J., Riedler, S. and Clement, W. (2000), Innovation in der Steiermark: Steigerung der Wettbewerbskraft der bestehenden Produktionswirtschaft und Öffnung in Richtung 'new economy'. IWI Arbeitsheft 55, Industriewissenschaftliches Institut, Wien.

Kline, S. J. and Rosenberg, N. (1986), "An Overview of Innovation", in R. Landau and N. Rosenberg (eds), *The Positive Sum Strategy*, Washington: National Academy Press.

Lagendijk, A. (1999), "Innovative Forms of Regional Structural Policy in Europe: The Role of Dominant Concepts and Knowledge Flows", in M.M. Fischer, L. Suarez-Villa and M. Steiner, (eds), *Innovation, Networks and Localities*, Springer, Berlin, pp. 272-99.

Lundvall, B. (ed.) (1992), *National Systems of Innovation Towards a Theory of Innovation and Interactive Learning*, Pinter, London.

Lundvall, B. and Borrás, S. (1998), "The globalising learning economy: Implications for innovation policy". Report to the DGXII, TSER, Bussels.

Maillat, D. (1991), "The Innovation Process and the Role of the Milieu", in E. Bergman, G. Maier and F. Tödtling (eds), *Regions Reconsidered. Economic Networks, Innovation, and Local Development in Industrialized Countries*, Mansell, London/New York, pp. 103-17.

Malecki, E. (1997), *Technology and Economic Development: The Dynamics of Local, Regional and National Competitiveness*, Longman, Essex.

Malecki, E. and Oinas, P. (eds) (1999), *Making Connections – Technological Learning and Regional Economic Change*, Ashgate, Aldershot.

Malmberg, A. and Maskell, P. (1999), "The competitiveness of firms and regions: 'Ubifiquation' and the importance of localized learning", *European Urban and Regional Studies*, vol. 6, no. 1, pp. 9-26.

Morgan, K. and Nauwelaers, C. (1999), *Regional Innovation Strategies – The Challenge for Less-Favoured Regions*, The Stationary Office, London.

Moulaert, F. and Tödtling, F. (1995), "The Geography of Advanced Producer Services in Europe", *Progress in Planning*, vol. 43, Parts 2-3 (Special Issue).

Nelson, R. (ed.) (1993), *National Innovation Systems - A Comparative Analysis*, Oxford University Press, Oxford.

Oinas, P. and Malecki, E. (1999), "Spatial Innovation Systems", in E. Malecki and P. Oinas (eds), *Making Connections*, Ashgate, Aldershot, pp. 7-33.

Ratti, R., Bramanti, A. and Gordon, R. (eds) (1997), *The Dynamics of Innovative Regions – The GREMI Approach*, Ashgate, Aldershot.

Saxenian, A. (1994), *Regional Advantage: Culture and Competition in Silicon Valley and Route 128*, Harvard University Press, Cambridge, Massachusetts.

Simmie, J. (ed.) (1997), *Innovation, Networks and Learning Region?* Regional Studies Association, London.

Steiner, M. (ed.) (1998), *Clusters and Regional Specialisation*, European Research in Regional Science, Pion, London.

Sternberg, R. (1995), *Technologiepolitik und High-Tech Regionen - ein internationaler Vergleich*. LIT Verlag, Münster.

Sternberg, R. (1998), Innovierende Industrieunternehmen und ihre Einbindung in intraregionale versus interregionale Netzwerke, *Raumforschung und Raumordnung*, vol. 4, Nol 56, pp. 288-98.

Storper, M. (1997), *The Regional World – Territorial Development in a Global Economy*, The Guilford Press, New York.

Storper, M. and Harrison, B. (1991), "Flexibility, hierarchy and regional development: The changing structure of industrial production systems and their forms of governance", *Research Policy*, vol. 20, no. 5, pp. 407-22.

Tödtling, F. (1992), "Technological Change at the Regional Level - The Role of Location, Firm Structure and Strategy", *Environment & Planning* A, vol. 24, pp. 1565-84.

Tödtling, F. (1994), "The Uneven Landscape of Innovation Poles Local Embeddedness and Global Networks", in A. Amin and N. Thrift (eds), *Globalization, Institutions, and Regional Development in Europe*, Oxford University Press, New York, pp. 68-90.

Tödtling, F., Kaufmann, A. and Sedlacek, S. (1998), *The State of a Regional Innovation System in Styria: Conclusions and Policy Proposals*. REGIS working paper no.5, Institute for Urban and Regional Studies, University of Economics and Business Administration, Vienna.

Tödtling, F. and Kaufmann, A. (1999), "Innovation systems in regions of Europe – A comparative perspective", *European Planning Studies*, vol. 7, no. 6, pp. 699-717.

Von Hippel, E. (1988), *The Sources of Innovation*, Oxford University Press, Oxford.

PART III:
THE CONSTRAINTS OF
LOCAL NETWORKS

9 Limits of Local Networks: Use of Local and External Knowledge in Technological Adaptation in the Seto Ceramics Industry

HIRO IZUSHI

An enigma of industrial districts is that only a small number of cases exist in spite of their popularity as a model of economic development (Piore and Sabel 1984; Best 1990). In mature industries, there are not many cases that have sustained their technological dynamism over the long term and made a successful transition from traditional products to more technology-intensive products.

The model of industrial districts, localized industries comprising small and medium-sized enterprises (SMEs), was first formulated by Alfred Marshal (1890) in the nineteenth century. It was resuscitated in the 1980s when a number of studies found contemporary regional economies resembling it, most notably Third Italy (Brusco 1982; Pyke et al. 1990; Pyke and Sengenberger 1992). SMEs in this model escape ruinous competition with large, mass-producing firms by making semi-custom products through the use of skilled workers and general-purpose machinery. The strategy of specialization by individual firms is associated with social divisions of labor through which firms manufacture products complementing one another within the region. It is such mutual dependence that facilitates information exchange among related producers. In addition, producers commit themselves to promoting the well being of their regional industry as a whole by supporting regional institutions. Proponents of industrial districts argue that such local networks have their strength in the capacity for innovation over the long term. The model sheds light on the potential of local networks for economic development and lent support for "reindustrialization" of declining mature industrial regions through innovation (Rothwell and Zegveld 1985).

However, such localized industries comprising SMEs are found to be a small minority of regional economies rather than a dominant type. In a study of four countries (US, Japan, Korea and Brazil), Markusen (1996) finds that most regions growing faster than the national average either revolve around one or several major corporations (or major government institutions in some cases) or are comprised chiefly of branch plants of multinational corporations. This is echoed by Harrison (1994) who argues that SMEs are increasingly integrated into networks of large corporations in which they are responsible only for tasks subcontracted out by their larger counterparts. In fact, cases of fast growing industrial districts in mature industries are largely limited to ones within Third Italy. Their prosperity is also a fairly recent phenomenon that started in the mid 1960s. Further, some districts in Third Italy have witnessed a rise of multinationals from indigenous firms and take-over by external corporations as well as collapse of local networks from within (Harrison 1994).

This raises the question why highly spatially concentrated networks of SMEs in mature industries are often unable to sustain their form and technological dynamism over the long term. Camagni (1991, 1993) suggests that the behavior of local networks is subject to explicit risks of aggregate and generalized decline, and local know-how and synergy may be unable to face big dynamic changes in markets or technologies. What happens in local networks of SMEs in mature industries when they attempt to enter more technology-intensive areas?

Further, it is suggested that intensive local networking is a privilege enjoyed by a small minority of regional economies (Grotz and Braun 1997), and promotion of networks reaching outside the region may be more effective for economic development than concentrating on indigenous firms within (Camagni 1991, 1993; Markusen 1996). Do inter-regional networks always produce an effective outcome? What distinguishes effective inter-regional networking from a less effective one?

Against the background, this chapter explores limits of local networks in mature industries. The next section outlines theoretical underpinnings of the dynamics in local networks of SMEs that account for their inability to sustain their form and technological dynamism. This is followed by a case study of the ceramics industry in Seto, Japan. The case study identifies three groups of firms that are distinct from one another in their networks, and suggests that, whether SMEs belong to local networks or networks reaching outside the region, they may lose technological dynamism unless they have a number of ties to different networks and constantly seek alternative sources of knowledge. The final section discusses policy implications of the findings.

Sources of Dynamics: Lock-in, Aging and Conflict

Local networks of SMEs in mature industries have a number of sources that define their dynamics. They are the time and resource-consuming nature of networking, locking of firms into previously successful networks, and resultant loss of flexibility and drive for innovation. When these are combined with the emergence of new technologies and markets, it causes conflict between old and new networks, leading to a breakdown of an industrial district. The same dynamics can take place in newer networks, too. The district's sustained renewal hinges upon the rise from within, or relocation from outside, of medium to large-scale firms that have multiple ties to different sources of knowledge. Otherwise the district eventually becomes an irrelevance.

It is often neglected that networking is a time and resource-consuming activity. In the original formulation of industrial districts by Marshall (1890), knowledge transmits between firms in the district through the local labor market (i.e., the "air" in his term). Here costs of knowledge sharing are hidden in replacement of workers. In contrast, proponents of contemporary industrial districts argue that firms in the region make more concerted efforts for sharing of knowledge through customer-supplier relations, trade associations and other collective institutions. Such knowledge sharing incurs costs explicit to the eyes of firms. For instance, compared with arm's-length relations, customers and suppliers under close relations disclose more information and communicate more frequently. They require more staff time and other resources in measuring each other's capabilities, setting goals and acting on tasks jointly. Until relationships stabilize, they incur larger costs than arm's-length market transactions. Participation in, and support for, collective organizations also incur costs as they reside outside the domain of essential business activity. In a similar vein, forming ties to universities and research institutes consumes significant staff time and other resources.

As the study of linkages to sources of technical knowledge outside the firm suggests, the time and resource-consuming nature of networking tends to favor firms with large technical staff that have a capability to explore, and exploit, external links (Rothwell and Dodgson 1991; Commission of the European Communities 1994). Large corporations or technologically advanced SMEs are likely to have many ties, strong or weak (Granovetter 1973), to external sources of technical knowledge, keeping their eyes open to see if there is any new opportunity. In contrast, technology-following SMEs are more likely to rely on a small number of strong ties (particularly key suppliers and customers) as an external source of technical knowledge.

Because of their limited resources, technology-following SMEs are often "locked in" the same network or the same type of networks that have brought success before. Networks may be more effective in communication than arm's-length market transactions and more flexible than internal resources within hierarchies. However, success often produces complacency and over-confidence about the formula of knowledge acquisition and development that has proved useful. Also, a reduction in transaction costs, which results from increased familiarity and trust between involved parties, discourages firms from starting networks with new partners from scratch, or experimenting with different types of networks. The combination of complacency and familiarity thus locks firms into their existing networks. As this goes on, the networks start to show their age. Unable to bring together information from different sources and perceive new opportunities, the networks become less flexible and less innovative than they used to be (Grabher 1993).

For an industry, the center of new knowledge changes its location over the long term along with the emergence of new technologies and new markets. The rise of new technologies, while creating new industries, often produces their applications in existing industries (e.g., use of microelectronics in numerically-controlled machinery). Also the rise of markets for new products often provides an opportunity of applying technology in existing industries in a new way or in conjunction with technology in other industries (e.g., use of fibers in previously unconventional areas like aircraft and spaceships). These alter the shape and boundary of industries and the opportunities for growth for firms in a mature industry (Mytelka 2000). Accordingly, the center of knowledge shifts and often moves outside the traditional district concerned.

In the process, some networks gain a link to a source of new knowledge outside the district while others continue to keep their old boundary and eventually lose their vitality. The two groups of networks do not always merge with each other. This is because firms in newer networks become reluctant as they protect the knowledge they obtain. It is also because firms in older networks are often unaware of the merits sources outside the district offer. The conflict enlarges gaps between them, causing a breakdown of industrial districts.[1]

Further, firms forming ties outside the district can also fall victim to the lock-in effects. The study of industrial districts, and networks of SMEs within them, has generally left unexplored their links to firms and institutions outside their locality (Markusen 1996). Given the generally observed dependence of SME owner-managers upon local knowledge and expertise (Bryson and Daniels 1998), there is an agreement that the external linkages of an industrial district are critical to its long-term vibrancy (Camagni 1993; Meyer 1998). However, technology-following SMEs can be locked into links reaching outside their region as well. For example, such firms may fail to perceive new opportunities emerging within their district. What causes lock-in is not the proximity between firms, but the combination of complacency and familiarity (i.e., decreased transaction costs) that develops over time. Whether a network can avoid lock-in depends on the degree to which its key members are able to search alternative sources of knowledge and to bring in new ties (Granovetter 1973, 1982).

Accordingly, the sustained renewal and vitality of industrial districts in mature industries eventually hinges upon the presence of medium to large-scale firms that are able to explore and exploit multiple ties to different sources of knowledge. They may appear through the following two main routes. First, one or a couple of technologically advanced firms within the district grow and become medium-sized and eventually large-scale over the long term. These advanced firms have many ties with firms and institutions outside the district. In the process of growth, they may merge other firms within the district. Second, one or a couple of large corporations relocate some of their functions, and most likely branch plants, to the district. Some SMEs in the district are integrated into the supply chain of the large corporations. In either way, the original networks of SMEs within the district change their forms, centering around the key medium to large-scale firms. If neither of the above happens, the district keeps losing its technological vibrancy and eventually becomes irrelevant.

The ceramics industry in Seto, Japan has undergone the stages described above and is at the crossroads between renewal and irrelevance. To this, the chapter now turns.

Three Pathways to Advanced Ceramics: the Seto Ceramics Industry

Seto is located within Aichi Prefecture in the middle of Japan's industrial belt between Tokyo and Osaka.[2] With an area of 112 square kilometers, the district had a population of 130,560 in 1998.[3] High-quality clay produced in the district gave rise to ceramics manufacturing in Seto as early as the 13th century. The industry has played an important part in its economy particularly since the late 19th century when the country's bustling period of industrialization started. However, the industry suffered a decline in recent years because of competition from manufacturers in newly emerging economies. The employment of the ceramics and related clay and stone industry declined in the district by 42 percent between 1986 and 1998. In

1998, the industry accounted for approximately 40 percent of the district's manufacturing employment.[4]

The manufacture of traditional ceramics (e.g., tableware, toys, ornaments) in Seto has three characteristics typically found in the model of industrial districts. Firstly, a great majority of ceramics manufacturers in the district are small firms. In 1990, when the most recent figure for the whole establishments was available, there were 1,350 establishments of ceramics and related clay and stone businesses, employing 10,118 workers.[5] This is an average of 7.5 employees per establishment. Except for several firms operating factories overseas, either on their own or in partnership with local manufacturers, the scale of production by Seto firms is small (Takeuchi 1994). Secondly, social divisions of labor are highly developed. Besides firms engaged in forming, firing, and decoration of ceramics, there are firms specializing in such production goods as glaze, saggers, refractory slabs, plaster casts, transfer paper, and coloring materials, as well as raw materials. With all these specialized producers, the district contains the whole production chain from raw materials to final goods. Lastly, producers have a strong sense of community in the district. Given the social divisions of labor and interdependence, local people often call the district's ceramics industry "Seto Ltd." as if it were a single firm. Supported by the partisanship, the district's association of ceramics producers, the Aichi Prefectural Pottery Industry Cooperation (abbreviated APPIC), has acted as a core of co-operative activities since its original body was founded in 1926. Among its key activities is supply of porcelain clay used in the manufacture of traditional ceramics. The association has quarrying rights at estates owned by the Aichi Prefectural Government and supplies its members with the raw material at cost (Seto Ceramic Trade Co-operative Association 1976).

In the district where a majority of firms manufactured traditional consumer ceramics like tableware, toys and ornaments, over 100 firms entered a market for industrial-use ceramics in the last century. The industrial-use ceramics that have the oldest history are insulators for electrical devices, such as ones for overhead power lines, indoor wirings and transformers (Kono 1984). Compared with them, the more recent, and technologically more demanding, are products called "advanced ceramics". The name comes from their use of man-made powder for raw materials and highly controlled manufacturing processes. Advanced ceramics produced in Seto include (1) parts and materials for electronic devices ("electronic ceramics" in technical parlance), such as cores for resistors, substrates for hybrid ICs, and materials for surface wave transducers and sensors, and (2) heat- and wear-resisting production goods, such as guides for spinning and weaving machinery, balls and linings for ball mills, and setters and saggers for the manufacture of piezoelectric devices.

In terms of the networking strategy adopted at the entry into the market for advanced ceramics, the firms in the district are divided into three groups: (1) manufacturers of insulators for electrical devices who attempted to enter the market for advanced ceramics through horizontal co-operation within the district; (2) a majority of the current manufacturers of advanced ceramics in the district who entered the market by forming close ties with a few key customer firms outside Seto; and (3) a small number of firms that make use of links with a diverse range of firms and organizations, rather than relying on a few customers.

Insulator Manufacturers and Early Entrants into Advanced Ceramics

Unlike consumer ceramics, the manufacturers of industrial-use ceramics supplied their products as intermediate input for other firms located elsewhere. In other words, the chain of production extended into firms in other regions. Insulators for electrical devices were no exception to this. Production of insulators for overhead power lines and indoor wirings in Seto began in the late 19th century. With an increase in the country's electric power supply, the number of firms producing the goods had amounted to approximately 100 in the district by the late 1950s. Their main customers were electric power companies and electrical work contractors located all over the country. Between Seto manufacturers and those customer firms, wholesalers (or trading firms) were often involved as an intermediary. When they supplied their customer firms directly (which was occasionally the case with electric power companies), their relationships were generally arm's-length (Izushi 1997).

In spite of the downstream linkages reaching outside the district, the insulator manufacturers were active in horizontal co-operation within the district, and particularly at a time when their market position was endangered. The first instance of co-operation on record went back to the shared ownership of a high-voltage generator introduced in 1936 (Kato 1997). After World War II in 1949, 62 manufacturers of the goods organized an association, which was merged with APPIC ten years later. The association soon worked on a plan for new shared testing facilities and established a laboratory that housed up-to-date equipment in 1952. The co-operation took place when the national government introduced a new regulation on insulators. The testing facilities served the association's members well, obtaining authorization for a mark of quality goods from the government. This gave the members a competitive advantage over small firms in other regions, a great majority of which were not authorized, because of the lack of testing facilities.

Producers of insulators for overhead lines and indoor wirings went on to do joint R&D in the early 1960s (Izushi 1997). When they faced declining demand for indoor wirings, and increased competition with large corporations in the market for overhead power line insulators, about 20 firms founded a research consortium in 1961. Their aim was to develop a new raw material compound for high-performance insulators so that they could enter the market that had been dominated by a few large corporations. The idea was encouraged by the Government Industrial Research Institute, Nagoya, a national research institute near the district, which had close relationships with Seto producers during an early part of the postwar period. With support from the institute, the consortium was successful in developing a new compound, but none of its members could penetrate into the market for high-performance insulators because of a conservative procurement policy on the part of electric power companies which valued brand names of large manufacturers. Nonetheless, the consortium laid the foundation of analytical services in APPIC. As a means of earning income for R&D, the consortium rendered analytical services for non-members as well as members, making use of its equipment for research. The services by the consortium continued until its breakup in 1983, and they were taken over by APPIC, which founded a new department for the activity that year. In 1998, APPIC strengthened and relocated the activity to its newly founded research institute, the first of this kind established by any association of ceramics manufacturers in the country.[6]

Of the manufacturers of insulators for electrical devices, a number of firms made an entry into the market for advanced ceramics as early as the 1930s. They generally started to manufacture advanced ceramics at the request of one or two key customers in other regions and gradually diversified their customer base (Izushi 1997). Those customers included large-scale final assemblers of electronic devices and appliances, their subsidiaries, and medium-sized manufacturers of components. Seto firms also did subcontracting work for large corporations engaged in manufacturing of new materials. These customers of Seto producers were in large part located in the industrial belt between Tokyo and Osaka, but none of them were in Seto. The use of man-made powder for an increasingly higher percentage of raw materials severed the upstream linkages within the district. With the exception of one supplier, the district's firms did not have the ability to produce the man-made powder used in the production of advanced ceramics. Large-scale chemical and ceramics firms in other regions increasingly supplied Seto manufacturers of advanced ceramics as their products were made from a greater percentage of man-made powder.

The advanced ceramics manufacturers in Seto kept long-term relationships with their key customer firms and made use of the customers' technological resources. They produced advanced ceramics by applying more refined, man-made raw materials to existing products so that they could meet requests for higher performance from their longtime customers. Their goals in R&D were more often set by their customers, than by detecting demand for novel products or potentially new customers. The reactive approach allowed them to avoid the risk of a cash flow crisis in case they needed to search a long time for customer firms after having developed a product. By taking semi-custom orders, they could also make use of technological resources of their customer firms. According to a survey conducted in 1987, about three out of four firms obtained technical information on advanced ceramics from their business connections including customer firms (Sugiyama 1987). Another more detailed survey revealed that some firms had also received technology transfer from their customers. To some Seto firms, joint R&D with customers was an indispensable part of developing every new product. Further, Scto firms were often dependent, in the product development stage, upon feedback from tests and evaluations conducted by their customers (Izushi 1997).

Conflict Between the Two Groups

Different interests of these two groups of firms clashed with each other when the insulator producers attempted to enter the market for advanced ceramics through joint R&D within the district (Izushi 1997). The strong market position held by the insulator firms eroded in the 1960s when large corporations made inroads into the market for high-voltage insulators for overhead power lines. The manufacturers also suffered a decline in demand for low-voltage insulators for indoor wirings. This forced them to turn to insulators for transformers, factory machines and others, and to even seek an opportunity in the market for advanced ceramics. In the mid 1960s, the insulator manufacturers considered an idea of establishing a co-operative to jointly develop and manufacture alumina-based advanced ceramics for electronic devices. To examine the state of technology, they organized meetings among APPIC's relevant members including the advanced ceramics firms as well as lectures by engineers of an Osaka-based electronics corporation and tours to its factories. After the preliminary survey, the insulator manufacturers set their target of a new co-operative on substrates for hybrid ICs, and called for participation from relevant members within the association. At the time, the majority of

Seto's advanced ceramics firms, with one probable exception, did not have much expertise that was either unique or advanced for developing ceramic substrates. Nonetheless, in spite of their earlier indication of interest, all the advanced ceramics firms declined the proposal. The negative reaction of advanced ceramics firms dampened enthusiasm among insulator manufacturers in the association. Finally, four top insulator manufacturers jointly founded a co-operative in 1970 with a view to developing ceramic substrates for hybrid ICs (Kato 1997). That was, however, much smaller in scale than had initially been planned by the association's secretariat.

The incidence was indicative of the locking of the insulator manufacturers into the formula of horizontal co-operation within the district. As noted earlier, the manufacturers had by then repeated horizontal co-operation efforts and achieved reasonable success (i.e., shared testing facilities founded in the late 1930s and early 1950s and joint R&D undertaken in the early 1960s). The previous success had created complacency and over-confidence about the formula. In spite of the evidence of the advanced ceramics manufacturers using the knowledge possessed by their customer firms elsewhere, the insulator firms attempted to enter the market through the use of resources available in the district alone. The co-operative started with one engineer hired locally as chief of its factory that was constructed at the site of one member firm. The engineer had no higher education qualification and had only worked at a traditional ceramics firm in the district before. Research and development in the co-operative, carried out mainly by the factory chief and the president of one firm, was weak and small in scale. In addition, they did not seek to gain any support and advice initially either from firms outside the district or from universities and research institutes. A blow to them in this regard was the new focus upon state-of-the-art technology by the Government Industrial Research Institute, Nagoya and their gradual retreat from more modest services to local SMEs. The co-operative soon faced difficulties in manufacturing ceramic substrates on their own, finding their production method too costly. It was only after this failed effort that they decided to ask for technology transfer from a large manufacturer of advanced ceramics by way of doing subcontracting work. The negotiations, however, ended in failure because of the lack of technology on the co-operative's side. Instead the co-operative was given subcontracting work of less advanced products such as tubes for thermoelectric couples. Failing to produce any sizeable profits, the four firms of the co-operative's board decided to dissolve it in 1982.[7] After the break-up, a new firm started as a spin-off under the management of the co-operative's former factory chief, but it eventually went out of business in 1993.

The failure of collaboration between the two groups of firms in the late 1960s also showed the reluctance of advanced ceramics manufacturers to engage in collaboration in the district. Their reluctance continued to prevail in the 1980s. In 1980, the Ministry of International Trade and Industry announced a ten-year R&D project on advanced ceramics for high-temperature machinery parts. This generated in the country's mass media and industrial circles a tremendous interest in advanced ceramics, with a new buzzword "fine ceramics". Amidst the interest, the Seto Municipal Government set up the Council on Promotion of New Ceramics Technology in 1982 to promote the entry of Seto firms into the market. While mainly addressing the lack of higher educational institutions on ceramics in the district, the council also planned a course of action in which Seto's advanced ceramics firms would work jointly toward new product development and introduction of new technologies.[8] This resulted in the establishment of a small study group of manufacturers within APPIC in 1983. The group consisted of those firms already engaged in advanced ceramics and those interested in the market. Its planned activities included: (1) lobbying the national and prefectural governments; (2) collecting and disseminating of information; (3) holding lectures and workshops; and (4) public relations and promoting advanced ceramics as one of the district's products.[9] However, the group accomplished few activities worthy of notice in the 1980s and the early 1990s, let alone joint R&D effort originally envisaged by the council. Meetings of the group were generally of little use in information exchange, since senior staff of many advanced ceramics firms seldom attended them to avoid contact with other firms.[10]

Instead of engaging in collaboration within the district, most Seto advanced ceramics firms gave priority to their ties with key customer firms as a source of technical knowledge. Further, for the first time in the history of the Seto ceramics industry, some advanced ceramics firms formed a financial affiliation with large corporations in Tokyo. For example, a producer of setters and saggers used in the manufacture of piezoelectric devices established a new firm in co-operation with a Tokyo-based chemical corporation in the late 1980s. In the new firm that manufactured electronic parts, the Tokyo-based Corporation undertook basic research and marketing, and the Seto producer mainly took the responsibility for their manufacturing.[11] Another case is a Seto firm, a sizeable percentage of whose stocks were acquired by a Tokyo-based manufacturer of new materials in 1990. The managing director of the Seto firm justified the alliance by stressing the need of SMEs to make the best use of the resources possessed by large corporations, and particularly in the areas of technology and marketing.[12] A sign of strengthened ties with customer firms also appeared locally. Since the mid 1980s, most medium-sized advanced ceramics firms in the district have set up their new factories at locations close to their customers. As noted earlier, Seto advanced ceramics firms had by then constituted only an intermediate part of the production chain. Most of the raw materials were supplied by firms in other regions, and their products were delivered to customers located elsewhere. Moreover, Seto's milieu, which fostered co-operation among producers in the earlier periods almost, if not entirely, broke down as regards advanced ceramics. This deprived the district of the previous advantages that had retained firms.

Rise of a New Entrepreneur and Fall of an Old Player

After the clash between the two groups and the breakdown of the district's milieu, a traditional ceramics firm made a sensational entry into the market for advanced ceramics. The firm, Yamaju Ceramics, represents a small but new group of Seto manufacturers that make use of links with a diverse range of firms and organizations, rather than relying solely on either horizontal co-operation within the district or close ties with a few customers outside the district. The firm was originally founded in 1925 as a manufacturer and exporter of tableware. When Hisao Kato, currently the firm's chairman, succeeded to his father's post of managing director in 1967, he saw imminent problems in the exporting of tableware, and decided to enter the advanced ceramics market. In searching for a new area of business, he first sought advice outside the district from a number of research institutes, including the Government Industrial Research Institute, Nagoya and the Research Laboratory of NHK (the country's public broadcasting company) in Tokyo. Advanced ceramics made from alumina, including substrates for hybrid ICs, were unattractive in Kato's view, since many firms, both within and outside Seto, were already engaged in research and production. Instead he found that a single crystal ruby would be promising for use in laser radiators. To study the Czochralski method of single crystal growth, Kato undertook joint research with the Institute of Metal Materials, Tohoku University from 1970 to 1971. Following the advice of the Institute, Kato dropped the initial target of a single crystal ruby and engaged in R&D of single crystal yttrium-aluminum-garnet. Although the research made progress, he had trouble manufacturing a product comparable to imports from the US. In addition, the domestic market for laser radiators proved very small in size. In 1973, after almost four years of research, Kato learned that single crystal $LiNbO_3$ had great promise for the use of surface wave transducers applied to intermediate wave filters in televisions and VCRs. Encouraged by an expert in single crystal use at Osaka-based Sumitomo Electric Industries, his firm started to research single crystal LiNbO₃ in 1974. Three years later, the firm finally succeeded in developing a mass-production technique for two-inch wide single crystal LiNbO₃ for the first time in the country. This news caused a sensation in the media, which hailed Yamaju Ceramics as an innovative entrepreneur from an old industrial district. After the product's introduction, Yamaju Ceramics then conducted joint R&D with Ibaraki-based Hitachi Ltd, one of its new customers, for three years. This enabled the Seto firm to make great strides in its quality control. It started to make profits from single crystal LiNbO₃ in 1983 and captured about a quarter of the worldwide market share by the late 1980s while closing down its original tableware business in 1991.[13]

The success in single crystal LiNbO₃, however, did not tie Yamaju Ceramics down to any customer firms, and in particular Hitachi Ltd. The careful search for a niche market and the early pioneering research in co-operation with a number of research institutes enabled the firm to initially establish a strong, independent position in the market where few firms had entered and whose size was too small to interest major electronics firms. Having established such a strong position, the firm then entered a co-operative relationship with Hitachi on equal standing. It helped the firm strengthen its technological base without falling victim to control by the giant customer firm.

In contrast, the vertical ties which many Seto advanced ceramics firms had with their key customers started to show their own "lock-in" effects in the 1990s. Confined to a number of vertical chains, a greater part of Seto's advanced ceramics firms failed to explore new possibilities. For instance, unlike the earlier periods when Seto firms had manufactured similar advanced ceramics, they became more specialized in their own product areas by the 1990s. This gave rise to new circumstances where Seto firms could jointly develop new products by combining their expertise in different areas. In fact, Yamaju's Kato saw an opportunity of combining his firm's thin film technology with advanced ceramics made by other Seto firms. Yamaju's thin film technology was originally developed in the late 1980s to manufacture pyroelectric infrared sensors by attaching a thin film of nickel chromium on a wafer of single crystal LiTaO₃. Having commercialized the infrared sensor in 1992, Kato developed a plan to create a new product by applying a thin film to advanced ceramic substrates manufactured by other Seto firms.[14] In spite of his approach within APPIC, this plan has not been realized to this date because of the lack of interest on the part of other Seto firms.[15]

A greater shock was caused by a financial difficulty of firm A, one of Seto's medium-sized manufacturers of advanced ceramics, in the late 1990s. As one of Seto's pioneers, firm A entered the market for advanced ceramics in 1939 by manufacturing ceramic cores for resistors for Osaka-based Matsushita Electric. Since then, the firm continued to supply over a half of its domestic sales to Matsushita throughout the postwar period.[16] By the 1970s, the firm had grown into a medium-sized manufacturer with over 250 employees, alongside the growth of the country's electronics industry including Matsushita. However, the reliance upon Matsushita forced firm A into a position of one of its low-cost component suppliers. It was stuck into the market for small-margin components like resistor cores, unable to establish a more lucrative position in the industry. Under the circumstances, firm A attempted to stay competitive by setting up factories in low-wage countries including China, India and the Czech Republic. The strategy, however, backfired as the firm's sales plummeted during the country's recession in the 1990s. Although it managed to avoid filing bankruptcy, it closed some of its factories, both domestic and overseas, and made about 110 employees redundant in 1998, reducing its employment to only 80, less than one third of the level in the 1970s.[17]

Present and Future

At the beginning of the new century, the Seto advanced ceramics industry is at crossroads between renewal and irrelevance. Although its position relative to the manufacture of traditional ceramics within the district grew larger as a result of the latter's decline, the sales of advanced ceramics produced in Seto has hardly kept pace with that in the country (Table 9.1). Further, the sales failed to grow in the 1990s at all. This in turn suggests that the industry has not produced employment growth in the district in recent years. In fact, since the clash between insulator manufactures and advanced ceramics manufacturers in the late 1960s, the entry of new firms into the market for advanced ceramics has been small. In the 1990s, the number of the district's firms operating in the market has remained largely unchanged at the lower twenties.[18] In addition, medium-sized firms have pursued the strategy of locating their new factories outside Aichi Prefecture. Lastly, but not least, the volume of trade between advanced ceramics firms within the district is almost non-existent. Overall, the conditions envisaged by the proponents of industrial districts, that is, intra-regional networks and growth deriving from their innovative nature, do not exist in the Seto advanced ceramics industry.

Table 9.1   Sales of Advanced Ceramics Produced in Seto

Year	Sales (million yen)	As percent of advanced ceramics produced in Aichi Prefecture	As percent of advance ceramics produced in the country
1967	758	28.1	7.9
1970	987	15.3	4.9
1973	1674	14.7	4.0
1977	1537	11.7	2.6
1981	2222	8.6	2.0
1986	5452	6.5	1.4
1990	7430	8.0	1.6
1994	7254	5.4	1.3
1998	7432	5.6	1.1

Notes: (1) The figures in the years of 1967-1981 are for electronic ceramics.
(2) Seto's figures in the years of 1986-1998 include advanced ceramics produced in Owari-Asahi, Seto's neighboring district.

Sources: For the years of 1967-1977, Aichi Prefectural Government, *Aichi Ken Seisan Dotai Tokei Nenpo (Yearbook of Statistics of Production in Aichi Prefecture)* cited in Kakino (1985), pp. 96-97. For the data of Seto and Aichi Prefecture in the year of 1981, Aichi Prefectural Government, *Aichi no Seisan Doko (Trend of Production in Aichi)*, 1982. For Seto's data in the years of 1986-1998, Kumiaiin Tojiki Seisan Jokyo (Statistics of Production of Syndicate Members) obtained by the author from Aichi Prefectural Pottery Industry Cooperation. For Aichi Prefecture's data in the years of 1986-1998, Aichi Prefectural Government, *Aichi no Kokogyo Doko (Trend of Mining and Manufacturing in Aichi)*, various years. For the country's data in the years of 1981-1998, Ministry of International Trade and Industry, *Zakka Tokei Nenpo (Yearbook of General Merchandise Statistics)*, various years.

On the other hand, there is a sign of change. As one of the district's few proponents of intra-regional collaboration, Hisao Kato of Yamaju Ceramics was elected as chairman of the study group of advanced ceramics manufacturers within APPIC in 1995. Kato started some new programs to facilitate learning from firms in other regions. One such program is tours the group makes once a year to visit firms in other regions and see their factories. The factories visited to this date include Murata Manufacturing's condenser factory in Shiga Prefecture and Sharp Corporation's liquid crystal display factory in Mie Prefecture. Also, the study group has started information exchange with a similar group of advanced ceramics manufacturers in Kyoto. The exchange, which includes visits to each other, aims to identify technologies possessed by firms in each group and to search for opportunities for collaborative businesses although such a business has yet to be realized.[19] The latest development added to these is the appointment of Yamaju's Kato as chairman of APPIC in 2000. He is the first person to take the post from the district's advanced ceramics firms, symbolizing the greater importance of advanced ceramics to the district's manufacture of ceramics. His appointment as the association's chairman will most likely lend support to the collaborative programs he has pursued in the advanced ceramics manufacturers study group.

Yet, Kato believes that such collaborative programs among SMEs are not enough for sustained renewal and growth of the Seto advanced ceramics industry. What is lacking, in his view, is the presence of a large corporation that would attract firms to Seto, creating intra-regional trade and draws upon a variety of sources of knowledge. Accordingly Kato intends to ask both the Seto Municipal Government and the Aichi Prefectural Government for inward investment support to attract a plant of a large manufacturer/user of advanced ceramics.[20] It remains to be seen if his plan will be realized. Nonetheless, there is little doubt that the Seto advanced ceramics industry will keep evolving into a form different from the model of an industrial district, rather than returning to its old form in the days of the traditional ceramics manufacture.

Conclusion

Given the time and resource-consuming nature of networking, success of a network tends to make technology-following SMEs blind to other opportunities or sources of knowledge and repeat the existing formulas of knowledge acquisition. This causes ageing of their networks, leading to a breakdown of industrial districts in mature industries.

For policy, it is useful to monitor networks operating in the region and to raise awareness about other sources of knowledge so that firms can prevent their networks from ageing. This is especially needed when networks stabilize and produce lock-in effects. On such occasions, government can obtain a larger picture of the situation within and outside the district than firms themselves do. It allows government to benchmark the region against others and help firms restructure their networks.

The best source of knowledge changes its location over the long term as an industry evolves, merges with another and create new markets. Technology-leader firms constantly look for new sources and, when appropriate, change their key partner organizations. This has an important implication to network programs that facilitate sharing of knowledge. The current tenet of network programs is based on the observation that technology-following SMEs are averse to risks and stick to their conventional sources of knowledge (i.e., suppliers and customers). Network programs hence often attempt to facilitate sharing of knowledge between trade partners. However, networks of trade partners are not always the best solution to problems facing firms. This depends partly on the phase of the industry, the type of knowledge targeted by programs, and the technical level of firms concerned. When running network programs, government needs to assess the sources of knowledge that participants draw upon and to ensure that they meet the programs' goal. In other words, there are occasions in which network programs should link parties who may appear unconventional in the eyes of technology-following SMEs.

Acknowledgements

I remain deeply grateful to AnnaLee Saxenian, Sir Peter Hall and Michael Gerlach for their generous support for the original study (Izushi 1994) that this chapter partly draws upon.

Notes

1   For instance, decentralized networks of SMEs in the Swiss watch industry failed to make a transition from mechanical movement to quartz-based electronic movement quickly enough to fend off Japanese competition, eventually replaced by some large corporations that emerged through mergers (Glasmeier 1991).
2   Edgington (1999) examines inter-relationships among core assembly firms, subcontractors, local governments and business associations in Chukyo Region consisting of the three adjoining prefectures of Aichi, Gifu and Mie.
3   Seto Municipal Government, *Seto-shi Tokeisho (Statistics of the City of Seto)*, 2000.
4   Ministry of International Trade and Industry, *Kogyo Tokeihyo (Census of Manufactures)*, 2000, and Seto Municipal Government, *Seto-shi Tokeisho*. The figures account for the employment of establishments with four employees and over and do not include the employment of establishments with fewer than four employees.
5   Seto Municipal Government, *Seto-shi Tokeisho*.
6   *Chubu Keizai Shinbun (The Mid-Japan Economist)*, 13 October 1998.
7   Interviews by the author with Isao Kato, Chairman of TG Keller, on 10 March and 30 July 1993.
8   *Chubu Keizai Shinbun (The Mid-Japan Economist)*, 9 August 1982.
9   *Chubu Keizai Shinbun (The Mid-Japan Economist)*, 27 January 1983.
10   Interview by the author with Takehisa Maeda, then Director of the Center for Technology and Skill Development, APPIC, on 17 April 1993.
11   Interview by the author with Rikichi Otake, Managing Director of Otake Insulators, on 30 June 1992.
12   Interview by the author with Kozo Kato, Managing Director of Maruju Co., on 24 June 1992.
13   Interview by the author with Hisao Kato, then Managing Director of Yamaju Ceramics, on 3 July 1992.
14   Ibid.

15   Interview by the author with Hisao Kato, Chairman of Yamaju Ceramics and Chairman of APPIC, on 23 August 2000.
16   Interview by the author with Akihiko Yamada, Managing Director of YS Porcelain Tubes Mfg., on 13 July 1992.
17   *Chubu Keizai Shinbun (The Mid-Japan Economist)*, 14 April 1998.
18   Data obtained by the author from APPIC.
19   Interview by the author with Hisao Kato on 23 August 2000.
20   Ibid.

References

Best, M. (1990), *The New Competition: Institutions of Industrial Restructuring*, Harvard University Press, Cambridge, Massachusetts.

Brusco, S. (1982), "The Emilian model: productive decentralization and social integration", *Cambridge Journal of Economics*, vol. 6, pp. 167-184.

Bryson, J.R. and Daniels, P.W. (1998), "Business Link, strong ties, and the walls of silence: small and medium-sized enterprises and external business-service expertise", *Environment and Planning C: Government and Policy*, vol. 16, pp. 265-280.

Camagni, R. (1991), "Local 'milieu', uncertainty and innovation networks: towards a new dynamic theory of economic space", in R. Camagni (ed.) *Innovation Networks: Spatial Perspectives*, Belhaven Press, London, pp. 121-144.

Camagni, R. (1993), "Inter-firm industrial networks: the costs and benefits of cooperative behaviour", *Journal of Industry Studies*, vol. 1, pp. 1-15.

Commission of the European Communities (1994), *Research and Technology Management in Enterprises: Issues for Community Policy*, Office for Official Publications of the European Communities, Brussels.

Edgington, D.W. (1999), "Firms, governments and innovation in the Chukyo Region of Japan", *Urban Studies*, vol. 36, pp. 305-339.

Glasmeier, A. (1991), "Technological discontinuities and flexible production networks: the case of Switzerland and the world watch industry", *Research Policy*, vol. 20, pp. 469-485.

Grabher, G. (1993), "The weakness of strong ties: the lock-in of regional development in the Ruhr Area", in G. Grabher (ed.) *The Embedded Firm: On the Socioeconomics of Industrial Networks*, London, Routledge, pp. 255-277.

Granovetter, M.S. (1973), "The strength of weak ties", *American Journal of Sociology*, vol. 78, pp. 1360-1380.

Granovetter, M.S. (1982), "The strength of weak ties: a network theory revisited", in P.V. Marsden and N. Lin (eds.) *Social Structure and Network Analysis*, Sage, London, pp. 105-130.

Grotz, R. and Braun, B. (1997), "Territorial or trans-territorial networking: spatial aspects of technology-oriented co-operation within the German mechanical engineering industry", *Regional Studies*, vol. 31, pp. 545-557.

Harrison, B. (1994), *Lean and Mean: The Changing Landscape of Corporate Power in the Age of Flexibility*, Basic Books, New York.

Izushi, H. (1994), *Fragmented Networks: Inter-firm Relationships in the Seto Ceramics Industry*, unpublished PhD dissertation, Department of City and Regional Planning, University of California at Berkeley.

Izushi, H. (1997), "Conflict between two industrial networks: technological adaptation and inter-firm relationships in the ceramics industry in Seto, Japan", *Regional Studies*, vol. 31, pp. 117-129.

Kakino, K. (1985), Nyu seramikkusu to Seto tojiki sangyo: sono yobiteki kosatsu (Advanced ceramics and the ceramics industry in Seto: preliminary study), in Nagoya Gakuin University (ed.) *Seto Tojiki Sangyo Kenkyu Senshu (Selected Studies of the Ceramics Industry in Seto)*, Seto, Nagoya Gakuin University, pp. 81-118.

Kato, I. (1997), *Seto Denjiki 100-nenshi (100-year Chronicle of Insulators for Electrical Devices in Seto)*, Seto, Aichi Prefectural Pottery Industry Cooperation.

Kono, S. (1984), Tojiki sangyo o meguru shomondai to gyokai no taio jokyo, sono 2 (Problems and responses of the ceramics industry, part 2), *Aichi Keizai Jiho (Review of Economy in Aichi)*, no. 143, pp. 1-50.

Markusen, A. (1996), "Sticky places in slippery space: a typology of industrial districts", *Economic Geography*, vol. 72, pp. 293-313.

Marshall, A. (1890), *Principles of Economics*, Macmillan, London.

Meyer, D.R. (1998), "Formation of advanced technology districts: New England textile machinery and firearms, 1790-1820", *Economic Geography*, vol. 74 (AAG special issue): pp. 31-45.

Mytelka, L.K. (2000), "Local systems of innovation in a globalized world economy", *Industry and Innovation*, vol. 7, pp. 15-32.

Piore, M.J. and Sabel, C.F. (1984), *The Second Industrial Divide: Possibilities for Prosperity*, Basic Books, New York.

Pyke, F., Becattini, G. and Sengenberger, W. (eds.) (1990), *Industrial districts and Inter firm Co-operation in Italy*, International Institute for Labor Studies, Geneva.

Pyke, F. and Sengenberger, W. (eds.) (1992), *Industrial districts and Local Economic Regeneration*, International Institute for Labor Studies, Geneva.

Rothwell, R. and Dodgson, M. (1991), "External linkages and innovation in small and medium-sized enterprises", *R&D Management*, vol. 21, pp. 125-137.

Rothwell, R. and Zegveld, W. (1985), *Reindustrialization and Technology*, Longman, Harlow.

Seto Ceramic Trade Co-operative Association (1976), *50-nenshi (50-year Chronicle)*, Seto Ceramic Trade Co-operative Association, Seto.

Sugiyama, S. (1987), Aichi-kennai no fain seramikkusu sangyo jittai chosa (Survey of the present situation of fine ceramics industry in Aichi Prefecture), *Aichi Keizai Jiho (Review of Economy in Aichi Prefecture)*, no. 153, pp. 21-50.

Takeuchi, E. (1994), Kokusai kyoso no gekika ni yureru tojiki no sogo sanchi (Ceramics district under pressure of increased international competition), *Kokumin Kin-yu Koko Chosa Geppo (Kokkin Monthly Report)*, no. 430, pp. 28-33.

10 Lean and its Limits: The Toyota Production System in Chukyo and Northern Kyushu, Japan

DAVID W. EDGINGTON

> Lean production is a superior way for humans to make things. It provides better
> products in wider variety at lower cost…It follows that the whole world should
> adopt lean production, and as quickly as possible (Womack, Jones and Roos, 1990,
> p. 225).

This chapter examines the idea of proximity and networks between firms
through an examination of Toyota's production system, especially
developments in the 1990s. The Toyota just-in-time production system has
often been seen as the epitome of efficiency, a system that aims to eradicate
waste wherever it may exist. Indeed, Toyota was the first company to earn
the attribute lean that was given to it by a group of researchers at the
Massachusetts Institute of Technology (Womack, Jones and Roos 1990;
Womak and Jones 1995, 1996). Certainly, Toyota-style manufacturing
aims to use as little labor, inventory, development time and factory space as
possible, and at its foundation is a spirit of innovation that tries to utilize
limited business resources efficiently. These key elements made it possible
for Toyota, and other firms that favored its approach, to achieve extremely
high levels of quality through absence of defects, and productivity
approaching two to three times higher than US or European automobile
plants in the late 1980s. Central to the success of lean management has
been Toyota's just-in-time (*kanban*) system of inventory-control in which
materials and parts are procured and delivered just before they are needed.[1]
The objective of just-in-time is to minimize the level of inventories,
especially when different models or parts are to be produced. Toyota Motor
Company (TMC) developed the system to initially coordinate in-plant
activities between different processes of production and before long to
control the timing of deliveries made by subcontractors. Centered on
Toyota City (located in Aichi prefecture, Japan), TMC perfected a unique
localized production system and close integration of its major suppliers and

sub-contractors. Eventually, this included not only the production and delivery of parts and components but also closer integration with their major suppliers into systems of research and design (Smitka 1991).[2]

There are many implications for the just-in-time (JIT) production system for the process of industrial clustering emphasized by economists, business scholars, and economic geographers (Krugman 1991; Storper and Harrison 1991; Storper 1997; Porter 2000). This is because its effective use is often considered to be facilitated by geographical proximity between firms and suppliers, and hence by industrial agglomeration. Indeed, TMC and its network of suppliers in Toyota City (and adjoining Aichi prefecture) has often been cited as a classic hub and spoke type of industrial district, one which has a single controlling firm linked through structured networks to satellite rings of supplier firms (Markusen 1996; Hayter 1997). As noted by Mair (1993), the mere adoption of Japanese-style production processes just-in-time has often given the illusion that spatial concentration and local embeddedness might be enhanced. Within the metaphor of the "Toyota JIT production complex" there is often a tendency to associate proximity itself with particular networks between suppliers and assemblers, including dedicated investments in production facilities oriented towards the assembly company's needs, the greater sharing of know-how, and more intensive communication over product design. The implicit hypothesis of many studies is that "Toyotaism" has fostered the spatial clustering of activities, in contrast to the principle of the spatial division of labor as characterized by "Fordism" (Hill 1989, 1990). Henry Ford, of course, was the recognized inventor of the branch plant that enabled a spatial fragmentation of the production process along with the decentralization of assembly plants to locations near the markets (Rubenstein 1992). However, such a viewpoint tends to attach a rather singular correspondence between an industrial model (supplier-assembler JIT networks) and a dominant spatial form (industrial agglomeration) (see Mair 1993).

By comparison, other scholars emphasize instead the importance of organizational proximity, meaning the networks that evolve between various actors, which are not fixed in space, but rather are structured around a common cognitive framework and decision rules. In "organizational space" the representations and structures that network actors use as a benchmark in order to define both their routine and strategic practices are more critical than geography alone (Kirat and Lung 1997). Returning to the JIT system, it has often been remarked that outside of Japan the impetus of the JIT to spatial agglomeration and proximity has been highly variable. Thus in North America, some Japanese companies have indeed tried to adopt just-in-time delivery methods and geographically closer relationships with local suppliers. By contrast, little evidence of local complexes of firms developing JIT clusters appears in Western Europe.[3] But what of Japan? Does the small size of the country, together with a traditional use of subcontracting in industry lead automatically to tightly clustered industrial districts, as suggested by Humphreys (1995, 1996). A significant body of work has now been published examining the nature of Toyota's lean production system (e.g., Schonberger 1982; Japan Management Association 1989; Womak, Jones and Roos 1990). However, much of the discussion is rather static and lacks an appreciation the dynamic interaction of this ideal model and its changing contexts. Clearly, the extent and significance of locational clustering and the importance of geographical proximity to Toyota's lean production system remains open for further research (Linge 1991).

In this chapter I seek to widen these issues by examining how TMC reacted to a new set of production problems in the late-1980s, problems that suggested there were practical limits to the gains achieved in manufacturing or engineering efficiency by continued geographical clustering. This study illustrates the limitations that Toyota itself has encountered through changes in the Japanese labor market, and the strains placed on lean production and the spatial integrity of JIT through increasing congestion costs and diseconomies of agglomeration. These in turn have necessitated TMC to revise its production system within Japan and embrace a certain degree of spatial restructuring. The central question in this chapter therefore is how adaptable has the JIT system been over time? The empirical analysis is based upon the author's research in the Chukyo production region of Japan (which includes Toyota City and Aichi prefecture) and at Toyota's first decentralized assembly plant in the northern Kyushu Island (see Figure 10.1).

The chapter commences by reviewing the origins of "lean production" and charting the history of Toyota in Aichi, paying attention to both geographical and organizational factors. The next section examines TMC's Kyushu assembly operation, opened in 1992 and located some 700 kilometers from Toyota City. The focus here is in terms of how JIT logistics have been re-arranged to allow for such long distances of supply chains, and the type of production innovations found in the new Kyushu plant. The conclusion summarizes these findings and speculates on the future of Toyota's production headquarters in Aichi prefecture in light of falling levels of automobile demand in Japan.

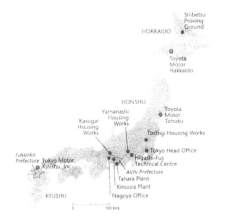
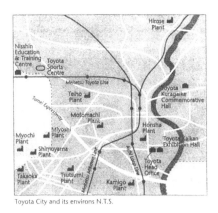

Source: Toyota Motor Corporation (1999a)

Figure 10.1   Location of Toyota's Major Operations in Japan

Toyota at Home in Aichi Prefecture

Figure 10.1 shows that a notable feature of Toyota's spatial production structure has indeed been the concentration of its major factories in one place. Indeed, up to 1990, all of TMC's twelve Japanese assembly and major components plants (e.g., for engines) were located in Aichi prefecture. Ten of these were situated in or on the outskirts of Toyota City, today a large industrial city located around 25 km due east from the major metropolis of Nagoya (population 2.2 million in 1995). Details of Toyota's car plants are in Table 10.1. Toyota City has a resident population of about 340,000, and the vast majority of them depend upon one of Toyota's factories or upon associated firms. The city grew most rapidly during both the 1960s domestic market boom and the 1970s export market boom as Toyota's annual production rose from 74,000 automobiles and trucks in 1960 to 1,068,000 in 1970 and 2,303,000 in 1980 (Fujita and Hill 1993). By this time, around ninety-five percent of industrial freight movements in the area were destined for Toyota's factories (Hoffman and Kaplinsky 1988, p. 130). The average component delivery rate at Toyota was then four times per day, with the most frequent deliveries occurring 16 times a day, and the least frequent delivery at least once per day (Hoffman and Kaplinsky 1988, p. 177).

Table 10.1   Toyota Car Plants in Japan, 1999

Name	Began operation	Land area (000m^2)	Employees	Main product/business
Honsha Plant	1938	555	2,800	Chassis (trucks, buses)
Motomachi Plant	1959	1,591	6,500	Passenger cars (Crown, Lexus SC400/300, Supra, Cressida)
Kamigo Plant	1965	874	3,600	Engines
Takaoka Plant	1966	1,360	5,000	Passenger cars (Corolla, Tercel, Corsa, Corolla II, Cynos, Paseo)
Miyoshi Plant	1968	334	1,800	Chassis parts
Tsutumi Plant	1970	933	6,200	Passenger cars (Lexus ES 300, Windon, Scepter, Vista, Camry)
Myochi Plant	1973	555	2,000	Engine parts, chassis parts
Shimoyama Plant	1975	415	1,800	Engines, exhaust emission control devices
Kinuura Plant	1978	808	2,700	Functional parts
Tahara Plant	1979	3,700	7,100	Trucks, passenger cars (Lexus LS 400, Celsior, Crown, Lexus GS300, Aristo, Corona EXIV, Carina ED, Celica, Hilux)
Teiho Plant	1986	287	2,000	Machinery, dies for casting and forging, molds for plastics
Hirose Plant	1989	247	1,400	Research, development, and production of electric parts and components
Toyota Motor Kyushu, Inc.	1992	1,060,000		Passenger cars (Mark II, Chaser, Windom Harrier)
Toyota Motor Hokkaido,Inc	1992	980,000		Transmissions, drive train parts, aluminium wheels
Toyota Motor Tohoku, Inc.	1992	294,000		Mechanical and electrical parts

Source: Toyota Motor Corporation (1999b)

Lean Production

Toyota developed its lean production system, however, in a particular historical and geographical context, and the allied themes of networks and propinquity enter this narrative in a number of ways. Hence, when Kiichiro Toyoda founded the Toyota Automatic Loom Works in 1926, the community known today as Toyota City was called Koromo, a historic silk weaving community in rural eastern Aichi with less than 30,000 population (Allison 1975; Miyakawa 1991). A pilot automobile factory was first set up in the nearby town of Kariya by his son Kiichiro Toyoda in 1934, and the Toyota Motor Company subsequently built its first full production factory in Koromo during 1938.[4] Cusumano (1985, pp. 180-181) notes that "Toyota actively recruited workers from Aichi or nearby prefectures because Kiichiro wanted to hire the same unskilled, malleable farm boys, with strong backs and communal loyalties, who had helped to make his father's companies so successful. Since there were not many alternatives for employment in that part of Japan, workers and residents tended to be grateful to the Toyota family, and Toyota group companies, for their economic contributions to the area". Kiichiro also scoured the Nagoya countryside and eventually succeeded in recruiting a number of supporting parts makers to supplement his efforts in Toyota's assembly factories (Fruin 1992, p. 262).

Significantly, the introduction of the famed just-in-time system following the Pacific War was facilitated by Toyota's geographical location. Toyota production engineer Taichi Ohno was most responsible for implementing JIT within the Toyota factories (Ohno 1988a,b). He began limited experiments in 1948 and gradually extended these throughout the company in the early 1950s. The immediate post-war period, however, was a turbulent environment in terms of Japanese management-labor relations and characterized by strong Japanese trade unions under left-wing control. Toyota's only strike of ten months was itself due mainly to the reforms in auto production that Ohno instituted in the machine shop (Cusumano 1985, p. 306). Yet in order to implement various lean production ideas it had to reduce around 2,000 jobs, create flexible teams and close down its main warehouses (Cusumano 1985). Resistance at Toyota to the new techniques were quelled at this time rather more easily than at Nissan, Toyota's major competitor based in metropolitan Tokyo-Yokohama, where there were a large number of strikes and lock-outs around the same period. This was largely because Toyota was able to control its union, in part due to its location in a rural area where workers had no previous experience of industrialization and few employment alternatives. Nissan, with a more resilient urban-based trade union, struggled with tight labor markets throughout the post-war period, whereas TMC's agglomeration in Toyota City drew upon a quasi-agricultural surplus labor for many years.

Besides a rather docile labor force, Fruin (1992, p. 292) notes that there was also willingness by local supply firms to join the Toyota production network. He observes "in the depressed economy of rural Nagoya during the 1930s or in the hard luck circumstances of post-war

Japan, business opportunities were rarely scorned" (Fruin 1992, p. 292). Other important factors included a welcoming local government willing to provide transportation infrastructure to facilitate the movement of materials and components between parts suppliers and assembly factories, just-in-time. Industrial estates, road building and traffic planning were oriented towards Toyota's needs and those of its major suppliers. Indeed, Koromo changed its name to Toyota City in 1959 in recognition of the local firm's growing importance and the opening of TMC's Motomachi Plant (Miyakawa 1991; Fujita and Hill 1993). Later on, Aichi prefecture upgraded the nearby ports of Nagoya and Gamagori to cope with increased exports from Toyota's car factories (Edgington 1996). By contrast, Nissan shared an urban transport infrastructure with many other firms in Tokyo-Yokohama, a situation that undermined Nissan's attempts to introduce the tight delivery scheduling and *kanban* command systems that Toyota used to operate JIT (Cusumano 1985; Mair 1992).

As the production of automobiles soared Toyota began teaching its in-house production system to major subsidiaries and affiliate suppliers. For instance, starting from 1958, Toyota instituted the custom of resident engineers whereby sub-contractors would regularly station engineers at Toyota (and vice-versa) to allow products to be continuously improved. Because this "learning" involved uncodified, tacit knowledge of assembly line skills and techniques, proximity to sub-contractors was a distinct advantage (Fruin and Nishiguchi 1993). Toyota taught its JIT approach to its major subsidiaries in Aichi prefecture by the late 1960s and early 1970s, allowing the synchronization of their production lines with its own. Thereafter Toyota demanded that subcontractors in other parts of Japan follow the JIT approach. "Firms in the Tokyo area were usually the last to convert their production lines and management systems" (Cusumano, 1985, p. 299). Nissan, by way of contrast, trailed Toyota in inventory control, precisely because its factories and suppliers were more dispersed throughout Japan than those of Toyota (Cusumano 1988, p. 36). So, in a very direct sense, Toyota was able to successfully adopt a hands-on teaching approach to JIT, in relation to its suppliers, because its production was so concentrated in a rather remote rural area.

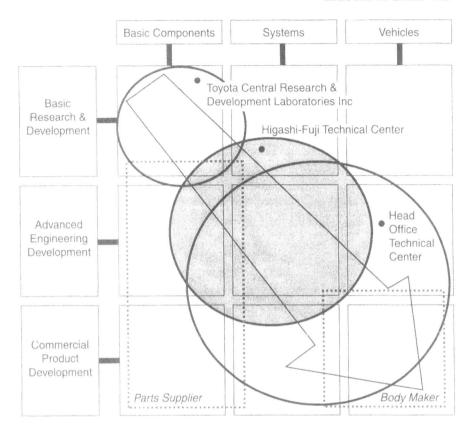

Source: adapted from Ohmori (1999)

Figure 10.2   The Toyota R&D System

Finally, Toyota's JIT system and its relations with suppliers and subcontractors entailed closer integration of R&D (research and development) effort as well as the supply of components. Indeed, the R&D facilities of Toyota's "focal factories" (Fruin 1992) in Toyota City have been important local sources of technology support for parts makers in the surrounding area. Ohmori (1999) shows that Toyota has three major R&D units (see Figure 10.2). The Toyota Central Research and Development Laboratories located close to Toyota City, carried out initial stage R&D and allowed TMC group members to collaborate in basic R&D. This was important when the technology levels of first-tier suppliers lagged behind that of Toyota itself. Moreover, the upgrading of suppliers' capability became critical when Toyota began to grant contracts on a "design-approved basis" from the late 1970s, meaning that suppliers were required to take responsibility for the design of products to TMC's performance specifications, often in conjunction with TMC engineers (Asanuma 1985, 1989). In the 1980s TMC required major suppliers to develop and incorporate new technology into parts system, such as electronics or advanced composite materials. Toyota's, wide-ranging R&D technical center in Higashi-Fuji, located on the western extremity of the Chukyo region in central Japan, of which Aichi prefecture is a part, assisted this. Another Technical Center at Head Office in Toyota City specializes in the more applied aspects of innovation and advanced engineering (Ohmori 1999).[5]

Beyond geographical proximity, however, organizational proximity also shaped the features of Toyota's production system. An initial illustration is that Toyota Motor Company long ago chose vertical disintegration as an organizational strategy. Thus Monden (1983) details how most of TMC's big first-tier suppliers were in fact once part of the original pre-war Toyota Motor Corporation (see Figure 10.3). In part, the process of gradually splitting off internal production divisions was triggered by the economic policies of SCAP (the allied supreme command occupying post-war Japan), which decreed that holding companies with a capitalization in excess of 5 million yen were to be dissolved. Accordingly, Toyota Industries Company, the holding company for the Toyoda family group, was dismembered and in 1945 Toyota spun-off its truck-body plant as Toyota Auto Body Company. In 1949 TMC sold its aircraft parts production facilities to Aichi Industries which later merged in 1965 with Shinkawa Industries to become Aishin Seiki, today one of Toyota Motor's most important suppliers. The trading functions performed by the holding company, however, were continued with the establishment of the Nisshin Tsucho Company in 1948, afterwards renamed the Toyoda Trading Company. Later, Toyota continued to spin off in-house supply operations into quasi-independent supplier companies. Hence, in 1949 TMC separated its electrical department as Nippondenso, and in 1950, the spinning and weaving department was uncoupled as the Toyoda Spinning and Weaving Company. Toyota Motor Sales was also split from TMC in 1950, but eventually they re-merged in 1982 (Figure 10.3).

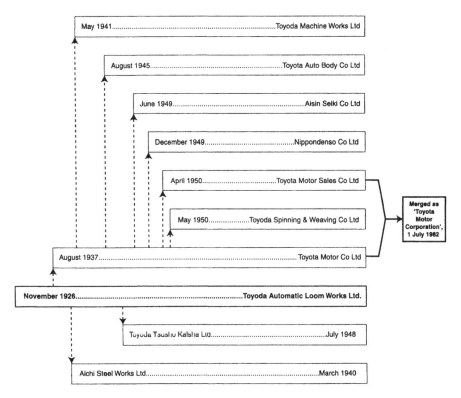

Source: adapted from Monden (1983)

Figure 10.3   The Vertical Disintegration of Toyota Motor Company, 1920s to 1980s

Table 10.2 shows the major Toyota subsidiaries associated with the Toyota group of companies and their headquarters location. This indicates that around its twelve assembly plants at Toyota City (Figure 10.1) are 9 major supply companies in which TMC has an equity position ranging from around 9 percent to 54 percent. Many of these firms have substantial cross-holdings in each other. TMC, for instance, holds about 23 percent of Denso (formerly called Nippondenso), which makes electrical components and engine computers, and sends about 60 percent of its output to Toyota. The rest it sells to virtually all other automotive companies apart from competitor Nissan. TMC also holds 40 percent of Toyoda Gosei, which makes seats and wiring systems; and 12 percent of Aishin Seki, which makes metal engine parts. In addition, it holds a major shareholding in affiliated assembly firms not located in Aichi; namely the Kanto Auto Works (located in the Tokyo-Yokohama region), Hino Motors Ltd (also in

Table 10.2   Toyota's Principal Subsidiaries and Affiliates in Japan, 1999

(1) Toyota Group

Company Establishment (#)	Main Business	Date of Establishment	Capital (mill. yen)	Employees	HQ Location
Toyoda Automatic Loom Works Ltd. (24.16)	textile machine	1926	40,133	9,200	Kariya, Aichi
Aichi Steel 1940 Works Ltd. (21.37)	specialty steel	1940	25,016	3,000	Tokai City, Aichi
Toyoda Machine Works Ltd. (21.00)	machine tools and auto parts	1941	24,783	4,300	Kariya, Aichi
Toyota Auto Body (41.76)	auto bodies and parts	1945	8,871	8,200	Kariya, Aichi
Toyota Tsusho Corp (21.70)	trading	1948	25,142		Nagoya, Aichi
Aishin Seiki Co Ltd. (22.13)	auto parts	1949	41,140	11,000	Kariya, Aichi
Denso (22.92)	electric auto parts	1949	151,166	39,390	Kariya, Aichi
Toyoda Gosei Co Ltd. (40.32)	rubber products	1949	26,412	6,300	Nishi-kasugaigun, Aichi
Toyoda Boshoku Corp. (8.98)	cotton auto parts	1950	4,558	1,300	Kariya, Aichi
Towa Real Estate Co Ltd.(49.00)	real estate	1953	23,750	100	Tokyo
Toyota Central R&D Laboratories Inc. (54.00)	technical research	1960	3,000	900	Aichi-gun, Aichi
Kanto Auto Works Ltd. (47.95)	auto bodies and parts	1946	6,850	5,900	Yokosuka City, Kanagawa
Hino Motors Ltd. (10.25)+ (1966)**	trucks and buses	1942	26,412	9,300	Hino City, Tokyo
Daihatsu Motor Co Ltd. (14.13)+ (1967)**	automobiles	1907	28,401	11,300	Ikeda City, Osaka

Table 10.2   Toyota's Principal Subsidiaries and Affiliates in Japan, 1999 (continued)

(2) Suppliers' Organization (*kyoryoku kai*)			
Association	*Date of Establishment*	*No of Companies*	*Description*
Kyohokai	1943	265	Manufacturers of auto parts and components
Eihokai	1983	101	Manufacturers of molds, gauges, jigs etc. and contractors for plant facilities

Note: Dates within brackets for Hino Motors and Daihatsu Motor Co. Ltd are for the establishment of business partnerships with TMC. All others are for company establishment.
(#) figures in parentheses indicates Toyota's equity participation
+ indicates business tie-up with Toyota
** date of tie-up

Source: Toyota Motor Corporation (1999c)

Tokyo), and Daihatsu (located in Osaka and Kyoto). As well as making their own trucks, these firms undertake commissioned production of certain small trucks and passenger vehicles for Toyota (Shiomi 1994).[6]

Secondly, following the need to upgrade the competitive capacity of its weaker supply base in the 1950s Toyota moved quickly to organize its group firms and independent suppliers into a assembler-supplier co-operative group, the *Kyoryoku Kai* (Table 10.2). Initially this type of arrangement was forced upon TMC by war-time government supply purchasing rules that mandated close connections with suppliers. But later on this Toyota association was used to create a totally different style of assembler-supplier relations from any seen before. For instance, Toyota used its supplier associations to teach its subcontractors JIT and arrange diffusion of new management techniques. In turn, Toyota often acquired new ideas from the more innovative suppliers which could then be implemented elsewhere in the subcontracting network (Ohmori 1999).[7]

Thirdly, to respond to the surge in demand in the 1950s, Toyota began to organize its suppliers into functional tiers, no matter what its financial relationship to the supplier. TMC retained control directly only over the larger first-tier firms of this network, relying on first-tier companies to control second-tier units and so on down the hierarchy of suppliers. Different responsibilities were then assigned to firms in each tier. As noted earlier, first-tier suppliers became responsible for working with new product. At the beginning of each four-year model cycle, Toyota directed them to develop, for example, a steering, braking, or electrical system compatible with other auto systems. Suppliers in the group therefore had to maintain close association with TMC and other firms at the design stage as well as the assembly and delivery stage, and were also involved in joint training and identification of development needs, precisely because of this organizational innovation (Fruin and Nishiguchi 1993).

Fourthly, critical to the success of this strategy was the combination of individual parts and their redesign into "sub-assemblies" during the 1960s. This had the advantage of reducing the number of items TMC itself had to purchase, leaving it to concentrate on helping existing suppliers improve (Smitka 1991). The first-tier suppliers in turn, reorganized lower-tiers of suppliers in the same manner. By the late-1960s, about half of the Toyota design and engineering of a new car was undertaken by its suppliers. It is important to note that Toyota did not control the whole supply system itself, even though it provided functional leadership and strategic direction. However, such an approach required TMC to invest in and manage institutional relationships with its suppliers. Consequently, Toyota often acted as banker for its suppliers groups, providing loans to finance the machinery required for new products. But because the suppliers of TMC retained considerable autonomy over their operations Aoki (1988) calls this an example of "quasi-integration", meaning that relations with suppliers were much more specific and enduring than in the case of spot contracting, although not as integrated as in American auto firms.

In sum, the Toyota spatial model has relied upon a mixture of proximity and organizational network dimensions in a more complex manner than is often realized. Its precise configurations are by no means universal in Japan and in some ways it is quite exceptional (Mair 1992). Certainly, concentration gave it four major advantages over its domestic rivals: a highly efficient logistics; quick, effective shifts of manpower and materials between factories in response to production swings; easy communication between the manufacturing and research and development departments (which made for the more efficient development of new models); and the absence of any need to maintain employee welfare facilities around the country, thus duplicating effort and capital expense (Fujita and Hill 1993).

The Limits to Lean

If proximity and dense networks around Toyota City comprised one of the keys to TMC's post-war manufacturing efficiency, by the end of the 1980s spatial concentration and Japan's over-heated "bubble economy" were leading to certain limits on "lean" production and the JIT system. To begin with, over-concentration led to traffic congestion on Nagoya and Aichi's crowded roads, as well as to a shortage of drivers. As a result, the *kanban* system had reached the extent where parts could no longer be supplied within the normal 15 to 20 minutes turnaround time (Cusumano 1994). In early 1990s, Toyota began to re-evalutate its logistics, and to cope with traffic congestion and accidents opened a buffer time zone, allowing suppliers' trucks to arrive as much as an hour earlier or later than scheduled (Nakajima 1991). TMC also began using the JR train service to deliver certain car parts because of the timing problems caused by traffic jams. In the years following, Toyota's JIT system also became vulnerable to a range of hazards and disruptions including earthquakes, labor disputes and a major fire at its largest parts supplier (Hsu 1999).

A more critical concern, however, was the impending shortage of young blue-collar workers who could be either found in, or attracted to, Aichi prefecture to work in TMC assembly factories. This phenomenon was linked not only to the rapid expansion of demand in the domestic car market, and therefore local production, but also to structural changes within the labor market. Thus, since the end of the 1980s the "bulge" of 18 year olds in Japan had peaked and the country began a trajectory towards a rapidly aging population (Seike 1997). Yet another constraint on local expansion was the poor image of factory work. In part, this was also a national problem as job expansion in the service sector led young workers to increasing reject what they perceived as the "three Ks" of factory work: *kitsui* (dangerous), *kitanai* (dirty), and *kiken* (dangerous). In part also, Toyota itself had a poor image problem and began to experience trouble attracting employees for the gruelling *kamban* regimen.[8] Price (1995) argues that constant rationalization at Toyota, including expanding job tasks, routinization of standard work movements, and long working hours, took its toll. This was expressed in the extremely high turnover of labor in the late 1980s and early 1990s, peaking at around 29 percent in 1990 (Hulme 1994). Moreover, the all-embracing conformity and conservativeness of Toyota City no longer appealed to younger Japanese recruits, most of which in recent times had to be attracted from locations far away throughout Japan. Despite the company's stellar profits and stability, young people tended to prefer the expanding office work and service jobs in the bright lights of major cities such as Tokyo and Osaka. Consequently, Toyota's challenge was therefore how to enhance the image of the company and make the workplace more appealing, in effect how to resurrect the factory as a positive career choice.

For Toyota, which has chose to avoid large-scale automation in favor of developing and maintaining a highly skilled factory workforce, these problems immediately became acute at the beginning of the 1990s. For instance, Toyota took over 1,600 new senior high-school graduates in 1992, but failed to meet its original recruitment target by some 11 percent for the first time since the end of the post-war era of rapid economic growth. Moreover, 23 percent of new recruits taken on in the spring of 1991 had resigned by the end of the same year. In short, it had become very difficult to retain young workers at such high production levels. In the over-heated "bubble economy" of the late-1980s Toyota City was a "jam-packed boom town" with an acute labour shortage, making major expansion impractical (Tomozawa 1992). For the future, Toyota projected that it would need 8,000 workers through to 1995 to replace retirees and accommodate growth, but it realistically anticipated hiring only half that number. Moreover, the working week was set to be reduced from 45 hours to 40 hours by 1993. Its parts suppliers, especially second- and third-tier companies had even more difficulty recruiting and relied more and more on illegal foreign workers in Japan. Toyota itself was adverse to hiring immigrant labor, say second- or third-generation Japanese from Brazil with bona-fide working visas, because of language difficulties and concerns over production quality (interview with T. Takahashi, Senior Executive, Toyota Motor Company, Toyota City, July, 1999).

Faced with these new challenges Toyota was forced to consider a radical change. In 1990 it announced extraordinary plans for developing a new vehicle assembly plant and two auto parts manufacturing outside of Aichi prefecture to supply the domestic market. These were to be built at industrial parks in the rural prefectures of Fukuoka (Kyushu), Hokkaido and Miyagi (Tohoku), located in southern and northern Japan, respectively. Details of the new factories are shown in Table 10.1, which indicates that that the Kyushu plant at Miyata-cho comprised the very largest plant of all, over one square kilometer of land that would be exceedingly hard to find at industrial estates close to Toyota City. While the Toyota group already had separate car assembly firms which produced outside of Aichi (the Kanto Auto Works and Hino plants based in Tokyo, and the Daihatsu plants based in Osaka, see Table 10.2), the newly announced projects represented the first of the company's own domestic factories to be located outside of Toyota's "corporate fortress" (*kigyo joka machi*), Aichi prefecture. However, there was an acute perception among top executives that lean production in-situ at Toyota City had "reached the limits" "We had no space to expand" (comment from TMC executive T. Takahashi, *op.cit.*).

A dispersal strategy to seek cheaper land and labor, of course, raised intriguing ramifications for production operations outside Aichi prefecture. By going into Japan's periphery would Toyota lose its legendary productivity, low cost production and competitive edge? The new plant certainly posed questions on just how the greater geographical distances in the JIT supply line might be managed. Moreover, could Toyota fit into a new local environment? Could it find and motivate employees that matched the levels of company loyalty cultivated over so many years in Aichi?

Outside the Fortress: Toyota in Northern Kyushu

In this section I examine these issues through a look at Toyota's Kyushu assembly plant built in 1992 at Miyata-cho, a small township set in an attractive rural area 30 kilometers from Fukuoka City.[9] The entire district was previously dependent upon coal mining. In fact, the new plant's 106 ha site was previously reclaimed for industry from coal waste when the local mine was closed in the 1960s. Construction was completed at a cost of 150 billion yen (about $US 1.5 billion). The plant produces four upper-mid range models of saloon cars, the Mark II, the Chaser, Windom and the Harrier. These are distributed through the domestic market, although some Windom and Harrier models end up as Lexus models for the North American market. Despite its potential for manufacturing 800 cars a year (around 200,000 a year) in 1998 the Kyushu plant was running at just over three-quarters capacity, or 680 cars a day, because of slumping demand for vehicles in the wake of the bubble economy collapse. Toyota runs two shifts per day at Miyata with about 340 factory workers per shift. I will focus on two aspects of Toyota's Kyushu plant, the logistics of JIT delivery of parts and components as well as improvements in the workers' environment, because here experimentation has been significantly original for TMC.

In principle, the traditional "lean" production methods of Toyota City apply also to cars made at Toyota Motor Kyushu (TMK), which are scheduled precisely on a monthly basis by orders from Toyota's nation-wide sales offices so as to reduce inventory. The plant's Production Control Division uses a similar computer system as TMC to integrate customer orders into the production schedule in the same sequence that it receives them. The same computer system also coordinates the TMK production line extremely efficiently with delivery of parts supplies. This is done along the JIT model that always assures that the right part reaches the assembly line at the right time. In practice, however, TMK has adopted an extended or "almost just-in-time" method in order to adapt to the local situation and to reflect the longer supply lines for certain parts delivered from Aichi. In fact, the TMC headquarters' solution to assembly in Kyushu has involved an innovative mix of nearby suppliers, in-house production and reliance on more sophisticated parts from "home" factories and suppliers in Aichi. Truck delivery from Aichi, 700 kilometers away, was certainly not feasible for all parts because of the transport cost alone. Consequently, the necessary know-how and lessons concerning long-distance supplier logistics had to be learned from Toyota's subsidiaries outside Japan in the USA - specifically New United Motor Manufacturing Inc (NUUMI) in California, and Toyota Motor Manufacturing USA Inc (TMM) in Kentucky. This involved how to transport parts by ship to distant ports and then on to "remote warehouses" prior to factory delivery, logistics that TMC never had to deal with at its Toyota City complex. Many consider this to be an indeed a supreme irony, especially considering the controversy involved in introducing Toyota's JIT system overseas (see Kenney and Florida 1993; Mair 1994). To begin with TMK followed Toyota's American practice of setting up a "parts distribution hub" at Hakata Port in Fukuoka, which in 1998 received about 40 percent of the 2,500 different car parts required by TMK by ship from Aichi, mainly sub-assembled auto components produced by Toyota suppliers. All engines, however, came from Toyota's main Kamigo, Shimoyama and Tahara plants, while transmissions originated from the Tsutumi and Kinuura plants (Table 10.1). Parts are ordered from these and other sources a week ahead of time instead of a few days. They are then delivered by boat four times during a week and arrive by a special Toyota boat at Hakata dock where they stay in the dockside warehouse one to two days until needed at the factory. The boats do not return empty but are used to carry cars back to the major distribution ports in Honshu island and elsewhere. Toyota trucks and trailers thereupon deliver engines and other parts to the factory entrance, and robots take the engines on pods and place them in the production line in correct sequence for the day's production. The JIT system operates so that the plant itself has three hours supply of engines, for instance, for any type of car within the factory.

A further 40 percent or so of parts are made by around 45 suppliers who are located in Kyushu, or in nearby Yamaguchi Prefecture, Honshu Island. Table 10.3 shows that only two of these are local firms; the overwhelming majority comprise Toyota first- or second-tier suppliers who were attracted to Kyushu (mainly Fukuoka and Saga prefectures) to supply directly to TMK, especially for lower value-to-weight or value-to-bulk components such as seats, car mufflers, heating and cooling equipment and auto trim parts. Because full production at Toyota's three new Japanese plants amount to about 10 percent of Toyota's domestic production, the company's primary suppliers felt obliged to follow Toyota outside of Aichi prefecture. TMK has never put any restrictions on parts suppliers' locations in Kyushu, however, other than to demand deliveries every hour, on time and in the right sequence and strictly by the quantities that are ordered. A special contingency of two hour's stock of any part on the factory premises allows suppliers to be late twice in a row with no disruption to supply. Most Toyota suppliers in Kyushu appear to have avoided sites close to Miyata-cho to avoid competing for local workers. Despite the greater distances than would be typical in eastern Aichi, Kyushu's lower urban density and its recently constructed inter-prefectural highway system facilitate the supply of parts on schedule in the traditional just-in-time manner. Thus, many suppliers' plants are located up to 100 kilometers from TMK in adjoining Saga, Kumamoto, Miyazaki and Kagoshima prefectures (up to two hours drive via the Kyushu Expressway), and some chose locations allowing relations with other vehicle manufacturers in Kyushu.[10] A final 20 percent of components are made on site, much more than in Toyota's other assembly plants. This includes the radiators and many plastic components such as the bumper.

Apart from introducing a hybrid JIT system, TMK has also been affected by spatial distance from Aichi and Toyota City in a more consequential way. Assistant Manager Tsutomu Nagata put it this way: "Because TMK could distance itself – both physically and psychologically from TMC, then many innovations could be tried out" (interview, December 1998, TMK, Miyata-cho). Certainly, the construction of the new plant allowed the introduction of dramatic improvements in working conditions when compared to Toyota plants constructed a generation or more earlier. Here, Toyota executives responsible for planning the Kyushu operation were convinced more had to be done to attract and retain young workers, and so learned from Volkswagen's Hanover plant in Germany where Toyota has co-produced light trucks since 1989. From the European experience they introduced a new concept of "more human, easy-to-work production line". Developments include the segmentation of traditional long-line structures into smaller mini-lines, which are typical of Dutch and Swedish socio-technical design at say Volvo's Uddevalla plant (Sandberg 1995).

The Kyushu plant at Miyata is indeed different. First, there has been close attention to environment and décor. Besides the rural setting and extensive landscaping of the factory, the inside has been painted in bright colors designed to soothe the eyes and the background sound muffled by gentle music. This compares rather well with the more stark interiors of traditional Toyota factories dominated by noisy air conditioning, machinery and bright lights. Indeed, noise is controlled in large part by substituting the traditional overhead chain system for transporting vehicle units with a moving platform system. Second, the continuous assembly line has been broken into eleven multiple short line segments, each corresponding to a major module or subsystem of the vehicle and separated by a small buffer of work-in-process inventory (with a capacity equivalent to five minutes of production time). The aim here is to group together a set of tasks related to one "whole job" or "product" and to train workers in teams of 20-25 to do all the tasks and to understand the underlying product design and manufacturing process for that particular line.

The Miyata plant tries to make factory work easier in other ways than merely dividing up the production line. A third innovation has been to use industrial robots to assist rather than replace the workforce and as much as possible avoid making assembly workers bend or twist in unnatural ways. An example is the in-line mechanical equipment that has replaced conventional belt conveyors with newly developed "friction moving floors", complete with miniature lifts. These wide "moving floors" are really just large moving platforms along which the car body, assembly worker and parts boxes run together. Workers can ride on these moving floors as they go about their jobs, so they operate as if they were standing still. The advantage is the relief of stress that comes from not having to "chase after the line". In addition to being psychologically relaxing it is also physically relaxing because the floor moves cars up and down depending upon the workers' posture and height, eliminating the physical stress that comes from having to work stooping over. Yet another innovative attempt to reduce workload is the "easy (*raku-raku*) seat" that is used in the interior assembly process. Inserting the interior means working within the narrow confines of the car body, with all the twisting and squeezing that such work entails. The *raku raku* seat is a semicircular arm with a chair attached to the end of it; the workers need merely to straddle it to be placed "easily" inside the car where they can work sitting down.

Fourth, the Miyata plant is operated as a Toyota subsidiary. Doing so allows TMC, the parent company, to introduce working conditions and a wage system that are different from those painstakingly worked out with labor unions at plants run directly by the parent firm in Toyota City. Innovatory labor-management relations in Kyushu have so far focused on efforts to hold down overtime, by running two back-to-back shifts, and plans to eventually abolish night shifts. Moreover, TMK has made continuous efforts to reduce workloads under the so-called TVAL (Toyota

Verification of Assembly Line) process, an index developed by Toyota for the Miyata plant to provide an objective measure of physical workloads in different assembly plant operations. This allows more flexibility in allocating older workers and female workers to jobs. It used to be that no one past 40 years was allowed to work on the assembly line, purely because of the demanding regime associated with *kanban* production. Now Toyota is finding ways to employ older workers and women. Indeed, the initial expectation was that a large proportion of assembly line workers at the new plant would be over 40 years and also women. In 1998, there were just 50 female workers in the factory, or roughly 3 percent out of a 1,600 strong workforce. This was set to be lifted, however, to around 5 percent, which can be compared more favorably to the estimated 0.4 percent female workforce in Toyota's major Aichi assembly plants the same year, none of whom were engaged in direct production.

Overall, therefore, there is the illusion at least that TMK's factory is a relatively pleasant place to work. And while no survey of workers' perceptions and opinions has yet been conducted, management is pleased by its high productivity and also by its ability to attract and retain young workers. Worker turnover rates reportedly approach those of the early 1980s (interview with Nagata, *op.cit.*). Indeed, many aspects of the "Kyushu experiment" have been introduced in the new Hokkaido and Tohoku plants, as well as transplanted back into Toyota City plants as opportunities for upgrading and retrofitting arise. For instance, the "automation assist" principles of using robots to assist rather than replace workers jobs have been used in the RAV4 sport utility line at the Motomachi plant, and at a fourth line in the Tahara plant. Of course, it is more troublesome to install all aspects of the new assembly line configuration in the old factories because they lack sufficient space (*The Economist* 1995; Fujimoto 1999). For their contributions to production engineering and technology in the design and construction of the Miyata assembly line, Toyota Motor and Toyota Motor Kyushu were awarded the Okochi Memorial Production Prize in March 1994 (Katayama 1996). Innovations at the "human-oriented" Miyata factory are of significance therefore far beyond Kyushu. Certain commentators predict that it may provide a blueprint for "post-lean" production lines of the future in all of Toyota's manufacturing plants. Certainly, aspects of the approach have been introduced into plants in Kentucky, USA, as well as Melbourne, Australia (Shimizu 1995; Fujimoto 1999).

Table 10.3 Major TMK Suppliers in the Kyushu-Yamaguchi Region

Company	Product	Location
Asahi Glass	Glass	(1) Kita-kyushu, Fukuoka Prefecture (2) Akike, Fukuoka Prefecture
Denso	Air conditioners	Kita-kyushu, Fukuoka Prefecture
Bridgestone	Tires	Kurume, Fukuoka Prefecture
Eitech	Soundproofing, anti-rust materials	Yamada, Fukuoka Prefecture
Asahi Koko*	Rubber molds	Yamada, Fukuoka Prefecture
Takehiro	Trim	Yame, Fukuoka Prefecture
Nihon Tokuhin Toryo	Soundproofing materials	Ikuhashi, Fukuoka Prefecture
Masekku	Interiors	Ogoori, Fukuoka Prefecture
Tsuchiya	Paint	Okagaki, Fukuoka Prefecture
Topii	Tires, wheels	Okagaki, Fukuoka Prefecture
Gowa	Paint	Inatsuki, Fukuoka Prefecture
Toyowa	Rear tray	Kaho, Fukuoka Prefecture
Sanou	Parts for piping	Eita, Fukuoka Prefecture
Inoac	Urethane	Hirokawa, Fukuoka Prefecture
Nihon Sekio	Bearings	Hirokawa, Fukuoka Prefecture
Kyushu Wheel	Wheels	Kanda, Fukuoka Prefecture
Hitachi Kinzoku	Cylinder block	Kanda, Fukuoka Preecture
Saga Tekko*	Bolts	Saga City, Saga Prefecture
Bridgestone	Seat cushions	Tosu, Saga Prefecture
Takata	Air Bag	Tosu, Saga Prefecture
Futuba	Muffler	Takeo, Saga Prefecture
Toyota Gyosei	Steering wheel	Takeo, Saga Prefecture
Arako	Door trim, seats	Kanzaki, Saga Prefecture
Hagatere	Carpets	Shiota, Saga Prefecture
Nagasaki Buhin	Wire harness	Higashionogi, Saga Prefecture
Kumamoto Buhin	Wire harness	Hondo, Saga Prefecture
Inoac	Chemicals Packing materials	(1) Kikuchi, Kumamoto Prefecture (2) Nagasu, Kumamoto Prefecture
Kyushu Judenso	Wire harness	Kikuchi, Kumamoto Prefecture
Aishin	Power seat, door locks	Jounan, Kumamoto Prefecture
Kumamoto Koki	Connectors	Nankan, Kumamoto Prefecture
Sanao Industrial Kyushu	Parts for power steering	Shichijo, Kumamoto Prefecture
Chokatan	Hub of accelarator	Otsu, Kumamoto Prefecture
JT Nifuko	Zippers	Goshi, Kumamoto Prefecture
Aoyama Seisakusho	Bolts	Takamori, Kumamoto Prefecture
Ichiko	Lamps	Nakatsu, Oita Prefecture
Judenso	Wire harness	Hita, Oita Prefecture
Kyoho	Auto machinery	Miyazaki City, Miyazaki Prefecture
Kito	Welding machinery	Saito, Miyazaki Prefecture

Table 10.3   Major TMK Suppliers in the Kyushu-Yamaguchi Region (continued)

Company	Product	Location
Asumo	Motors	Kunitomi, Miyazaki Prefecture
Miyazaki Buhin	Wiring	Kadogaira, Miyazaki Prefecture
Taiho	Metals	Izumi, Kagoshima Prefecture
Toyota Shatai	Research and development	Kokubu, Kagoshima Prefecture
Nihon Tokuhu	Spark plugs	Miyanojo, Kagoshima Prefecture
Nishikowa Gomu	Door seals	Shimonoseki, Yamaguchi Prefecture
Bridgestone	Tires	Hoku, Yamaguchi Prefecture

* indicates a local independent firm

Source: compiled from Kyushu Economic Research Center (1998)

Conclusion

This case study of Toyota's production system in Japan shows that geography and proximity certainly played an important part in the success story of the Toyota lean production system. Indeed, Toyota City should be seen as extreme case of a production site located amidst a heavy clustering of supplier plants dotted around the TMC assembly facilities. From the very beginning, eastern Aichi provided a docile workforce together with willing suppliers and a conducive local government. Over the following 50 years or so, geographical clustering allowed Toyota to capitalize on agglomeration economies, minimize its JIT transaction costs, and interact frequently with suppliers in design, development and production, as well as in sharing information and knowledge.

However, organizational proximity, characterized by quasi-integration arrangements between TMC and its major suppliers, the nurturing of the *kyoryoku kai*, the structuring of suppliers into a well-ordered hierarchy, were also important prerequisites for successful JIT and the nurturing of an industrial innovation system. In addition, external factors, such as the role of local governments in supporting industrial development more generally in Aichi were material factors (see Edgington 1999). So, while lean production and JIT gave TMC an edge over both Nissan and US competitors in the 1980s, geography was not the sole determining factor. The successful management of organizational space also proved important, and proximity was just one factor in how that was arranged. Geographical proximity, while it certainly played a role in nurturing those interactions within the Toyota group was, therefore, a necessary but not a sufficient precondition for the accomplishments of TMC and its lean production system.

This chapter also focused on the long-term viability of the Toyota JIT production complex. The spatial integrity of the JIT system in Aichi was indeed challenged by new pressures at the end of the 1980s, pressures which tested the "spatial proximity is everything" hypothesis. Higher levels of traffic congestion, labor shortages and worker discontent appeared to establish the "limits to lean", at least in the TMC context within Aichi. Because of its exceptional size and dominance in the region's labor markets, Toyota was forced to adopt what at the time was considered a rather extreme response to rising wage costs, shortages of labor, urban congestion costs, and also a dearth of suitably priced land for expansion. These factors led Toyota to modify key elements of lean techniques by relaxing JIT procedures in a rural environment far from Aichi, and re-arranging production within the assembly factory. Nonetheless, the ability of Toyota to move beyond Aichi and establish a successful car plant in far-away Kyushu demonstrated that the JIT system could be "stretched" without loss of productivity. If "geography is everything" then Toyota could not have sustained its high levels of productivity outside of Toyota City and Aichi prefecture. However, a certain institutional learning proved necessary at TMK, including understanding how to manage inter-firm relations with local and Aichi-based suppliers. Institutional proximity to Toyota's first-tier suppliers was critical, and so successfully used that strict geographical proximity became dispensable.

But distance itself provided a surprising bonus. The new Miyata plant in Kyushu gave Toyota engineers the "space" to re-think and re-design the approach to making a car. In fact, so powerful were the labor enhancing innovations as Miyata that many of the features have become installed in previously "lean" factories in Aichi that took little account of worker amenity and comfort. The experience of Toyota at Kyushu became therefore a "laboratory of change". In this respect, "Toyotaism" has proved to be an unexpectedly flexible ideology, one that has moved beyond the more severe interpretation of "lean production" provided by Taichi Ohno. This case study also has wider implications for our assessment of hub and spoke industrial districts and the concept of proximity. While retaining "organizational proximity" with major suppliers, the spokes from the hub firm in Toyota City now extend far beyond the local Aichi economy, south to Kyushu and also north to Hokkaido and Tohoku. This has in turn assisted local development back in Toyota City by facilitating access to ideas and techniques that are new to the region.

Does this mean that TMC will rethink the logic of its own industrial district centered on Toyota City? Will Toyota continue to move out of Aichi? Two features of Toyota's contemporary corporate strategy are relevant here. Firstly, despite the Miyata experience TMC has continued to commit to the JIT system. Even as the severe labor shortages of 1990 receded, Toyota's new challenge was to remain competitive in the slower growth domestic markets of the post-bubble era. Accordingly, TMC drastically reduced its annual production costs and reduced the time to develop new models in half. In achieving this goal Toyota managers reported that long-term relations with regional suppliers were vital to improving the company's situation and profitability, especially through identifying ways to produce cars and trucks even more efficiently (interview with Takahashi, *op.cit.*). One way was to work with a much wider array of second-tier and even third-tier parts suppliers to implement JIT production techniques. Formerly, the JIT system was not taught directly to lower-ranking suppliers (Yamamoto 1995; Toyota Motor Company 1993, 1994, 1995; Fujimoto and Takeishi 1997). Moreover, Nishiguchi and Beaudet (1998) document TMC's continued commitment to JIT production even in light of disruption caused by the Kobe earthquake and a devastating fire at a major supplier.

Secondly, Toyota has renewed its commitment to the industrial cluster in Aichi by expanding its own local research capability. It is currently concentrating on producing a new generation of "hybrid electric cars" (the Prius) and is conducting research into new commercial navigation systems and equipment for motor vehicles and other "smart car" devices (interview with Takahashi, *op.cit.*). Thirdly, Toyota has increased its non-automobile business from a mere 2 percent in the early 1990s to over 13 percent in 2000. New business ventures include web site retailing, telecommunications and aerospace (Miyata and Russell 1996; Toyota 2000). While not all of these concerns will be located in Aichi, Toyota's initial foray into the aerospace business will in particular support the region's long-range economic development goals (Edgington 1999, 2000).

Clearly, the era of continuous growth in Japanese automobile production is over.[11] Still, the Toyota City industrial district is not "dead" or static, even though TMC has expanded out of Aichi into Kyushu and other peripheral locations - it is still evolving. While facing tangible limits to lean production, the model of long-term collaboration between Toyota and its suppliers, the product of decades of investments in capabilities, together with trust and commitment, are still in place. This case study illustrates that the link between proximity and networks is complex and always set within a mass of different, often contending forces, and the tendency to link networks and proximity in any simple way should not be over-exaggerated. As Storper and Walker (1989) note, capital accumulation has never led to a single universal type of spatial outcome, and there are many examples of changes over time. The outcome of TMC in Japan during the 1990s is such a case.[12]

Acknowledgements

The author wishes to acknowledge the help of various TMC and TMK managers interviewed in 1998 and 1999, and assistance provided by Professor Kenkichi Nagao, Osaka City University, and Mr. T. Niwa, Director, Institute for International Economic Affairs. Cartography for this chapter was drawn by Eric Leinberger.

Notes

1   Literally a "shop sign", a *kanban* card comes in the form of a small piece of paper in a square vinyl holder. It indicates the type and quality of parts needed and the production process using them, and is attached to the container holding the parts. When the parts are assembled, the workers at the process returns the kanban to the proceeding process then produce and supply the amount of parts written on the just returned kanban. For the production-ordering *kanban* card to a subcontractor, delivery times, the store shelf to deliver, and the gate to receive, for example, are also specified. In this way, the parts are produced or delivered just-in-time to eliminate or minimize inventories. The system has been characterized as a "pull" system because parts are pulled from parts fabrication into assembly just when they are needed in accordance with the latter's production schedule. By contrast, in the traditional "push" system, parts are produced according to a separate schedule and pushed into inventories regardless of subsequent processing needs. More specialized references to the Toyota production system include Monden (1983), Cusumano (1985, 1988), Ohno (1988a,b), Fruin (1992) and Fujimoto (1999).

2   Beyond any consideration of spatial outcomes the very basis of Toyota's lean production approach has not been uncontested. Thus critics of lean production argue that Japanese manufacturing methods have been essentially negative and stressful upon plant employees due to greater work intensification and exploitation of the workforce than in previous manufacturing regimes (see for example, Williams et al. 1992; Harrison 1994; Leslie and Butz 1998; Danford 1999).

3   Kenney and Florida (1993) and Mair (1994) have identified a "transplant corridor" in the USA that contains most of the auto assembly plants set up by Japanese companies during the 1980s. While this has indeed attracted a components industry, close to 40 percent of suppliers have located over 400 kilometers away from the particular Japanese assembly plant supplied. Morris (1992) and Sadler (1994) note there is little evidence of the relocation of existing component plants in response to pressures for just-in-time production in Europe. Such a discrepancy can be found in the different approach taken by Japanese auto supply companies and their role in local automobile production chains. Elger and Smith (1994) argue that outside Japan just-in-time systems have encouraged agglomeration only in a limited number of

situations, and throughout Europe Japanese companies have modified their logistical arrangements through sophisticated freight handling companies in order to adapt to extensive geographical linkages.

4   Fruin (1992) makes the observation that history of the Toyota Motor Company began as another Toyota story finished. Thus, in 1930, Sakichi Toyoda, on his deathbed at the age of 63, confided to his son Kiichiro "The automatic loom business was my life's work. I had nothing but ideas and my two hands when I first started out. You should have your own life's work. I believe in the automobile. It will be indispensible in the future. Why not make it your life's work?" (cited in Fruin 1992, p. 260).

5   Ohmori (1999) notes that the R&D units of Toyota are only open to the assembler and the first-tier and selected second-tier members. Lower down the supply network hierarchy, small firms must fend for themselves and frequently make use of local and regional public sector technical support institutions, as do independent firms. This finding underlines Florida's (1995) argument that the significance of proximity may be less in terms of inter-firm relations than the way in which local cultures and networks of promotion and support influence business organizations. Hence the importance of "institutional proximity" and the "learning region" concept, with its public-private interface (Florida 1995; Amin and Thrift 1995). In the industrial region of Chukyo, where Toyota City is located, the availability of local public sector institutional support (mainly in the form of both financial, technical, marketing, infrastructure and business services) has meant that proximity has became a significant advantage to certain firms. This regional advantage clearly goes beyond the strictly private forms of networks and business cooperation that would otherwise have existed (Edgington 1999).

6   TMC also has minority shares in a large number of other first-tier suppliers, not normally considered part of the Toyota group of companies. This includes 19 percent of Koito, which makes trim items, upholstery, and plastics, and which is located in Tokyo (Fruin 1992, pp. 289-291).

7   In fact, two supplier organizations help coordinate the relationship between the Toyota parent and its first-tier subcontractors (Table 10.2). *Kyohokai*, founded in 1943, includes about 265 companies that manufacture auto parts and components. *Eihokai*, founded in 1983, brings together around 100 companies that manufacture items such as moulds, gauges, and jigs as well as contractors for plant facilities. Each of these primary suppliers has between two hundred and three hundred second-tier subcontractors, and each of those subcontractors has many smaller third-tier suppliers (see Smitka 1991).

8   See the graphic "factory of despair" image of Toyota presented by journalist Satoshi Kamata in the early 1970s (Kamata 1982).

9   Material in this section was collected at a site visit in December, 1998, and an interview with T. Nagata Assistant Manager, General Affairs Department, Toyota Motor Kyushu Inc., Miyata-cho, Fukuoka. See also commentary on the Toyota Kyushu plant in Miyata by Rafferty (1995); Katayama, (1996); Mishina, (1998); Nohara, (1999); and Fujimoto (1999).

10   Kyushu has also attracted major auto assembly firms such as Nissan, Mazda, Mitsubishi and Honda, and by the 1990s accounted for about 8 percent of automobile-related production in Japan (Oishi 1992). This shift, together with the dispersion of Toyota's operations in Japan has opened up or expanded the ability of Toyota's first- and second-tier suppliers to serve competing enterprises by re-locating to Kyushu. Conversely, certain factories in the Nissan and Mazda groups

who had already located in Kyushu have now begun to supply their products to Toyota Kyushu (Funaki 1990; Tomozawa 1992).

11 Toyota's domestic production of automobiles peaked at 4.2 million vehicles in 1990 and dropped throughout the decade to 3.2 million in 1998. In the same year overseas production increased to 1.5 million vehicles, a fifty percent increase since 1993 (Toyota Motor Corporation 1999a). Labor adjustments to smaller production quantities have been achieved by reducing overtime hours, severe cutting of part-time labor and by natural attrition (Ishida 1997).

12 While there is no more pressure to build further assembly capacity in other parts of Japan, Toyota's JIT complex in Aichi continues to face challenges by the need to expand production chains into new markets in locations such as Asia, Latin America and Eastern Europe. Toyota must look outside Japan for most of its growth in the near future. A key part of its strategy now involves continuing to replace exports from Japan with more competitive offshore production. The further internationalization of production may therefore severe implications for the long-term future of Toyota in Aichi (Humphrey et al. 2000).

References

Allison, G. (1975), *Japanese Urbanism: Industry and Politics in Kariya, 1872-1972*, University of California Press. Berkeley.

Amin, A. and Thrift, N. (1995), "Globalization, Institutional 'Thickness' and the Local Economy", in P. Healy et al. (eds), *Managing Cities: The New Urban Concept*, John Wiley, Chichester, pp. 91-108.

Aoki, M. (1988), *Information, Incentives, and Bargaining in the Japanese Economy*, Cambridge University Press, Cambridge.

Asanuma, B. (1985), "The Organization of Parts Purchases in the Japanese Automotive Industry", *Japanese Economic Studies*, vol.XIII (4), pp. 32-53.

Asanuma, B. (1989), "Manufacturer-Supplier Relationships in Japan and the Concept of Relation-Specific Skill", *Journal of Japanese and International Economies*, vol. 3, pp. 1-30.

Cusumano, M.A. (1985), *The Japanese Automobile Industry*, Harvard East Asian Monographs 122, Harvard University Press, Cambridge, Mass.

Cusumano, M.A. (1988), "Manufacturing Innovation: Lessons from the Japanese Auto Industry", *Sloan Management Review*, Fall, pp. 29-39.

Cusumano, M.A. (1994), "The Limits of 'Lean'", *Sloan Management Review*, vol. 35(4), pp. 27-32.

Danford, A. (1999), *Japanese Management Techniques and British Workers*, Mansell, London.

The Economist (1995), "The Kindergarten that will Change the World", 4 March, pp. 63-64.

Edgington, D.W. (1996), *Planning for Industrial Restructuring in Japan: The Case of the Chukyo Region*, AURN WP#11, Centre for Human Settlements, University of British Columbia, Vancouver.

Edgington, D.W. (1999), "Firms, Governments and Innovation in the Chukyo Region of Japan", *Urban Studies*, vol. 36, pp. 305-339.

Edgington, D.W. (2000), "New Directions in Japanese Urban Planning: A Case Study of Nagoya", in P. Bowles and L.T. Woods (eds) *Japan After the Economic Miracle: In Search of New Directions*, Kluwer Academic, Dordrecht, pp. 145-168.

Elger T. and Smith, C. (1994), *Global Japanization? The Transnational Transformation of the Labour Process*, Routledge, London.

Florida, R. (1995), "Toward the Learning Region", *Futures*, vol. 27, pp. 527-536.

Fruin, W.M. (1992), *The Japanese Enterprise System: Competitive Strategies and Cooperative Structures*, Clarendon Press, Oxford.

Fruin, W.M. and Nishiguchi, T. (1993), "Supplying the Toyota Production System: Intercorporate Organizational Evolution and Supplier Subsystems", in B. Kogut (ed.), *Country Competitiveness: Technology and the Organizing of Work*, Oxford University Press, New York, pp. 225-246.

Fujimoto, T. (1999), *The Evolution of a Manufacturing System at Toyota*, Oxford University Press, New York.

Fujimoto, T. and Takeishi, A. (1997), "Automobile Industry in Japan Commission on Industrial Performance" (ed), *Made in Japan: Revitalizing Japanese Manufacturing for Economic Growth*, The MIT Press, Cambridge, Mass., pp. 71-95.

Fujita, K. and Hill, R.C. (1993), "Toyota City: Industrial Organization and the Local State in Japan", in K. Fujita and R.C. Hill (eds), *Japanese Cities in the World Economy*, Temple University Press, Philadelphia, pp. 175-200.

Funaki, T. (1990), "Toyota Diaspora Seen as Timely", *The Japan Economic Journal*, 27 October, p. 27.

Harrison, B. (1994), *Lean and Mean: The Changing Landscape of Corporate Power and Flexibility*, Basic Books, New York.

Hayter, R. (1997), *The Dynamics of Industrial Location: The Factory, The Firm and the Production System*, John Wiley and Sons, Chichester.

Hill, R.C. (1989), "Comparing Transnational Production Systems: The Case of the Automobile Industry in the United States and Japan", *International Journal of Urban and Regional Research*, vol. 13, pp. 462-480.

Hill, R.C. (1990), "Industrial Restructuring, State Intervention and Uneven Development in the United States and Japan", in J.R. Logan and T. Swanstrom (eds), *Beyond the City Limits: Urban Policy and Economic Restructuring in Comparative Perspective*, Temple University Press, Philadelphia, pp. 60-85.

Hsu, R.C. (1999), "Just-in-time System", in *The MIT Encyclopedia of the Japanese Economy* (second edition), The MIT Press, Cambridge, Mass., pp. 248-250.

Hulme, D. (1994), "Things Keep Going Right", *Asian Business*, vol. 30, no. 12, pp.14-16.

Humphreys, G. (1995), "Japanese Integration and The Geography of Industry in Japan", in R. Le Heron and S.O. Park (eds), *The Asian Pacific Rim and Globalization*, Avebury, Aldershot, pp. 129-150.

Humphreys, G. (1996), "Japanese Industry at Home", *Geography*, vol. 8, pp. 15-22.

Humphrey, J., Lecler, Y. and Salerno, M.S. (eds) (2000), *Global Strategies and Local Realities: The Auto Industry in Emerging Markets*, Macmillan Press, Houndmills.

Ishida, M. (1997), "Japan: Beyond the Model for Lean Production", in T.A. Kochan, R.D. Lansbury and J.P. MacDuffie (eds), *After Lean Production: Evolving Employment Practices in the World Auto Industry*, Cornell Univesity Press, Ithica, pp. 45-60.

Japan Management Association (1989), *Kanban: Just-In-Time at Toyota*, Productivity Press, Cambridge, Mass.

Kamata, S. (1982), *Japan in the Passing Lane*, Pantheon, New York.

Katayama, O. (1996), *Japanese Business in the 21st Century: Strategies for Success*, Athlone, London.

Kenney, M. and Florida, R. (1993), *Beyond Mass Production*, Oxford University Press, New York.

Kirat, T. and Lung, Y. (1997), *Innovation and Proximity: Territories as Loci of Collective Learning Procesess*. Paper presented a the 93rd Annual Meeting of the Association of American Geographers, Fort Worth, Texas (mimeo).

Krugman, P. (1991), *Geography and Trade*, Leaven University Press, Leaven.

Kyushu Economic Research Center (1998), *Directory of Automotive Firms in Kyushu and Yamaguchi* (mimeo) (in Japanese).

Leslie, D. and Butz, D. (1998), "GM Suicide: Flexibility, Space, and the Injured Body", *Economic Geography*, vol. 74, pp. 360-378.

Linge, G.J.R. (1991), "Just-In-Time, More or Less Flexible", *Economic Geography*, vol. 67, pp. 316-332.

Mair, A. (1992), "Just-in-Time Manufacturing and the Spatial Structure of the Automobile Industry: Lessons from Japan", *Tijdschrift Voor Economie and Sociale Geografie*, vol. 83, pp. 82-92.

Mair, A. (1993), "New Growth Poles? Just-in-time Manufacturing and Local Economic Development Strategy", *Regional Studies*, vol. 27, pp. 207-221.

Mair, A. (1994), *Honda's Global Local Corporation*, Macmillian, Houndmills.

Markusen, A. (1996), "Sticky Places in Slippery Space: A Typology of Industrial Districts", *Economic Geography*, vol. 69, pp.157-181.

Mishina, K. (1998), "Making Toyota in America: Evidence From the Kentucky Transplant, 1986-1994", in R. Boyer, E. Charron, U. Jurgens and S. Tolliday (eds), *Between Imitation and Innovation: The Transfer and Hybridization of Productive Models in the International Automobile Industry*, Oxford University Press, Oxford.

Miyakawa, Y. (1991), "The Transformation of the Japanese Motor Vehicle Industry and its Role in the World: Industrial Restructuring and Technical Evolution", in C.M. Law (ed.), *Restructuring the Global Automobile Industry*, Routledge, London, pp. 88-113.

Miyashita, K. and Russell, D. (1996), *Keiretsu: Inside the Hidden Japanese Conglomerates*, McGraw-Hill, New York.

Monden, Y. (1983), *The Toyota Production System*, Atlanta, Institute of Industrial Engineers.

Morris, J. (1992), "Flexible Specialization or the Japanese Model: Reconceptualizing a New Regional Order?", in H. Ernste and V. Meier (eds), *Regional Development and Contemporary Industrial Response: Expanding Flexible Specialization*, Belhaven Press, London, pp .67-80.

Nakajima, A. (1991), "Firms Sharpen Kanban to Hone Competitive Edge", *The Japan Economic Journal*, 6 April, pp. 1,19.

Nishiguchi, T. and Beaudet, A. (1998), "The Toyota Group and the Aisin Fire", *Sloan Management Review*, vol. 40(1), pp. 49-60.

Nohara, H. (1999), "The Historic Reversal of the Division of Labour? The Second Stage of the Toyota Production System", in J-P Durand, P. Stewart and J.J. Castillo (eds), *Teamwork in the Automobile Industry: Radical Change or Passing Fashion?*, MacMillan Press, Houndmills, pp. 37-53.

Ohmori, T. with S. Kojima et al. (1999), "Auto Parts Industry", in Y. Okada (ed), *Japan's Industrial Technology Development: The Role of Cooperative Learning and Institutions*, Springer, Tokyo, pp. 103-132.

Ohno, T. (1988a), *Workplace Management*, Productivity Press, Cambridge, Mass.

Ohno, T. (1988b), *Toyota Production System: Beyond Large-Scale Production*, Productivity Press, Cambridge, Mass., Oishi, N. (1992), "Automakers Escalate Kyushu Buildup", *The Nikkei Weekly*, 23 May, pp. 6.

Porter, M. (2000), "Clusters and the New Economics of Competition", in J.E. Garten (ed.), *World View: Global Strategies for the New Economy*, Harvard Business School Press, Boston, pp. 201-225.

Price, J. (1995), "Lean Production at Suzuki and Toyota: A Historical Perspective", in S. Babson (ed), *Lean Work: Empowerment and Exploitation in the Global Auto Industry*, Wayne State University Press, Detroit, pp. 81-107.

Rafferty, K. (1995), *Inside Japan's Power Houses: The Culture, Mystique and Future of Japan's Greatest Corporations*, Weidenfeld and Nicolson, London.

Rubenstein, J.M. (1992), *The Changing U.S. Auto Industry: A Geographical Analysis*, Routledge, London.

Sadler, D. (1994), "The Geographies of Just-In-Time: Japanese Investment and the Automotive Components Industry in Western Europe", *Economic Geography*, vol. 70, pp. 41-59.

Sanberg, A. (1995), *Enriching Production: Perspectives on Volvo's Uddevalla Plant as an Alternative to Lean Production*, Avebury, Aldershot.

Schonberger, R.J. (1982), *Japanese Manafacturing Techniques: Nine Hidden Lessons in Simplicity*, The Free Press, New York.

Seike, A. (1997), "Aging Workers", in M. Sako and H. Sato (eds), *Japanese Labour and Management in Transition*, Routledge, London, pp. 151-167.

Shimizu, K. (1995), "Humanization of the Production System and Work at Toyota Motor Co and Toyota Motor Kyushu", in A. Sandberg (ed.), *Enriching Production: Perspectives on Volvo's Uddevalla Plant as an Alternative to Lean Production*, Avebury, Aldershot, pp. 383 404.

Shiomi, H. (1994), "The Formation of Assembler Networks in the Automotive Industry: The Case of Toyota Motor Company (1955-80)", in H. Shiomi and K. Wada (eds), *Fordism Transformed: The Development and Production Methods in the Automobile Industry*, Oxford University Press, Oxford, pp. 28-48.

Smitka, M.J. (1991), *Competitive Ties: Subcontracting in the Japanese Automobile Industry*, Columbia University Press, New York.

Storper, M. (1997), *The Regional World: Territorial Development in a Global Economy*, Guilford Press, New York.

Storper, M. and Harrison, B. (1991), "Flexibility, Hierarchy and Regional Development: The Changing Structure of Industrial Production Systems and Their Forms of Governance in the 1990s", *Research Policy*, vol. 20, pp. 407-422.

Storper, M. and Walker, R. (1989), *The Capitalist Imperative: Territory, Technology and Industrial Growth*, Basil Blackwell, Oxford.

Tomozawa, K. (1992), "Recent Technological Innovation in the Japanese Automotive Industry and its Spatial Implications for the Kyushu-Yamaguchi Area in Southwestern Japan", *The Science Reports of the Tohoku University, 7th Series (Geography)*, vol. 42, no. 1, pp. 1-19.

Toyota Motor Corporation (1993), *What We Need to Do (And Why): Toyota 1993 Annual Report*, Toyota City, TMC.

Toyota Motor Corporation (1994), *Toyota Annual Report 1994: How We Saved $1.4 Billion*, Toyota Motor Corporation, Toyota City.

Toyota Motor Corporation (1995), *Toyota Annual Report 1995: You Ain't Seen Nothing' Yet!*, Toyota Motor Corporation, Toyota City.

Toyota Motor Corporation (1999a), *Toyota*, Toyota Motor Corporation, Toyota City.

Toyota Motor Corporation (1999b), *Outline of Toyota* (mimeo).

Toyota Motor Corporation (2000), *Annual Report 2000: Growth, Innovation*, Toyota Motor Corporation, Toyota City.

Williams, K., Haslam, C., Williams, J. and Cutler, T. with Adcroft, A. and Johal, S. (1992), "Against Lean Production", *Economy and Society*, vol. 21, pp. 321-354.

Womack, J.P. Jones, D.T. and Roos, D. (1990), *The Machine that Changed the World*, Ravan Associates, New York.

Womack, J.P. and Jones, D.T. (1995), *The Lean Revolution in North America and Europe: A Progress Report*, IIES Seminar Series No. 9503, Institute for International Economic Studies, Tokyo.

Womack, J.P. and Jones, D.T. (1996) *Lean Thinking: Banish Waste and Create Wealth in Your Corporation*, Simon Schuster, New York.

Yamamoto, T. (1995), "Toyota vs. the Rising Yen", *Tokyo Business Today*, vol. 63(7), pp. 42-44.

11 Local and Global Networks in the Economics of SMEs - Is Proximity the Only Thing that Matters?

MARIO A. MAGGIONI AND ALBERTO BRAMANTI

This chapter aims at showing - both from a theoretical and an empirical perspective - that local identity, which is a social, economic and technological by-product of *proximity*, is one of two opposite but complementary engines which drives the growth and development of spatial systems of production and innovation (SSPIs), the second being the existence of an efficient *network* of global relationships.

This hypothesis constitutes the basis of the so-called "economics of SMEs", sometimes seen as a rather spurious discipline which emerged in the middle 1980s from different theoretical approaches - the Italian School of Industrial Districts, the French School of Regulation, the Californian School of Industrial Geography, The European GREMI research network, to name only a few - as a challenge to the neo-classical orthodoxy with its focus on the profit maximizing individual firms whose relationships with other agents are exclusively structured as market interactions.

The first stage of this composite approach stressed the role of local identity as a comparative advantage which could explain the survival of SMEs in the economic framework of the late 1960s and early 1980s, dominated by economies of scale, a stable rate of technological change and standardized demand, and justify its success in the post-fordism framework of the middle of the 1980s, characterized by technological and demand shocks and the "flexible specialization" organizational paradigm.

As time passed, it became self-evident that SSPIs were gradually changing their whole organizational structure in order to open their boundaries to new markets and suppliers to cope with the globalization and internationalization processes; in the meantime large multinational companies were changing their corporate strategies and organizational model from a monolithic and vertical structure to a flatter and interactive web of divisions, departments and co-operative agreements. The effect on the theoretical side was a spur of interest on the analysis of networks, both within and outside the firm's boundaries.

At the beginning of the 21st century it seems possible now to look at local identity (proximity) and global relationships (networks) as two complementary elements, which are needed in order to ensure a stable path of "sustainable growth" and "endogenous development". These two terms call for further explanations since they seem to mimic and mix two buzzwords of mainstream economics: "endogenous growth" and "sustainable development". On the contrary, with these concepts we refer to the essential patterns of evolution of a SSPI. *Sustainable growth* refers to a given set of production and innovation dynamics and concerns the existence of enabling conditions for the re-production of the local endowment of (human, technological, natural and social) resources which solely grant the realization of positive performance and the persistence of the SSPI in the long run. *Endogenous development* refers to the governance of the SSPI and concerns the capability of local agents (namely firms, entrepreneurs and public decision makers) to control and guide (at least partially) the patterns of qualitative and quantitative expansion of the system, in order to escape from undesired external influences and constraints.

The relevance of the role played by local and global relationships in determining the economic performance of a SSPI is witnessed by its current centrality in the theoretical and empirical literature, and in the policy debate. From a theoretical viewpoint, the analysis of spatial problems (of geography and trade) has recently been re-admitted to the realm of economic theory after long years of exile (Krugman 1991a; 1991b). From an empirical perspective, the analysis of geographical spillovers and inter-industrial linkages is getting much attention from scholars (Glaeser et al. 1992; Jaffe et al. 1993; Feldman 1995). Finally, from a policy-oriented standpoint, the current worldwide globalization process, together with processes of sovra-national integration, has gradually but crucially shifted the focus of economic policies far from the national toward the sovra-national[1] and local levels.

The chapter is organized as follows: after the introduction, the second section discusses the economic principles of agglomeration economies and network externalities; the third looks at the very engine of growth - i.e., innovation - highlighting four building blocks of the innovation process, namely: information, knowledge, competence and creativity. The fourth section deals with collective learning mechanisms while the following presents some sketched empirical evidence on the role of proximity and networks in sustaining innovation and growth of SSPIs. The final section concludes the Chapter by dealing with the notion of governance, as a way to preserve local identity and global openness, and draws some policy suggestions.

Microeconomics Behind Proximity and Network: Agglomeration Economies, Network Externalities and Club Goods

The reference to "the economics of SMEs" in the paper calls for a redefinition of two main concepts, namely proximity and networks. The aim of this section is to show, and briefly discuss, the economic principles that lie under and behind these two terms.

Let us start the analysis from the concept of "proximity". According to Veltz (1993), proximity does not necessarily refer to geographical space; in other words it may well not mean contiguity. Dupuy and Gilly (1993) list several different conceptualizations of proximity:

- *industrial proximity*, which refers to the degree of industrial similarity and complementarity;
- *organizational proximity*, which defines appropriate levels of integration/disintegration of the production process;
- *cultural proximity*, which echoes the Marshallian concept of "industrial atmosphere", but may also refers to a-spatial networks of professionals;
- *temporal proximity*, which deals with the timing of different forms of co-operation.

Proximity - in the new competitive scenario - is a precondition for territory to become an "innovative milieu" (Ratti, Bramanti and Gordon 1997): a production system, a set of actors, a system of representations and an industrial culture which generates a dynamic localized process of collective learning and which acts as an operator for uncertainty reduction in the innovative processes (Camagni 1995).

All these different definitions are able to capture a single aspect of the concept of proximity at the expense of the remaining ones and seem scarcely operational.

Perhaps it is worth going back to some basic economics and analyze a more traditional but definitely more solid notion of agglomeration economies.

Alfred Marshall (1921) defines agglomeration economies as a special case of external economies of scale; however one may also refer to a previous contribution by Alfred Weber (1909) who defines the locational choice of firms as dependent on three main forces: transport costs, labor costs and agglomeration.

In our opinion, Weber's contribution is crucial to the topic at study since the German scholar explicitly takes into account both positive and negative effects arising from other firms' location. In particular Weber assumes agglomeration forces it to be a parabolic (hence non monotonic and concave) function of the number of located firms while deglomeration forces it to be linear.

Such an hypothesis is crucial to the issue at study since it determines the existence of a maximum dimension of a cluster and, consequently, it draws a line between local and global, between proximity and networks.

Agglomeration Economies and Proximity

Referring to the abovementioned Weberian framework and following Maggioni (1999)[2] one can think at agglomeration economies (or benefits) as the difference between the costs and benefits one firm experiences in a given location because of the location of other firms.

More formally, let us assume agglomeration benefits for firm f, located in cluster q, $A_{fq}(n_q)$ to be a concave non-monotonic function of the number of incumbents (i.e., firms already established in cluster q) n_q. The assumption of concavity and non monotonicity in A_q implies that, as the number of firms located in cluster q increases, gross benefits firstly increase because of agglomeration economies (due to productive specialization; scientific, technical and commercial spillovers; reduction in both transport and transaction costs, increases in the quality of the local pool of skilled labor force and in the efficiency of the local credit market); then decrease when congestion more than negates agglomeration economies.

Agglomeration diseconomies a_q, are assumed to be a convex non-monotonic function of the number of regional incumbents n_q. The assumption of convexity and non monotonicity in a_q implies that, as the number of firms in cluster q increases, locational costs initially decrease until some optimal number of users for a given set of urban, industrial and environmental infrastructures and resources is reached. They then increase due to the competition, between larger numbers of firms, for a limited pool of local inputs (i.e., capital, labor, business services, land and public infrastructures), which raises their prices.

Net agglomeration economies $N_{fq}\left(n_q\right)$ can therefore be calculated as the difference between gross agglomeration economies and diseconomies:

$$N_{fq}\left(n_q\right) = A_{fq} - a_{fq} \tag{11.1}$$

It is easy to see that the locational net benefits function is always concave, since N_{fq} is equal to the difference between a concave function $A_{fq}\left(n_q\right)$ and a convex one $a_{fq}\left(n_q\right)$ (see Figure 11.1). In other words, each marginal firm, which enters the cluster, increases the average profitability of locating there only up to a threshold. After that point, any new entrant lowers the average net benefits available to each resident firm and new entrant.

A is the minimal sustainable dimension of the cluster (i.e., where agglomeration net benefits start to be positive. Prior to **A** no firm will spontaneously enter the region (because agglomeration benefits are negative). **A** can be called the critical mass of the region. **A** can be reached only by a group of coordinated firms entering together, or by direct intervention of a public authority aimed at subsidizing entries until $n(t) = \mathbf{A}$.

The recent history of Irish FDIs may be seen as an example of tax incentives, used by public authorities as a policy instrument (together with business services provision) to reach an appropriate critical mass of industrial clusters.

B is the cluster dimension where average agglomeration costs are minimum. **B'** is the dimension that maximizes gross average agglomeration benefits. **B** and **B'** underline the importance of analyzing both costs and benefits of location to avoid harmful misrepresentation of the economic reality, as in some early contributions of location theory. Obviously, it could also be the case that **B' < B**.

C gives the maximum per firm net benefits (i.e., average net benefits). Up to **C** every new entrant increases (by its very entry) the average benefits of all incumbents; after **C** the average benefits decrease. **C** is therefore the optimal size of cluster for incumbent firms; however, it is neither the social efficient outcome (given that marginal benefits are still greater than marginal costs) nor the maximum possible dimension (average benefits are still positive). At **C**, several firms outside the cluster might still want to enter, while firms already in the region would like to deter further entries. Here we have a contrast between incumbents, outsiders and public authorities, each of them with a different view of what is the optimal outcome.

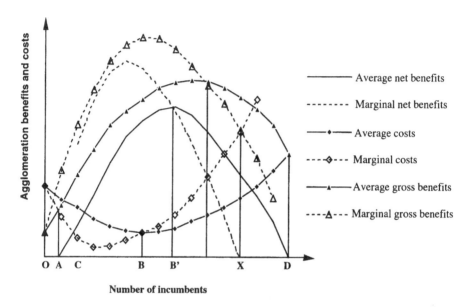

Figure 11.1   Agglomeration Economies, Diseconomies and Critical Sizes of a Cluster

X is the economically efficient (i.e., social optimum) dimension of the cluster. At **X** marginal costs equal marginal benefits, therefore the total benefits (number of firms times *per capita* benefits) are maximized. However, as the average benefits at **X** are still positive, some outsiders would still like to enter. Such entries would reduce the total amount of benefits available to incumbents.

D is the maximum dimension of the cluster (in terms of its economic mass) since average costs equal average gross benefits. From **D** onwards no more net entry is deserved because, after this point, average net benefits are negative and therefore there are no incentives to enter. However, new entries are still possible but these would be at the expense of some incumbents who would be driven out of the cluster. After **D** new entries thus support a turnover process without causing relevant changes to the equilibrium level.

Brianza - the most important wooden furniture industrial cluster in Italy - has already approached, at the end of the 1980s, its **D** point. From that moment, it has witnessed a de-location process, toward other regions in Central Italy and countries in Eastern Europe in order to avoid the raising costs of production factors (mainly, urban rents and wages) and the congestion of infrastructures caused by the high density of SMEs.

One may also define agglomeration economies as a special case of externalities i.e., a situation in which the behavior of one economic agent (in this case the location of a firm) influence the actions and payoff of another agent through a non-market mechanism.

In both ways the analysis of proximity is built on the basis of economic theory and can thus avoid the danger of being solely defined through case histories and success stories, which doomed it to inescapable parochialism or blind localism.

In the meantime the strategic management approach has stressed that the key to competitive advantage lies in the exploitation of core competencies. The connection of core knowledge across different firms creates the web of information and knowledge flows, which yields improvements in quality and timing required by customers, within a global market. In implementing this strategy a SSPI should open its boundaries and build global linkages to gain economies of scale (in the knowledge creation process), economies of scope (in the generation of variety) and economies of complexity (in the organisation of multi-process production).

Thus, strategic management literature widely recognized that knowledge development, especially by SMEs, is strictly linked both to their territorial embeddedness and in the network of technology channels established with universities, large firms, and innovative customers outside the local area.

Network Externalities and Openness

Let us now deal with networks. Mitchell (1969) defines network as "a specific type of relation linking a defined set of persons, objects and events". More specifically network relationships identify selected and explicit linkages with preferential partners in the firm's space of complementary assets and market relationships (Bramanti and Maggioni 1997).

According to Bressand et al. (1989) a network may be defined as: "a set of technical means (or infrastructures) and strategic norms (or infostructures) enabling actors with rights of access to set up and manage value-creating relationships among themselves". Infrastructure refers to information and communication technologies, media and devices while infostructure refers the communication code and language (mutual expectation and/or behavioral norms) (Bramanti and Senn 1993).

Modern microeconomics (and in particular, the industrial economics literature and, more recently, the papers on ICTs and the New Economy) deals with network relationships and structures under the heading of "network externalities". Network externalities are defined as a specific type of consumption externality, which derives from direct or indirect complementarity between the components of a (real or virtual) network, in which "the value of a unit of the good increases with the expected number of unit sold" (Economides 1996). One of the most established results is that network externalities cause allocative inefficiencies and welfare losses (Varian 1999). Perfect competition becomes inefficient since it provides a smaller network than is socially optimal; furthermore, for some relatively high marginal costs, the good may not be provided despite the socially optimality of its production.

However it must be also remembered that a monopolist - unable to price discriminate its customers - will support a smaller network and charge higher prices, in presence of network externalities, than the competitive case.[3]

Public Goods and Club Goods

Another way to look at proximity and network as different types of inter-firms relationships refers to the concept of public goods. Public goods are defined as particular type of goods whose consumption is both non rival and non excludable.

The benefits enjoyed by a SME located within a traditional industrial district in terms of information sharing, labor market pooling, access to specialized intermediate inputs can be easily classified as public goods. It is not by chance that the Marshallian term, "industrial atmosphere", refers to the best example of pure public good: "air".

Referring back to Figure 11.1, the development path of a SSPI, in which exclusion is unfeasible, may thus be divided in three distinct phases. In the first phase $(A < n \le C)$, which follows immediately after the critical mass is reached, the cluster behaves as a pure non-marketable public good.

Each firm produces its output (private good) and indirectly produces a positive externality, which directly benefits every firm located there. At this stage, the level of externality is an increasing (concave) function of the number of local firms. In the second phase $(C < n \leq X)$ the cluster acts as a non-marketable impure public good. The incumbents (i.e., the firms already located in the cluster) would like to restrict any entry, since at C the average agglomeration net benefits are maximized and any further entry reduces them. A simple welfare analysis shows that entry should continue (from a cluster social planner's point of view) until the cluster industrial mass (i.e., the number of located firms) reaches X, where marginal costs equal marginal benefits. However the entry process continues, driven by the existence of positive average benefits and, once X is exceeded, the cluster initiates its third phase $(X < n \leq D)$ becoming a common resource which is inevitably bound towards over-exploitation. Finally the net entry process ends in D when the excessive entry of firms drives the agglomeration benefits to zero.

Networks, despite a certain similarity to public goods, may be classified in a contiguous but distinct typology, namely: club goods, which are defined as goods for which exclusion is feasible and congestion effects arise after a certain threshold of membership is reached. Referring to Figure 11.1 one may describe the evolution of a network, as function of its membership, as follows. In the first phase (from A to C), the cluster behaves as a marketable public good, which thanks to the feasibility of exclusion, is provided by leader firms. After that, the network can be managed as a club in order to control the effects of congestion in a way that allows it to reach the optimal social dimension X. Once this dimension has been reached, the network's leading core acts to keep it stable.

According to this analytical perspective, feasibility of exclusion constitutes the main difference between network and proximity. A different way to describe the same phenomenon refers to the explicit willfulness of relations implied by network *membership* as opposed to the implicit "sense of belonging" which characterize inter-firms relations within an industrial district.

Such an approach is also supported by a different, but complementary, perspective put forward by Parr (2000). In his work he stresses the "very wide ranging nature of the concept of agglomeration economies" and proposes a taxonomy, which is able to describe the existence of different types of agglomeration economies and, to a certain extent, to contribute to the proximity versus network debate.

The Innovative Process: A Dynamic Learning Approach

Innovation is the engine of growth for every economic system and SSPIs are not exceptions. This perspective is consistent with a systemic, dynamic, and self-organizing view of growth, which encompasses the explanation offered by "new growth theory" and by the "evolutionary economics" approach. The innovative process may be understood in terms of the following propositions, jointly considered:

- innovation is the outcome of a network of activities and resources exchanged between the actors involved (Håkansson 1987), rather than the product of an isolated heroic entrepreneurial process (Bianchi and Miller, 1994);
- innovation is a complex and interactive process in which the firm depends on the knowledge, competence and expertise of different agents, such as public authorities and research institutions (Amendola and Gaffard 1988; Maggioni 2001);
- innovation stems from a creative combination of generic know-how and specific competencies (Becattini and Vaccà 1994);
- territorial organisation is an essential component of the process of techno-economic creation (Malecki 1991; Bramanti and Miglierina 1995).

In this perspective innovation refers both the Schumpeterian process of creative destruction and to the recent debate on the role of institutions, social norms, interactions, and governance structures in spreading innovations (Maillat 1995). Furthermore, in a dynamic and evolutionary framework, it is possible to consider space as a crucial factor in the process of innovation creation and diffusion and not as a extra dimension, superimposed to a technologically pre-defined dynamics.

If the firm is considered as a crucial knowledge reservoir, then the relevant information and knowledge - on which innovation is based - become "sticky", i.e., difficult to transfer from place to place, due to the partial tacitness of the firm-specific knowledge, embedded in its operational routines. All the above calls for the coexistence of two different, but highly complementary, circuits: the first, which refers to the internal structure of the firm and of its closest local environment, and the second which concern the set of external relations, dealing with both production and research processes on a wider global scale.

The Four Stages of Innovation Process

In order to understand how territory may become the catalyst of the innovation process, it may be useful to split the innovative process into four logical stages. Information, knowledge, competence and creativity are the four building blocks on which innovation process develops.

- *Information* is the first and most general input of the innovation chain. Information is produced in a diffused way; it is easily exchanged at a relatively low price, and becomes rapidly obsolete because of the production of new information. Moreover, since it cannot be fully appropriated, it generates spillovers and cross-fertilization of different industries and territorial system.
- *Knowledge* implies some specific ability in the receiver of the message, and adequate receptive structures. In general, pure information cannot, be used by the receiver since he/she is not always able to translate it and internalize into his/her own information set. Therefore information is selected to become knowledge, and some selection criteria are territorially based.
- *Competence* adds a further element, namely "know-how". Competence refers to the individual and the collective learning processes and is strongly connected to the very stages of the production process where learning by doing activities takes place.
- *Creativity* emerges from the synergetic meeting of the previous stages - information, knowledge and competence - combined in a specific cultural and territorial context. For this reason it is a non-exchangeable resource.

Figure 11.2, illustrates the innovative circle which links together the four "building blocks" in a dynamic process where positive feed-back and self-enforcing mechanisms play a major role.

Tacit and Explicit Knowledge

At this stage we may introduce a largely accepted definition of knowledge, which refers to two main typologies. Following Polanyi (1962) a distinction is made between "objective" and "tacit" knowledge, the former being abstract, communicable and conveyed by symbols and language; the latter being incommunicable and embedded in practice, people and organization, specific to particular problem-solving activities, and somewhat idiosyncratic.

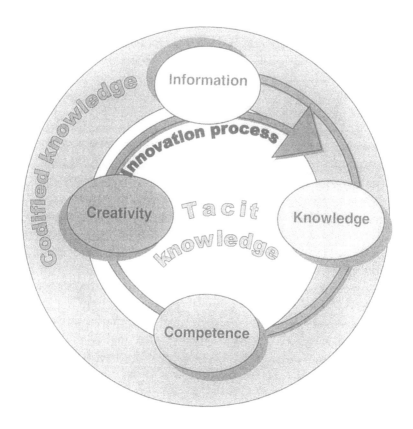

Figure 11.2   Innovation Processes and the Role of Knowledge

Real life organizations contain both types of knowledge and individuals within organizations are able, through social interactions, to create and expand knowledge by performing what Nonaka (1991) calls "knowledge conversion".

The assumption that knowledge is created through the interaction between tacit and explicit knowledge allows the Japanese scholar to postulate four different modes of knowledge conversion:

> (1) from tacit knowledge to tacit knowledge, which we call socialization; (2) form tacit knowledge to explicit knowledge, or externalization; (3) from explicit knowledge to explicit knowledge, or combination; (4) from explicit

knowledge to tacit knowledge, or internalization (Nonaka and Takeuchi, 1998, p. 220).

The interactions between the building blocks of the innovation processes - information, knowledge, competence and creativity - can be better understood with specific reference to tacit and codified knowledge.

The production and exchange of *information* are mainly related to aspatial networks in which codified knowledge is exchanged on a global scale. *Knowledge* and *competence* feed on both circuits (codified and tacit), despite a clear evidence of a major role played by proximity, and face-to-face contacts. *Creativity*, being the more specific and firm based dimension of the innovation process, refers to tacit knowledge and needs both frequent interactions with the other building blocks and a strong territorial contextualization.

An unbalanced emphasis on tacit knowledge produces an inward looking SSPI. The learning ability of economic agents within the SSPI are reduced to learning-by-doing and learning-by-using activities which generates incremental innovation. This may be optimal when stable market and technological conditions prevail; on the contrary, when it is necessary to radically innovate the product (or the production process) in order to cope with a major change in the external conditions, a weak access to codified knowledge reduces the spectrum of technological opportunities. The SSPI may thus experience a decaying process caused by the emerging of spatial competition among different SSPIs, which displays a more efficient set of external connections.

When the SSPI exhibits an unbalanced emphasis on codified knowledge but poor internal relations, learning can only be performed through external channels. The SSPI will not learn through the interaction of each and every individual agent, but rather through a selection process. The turnover rate within the system will be high and the weakest firms will be forced to leave the system and give way to a new generation of externally based subjects which have the distinctive competencies to stand competition. The most likely result is the loss of the local identity and the delocalization of the production process along the line of the lowest input costs.

A good balance of the two dimensions supports and strengthens the innovation process, which can in turn, grant the creation and re-creation of a dynamic competitive advantage for the SSPI and for each and every firm within it.

Internal and External Channels of Collective Learning

In the economic literature, learning dynamics have been modeled in different ways:

- as positive externalities in a production function in the endogenous growth literature framework (Romer 1986; Lucas 1988);
- as an error correction procedure which assure a Bayesian adjustment mechanism of the expected value of a given variable, in the rational expectation literature (Lucas 1972);
- as a diffusion process of a better techniques in the economics of technological change (Grilliches 1957; Mansfield 1968; Karshenas and Stoneman 1995).

We build upon the latter stream of literature in order to analyze two different but complementary types of collective learning. Collective learning is defined as the process through which a SSPI, without the existence of a central mastermind, improves overtime its performance through the comparison of identified targets and accomplished tasks.

Learning, within this theoretical perspective, is conceived as a self-organizing process. A SSPI, therefore, learns through the diffusion of best practices and innovations and through a benchmarking activity performed independently, but not separately, by each and every firm.

When learning is represented as a diffusion process, it implies a complex intertwining of competitive and co-operative relationships, which rely on two different communication channels: the internal and the external channel. Such a twofold structure directly determines the existence of two different diffusion processes: an endogenous and an exogenous one.

The endogenous diffusion process refers to the incremental innovation process which origins from a continuous imitation of best practices within a SSPI. Such a process can be analytically described as an internal influence[4] version of an epidemic diffusion model (Mahajan and Peterson 1985). Formally:

$$\frac{dn_q}{dt} = bn_q(t)\big(K_q - n(t)\big) \tag{11.2}$$

where $n_q(t)$ is the number of firms in cluster q which have already adopted the best practice at time t and K_q is the total number of firms in the cluster.

Equation (2) states that the speed of the diffusion process is proportional to the frequency of contacts (or social interactions) between the firms that have already adopted $n_q(t)$ and those, which have not yet adopted the best practice $K_q - n_q(t)$. b is a behavioral parameter which describes the potential adopters' propensity to imitate.

When $n_q(t)$ is plotted against time, equation (11.2) describes a logistic curve, an S-shaped curve, which is often chosen for modeling diffusion processes for its convenient mathematical features.[5]

The exogenous diffusion process refers to a radical innovation process which is determined outside the SSPI and influences the cluster through the periodical "exposure" of leading firms to a "technological window" Such a process can be analytically described according to an "external influence" version of an epidemic diffusion model (Mahajan and Peterson 1985). Formally:

$$\frac{dn_q}{dt} = a\left(K_q - n_q(t)\right) \tag{11.3}$$

where a is a parameter describing the efficiency of the external information spreading mechanisms. In this case, the time path of the learning dynamics becomes a decaying curve in which, over time, the cumulative number of "innovated" firms increases, but at a constant decreasing rate.[6]

We have looked separately at these different types of collective learning for the sake of exposition. In real life, a SSPI learns thanks to a combination of both channels. The easiest way to model such a situation is through a linear combination of equations (11.2) and (11.3). The resulting model allows both internal and external factors to influence the learning process. Formally:

$$\frac{dn}{dt} = \left(a + bn_q(t)\right)\left(K_q - n_q(t)\right) \tag{11.4}$$

the prevalence of either the external channel of communication or the external one is directly dependent on the governance structure of the SSPI.

Some Empirical Evidence

The aim of this section is to present a collection of empirical analyses - which have been performed by the authors and extensively discussed elsewhere[7] - in order to measure and assess the validity of a number of theoretical hypotheses, stylized facts and logical conjectures on the role played by network and proximity in the structure and evolution of SSPIs.

Because of the multifaceted nature of the issues at study, different empirical exercises have been performed in order to look at the same issues from several empirical perspectives.

The Determinants of High-tech Clusters in Four OECD Countries

If classical location theory (*à la* Weber, Christaller and Von Thünen) can be summarized by the claim "geography matters", in the sense that the exogenous spatial distribution of inputs (and, sometimes, consumers) crucially determines firms' location decisions, more recent approaches (such as the New Economic Geography on the one hand and the Californian School of Industrial Geography on the other) seem to state that "history and expectations", matter most.

Krugman (1991a, 1991b) - referring explicitly to Marshall (1920) - stresses the role of economies of scale (which are internal to the individual firm) as the main centripetal force determining firms' location; while other authors (Storper and Walker 1984; Scott 1986; Arthur 1990; Becattini 1998) - quoting almost the same passages from Marshall (1920) - identify agglomeration economies (which are external to the individual firm) as the key determinants of industrial clustering. The contrast is extended also to the interactions between scale and agglomeration economies. According to Krugman, economies of scale are a pre-condition for the existence of agglomeration economies[8] (thus these two factors coexist and, in general, they are mutually re-enforcing). On the contrary, according to Scott, the very trade-off which exists between agglomeration and scale economies can explain why, in certain industrial sectors and in certain areas, large firms prevail; while in other industries and/or locations, small interdependent firms seem to be the general rule.[9]

Maggioni (1999) presents an econometric model able to take into account (a part from scale and agglomeration economies) three major phenomena which play a crucial role in the development of industrial clusters: the presence of inter-industry linkages, the role of geographical spillovers and the existence of locational shadowing. In particular geographical spillovers are modeled as the effects on the cluster caused by the industrial specialization of a larger area (i.e., a region for a county), while industrial spillovers are modeled as the effects caused by the specialization of the same area in other industries.

The model is tested on an original dataset based on five high-tech industries[10] at the county level for four major OECD countries (United States, United Kingdom, Italy, and France). Each industry-specific regression has been estimated on a sample of some 250 observations.

The results show that, in general, scale economies seem to prevail over agglomeration economies, the exception being the Instruments sector. It is interesting to note that scale economies seem to perform a larger role in Pharmaceuticals (this is consistent with the structure of the industry where larger plants prevail), while agglomeration economies largely contribute to the geographical concentration of the Instrument industry (where customized production and tailor made products are the rule).[11] In absolute terms, scale economies are very relevant also for computers and office machinery, and aerospace. In relative terms, for the electronic components industry, while scale economies effects are not as important as in other high-tech sectors, agglomeration economies play an absolutely insignificant role in determining the industrial specialization of the area.

A further remark concerns the relevance of inter-industry linkages. All regression equations record a positive coefficient for this variable even if this phenomenon appears to be stronger in the electronic components and in the aerospace industries, which are benefiting more from the closeness to other high-tech sectors. One can explain this result in term of strong forward linkages for electronic components (whose products are inputs in several high-tech industries) and of backward linkages for aerospace (which uses, as inputs, several products of other high-tech sectors).

A further test concerns the presence of spatial positive spillovers or the emergence of locational shadowing. For all but one sector, the variable used to measure spatial spillovers displays a positive and significant coefficient signaling that a positive relation exists between the specialization in an industry at the county and at the regional level. However it is worth noting that the negative coefficient for the instruments industry suggests the existence of locational shadowing phenomena.[12]

Finally, inter-industry linkages (or technological externalities) - derived from the co-location of firms belonging to others high-tech industries - record higher coefficients than geographical knowledge spillovers.

One may, at a first glance, assume global network relationships to be associated with larger than average SMEs and agglomeration economies to be the building blocks of proximity-based relations. If this hypothesis is true, then the empirical exercise presented above would suggest that network relationships better fit the specialization patterns of high-tech industries. However the comparison of the coefficients attached to inter-industry linkages and geographical knowledge spillovers clearly shows that tacit knowledge and technological know-how do not travel easily outside the county border. Therefore one may conclude that while the empirical results directly show the relative importance of proximity relationship, they also, indirectly, show that - in order to overcome long distance - a stronger type of relationship is needed. Such a relationship, i.e., a set of selected and explicit linkages with preferential partners, constitutes what may be defined as a "network".

High-growth Firms in Italy

In the last decade there has been a renewed interest in the analysis of SMEs mainly due to the evidence of their job-creation ability not only in Italy, but also on a European scale.

A recent extensive study, carried out by CERTeT on behalf of the OECD,[13] has focused, for the Italian case, on the following three main questions:

1. which type of firm is the best job-creator? (i.e., which is the fastest growing type of firm?)
2. do SMEs grow faster than large firms?
3. what are the explanations for such a rapid growth?

The analysis has been developed on a twofold basis. In the first step we built an original national dataset regarding the total population of Italian SMEs - ranging from 20 up to 500 employees - defined as "permanent" - i.e., founded in 1990 or before and still active in 1995 - operating in manufacturing and business services sector, with at least one employee. The dataset - composed by 29,140 enterprises with some 1.8 million persons employed in 1995 - is illustrated in Table 11.1 according to four size classes, four territorial macro areas (Northwest, Northeast, Center, South and Islands) and two industrial classes (Manufacturing and Business Services).

The second step of the research project concerned a qualitative analysis, performed on a sample of 415 Italian SMEs, which is described in Table 11.2. For the selection of the sample we have proceeded in two phases.

Firstly, six representative Italian regions have been chosen according to a balanced geographical distribution (Lombardy and Piedmont in the North, Marche in the Center, Basilicata, Apulia and Sardinia in the South). Secondly, a number of interviews, proportional to the regional presence of HG firms, has been assigned to each region. The selected 414 growing firms have been finally split in two groups: 117 HG firms - which display a Birch index[14] value larger than four - and the rest of 297 growing firms (with Birch index value less than four).

The main results of the analysis are as follows:

- The 117 high growth firms (HGs) represent the 8 percent of total Italian HG SMEs in manufacturing and business services;
- HGs have a smaller average size in 1990 than average growing firms. Obviously the result is completely overturned at the end of the period, due to the faster growth rate of HG;
- the spectacular employment growth of HG is matched by the global increase of turnover but sales per employee are decreasing in the same period for manufacturing firms (from 105,300 Euro down to 86,000 Euro). To some extent, employment growth has been traded off with a reduction in labor productivity.

A few comments on the sample firms are as follows: first, fast growing SMEs are more export-oriented than the rest of the sample; secondly, innovativity is a sufficient but not necessary condition for ensuring fast growth. In other words, while innovative performance is not the only way to grow fast, when successful innovation takes place, the firm experiences relevant consequences on employment and sales growth.

A first possible conclusion of the sketched research findings is that SSPIs can help, support and strengthen the export performance and the innovation activities of located firms, and by doing so, they offer an important contribution to the growth process of the system as a whole, i.e., they achieve the goal of a "sustainable growth".

At the same time one must consider that, despite the common wisdom of Italian local system being locked-in low-tech sectors, the innovative level of firms locates within SSPIs is generally on equal and in some cases even higher, then that of the average Italian SMEs.

Table 11.1 Net Jobs Created in Permanent SMEs: Size-classes, Sectors, and Territories

Macro Areas	20-49	50-99	100-199	200-499	Total	Manuf.	Serv.
N-W	14,113	8,890	535	2,199	25,737	20,532	5,205
N-E	17,528	11,589	3,310	−283	32,144	24,958	7,186
C	2,668	11,640	−964	−4,597	8,747	3,157	5,230
S-I	777	2,606	−1,499	−7,892	−11,220	−14,171	2,951
Italy	35,086	29,513	1,382	−10,573	55,408	34,836	20,572
Manuf.	25,909	22,545	121	−13,739	34,836		
Services	9,177	6,968	1,261	3,166	20,572		
Total	35,086	29,513	1,382	−10,573	55,408		

Source: elaboration on OECD-CERTeT research project

One may thus connect the good performance experienced by SSPIs - as measured by exports and innovation performance - with some proximity effect. However, the evidence of the reported analysis is not clear-cut, since the study was not originally designed for that purpose.

Nevertheless, we can observe a relatively larger diffusion of skilled labor poaching performed by HG firms in their territorial context. This result confirms a largely accepted conclusion about the role of local labor market and the mechanism of collective learning within SSPIs. In addition, a relevant turnover of skilled workers fosters those processes of knowledge conversion, combination and socialization, which are of the greatest importance for innovation.

Finally, the data show a large use of business services offered by local Chambers of Commerce as well as industry-specific Employers Associations. The sense of belonging to the same territorial and socio-cultural background seems thus to reinforce the effectiveness of business services on the growth of SMEs.

Structure and Evolution of Italian SSPIs

The literature on Italian SSPIs is almost infinite and multifaceted. Its most recent developments are influenced by a worldwide debate on the process of local development in which synergetic effects - based on a socio-cultural atmosphere - go hand in hand with a fast expansion of different cognitive circuits.

Table 11.2   Distribution of the Sample: Sectors, Employment, and Turnover

	Manufacture	Business Services	Total
	number of firms		
HG firms	75	42	117
Growing firms	230	67	297
Total	305	109	414
	employees per firm (1990)		
HG firms	22	28	24.1
Growing firms	47	37	44.7
Total	41	33.5	39
	employees per firm (1995)		
HG firms	101	130	111.4
Growing firms	78	66	75.3
Total	83.6	90.7	85.5
	turnover per firm (1990): thousand Euro		
HG firms	2,391	1,054	1,911
Growing firms	4,254	2,202	3,791
Total	3,796	1,760	3,260
	turnover per firm (1995): thousand Euro		
HG firms	8,614	4,952	7,300
Growing firms	7,227	4,381	6,585
Total	7,568	4,601	6,787

Source: elaboration on OECD-CERTeT research project

Within a general macroeconomic framework influenced by globalization dynamics, regional integration processes and the diffusion of ICTs, almost every SSPI should be widening the local system of value and enlarging the actual set of local linkages in order to preserve its competitive advantages.

Since the easiest way to open the production structure of a SSPI to the outer environment is to raise the hierarchical status of some leading-firms - whose decisional processes have a strong impact on SSPI relations - it is worthy to analyze the specific governance structure which SSPIs are endowed with.

Figure 11.3 plots the evolution of SSPIs along two critical dimensions: governance structures and knowledge formalization. Along the horizontal axis we classified three different *governance structures* of SSPIs, following Storper and Harrison (1991) and Bramanti and Maggioni (1997). There is a progression from the idealized "a-hierarchical network" without leading firms (all ring–no core) towards a more hierarchic network (core-ring with leading firm) in which the leader is almost independent from its suppliers and there is a quite strong asymmetry of role and bargaining power.

Co-coordinating or leading firms are those agents able to introduce radical and systemic innovation, and to modify entrepreneurial and organizational models thanks to their closeness to the "technological windows". The introduction of radical innovation by some leader-firms may cause the evolution of the whole SSPI if and only if the system as a whole is able to respond to the new cycle of innovation.

Along the vertical axis - following Belussi and Pilotti (1999) - we plot different degrees of knowledge formalization: from tacit to highly codified one as previously defined.

Two concave areas identify the operational space for local proximity and trans-national networks. The lens-like figure in the middle represents the area of co-existence of internal and external networks, the local-global dimension, where the mutual presence of short and long links feeds the innovation process.

Innovation may be seen as a successful application of new knowledge, which is not simply added to the pre-existing one, but is something that transforms it. Thus, knowledge creation is achieved through knowledge transformation. The lens space in Figure 11.3 represents a space where knowledge is continuously created, modified, updated, disseminated and shared.

The arrow describes the most likely evolutionary pattern in the contemporary economy: the process by which knowledge and information evolve towards a process of strong codification thanks to the pervasiveness of ICTs, while the governance structure of SSPIs evolve toward more hierarchical organizational forms.

Three circles capture different "stylized SSPIs" and may be seen as their possible evolutive path: from a first phase characterized by a classical Smithian division of labor, through a second phase based on a more innovative Marshallian division of labor in which actors and firms share culture, atmosphere and externalities, towards a third phase of "cognitive division of labor".[15]

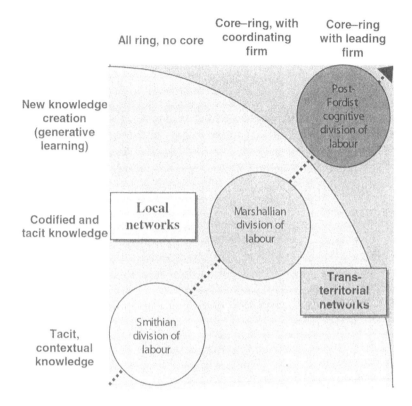

Figure 11.3   A Diagrammatic View of SSPI Dynamics

It is not difficult to classify a number of Italian SSPI (including some well known traditional industrial districts) within the table.

The exercise is reported in the following Table 11.3, showing some forty SSPIs, derived from an extensive survey of empirical literature as well as from previous direct analyses performed by the authors.

There is a growing evidence that "all ring–no core" governance structure is not the most appropriate to preserve SSPI's competitive advantage in the current economic condition. A number of SSPIs classified in the most left column, are not able to manage radical innovation due to certain lack of external linkages. In addition, the strong presence of tacit knowledge alone, is not a sufficient barrier against price competition, and many SSPIs, classified in the bottom line, are experiencing an erosion of their competitive advantage in front of other production systems located outside Italy.

Finally, in the up-right corner, four cells (shaded area) represent different success stories, which have established a proper mix of tacit and codified knowledge, which is functional and coherent with their specific governance structure.

Initial attempts to measure the performance of firms operating in SSPIs have been offered by Signorini (1994) and Fabiani and Pellegrini (1998). These researches are based on the balance sheets of "distrectual" firms comparing their financial and economic indexes with the industry average. More recently, a research project developed by the Bank of Italy, has measured the performance of firms belonging to SSPI. The profitability and productivity ratios of firms belonging to SSPIs - as defined by Istat (1997) - are analyzed in comparison to a control sample of firms having the same characteristics in terms of size and specialization. These analyses confirm the existence of positive externalities in belonging to SSPIs, such as a higher profitability measured by ROE, ROI, gross operating margin over sales, and superior technical efficiency. A further agglomeration advantage yielded by SSPI is a lower per capita cost of labor. Profitability always appears to be higher even when different industries and average size of firms are taken into account. The authors thus conclude that SSPIs are efficient organizational models.

Governance: The Balance Between Global Networks and Local Identity

All the above seems to suggest that the competitiveness of a SSPI is related to the co-evolution of an appropriate governance structure and a coherent learning mechanism. Furthermore the process of globalization, with its effects of shifting sovereignty and loyalties at all levels (European, national, regional, local) calls for a re-definition of the collective governance mechanisms in contemporary democracies.

Among the most recent contributions to this issue, the "associational model", proposed by Cooke and Morgan (1998) that is based on a more social and collaborative mode of economic organization is of some relevance for the issue at study. The strong emphasis on governance is due to the fact that interactions - plus shared history and culture - facilitate the development of trust-based social capital in local business communities.

Social capital is a metaphor to describe the embeddedness of economic activity in the social structure.

Economic Governance in SSPIs

Governance in not regarded as a universally applicable blueprint for territorial success, but it certainly plays - by addressing the relational dimension of development - a central role in the contemporary theory of economic organizations.

The term *governance* has been applied to the regulation of such relations, being the result of the combination of different forms: hierarchy, sub-contracting, partnership, "milieu", public and non-public agencies. Storper and Harrison (1991), among others, show the great variety of governance forms, and elsewhere we have already applied this very scheme to the analysis of a certain number of Italian productive systems (Bramanti and Maggioni 1997) in order to show an emerging trend in the process of reorganization of SSPI caused by the process of increasing global competition and fast technological change.

Within a territorial perspective the relational approach has important impact on organizational models. The actors' embeddedness, and their behavior, develops and creates a social environment, a sort of "cultural software" which is continuously fed and modified during an ever-lasting process of interaction.

Hence the concept of institutional proximity (Kirat 1993) - which is based upon local conventions and institutions created, adapted and participated by local actors - ensures the social cohesiveness of the local productive systems.

Organizational theory becomes a necessary step to describe and forecast the industrial dynamics. An organization is interpreted as a place for co-coordinating the behavior of different agents; a place for solving the problems caused by a changing environment, a mean of conversion of individual learning into collective learning; a place for the management of conflicts and the experimentation of new procedures for the distribution of locally produced value added.

Governance is an efficient way to co-ordinate self-interest and micro-economic choices, of resolving disputes, of assigning property rights, of distributing power among community's members, of enforcing entitlements, of assuring social embeddedness, of pursuing shared visions of development, of producing relational public goods, of strengthening trust, confidence and participation.

Table 11.3 A Bi-dimensional Taxonomy of Italian SSPIs

	All ring, no core	Core–ring, with coordinating firm	Core–ring with leading firm
New knowledge creation (generative learning)		Mirandola (biomedical instruments) Baxter Travenol – Gambro Casale (refrigeration industry) Mondial Frigor-Franger – Framek – Cold Car	Treviso (knitwear) Benetton Catania (microelectronics) SGS Thomson – Nokia Milan (multimedia) Rizzoli – Mondatori Bologna (packaging machinery) IMA – ACMA
Codified and tacit knowledge	Carrara (marble) Lumezzane (taps & fittings) Omegna (pots & pans) Reggio Emilia (agriculture machinery) Santo Stefano (balances) Valenza Po (jewellery) Varese (car alarms) Vicenza (jewellery)	Biella (wool fabrics) Loropiana – Fila Brianza (wood furniture) Poliform – Molteni Como (silk) Ratti – Mantero Parma (food valley) Parmalat – Barilla Varese (frames – glasses) Polinelli – IC Optics Castelfidardo (musical instruments) Bontempi	Santeramo (leather sofa) Natuzzi Montebelluna (skiboots & footwear) Nordica–Brixia– Lotto–Nike Cadore (frames– glasses) Luxottica – Safilo Sassuolo (ceramic tiles) Marazzi – Ires Ceramiche
Tacit, contextual knowledge	Arzignano (leather) Barletta (footwear) Carpi (knitting & clothing) Frosolone (cutlery) Maniago (cutlery) Murano (glasses) Prato (textile) Premana (scissors) Settimo Torinese (felt pens) Solfora (leather) Valduggia (valves) Val Vibrata (clothes)	Cerea-Bovolone (furniture) Selva Grumello (buttons) Zaravit – Mpd Udine (chairs) Calligaris – Euroline Cremona (musical instruments) Batta-Morassi – Bussolotti	Casarano (footwear) Filanto Arezzo (Jeweller's craft) Uno A Erre Tolentino (leather goods) Nazareno Gabrielli Castelgoffredo (nylon stokings) Golden Lady – Csp International

Note: the Table shows the present situation of some forty Italian SSPIs through the following symbols: name of the SSPI; prevalent or dominant production (in brackets); name of the leader firms in the area.

Governance describes furthermore the capacity of political institutions - jointly with civic society - to manage, through public policies and democratic representation, conflicting interests within the political arena. Whereas government refers to sovereignty and political autonomy, governance refers to social mediation and institutional interdependence.

This is particularly evident within the evolving patterns of European governance where the cohesion policy has already evidenced that it is impossible to identify a leading actor. Every time there is no leading actor, control is shared in such a way that actors are mutually dependent from one another. Each player needs to exchange resource with others in order to exert power and this situation force all players to consolidate their relationship in more or less durable arrangements.

The major role of governance within SSPIs is to design local development policy based on partnerships between public and private institutions rather than on pure public authority. The aim of this "partnership approach" is to create a more flexible mechanism of growth and establish a strategic agenda for technical and institutional change.

There is increasing evidence that modifications in the learning processes, and in their underlining governance structures, are not the result of a spontaneous dynamic of regions and SSPIs. This calls for the presence *system integrators* - these being individuals, public agencies, interest groups, or lobbies - which pursue an active role of balancing the centripetal and centrifugal forces of local development in order to achieve "sustainable growth" and "endogenous development".

Acknowledgements

The chapter is the outcome of joint research and discussion between the authors, nevertheless, the 1st, 2nd and 4th sections plus the empirics on high-tech clusters can be attributed to Mario A. Maggioni, while the 3rd and 6th sections plus the empirics on HG firms and on Italian SSPIs to Alberto Bramanti. We wish to thank Simona Beretta and Massimiliano Riggi for useful comments. The usual caveats apply.

Notes

1   NAFTA, the North-American free-trade agreement and, above all, the European Union are the best examples of the above mentioned dynamics.

2   In which a main difference is introduced by modelling also agglomeration diseconomies in a non linear (convex) way.

3   Therefore the existence of network externalities cannot be claimed as a reason in favour of a monopolistic market structure.

4   The internal influence model is most appropriate when: (i) the adoption decision is complex and socially visible (i.e. not adopting the best practice places firms at a competitive disadvantage in business; (ii) the number of firms in the SSPI is relatively small and homogeneous; and (iii) there is a need for experiential or legitimising information, prior to adoption (Mahajan and Peterson, 1985).

5   The logistic curve is symmetrical, has an inflection point at $n(t)/2$, and can be linearly estimated through a logarithmic transformation.

6   The rationale for such a model is the following: the source of innovation is external to the SSPI. The rate of location becomes therefore dependent only on the number of potential adopters at each moment of time (and this number is always decreasing as more and more firms adopt the innovation).

7   Mainly in Bramanti and Maggioni (1997), OECD-CERTeT (1998), and Maggioni (1999).

8   "If each firm could produce in both locations (...), then the full portfolio of firms and workers could be replicated in each location and the motivation for localisation would be gone." (Krugman 1991a, p. 40-41).

9   "Vertical disintegration encourages agglomeration and agglomeration encourages vertical disintegration". (Scott 1986, p. 224).

10   These being: Pharmaceutical, Computers and office equipment, Electronic components, Instruments, and Aerospace.

11   One must also consider that Instruments industry (especially in Italy and France) includes many different sub-sectors whose technological level (in certain countries) is not very high.

12   By "locational shadowing" we define a situation in which a county, which is highly specialised in a given industry, become so attractive for outsider firms that no other counties in the region develop a cluster in the same industry.

13   The whole section is constructed on the result of the research project OECD-CERTeT (1998) related to: *"High-Growth SMEs and Employment: Assessment of Best Practice Policies"*, coordinated by A. Bramanti.

14   A composite index which takes into account both absolute and relative dimension of growth.

15   The interested reader may compare our taxonomy with the one put forward in Markusen (1996).

References

Amendola, M. and Gaffard, J.L. (1988), *The Innovative Choice: An Economic Analysis of the Dynamics of Technology*, B.H. Blackwell, Oxford.
Arthur, W.B. (1990), "Silicon Valley Locational Clusters: When Do Increasing Returns Imply Monopoly?", *Mathematical Social Sciences*, Vol. 19, n. 3, pp. 235-251.
Becattini, G. (1998), *Distretti industriali e Made in Italy*, Bollati Boringhieri, Torino.
Becattini, G. and Vaccà, S. (eds) (1994), *Prospettive degli studi di economia e politica industriale in Italia*, Franco Angeli, Milano.
Belussi, F. and Pilotti, L. (1999), "Knowledge Creation and Learning in the Institutional Governance of Italian Local Production Systems", Paper presented at the Conference *Il*

futuro dei Distretti. Lavoro, tecnologia, organizzazione, istituzioni, University of Padova, June, Vicenza.

Bianchi, P. and Miller, L.M. (1994), "Innovation, Collective Action and Endogenous Growth: an Essay on Institutional and Structural Change", *Dynamis-Quaderni IDSE*, 2, IDSE-CNR, Milano.

Bramanti, A. and Maggioni, M.A. (1997), "The Dynamics of Milieux: The Network Analysis Approach", in R. Ratti, A. Bramanti and R. Gordon (eds), *The Dynamics of Innotive Regions*, Ashgate, London, pp. 321-342.

Bramanti, A. and Miglierina, C. (1995), "Alle radici della crescita regionale: fattori, fenomeni, agenti", *L'Industria*, n. 1, pp. 5-31.

Bramanti, A. and Senn, L. (1993), "Entrepreneurs, Firms, "milieu": Three Different Specification of Networking Activities. Some Evidences from the Case of Bergamo", in D. Maillat, M. Quévit and L. Senn (eds), *Réseaux d'innovation et milieux innovateurs: un pari pour le développement régional*, GREMI–EDES, Neuchâtel, pp. 181-207.

Bressand, A., Distler, C. and Nicolaidis, K. (1989), "Networks at the Heart of the Service Economy", in A. Bressand and K. Nicolaidis (eds), *Strategic Trends in Services*, Harper & Row, London, pp. 14-33.

Camagni, R. (1995), "Global Network and Local Milieu: Towards a Theory of Economic Space", in S. Conti, E.J. Malecki and P. Oinas (eds), *The Industrial Enterprise and its Environment: Spatial Perspectives*, Avebury, Aldershot, pp.195-214.

Cooke, P. and Morgan, K. (1998), *The Associational Economy. Firms, Regions, and Innovation*, Oxford University Press, Oxford.

Dupuy, C. and Gilly, J.P. (1993), "Les stratégies territoriales des grands groupes industriels", in A. Rallet and A. Torre (eds), *Économie industrielle et économie spatiale*, Economica, Paris, pp. 129-146.

Economides, N. (1996), "The Economics of Networks", *International Journal of Industrial Organization*, vol. 14, n. 6, pp. 673-699.

Fabiani, S. and Pellegrini, G. (1998), "Un'analisi quantitativa nei distretti industriali italiani: redditività, produttività e costo del lavoro", paper presented at Convegno de L'Industria, September, L'Aquila.

Feldman, M.P. (1995), *The Geography of Innovation*, Kluwer, Dordrecht.

Glaeser, E.L., Kallal, H.D., Scheinkman, J.A. and Shleifer, A. (1992), "Growth in Cities", *Journal of Political Economy*, vol. 100, n. 6, pp. 1126-52.

Grilliches, Z. (1957), "Hybrid Corn: An Exploration in the Economics of Technological Change", *Econometrica*, vol. 25, n. 4, pp. 501-522.

Håkansson, H. (ed.) (1987), *Industrial Technological Development. A Network Approach*, Croom Helm, London.

Jaffe, A.B., Henderson, R. and Trajtenberg, M. (1993), "Geographic Localization of Knowledge Spillovers as Evidenced by Patent Citations", *Quarterly Journal of Economics*, vol. 63, n. 3, pp. 577-598.

Karshenas, M. and Stoneman, P. (1995), "Technological Diffusion", in P. Stoneman (ed.), *Handbook of the Economics of Innovation and Technological Change*, Blackwell, Oxford, pp. 265-297.

Kirat, T. (1993) "Innovation technologique et apprentissage institutionnel: institutions et proximité dans la dynamique des systèmes d'innovation territorialisés", *Revue d'Economie Régionale et Urbaine*, n. 3, pp. 547-563.

Krugman, P. (1991a), *Geography and Trade*, MIT Press, Cambridge, Mass.

Krugman, P. (1991b), "Increasing Returns and Economic Geography", *Journal of Political Economy*, Vol. 99, n. 3, pp. 483-499.

Istat (1997), *I sistemi locali del lavoro 1991*. Collana Argomenti, Istat, Roma.

Lucas, R.E. (1972), "Expectation and the Neutrality of Money", *Journal of Economic Theory*, n. 4, pp. 103-124.

Lucas, R.E. (1988), "On the Mechanics of Economic Development", *Journal of Monetary Economics*, Vol. 22, n. 1, pp. 3-42.

Maggioni, M.A. (1999), *Clustering Dynamics and the Location of High-Tech Firms*. Ph.D. Thesis, University of Warwick, forthcoming by Springer Verlag, Heidelberg.

Maggioni, M.A. (2001), "The Development of High-Tech Clusters: Theoretical Insights and Policy Implications", in M. Feldman and N. Massard (eds.), *Knowledge Spillovers and the Geography of Innovation*, Kluwer, Dordrecht (forthcoming).

Mahajan, V. and Peterson, R.A. (1985), *Models for Innovation Diffusion*, Sage, Newbury Park.

Maillat, D. (1995), "Milieux innovateurs et dynamique territoriale", in A. Rallet and A. Torre (eds), *Économie industrielle et économie spatiale*, Economica, Paris, pp. 211-231.

Malecki, E.J. (1991), *Technology and Economic Development*, Longman Scientific & Technical, Harlow.

Mansfield, E. (1968), *Industrial Research and Technological Innovation*, Norton, New York.

Markusen, A. (1996), "Sticky Place in Slippery Space: A typology of Industrial Districts", *Economic Geography*, n. 72, pp. 293-313.

Marshall, A . (1920), *Principles of Economics*, Macmillan, London.

Marshall, A . (1921), *Industry and Trade*, Macmillan, London.

Mitchell, J.C. (ed.) (1969), *Social Networks in Urban Situation*. Manchester University Press, Manchester.

Nonaka, I. (1991), "The Knowledge Creating Company", *Harvard Business Review*, Novembre-December, pp. 96-104.

Nonaka, I. and Takeuchi, H. (1998), "A Theory of Firm's Knowledge-Creation Dynamics", in A.D. Jr. Chandler, P. Hagström and Ö. Sölvell (eds), *The Dynamics Firm. The Role of Technology, Strategy, Organization, and Regions*, Oxford University Press, Oxford, pp. 214-241.

OECD–CERTeT (1998), *High-Growth SMEs and Employment: Assessment of Best Practice Policies*. DSTI/IND/PME(98), October, Milan.

Parr, J.B. (2000), "Agglomeration Economies: Some Missing Elements", Paper presented at the 6th RSAI World Congress, 16-20 May, Lugano.

Polanyi, C. (1962), *Personal Knowledge: Towards a Post-Critical Philosophy*, Chicago University Press, Chicago.

Ratti, R., Bramanti, A. and Gordon, R. (eds) (1997), *The Dynamic of Innovative Regions: the GREMI Approach*, Avebury, Aldershot.

Romer, P. (1986), "Increasing Returns and Long-run Growth", *Journal of Political Economy*, vol. 94, n. 5, pp. 1002-1037.

Scott, J. (1986), "Industrial Organization and Location: Division of Labour, the Firm, and Spatial Process", *Economic Geography*, vol. 62, n. 3, pp. 215-231.

Signorini, L. (1994), "The Price of Prato, or Measuring the ID Effect", *Papers in Regional Science*, n. 73, pp. 369-392.

Storper, M. and Harrison, H. (1991), "Flexibility, Hierarchy and Regional Development: the Changing Structure of Industrial Production Systems and their Forms of Governance in the 1990s", *Research Policy*, n. 5, pp. 407-422.

Storper, M. and Walker, R. (1984), *The Capitalist Imperative. Territory, Technology and Industrial Growth*, Basil Blackwell, New York.

Varian, H.R. (1999), Market structure in the Network Age, paper presented at the Depatment of Commerce Conference on "Understanding the Digital Economy", 25-26 May, Washington (DC), http://www.sims.berkeley.edu/~hal/papers/doc/doc.html

Veltz, P. (1993), "D'une géographie des coûts à une géographie de l'organisation. Quelques thèses sur l'évolution des rapports entreprises/territoires", *Revue économique*, n. 4, pp. 671-684.

Weber, A. (1909), *Theory of the Location of Industry*, Chicago University Press, Chicago.

12 The Spatial Configuration of Inter-firm Networks in Producer Service Agglomerations

NEIL M. COE AND ALAN R. TOWNSEND

Many accounts of contemporary economic change focus upon the world economy as a mosaic of interconnected regional economies (e.g., Scott 1998). To put it another way, cities and/or city-regions act as key nodes and grounding points in global economic networks (Amin and Thrift 1992). These nodes of expertise and interaction, it is argued, are perhaps becoming *more* important as dense transnational connections are formed as part of broader globalization processes. The success of these "regional motors of the world economy" (Scott 1996) is seen to lie in local networks of interaction, whether they be formal input-output linkages (e.g., Scott 1998), or more diffuse socio-cultural practices associated with conventions, norms, and processes of collective learning and innovation (e.g., Maillat 1995; Malmberg and Maskell 1997). The study of spatial agglomerations of economic activity is, of course, nothing new, dating back to the pioneering work of Marshall (1916) and Weber (1929). Since the late 1980s, however, there has been an increasing re-discovery of interest in detailed analysis of industrial organisation in particular localities, largely based upon the economic analysis of agglomerations of production (see Storper 1995 for an account of this resurgence). Much of the debate has focused around the emergence of new, flexible industrial districts or spaces, reflecting a transitional phase in, or perhaps a total breakdown of, the traditional Fordist mode of mass production (Piore and Sabel 1984; Hirst and Zeitlin 1989). However, as Malmberg (1996) notes, this new literature on industrial agglomeration is by no means homogeneous, with vastly different interpretations, for example, of the sectoral bases, operational scale and key mechanisms behind such clustering.

With somewhat less discipline still, the idea has been further extended in the 1990s under the banner of "clusters". Under the international neo-liberal agenda, the cluster has been seen in different countries as an aid to the promotion of competitiveness, often by business studies interests and by a new generation who, in the UK, knew none of the lessons of locational policies adopted before the Conservative era of the 1980s. Porter (1990; 1998) concentrated his analysis on regional economies that were "competitive high points", identifying geographic concentrations of industry, if necessary irrespective of known linkages that had the potential for business-to-business co-operation. This type of view was taken up by the business and policy advisers to the New Labour government in the Department of Trade and Industry (1999) in *Our Competitive Future: building the knowledge driven economy*. Practitioners such as Wood and Atherton extended the search for clusters beyond long-included non-market linkages to informal social networks of entrepreneurs, membership associations, and common needs and interests which we used to call the economies of urbanization. In work for a Regional Development Agency (RDA) their role in identifying 53 areas of potential clustering (Foundation for SME Development 2000) merged into conventional description of local employment data and forecasting of regional export prospects. This feeds the need of RDAs to develop promotional business strategies. There the matter might rest, except that the "knowledge driven economy" was given priority over traditional locational restraints in South East England. There were arguably prospective new linkages between new development in the biotechnology industry (but in Oxfordshire, Smith, Mihell and Kingham 2000, emphasize rather the scientific labor market and common infrastructure) and thus the government was obliged to make some concessions over planning constraints as they applied to the industry in Cambridgeshire, also later in Lothian. In turn, most RDAs have adopted clusters or new technology corridors in their Economic Strategies and it is suggested that Treasury finance will in future depend on the Agencies' prosecution of clusters. It is surely relevant now to test the precedent of small and medium sized firms in the fastest-growing sector of the South East, providing computer services.

This chapter uses a case study of the producer service industries of South East England to contribute to these debates in three ways. Firstly, we make the simple, but nonetheless important argument that many agglomerations are dominated by service sector employment. Secondly, in terms of identifying the scale at which agglomerations can be delimited, we argue that it may not be possible to identify relatively self-contained growth clusters at the sub-regional level (i.e., town, district or county).

Rather, in the case of the South East, businesses and localities appear tied in to a particular mode of growth at the greater regional level. In essence, we argue that local producer service networks need to be understood in the context of a regionalized mode of service growth across the whole South East, as suggested by Allen (1992, p. 296):

> ... a highly "open" economy such as the UK is characterized by regionalized modes of economic growth, of which the most significant in recent times is service sector growth across the London city region and beyond.

Thirdly, with regards to the processes creating and sustaining agglomerations, we propose that historical processes of cumulative causation are a far more crucial component than is suggested by the existing literature, preoccupied as it is with local networking.

This chapter synthesizes a combination of secondary sources about South East England with detailed evidence from a large-scale survey of the UK computer services sector[1] conducted in the mid-1990s (see Coe 1996a; 1996b; 1998 for more details). In this research, managers from 84 firms were interviewed in the South East: 43 in Hertfordshire (September 1994) and 41 in Berkshire (February 1995). Berkshire was chosen as the traditional "hub" of the UK IT industry, while Hertfordshire was selected to provide a basis for comparison within the South East region. Firms were sampled from the best available lists of the total population of computer service establishments at the time to meet a target of around 40 firms in each county, and the samples were stratified by size-band to mirror the total population. It is important to remember that the survey results cover establishments (i.e., single site firm, HQ or branch) and not necessarily a whole company. The response rates were 67 percent in Berkshire and 69 percent in Hertfordshire. The remainder of the chapter is structured into three main sections corresponding to our three main arguments.

The South East as a Service Economy

The first argument of this chapter is that many agglomerations in advanced economies are in fact concentrations of service activity. Since the mid-to-late 1980s, both the re-emergence of agglomerations of economic activity and the growth of knowledge-based service industries have attracted a great deal of research in economic geography. However, with limited exceptions

(Christopherson 1989; Coffey and Bailly 1991; 1992; Wood 1991) very few commentators have drawn links between the two issues. This is particularly surprising given that

> modern agglomerations of economic activity, whether in high technology Silicon Valley, business service dominated South-East England, or the "Third Italy", are essentially agglomerations of service expertise (Wood 1991, p. 166).

Further, Lash and Urry (1994) have attacked Storper and Walker's (1989) analysis of the connections between territory, technology and growth as lacking any appreciation of the importance of services in the development of "territorial production complexes". Indeed, much of the recent research into agglomerations emerges from a school of thought in which service activity is seen only as a dependent adjunct to material production (Cohen and Zysman 1987; Britton 1990; Sayer and Walker 1992), with a stress on business services simply taking in work previously done in-house by manufacturing firms. However, empirical evidence from South East England suggests that theories of growth should concentrate on the dynamics of service activities and expertise.

The dependence of the South East's economy upon various service sectors is plainly evident from a variety of data. Services now represent well over 80 percent of the economy of the Region, including 87.6 percent of employees in employment at September 1998 (see Table 12.1). The respective figures for Greater London and the Rest of the South East (ROSE) stand at 91.8 and 84.2 percent, representing a very substantial level of both decentralization and new growth in the 1990s (see Table 12.1). Services represent 86.8 percent of the value of production for Greater London, with financial and business services over 40 percent alone and more than 30 percent in ROSE, compared with 11.5 and 16.8 percent respectively in manufacturing. These two groups of services – collectively known as producer services – are the main focus of this chapter due to their extremely high concentration in the South East: "financial services" covers activities such as banking, insurance and pension funds, while "business services" represent a more diverse group including the older professions such as law, accountancy, architecture, surveying and engineering consultancy, as well as newer activities such as manpower agencies, market research, computer services, security and industrial cleaning. In terms of the breakdown between these two groups of services, in September 1998 the South East accounted for 536,000 financial services jobs, or exactly half the UK total, and 1,638,000 business service jobs, 49 percent of the total. As would be expected, financial services show a higher level of concentration in Greater London itself, which accounts for 63 percent of the South East total, compared to 52 percent in the business services.

Table 12.1   Financial and Business Services' Share of South East Employment

	Financial and Business Services[2]		Services, total	
	Employees in employment (thousands)			
	1991	1998	1991	1998
Greater London[1]	862	1156	2898	3317
Rest of South East	725	1018	3186	3804
South East (total)	1589	2174	6085	7121
	Share of employees in employment (percent)			
Greater London	26.5	32.0	89.1	91.8
Rest of South East	18.3	22.5	80.4	84.2
South East (total)	22.0	26.7	84.3	87.6

Source: Labour Market Trends

[1] Standard Statistical Region.
[2] Defined as sectors J and K of the Standard Industrial Classification (1992).

Figure 12.1 illustrates the spatial distribution of financial and business service employment at the time of the 1998 Census of Employment, clearly showing the extent of the concentration in South East England. The counties containing Bristol, Cardiff and Edinburgh are the only ones outside the South East with above average employment levels in these sectors, with the former two being clearly linked to the South East by the M4 corridor. The "Western Crescent" of growth around London identified by Hall et al. (1987) in the mid-1980s has expanded northwards, westwards and southwards to produce a contiguous zone of high levels of producer service employment that covers much of Southern England, although the under-representation of these activities in the eastern counties of the region (Norfolk, Suffolk, Essex and Kent) still persists. This overall pattern speaks of the importance of "centrality within southern Britain's space-economy for reasons of access not only to London but also to clients nation-wide" (Keeble et al. 1991, p. 450). The growth rates in many of the counties in the expanded

Western Crescent have been very impressive during the 1990s. For example, between 1991 and 1998, Surrey, Berkshire, Buckinghamshire and Oxfordshire expanded employment in Financial and Business Services by 50 to 70 percent, and East and West Sussex, Hampshire and Hertfordshire by 35 to 45 percent. The rapid growth in the ROSE region is being driven by a combination of new, demand-lead growth, and decentralization from Greater London. These twin processes of growth are increasingly over-spilling the rather arbitrary boundaries of the South East Standard Region, justifying the common usage of the "Greater South East" to describe the zone of growth (Figure 12.1).

By any measure, then, the South East is a service-based economy. However, it is important to realize that, as Dunford and Fielding (1997, p. 263) describe:

> The characteristics of the London and South East economies did not just appear in the recent period. They reflect long-term economic processes, some of which are so deeply rooted in the economic geography of the UK that they can be traced back to the earliest stages of modern capitalist development, if not earlier.

Taking a historical perspective, the South East emerged as center of growth in the 18th century based upon the twin pillars of accumulated wealth from trade and finance, and land (Lee 1986). By the 19th century, the London-based finance capital elite effectively dominated the country. Dunford and Fielding illustrate how post-Fordist economic restructuring since the 1970s has also shaped the nature of the South East's economy. A wide variety of processes - namely de-industrialization, privatization, flexible specialization, feminization, multi-culturalism, social polarization, and globalization - has reinforced the position of the South East as a producer service based economy. A political move to the right in the 1980s in the UK ensured that the booming post-Fordist growth of the South East economy was allowed to continue unchecked by strategic or regional planning, thereby accenting the depth of the temporary regional downturn in the early 1990s. Thus, not all scholars see the development of the South East's economy in a positive light. For example, Allen et al. (1998, p. 120), when considering the recession of the early 1990s, stated, "the economic base turns out to be rather narrow, precisely because of the extent of concentration in a relatively limited space".

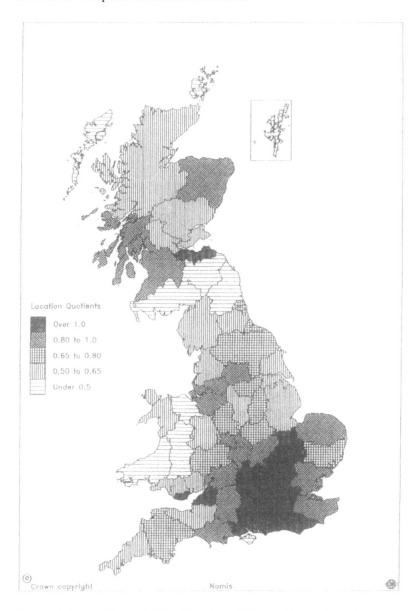

Location Quotients

- Over 1.0
- 0.80 to 1.0
- 0.65 to 0.80
- 0.50 to 0.65
- Under 0.5

© Crown copyright   Nomis

Figure 12.1   **Spatial Distribution of Financial and Business Service Employment, 1998**

The Scale of Agglomeration: Regionalization not Localization?

Having established the need to take service sector agglomerations seriously, we now move on to consider the spatial scale at which such concentrations can be identified, a field of considerable debate in the literature. While some accounts identify critical growth dynamics within particular localities such as Hollywood, Toulouse, Toyota City or Cambridge, commentators are increasingly suggesting that agglomeration processes are active at some kind of regional level, such as Orange County, northeast-central Italy or Baden-Wuerrtemburg. Due to the hierarchical nature of employment in service industries, service sector research tends to focus on metropolitan areas and on decentralization to their hinterlands (e.g., Coffey 1992). Using the core region of the UK as a case study, in this section we argue that while the dynamics of service activity are in many cases contained within some kind of Greater South East, there is very little evidence for more localized clusters of inter-related growth activity outside central London, even at the sub-regional level in, say, Berkshire, Cambridgeshire or Oxfordshire (see Lawton-Smith et al. 2000, on the last of these).

The argument, then, is that geographical concentrations of economic activities need not be functionally defined clusters of dense local networking, although our view is still unfashionable. While some research in the UK context does identify the occurrence of strong and effective local networks (e.g., Bryson et al. 1993; Sweeting 1995; Crewe 1996), an increasing number of studies question the extent and significance of local relationships (e.g., Penn 1992; Clark 1993; Baker 1995; Hardill et al. 1995; McCann 1995; Garnsey and Cannon-Brookes 1993). Several empirical studies of portions of the South East economy bear out the same argument. For example, two studies of innovative high technology firms in Hertfordshire struggled to find any containment of network relations at that sub-regional scale. In his survey of 177 high technology firms in Hertfordshire, Henry (1992, p. 388) found that only 19 percent of the major production links identified were internal to the county. Although any county's boundary is arbitrary:

> it may be argued that the spatial scale of Hertfordshire is too restrictive. It must be remembered that Hertfordshire is part of the Western Crescent agglomeration and possibly this is the spatial scale at which the analysis should be taking place.

His analysis showed that 54 percent of all major production linkages occurred within the "Greater" South East: a further 16 percent went overseas, 3 percent to the West Midlands, and 27 percent to the rest of the UK. Similarly, in his study of 35 award-winning innovative firms in Hertfordshire, Simmie (1998, p. 1264) asserts that

> Agglomerated firms do not necessarily maintain links with each other ... in addition, empirical research in a variety of high-technology agglomerations ... has cast doubt on the local existence of these local production networks for innovative firms – or at least, have questioned their apparently assumed universality ... Contrary to much network theory, the level of their mutual and local input-output trading relationships could, in fact, be more or less zero.

This argument is reiterated by Jones' (1998) two surveys of business and professional services in London. The key advantages of a central location were found to lie in accessibility to clients, a wide recruitment pool, and a prestige address. He found that lateral linkages between the firms were "weak and unstable" (p. 156). In terms of locational factors, proximity to similar businesses was highlighted by only four percent of businesses. While proximity to clients was mentioned as the most important factor by 29 percent of businesses, Jones pointed out that the markets were geographically relatively dispersed across the UK and abroad. Overall, Jones (1998, p. 164) hoped that his evidence would

> counteract causal assumptions that propinquity between similar businesses necessarily indicates the existence of strong, localized inter-firm networks, or the automatic characterization of geographical concentrations of industries as "clusters".

The lack of evidence of significant patterns of local networking shifts the focus of attention to relations at the national and international scales. In particular, it is now increasingly difficult to separate the growth of local economies from global economic forces (Amin and Thrift 1994). Agglomerations are clearly both constitutive of, and affected by, wider processes of global economic restructuring. One conceptualization of the emergence of key agglomerations is to view them as nodes in the global networks of increasingly powerful and integrated transnational corporations (Amin and Thrift 1992; Amin 1993). In such an account, nodes or agglomerations remain important in contemporary economies as sites for the actuation of processes of authority, interaction and innovation. It is only through such geographical centers that the competitive advantages of certain global production chains can be maintained. Others such as Castells (1996) and Cooke (1996) also argue that globalization processes are reinforcing the importance of regional agglomerations, and that the most dynamic sectors in such areas are integrated into international networks. These arguments resonate with the service sector research of Moulaert et al. (1997, p. 106), who suggest that agglomerations of service activity must be considered in the context of the global corporate networks in which they are situated:

> the economic interactions that give rise to external economies take place at different spatial levels. In some cases, they are confined to a single metropolitan region; in other cases, they spill over into networks of agglomeration ... a wide-area network of agglomerations located at significant physical distance from each other but with strong functional interdependencies.

Such arguments are central to Allen's (1992) notion of a regionalized service economy. He asserts that much service growth in the South East has become reliant upon the internationalization of key service markets and the consequent strategies of many financial and service sector multinational companies. The overlapping geographies of internationally oriented growth sectors such as financial services, high-technology services (including computer services) and tourism combine to produce a discernible "varied and somewhat cumulative mode of service growth which has moved across London and much of the south, but little further" (p. 300).

A key contention of this article is that while visible foreign trade in services actually remains fairly low, the ownership of service facilities is becoming significantly more internationalized through foreign direct investment, with merger and acquisition activity particularly prevalent in many producer service sectors. Such processes reinforce the primacy of core regions. For example, Sjoholt (1994) suggests that the pre-existing spatial structure of the host country's economy is a centralizing force for international investments across all producer service sectors: in particular, acquisitions, and joint ventures established by multinationals tend to focus on the core region.

Given that local linkages may be being over-emphasized at the expense of national and international level connections, how then, in spatial/functional terms, can we begin to delimit the agglomeration of producer service activity in southern England? Aggregate statistical analyses are unrevealing. For example, Bennett et al. (1999, p. 412), while identifying some 126 business clusters in the UK through statistical procedures, conclude that

> the zone from Lancashire/Yorkshire to London and the South East is an area of almost continuously overlapping clusters. We might correctly identify this area of Britain therefore as a *metacluster* (original emphasis).

Some of the ensuing analysis, however, is rather vague:

> at the scale of the metacluster, the main competitive advantage for the British economy would appear to lie in the overlapping of advantages of very local closeness within the microclusters, as well as broader cluster overlaps. At the level of the metacluster, it will be commonalities of factor conditions that are most important to business growth, rather than close supply chain interlinkages.

The assumption appears that there will be dense patterns of networking within very local clusters, sustained by common factor conditions at the level of the metacluster. We want to argue that the appropriate scale of analysis lies somewhere in between Bennett et al.'s notions of the micro- and metaclusters.

We suggest, in line with Allen (1992), that the service economy of the South East is a distinguishable, albeit porous, space within the UK economy. In other words, we are proposing that there is a significant level of coherence and commonality, which Harvey (1985) refers to as the "structured coherence" of regional spaces, in evidence at the scale of the Greater South East. However, building on the work of Allen et al. (1998), several caveats should be born in mind. Firstly, the Greater South East does not map neatly onto the standard statistical region, or those of the Government Offices for the Regions. As Figure 12.1 shows, it clearly extends significantly northwards and westwards beyond the standard region, into counties such as Cambridgeshire, Avon and Wiltshire. Secondly, the boundedness of the South East agglomeration should not be overemphasized. Allen et al. (1998, p. 54) develop a notion of the region as a nexus of social relations, which leads them to conclude that

> The South East as we think of it is not bounded off from but linked to, and in part constituted in its character through its linkage to, other regions. This is clearest in relation to the interactions between activities in the South East and the rest of the UK. It is also clearly apparent in international links, and in the specificity of the nature of those links, which distinguish this part of the country from other regions. Many economic activities in the South East form a link between the extra-UK economy and the national economy. There is also a sense in which parts of the economy of the South East form an international enclave within the wider UK space.

Thus the nature of the wider national and international linkages emanating from the South East can be as crucial in delimiting its unique character as local networks of interaction. Thirdly, the growth region is by no means spatially continuous, but has a number of significant holes in it. At the County level, Essex and Kent are not fully integrated into the service mode of growth (see Figure 12.1). At the smaller scale, a wide variety of localities employment appears to have been left out: Allen et al. (1998) highlight the Medway towns as examples of such a plight. Fourthly, within the broader pattern, there are great intra-regional variations in the rates and nature of growth. Cambridge, for example, may stand out as a hot spot of high technology industry, in the same way as Bracknell has seen spectacular growth in the software industry. In no way, however, does this observation suggest that these localities are self-contained or disembedded from the broader region.

This argument can be illustrated by considering the spatial extent of the linkages of computer service firms, which clearly shows the dangers of "reading off" localized transactions from the existence of agglomerations. Table 12.2 describes the geography of the market linkages of the South East-based survey firms. Several points are worth noting here. Firstly, the levels of sales to the immediate local market (same county) are very low, being just five percent in Hertfordshire and four percent in Berkshire, thus adding to the evidence that suggests local linkages are not a necessary condition for agglomeration to occur. Secondly, there is a fairly high degree of containment of sales within London and the South East, which together account for some 65 percent of sales from Hertfordshire firms, and around 50 percent from those in the Berkshire survey. This general pattern accords with the data of Wood et al. (1993), whose survey of management consulting firms in the South East found half their trade to be regionally based, but only about ten percent of trade to lie within 20 miles of the firm. Thirdly, Greater London itself represents a very important market, constituting 30 percent of the total sales of firms in Hertfordshire, the same as the rest of the South East put together. For firms in Berkshire, the metropolis accounts for 19 percent of sales, with 28 percent coming from the outer South East. While these figures largely reflect the scale of the producer service and headquarters complex that exists in London, it also indicates how firms retain London clients when decentralizing to the Home Counties. Fourthly, the breakdown of the rest of the South East markets strongly supports Allen's (1992) concept of a regionalized service economy, within which distance from clients is largely irrelevant. This is shown by the results for Hertfordshire; despite the fact that the county is directly north of London, the split in revenues between counties north of the Thames and south of the Thames (see Table 12.2 for definitions) is almost exactly even. Although inconclusive, the Berkshire data suggests that there may be a slight western bias to activity within the region, with three times as much revenue (20.7 to 7.3 percent) being derived from the seven western counties as the three eastern counties (again, see Table 12.2 for categories).

Fifthly, and perhaps most interestingly given the frequent portrayal of the South East as "internationally connected", these data highlight the low level of direct international sales of computer services (five percent). At first glance these results may appear contrary to Allen's notion of an internationally connected regional economy: however, the crucial point when conceptualizing producer service firms within their international networks is to recognize the increasing importance of international *ownership* through acquisition. For example, while the research and development and marketing functions of computer service firms are increasingly being coordinated at the continental, or global levels, by the very nature of many service activities the provision of expertise usually occurs locally (Coe 1997). However, in terms of the firms supplying these services to UK clients, the industry is characterized by a high level of foreign ownership. As an indicator, foreign owned firms accounted for 53 percent of the total sales of the Hertfordshire sample, and 65 percent in Berkshire. These results can be compared with those from other research. In assessing a wide variety of different surveys, both Cornish (1996) and

Illeris (1996) suggest that, on average, producer service firms export between five and 10 percent of their total sales. Interestingly, Cornish concludes that, along with management and engineering consultancy services, computer services are in general among the most internationally mobile producer services in terms of sales.

Table 12.2   The Geographical Distribution of the Survey Firms' Sales

HERTS: percent of business in	Herts.	Greater London	SE[1] counties North of Thames	SE[2] counties South of Thames	Rest of the UK	Rest of the EU	Rest of the World	Total (%)
Unweighted	18.6	25.5	14.9	12.0	25.0	3.5	0.6	100.0
Weighted*	5.1	30.0	15.3	15.4	29.1	4.5	0.5	100.0

BERKS: Percent of business in	Berks.	Greater London	SE counties East of London[3]	Other SE counties[4]	Rest of the UK	Rest of the EU	Rest of the World	Total (%)
Unweighted	7.8	21.7	4.9	15.7	36.9	7.8	5.3	100.0
Weighted*	3.6	18.9	7.3	20.7	44.2	2.8	2.2	100.0

Source: Coe (1996a)

[1] Defined here as Bedfordshire, Buckinghamshire, Essex and Oxfordshire.
[2] Berkshire, East Sussex, Hampshire, Isle of Wight, Kent, Surrey and West Sussex.
[3] Essex, East Sussex and Kent.
[4] Bedfordshire, Buckinghamshire, Hampshire, Hertfordshire, Isle of Wight, Oxfordshire, Surrey, West Sussex.
* Here the figures have been weighted by employment (used here as the best available measure of business volume) to show the overall importance of market areas when the different sizes of firms are accounted for.

More direct comparison can be drawn with other studies focusing on southern England, suggesting that direct overseas exports from our surveys are lower than, but still comparable, with other surveys. For example, in a study of small market research and management consultancy firms in the South East, Wood et al. (1993) found only slightly higher levels of international export activity (approximately 11 percent, the figure being lower for market research). Most authors agree that the South East is more oriented to international markets for financial and business services than are other regions of the UK. For example, O'Farrell et al. (1996, p. 102) argue that, with reference to their earlier work, "South East business service companies achieved a greater degree of international export penetration (17 percent) than either Scotland (four percent) or Nova Scotia (four percent)". London firms in particular appear more deeply entrenched in foreign markets (O'Farrell et al., 1996); according to Wood (1996, p. 662), the South East is "exploiting agglomeration advantages and developing a growing global role". As stressed by O'Farrell et al. (1996) there is a cumulative element to these patterns of networking within the South East; exposure to foreign competition has a strengthening effect on competitiveness, in turn encouraging the development of more internationally oriented and competitive businesses.

To investigate the nature and spatial pattern of backwards linkages, often a gap in the producer services literature, the surveyed computer service firms were asked about any tasks they subcontracted (apart from standard legal and accountancy activities), with just under two thirds of firms being found to subcontract some kind of operation. The most common functions to be subcontracted were the support and maintenance of computer hardware (23 percent of firms), and the provision of networks and cabling (20 percent of firms), both representing other parts of the computer services sector. However, the survey evidence strongly supported Michalak and Fairbairn's (1993) assertion that computer services are not strong *local* purchasers of services. Not a single company responded that the local availability of suppliers or potential subcontractors was important in the locational decision, or furthermore, was crucial to the firm's subsequent growth and development. The most commonly externalized services, hardware maintenance and network services, were subcontracted to a mixture of local and non-local firms, of varying sizes. Analysis of the horizontal linkages of computer service establishments to other IT businesses produces a similar picture. Some 62 percent of the survey firms engaged in some kind of formal link or joint venture with other IT companies: the most common kind of scheme undertaken was some kind of joint marketing or selling, with firms offering the services or products of other IT companies in conjunction with their own core activity. Again, it is the geographical content of these links that is particularly interesting. As with subcontracting links, the survey firms failed to cite the need for proximity to other IT businesses as an important locational factor or influence on development. While many links involved businesses in the South East due to the national structure of the IT industry, longer distance links were also common. In particular, joint selling agreements did not require long-term close interaction. When coupled with the relatively high spatial range of computer service sales (see above), these results cast severe doubt on the applicability of theories of growth based on flexible production districts (e.g., Scott 1988a; 1988b) to service activities, which, as described earlier, represent a substantial proportion of advanced economies. Thus the evidence suggests that although there is some degree of spatial containment of producer service firm linkages within the greater South East (and certainly not at any smaller spatial scale), many firms located within the South East exhibit a considerable degree of extra-regional linkage. While direct international sales are limited, producer service firms in the South East are undoubtedly "plugged into" international networks through their ownership structures.

Accumulated Advantages: Processes of Agglomeration Formation

Unsurprisingly, the task of identifying the actual processes that lie behind the agglomeration of economic activity has prompted great debate in the literature. The static interpretations of growth identified by Malmberg et al. (1996) assert that location in an agglomeration can improve the economic performance of a firm by reducing the costs of transactions both for tangible goods and for services (Appold 1995). In Scott's (1988a) view, such savings (and hence the formation of regionalized industrial systems) will be strongest in situations where linkages are small-scale, unstable and unpredictable. Many explanations of service agglomeration have sought similar explanations. For example, Coffey (1992, p. 142) suggests that:

> where both forward and backward linkages are concerned, the concentration of producer services in a small number of large cities enables the transaction costs associated with the production and delivery of such services to be minimized. In particular, it is the cost of maintaining face-to-face contact between the producers, on the one hand, and their inputs and markets, on the other hand, that is potentially the most expensive element of intermediate-demand service production: this expense can be significantly reduced by spatial agglomeration.

In such accounts, the geography of producer service employment is often equated with the local geography of demand and the decisive need to be located in "information dense environments" (Illeris 1996, p. 118). However, there are increasing doubts about the generality and transferability of the transaction cost argument. Remarkably, the empirical evidence for intense and efficient localized linkages has proved to be fairly weak, especially in service sector activities. For example, Henry (1992, p. 388) has argued that the transaction cost mechanism may be only one of many processes causing agglomerations:

> the mechanism's operation to create agglomeration is a contingent and not a necessary relation. The possibility exists that the causal mechanism may operate without creating the outcome of agglomeration.

Attention shifts, then, to the many other mechanisms that may produce agglomerations, such as localized processes of externalization, labor market externalities, and socio-cultural factors. Despite the central importance of these processes to contemporary economic geography, conceptual understanding and delimitation of these dynamics are still very uneven, as Gordon and McCann (2000, p. 515) describe:

> discussion of industrial clustering has tended to conflate ideas arising from quite different perspectives, which are sometimes complementary, and sometimes contradictory. Empirical observations of industrial clustering can then be interpreted in quite different ways, depending on the observer's initial perspective, with little consciousness of alternative ways in which these might be understood.

They go on to develop a useful threefold typology of processes that may be stimulating agglomeration. Firstly, Gordon and McCann identify a "model of pure agglomeration". This is based upon the work of writers such as Marshall (1916) and Hoover (1937, 1948). Marshall detailed three reasons why firms would group locally: the development of a specialized pool of labor, the local provision of important non-traded inputs (e.g., capital finance), and benefiting from flows of information and ideas. Hoover's classification was more alert to sectoral specificities. His three categories were the internal economies of scale from serving a large market, sector-specific localization economies, and non-sector-specific external economies, known as urbanization economies. In general, this model of agglomeration assumes that actors respond purely on self-interest in a competitive environment. Secondly, Gordon and McCann describe the "industrial complex model" based on the reduction of spatial transaction costs, as posited by Scott and others. In this scheme, individual firms determine that they can best keep down their transaction costs by locating close to other firms in the particular input-output production and consumption hierarchy in which they are embedded. Thirdly, they identify a "social network model", a more dynamic interpretation of events that has emerged in response to the shortcomings of the more static approaches just described (Malmberg et al. 1996). This interpretation builds on the observation that spatial clustering may well be in evidence without any significant local input-output relationships. In this view, economic systems are made up not only of physical flows, but also of exchanges of business information and technological expertise, both in traded and untraded forms (Scott 1995; Storper 1993; 1995). Notions of knowledge creation and the learning economy thus place the emphasis upon invisible territorialized synergies and interdependencies that are embedded in networks of actors. Such arguments again appear to be tailor made to explain developments in concentrations of service activity (for example, in the circulation of experienced and expert staff in the local labor market), but have tended to focus on the benefits of technological progress (see Storper 1995). However, the territorial basis of informal networks is also open to question. In research on the gaining of market intelligence in the software products industry, for example, Cornish (1997) concludes that proximity is not always necessary for the establishment of informal networks, because of their basis in social relations or "social capital" (Coleman 1988).

Three further points are worth noting. Firstly, there is a wide variety of processes that may lie behind the agglomeration of economic activity, and they are often operating simultaneously to varying extents. For example, Simmie (1998, p. 1266) concludes his study of innovation in Hertfordshire by stating that "no single one of the contemporary theories ... can account for even a majority of innovative firm agglomerative behavior." He goes on (p. 1285);

> The reasons for innovating there [Hertfordshire] are a complex mixture of the costs and benefits involved in arranging production between Hertfordshire and other places, special production factors within the county, the need to accommodate production changes, and the relationships between all these

production considerations and interactions with major, often international customers.

Secondly, the nature of the processes in operation may vary from sector to sector. For example the evidence presented by Gordon and McCann (2000, p. 527) from the London Employer Survey (LES) suggests that the financial sector exhibits different characteristics to other industries:

> City financial services stand out from other groups of respondents to the LES in terms of both their strong positive evaluation of proximity to related activities and the specific emphasis on local intelligence as the crucial externality ... Their main difference from other London businesses appears to be in the value attached to (sector-specific) localization economies.

This is consistent with Amin and Thrift's (1992) notion of the City as an international center for discourse construction, interaction and innovation (see also Thrift 1994 on the socio-cultural processes maintaining agglomeration in the City).

Thirdly, and most intriguingly, Gordon and McCann's empirical evidence from the 1996 LES throws doubt on the extent to which firms are even aware of the positive externalities that may be associated with co-location. They found that only 25 percent of private sector employment was in firms that perceived that being close to related activities was an advantage, with 25 percent stating it was actually a disadvantage due to increased competition, suggesting that the academic consensus has wrongly neglected the whole Loeschian landscape in which firms seek respectively to dominate their own spatially distinct markets. Many firms were not aware of spatial externalities, moving location primarily for reasons of cost and premises.

A key problem in this debate is the difficulty in empirically separating the agglomeration or localization economies attributable to firm location from other locational and structural influences - i.e. urbanization economies (Phelps 1992; Harrison et al. 1996). In particular, many of the mechanisms which are seen to create localization are connected to various forms of cumulative causation, i.e. the concept that the growth of a sector in an area has an impact on that area's attractiveness as a location for other sectors, through its impact on entrepreneurship, capital supply, labor supply and the institutional framework. In such an argument, spatial order is seen as process dependent, with new industry laid down in a layer-like fashion on inherited locational patterns. Such ideas are also receiving renewed interest in economics, for example in the work of Krugman, who argues strongly that "history matters", and that regional economic development is, by its very nature, a historical, path dependent process (see for example, Krugman 1991; Martin and Sunley 1996).

A central argument of this chapter must emerge, that existing research may have over-emphasized the importance of localization economies, and neglected these cumulative causation processes based on an area's pre-existing industrial and occupational structure. According to Maskell and Malmberg (1995), there are two important processes involved in this continuous reproduction of agglomeration. Firstly, entrepreneurs in a given industry will concentrate in geographical areas where the sector is already concentrated. Secondly, a cluster of firms in a certain sector will make the region especially suited to meet the locational requirements of such firms. Several service sector studies have identified how processes of externalization and new firm formation can cause co-location (e.g., Howells 1987, 1989; Marshall et al. 1988). A large-scale study of the UK computer services sector in the mid-1990s (Coe 1996a, 1996b, 1998) clearly illustrates the locational inertia inherent in new firm formation. We argue that new firm formation processes, which vary both quantitatively and qualitatively across the UK, underlie the most recent agglomeration of fast growing producer service sectors in the Greater South East. The computer services industry is a relatively young one, with the majority of growth occurring from 1980 onwards (Howells 1987), and hence it is vital to understand how computer service firms start up.

It can be asserted that computer service firms are essentially a product of the existing industrial structure of an area (Coe 1996a; 1996b). A crucial, but not unexpected, point to arise out of the survey was that the most important locational factor was *that the firms' original founders already lived locally*; for 58 percent of firms in both Hertfordshire and Berkshire. When firms decentralizing from London (14 percent in Hertfordshire, 17 percent in Berkshire) and those established due to links with existing companies in the county (19 and 7 percent respectively) were also taken into account, it was apparent that only a minority of firms were set up by investments from outside the local area (9 and 17 percent). The exact location chosen was not an important priority for decision-makers, rather proximity to the home of the founders and key staff was the crucial factor.[2] Subsequent to start-up, the survey firms showed an extremely low level of long-distance (inter-county, or inter-regional) mobility, and therefore, to explain development trends, the underlying local structural conditions, which create, (or hinder) the conditions for such new firm formation must be considered.

Table 12.3   The Mode of Establishment for Surveyed Firms

Mode of establishment	Herts.	Berks.	Total firms
New start up (in same area)	15	13	28
Spin-off	10	12	22
New start up (from outside the area)	4	8	12
Management buy-out	7	5	12
Take-over of existing company	3	2	5
Merger of existing companies	3	1	4
Management buy-in	1	0	1
Total	43	41	84

Source: Coe (1996a)

In line with the results of much producer services research (for example Beyers 1989; Illeris 1989; Keeble et al. 1991; O'Farrell et al., 1993; Perry 1992), new firm formation in the computer services industry would now appear to be occurring independently of any processes of vertical disintegration in manufacturing or service sectors. The majority of survey firms were either new local start-ups, or spin-offs from existing firms[3] (see Table 12.3). These two methods alone accounted for the establishment of nearly two-thirds of the surveyed firms, with the vast majority being initiated by the movement of individuals from existing employers, and not a process of larger scale externalization of groups of staff. In other words, many computer service businesses are being created independently of changes in established enterprises. Management buy-outs (MBOs) and new start-ups from outside the area (i.e., branches set up for geographical reasons) are the other two main modes of start up. A particularly important feature of the new firm formation process is that the vast majority of founders come from the same sector, in this case the IT industry. Indeed, the survey results indicate that firm formation in the computing industry is to a large extent self generating, with founders originating from computer hardware and services companies together accounting for some 75 percent of new firm formations in Hertfordshire and Berkshire. These results confirm that disintegration within the computer industry rather than between sectors is stimulating growth. The nature of this growth means that the historical origins of the UK computer services industry in central London and its subsequent dispersal since the mid-1970s (see Coe, 1996a, for a fuller account) have been crucial to the current levels of employment in the sector in the South East, and similar processes can be identified in other service sectors such as management consulting, market research and financial services (see Coe and Townsend, 1998, on East Surrey).

Obviously, the new firm formation process is not a free-floating, structurally determined phenomenon, as it is both socially and culturally grounded. Indeed, there is now a consensus that there is a whole suite of supply side factors unique to the core region that supports the apparently self-propelling processes of new firm creation. The labor market is undoubtedly a crucial factor, with the growth processes depending on a ready supply of highly skilled computer professionals and managers. This critical mass of employees is not only tied to the historical roots of the industry in South East England, but also to a series of quality of life and amenity choices made by relatively mobile high income professionals. In particular, the Greater South East appears to be an attractive residential location, offering a wide range of high quality, affordable suburban housing within commuting distance of London and the Western Arc. What is crucial though, is that new firm formation processes in the computer services industry appear to have powerful spatial underpinnings. The importance of the historical roots of the computer services industry in the south of Britain for the consequent spatial development of the sector suggests that the development of such industries is largely a historically specific, path dependent, process. Here our argument overlaps considerably with the more general point made by Webber and Rigby (1996, p. 201), who argue that:

> the emergence of high technology industrial regions is perhaps best "explained" by the path dependence that follows small, chance events. Continued competitive success of the region is then a matter of the creativity of the firms within it.

For example, the attraction of scientific and technical staff to the whole Western Arc was founded on the decentralization of the research laboratories of public and private national organizations to the area since the 1930s, but it is acknowledged that this was greatly assisted in the M4 corridor by chance events such as the foundation of establishments like

Aldermaston or Harwell. The locally-embedded nature of the new firm formation process is thus crucial in both creating and maintaining the agglomeration of computer service firms in the outer South East, with foreign investment being drawn to, and accentuating the dominance of the core region. In this sense, cumulative causation processes are a vital driver of the concentration of activity, and it is imperative that any subsequent linkage patterns of firms once established are not simply "read off" as the reason for co-location. However, we are not suggesting that this is the *only* form of cumulative causation in operation - for example, the emergence and maintenance of a well qualified and entrepreneurial workforce clearly has self-reinforcing effects within the Greater South East - rather it is one clear and powerful example of how history matters.

Conclusion and Policy Implications

Our aim in this chapter has been to identify three important caveats with respect to the burgeoning literature on local networks and agglomerations. Firstly, debates surrounding agglomerative processes need to focus more explicitly on service sectors, activities that dominate dynamic regional economies, and especially core regions such as the South East of England. While this can create difficulties due to the more varied, diffuse and less visible nature of linkages in service sectors, this shift is an important one if economic geography is to maintain its relevance to contemporary economic realities. Secondly, we have endeavored to expose what we have elsewhere termed the "myth of localized agglomeration" (Coe and Townsend 1998) by suggesting that the appropriate level for studying the network relations of producer service firms is the Greater South East as a whole. In other words, we feel that networked clusters at smaller spatial scales have been overemphasized. This conclusion does not necessarily undermine the arguments of proponents of localized agglomerations in certain manufacturing sectors, and indeed, it may be dangerous to generalize about the dynamics of the whole region's economy from studies of producer service sectors. Equally, there will be different spatial patterns of network relations in different producer service sectors: as we have shown, localized networks of interaction may typify the activity patterns of financial institutions in the city, but the linkage patterns of many computer service and computer-using firms in the South East stretch across the country.

Overall, however, we feel our argument is a useful corrective to the implicit assumption in much of the literature that co-locating firms in the same sector are *necessarily* interacting. In traditional areas of industrial production where this was historically true, the surviving firms may have no linkages left between them and may attract no firms whatsoever to the area, a fact frequently born out by empirical analysis. Equally we argue that a jump to the opposite extreme, of seeing producer services as being dominated by international or global forces, is equally fallacious. Despite the inroads of globalization processes, especially on the City of London, and the efforts of the EU to harmonize international trade in services, the sales of surveyed establishments to locations beyond the UK rarely amounted to more than a small fraction. Thirdly, in the absence of these dense local networking patterns, there are obvious doubts about their influence as a causal factor leading to the development of agglomerations. We argue that there are important historical processes at work, and that cumulative causation processes are at the heart of the agglomeration of producer service firms in London and the Western Arc. In particular, in new sectors such as computer services, the locational logics inherent to the new firm formation process, be that by indigenous firms, or foreign investors looking for a foothold in the leading region in the UK through acquisition, have a massive impact on patterns of co-location. Evidently, more refinement and discrimination are needed as to the possible causes of agglomeration, and in particular among the urbanization economies or cumulative causation processes that may be operating at a regional, or even wider level.

In one respect these conclusions support present government policy. The new Labour government of 1997 failed to assert previous policies which sought to re-direct growth from the South East to other, needy regions. In part, this was no doubt to avoid being seen to restore intervention in the affairs of industry; in part is was because their advisers were unaware of past policies of the 1970s and were swimming with the tide of new patterns. It would also be true, however, given the size structure and dynamics of computer services, that this key growth industry would be difficult to move from the South East (Coe 1999), although this need not apply to all producer services (Coe and Townsend 1998). All regions, including those of the South East, have now been given Regional Development Agencies, most of which are advocating development through clusters of growth. There may be a variety of ways in which clusters may be of some little assistance to development; they will generally do no harm in the receiving areas, although they may in the neglected ones. There may be a few industries in which the arguments for clusters are more specific, as may be the case with biotechnology. However, for the most part, the policy advisers are following the same exaggerated fashions that are so heavily qualified in this chapter, and, when endorsed by the UK Treasury, may lead to distortions in spending.

Notes

1   A fairly broad definition of the sector is favored here, covering the following activities: software products, custom software, total systems/systems integration, consultancy, IT facilities management, hardware maintenance, data processing, IT training, IT recruitment and contract staff, database services, software maintenance, value added reselling, value added networks and contingency planning (i.e., disaster planning).
2   The major motivation for entrepreneurs to start new firms was the perception of a market opportunity, and it is important to remember the processes of corporate restructuring (in response to an increasingly complex external environment) that are stimulating demand for such services. See Coffey (1992) for a summary of these processes.
3   Spin-offs were defined in the situation where a founder used a product, service or skill developed in their previous employment to establish a new firm, while new start-ups represented founders moving into a slightly different area of expertise to establish a firm.

References

Allen, J. (1992), "Services and the U.K. space economy: regionalization and economic dislocation", *Transactions of the Institute of British Geographers New Series*, vol. 17, pp. 292-305.
Allen, J., Massey, D. and Cochrane, A. (with Charlesworth, J., Court, G., Henry, N. and Sarre, P.) (1998), *Rethinking the region*, Routledge, London.
Amin, A. (1993), "The globalization of the economy: an erosion of regional networks?", in Grabher, G. (ed), *The embedded firm: on the socio-economics of industrial networks*, Routledge, London, pp. 278-95.
Amin, A. and Thrift, N. (1992), "Neo-Marshallian nodes in global networks", *International Journal of Urban and Regional Research*, vol. 16, pp. 571-87.
Amin, A. and Thrift, N. (1994), *Globalization, institutions, and regional development in Europe*, Oxford University Press, Oxford.
Appold, S.J. (1995), "Agglomeration, inter-organizational networks, and competitive performance in the US metalworking sector", *Economic Geography*, vol. 71, pp. 27-54.

Baker, P. (1995), "Small firms, industrial districts and power asymmetries", *International Journal of Entrepreneurial Behaviour & Research*, vol. 1, pp. 8-25.

Bennett, R.J., Graham, D.J. and Bratton, W. (1999), "The location and concentration of businesses in Britain: business clusters, business services, market coverage and local economic development", *Transactions of the Institute of British Geographers New Series*, vol. 24, pp. 393-420.

Beyers, W. (1989), *The producer services and economic development in the US: the last decade*, Final report for the US Department of Commerce, Department of Geography, University of Washington, Seattle.

Britton, S. (1990), "The role of services in production", *Progress in Human Geography*, vol. 14, pp. 529-46.

Bryson, J.R., Wood, P.A. and Keeble, D. (1993), "Business networks, small firm flexibility and regional development in UK business services", *Entrepreneurship and Regional Development*, vol. 5, pp. 265-77.

Castells, M. (1996), *The rise of the network society*, Blackwell, Oxford.

Christopherson, S. (1989), "Flexibility in the US service economy and the emerging spatial division of labour", *Transactions of the Institute of British Geographers New Series*, vol. 14, pp. 131-43.

Clark, G.L. (1993), "Global interdependence and regional development: business linkages and corporate governance in a world of financial risk", *Transactions of the Institute of British Geographers New Series*, vol. 18, pp. 309-25.

Coe, N.M. (1996a), *The growth and locational dynamics of the UK computer services industry, 1981-1996*, Unpublished PhD Thesis, Department of Geography, University of Durham.

Coe, N.M. (1996b), "Uneven development in the UK computer services industry since 1981", *Area*, vol. 28, pp. 64-77.

Coe, N.M. (1997), "Internationalization, diversification and spatial restructuring in transnational computer service firms: case studies from the UK market", *Geoforum*, vol. 28, pp. 253-70.

Coe, N.M. (1998), "Exploring uneven development in producer service sectors: detailed evidence from the British computer services industry", *Environment and Planning A*, vol. 30, pp. 2041-68.

Coe, N.M. (1999), "Local economic development strategies for the UK computer services sector", *Local Economy*, vol. 14, pp. 161-74.

Coe, N.M. and Townsend, A.R. (1998), "Debunking the myth of localised agglomerations: the development of a regionalised service economy in South-East England", *Transactions of the Institute of British Geographers New Series*, vol. 23, pp. 385-404.

Coffey, W.J. (1992), "The role of producer services in systems of flexible production", in Ernste, H. and Meier, V. (eds), *Regional development and contemporary industrial response: extending flexible specialisation*, Belhaven, London, pp. 133-46.

Coffey, W.J. and Bailly, A.S. (1991), "Producer Services and Flexible Production: An exploratory analysis", *Growth and Change*, vol. 22, pp. 95-117.

Coffey, W.J. and Bailly, A.S. (1992), "Producer services and systems of flexible production", *Urban Studies*, vol. 29, pp. 857-68.

Cohen, S. and Zysman, J. (1987), *Manufacturing matters: The myth of the post-industrial society*, Basic Books, New York.

Coleman, J.S. (1988), "Social capital in the creation of human capital", *American Journal of Sociology*, vol. 94, Supplement, pp. S95-120.

Cooke, P. (1996), "Reinventing the region: firms, clusters and networks in economic development", in Daniels, P.W. and Lever, W.F. (eds), *The global economy in transition*, Longman, Harlow, pp. 310-27.

Cornish, S.L. (1996), "Marketing software products: the importance of 'being there' and the implications for business service exports", *Environment and Planning A*, vol. 28, pp. 1661-82.

Cornish, S.L. (1997), "Strategies for the acquisition of market intelligence, and implications for the network paradigm", *Annals of the Association of American Geographers*, vol. 87, pp. 451-70.

Crewe, L. (1996), "Material culture: embedded firms, organizational networks and the local economic development of a fashion quarter", *Regional Studies*, vol. 30, pp. 257-72.

Department of Trade and Industry (1999), *Our Competitive Future; building the knowledge driven economy*, White Paper, HMSO.

Dunford, M. and Fielding, A.J. (1997), "Greater London, the South-east region and the wider Britain: metropolitan polarization, uneven development and inter-regional migration", in H.H. Blotevogel and A.J. Fielding (eds), *People, jobs and mobility in the New Europe*, Wiley, Chichester. pp. 247-76.

Foundation for SME Development (2000), *A regional overview and initial mapping of potential areas of clustering in the North East of England*, Foundation for SME Development, University of Durham.

Garnsey, E. and Cannon-Brookes, A. (1993), "Small high technology firms in an era of rapid change: evidence from Cambridge", *Local Economy*, vol. 8, pp. 318-33.

Gordon, I.R. and McCann, P. (2000), "Industrial clusters: complexes, agglomeration and/or social networks?", *Urban Studies*, vol. 37, pp. 513-32.

Hall, P., Breheny, M., McQuaid, R. and Hart, D. (1987), *Western sunrise: the genesis and growth of Britain's major high tech corridor*, Allen and Unwin, London.

Hardill, I., Fletcher, D. and Montagne-Vilette, S. (1995), "Small firms' 'distinctive capabilities' and the socio-economic milieu: findings from case studies in Le Choletais (France) and the East Midlands (UK)", *Entrepreneurship and Regional Development*, vol. 7, pp. 167-86.

Harrison, B., Kelley, M.R. and Gant, J. (1996), "Innovative firm behaviour and local milieu: exploring the intersection of agglomeration, firm effects, and technological change", *Economic Geography*, vol. 72, pp. 233-58.

Harvey, D. (1985), "The geopolitics of capitalism", in Gregory, D. and Urry, J. (eds), *Social relations and spatial structures*, Macmillan, Basingstoke.

Henry, N. (1992), "The new industrial spaces: locational logic of a new production era?", *International Journal of Urban and Regional Research*, vol. 16, pp. 375-96.

Hirst, P. and Zeitlin, J. (1989), *Reversing industrial decline? Industrial structure and policy in Britain and her competitors*, Berg, Oxford.

Hoover, E.M. (1937), *Location theory and the shoe and leather industries*, Harvard University Press, Cambridge, MA.

Hoover, E.M. (1948), *The location of economic activity*, McGraw-Hill, New York.

Howells, J. (1987), "Developments in the location, technology and industrial organisation of computer services: some trends and research issues", *Regional Studies*, vol. 21, pp. 493-503.

Howells, J. (1989), "Externalisation and the formation of new industrial operations: a neglected dimension in the dynamics of industrial location", *Area*, vol. 21, pp. 289-99.

Illeris, S. (1989), *Services and regions in Europe*, Avebury, Aldershot.

Illeris, S. (1996), *The service economy: a geographical approach*, Wiley, Chichester.

Jones, A. (1998), "Local economies and business networks revisited: a case study of business and professional services in London", *Local Economy*, vol. 13, pp. 151-65.

Keeble, D., Bryson, J. and Wood, P. (1991), "Small firms, business services growth and regional development in the U.K.: some empirical findings", *Regional Studies*, vol. 25, pp. 439-57.

Krugman, P. (1991), "History and industrial location: the case of the manufacturing belt", *The American Economic Review*, vol. 81, pp. 80-3.

Lash, S. and Urry, J. (1994), *Economies of signs and spaces*, Sage, London.

Lawton-Smith, H., Mihell, D. and Kingham, D. (2000), "Knowledge-complexes and the locus of technological change: the biotechnology sector in Oxfordshire", *Area*, vol. 32, pp. 179-88.

Lee, C.H. (1986), *The British economy since 1700: a macroeconomic perspective*, CUP, Cambridge.

Maillat, D. (1995), "Territorial dynamic, innovative milieus and regional policy", *Entrepreneurship and Regional Development*, vol. 7, pp. 157-65.

Malmberg, A. (1996), "Industrial geography: agglomeration and local milieu", *Progress in Human Geography*, vol. 20, pp. 392-403.

Malmberg, A. and Maskell, P. (1997), "Towards an explanation of regional specialization and industry agglomeration", *European Planning Studies*, vol. 5, pp. 25-42.

Malmberg, A., Solvell, O. and Zander, I. (1996), "Spatial clustering, local accumulation of knowledge and firm competitiveness", *Geografiska Annaler*, vol. 78B, pp. 85-97.

Marshall, A. (1916), *Principles of economics: an introductory volume*, (7th edn.), Macmillan, London.

Marshall, J.N., Wood, P.A., Daniels, P.W., McKinnon, A., Bachtler, J., Damesick, P., Thrift, N., Gillespie, A., Green, A. and Leyshon, A. (1988), *Services and Uneven Development*, Oxford University Press, Oxford.

Martin, R. and Sunley, P. (1996), "Paul Krugman's geographical economics and its implications for development theory: a critical assessment", *Economic Geography*, vol. 72, pp. 259-92.

Maskell, P. and Malmberg, A. (1995), *Localised learning and industrial competitiveness*, BRIE Working Paper 80, Berkeley Roundtable on the International Economy.

McCann, P. (1995), "Rethinking the economics of location and agglomeration", *Urban Studies*, vol. 32, pp. 563-77.

Michalak, W.Z. and Fairbairn, K.J. (1993), "The producer service complex of Edmonton: the role and organisation of producer service firms in a peripheral city", *Environment and Planning A*, vol. 25, pp. 761-77.

Moulaert, F., Scott, A.J. and Farcy, H. (1997), "Producer services and the formation of urban space", in F. Moulaert and A.J. Scott (eds), *Cities, enterprises and society on the eve of the 21st century*, Pinter, London, pp. 97-112.

O'Farrell, P.N., Moffat, L.A.R. and Hitchens, D.M. (1993), "Manufacturing demand for business services in a core and peripheral region: does flexible production imply vertical disintegration of business services?", *Regional Studies*, vol. 27, pp. 385-400.

O'Farrell, P.N., Wood, P.A. and Zheng, J. (1996), "Internationalization of business services: an interregional analysis", *Regional Studies*, vol. 30, pp. 101-18.

Penn, R. (1992), "Contemporary relationships between firms in a classic industrial locality: evidence from the Social Change and Economic Life initiative", *Work, Employment & Society*, vol. 6, pp. 209-27.

Perry, M. (1992), "Externalisation and the interpretation of business service growth", *Service Industries Journal*, vol. 12, pp. 1-16.

Phelps, N.A. (1992), "External economies, agglomeration and flexible accumulation", *Transactions of the Institute of British Geographers New Series*, vol. 17, pp. 35-46.

Piore, M. and Sabel, C. (1984), *The Second Industrial Divide*, Basic Books, New York.

Porter, M.E. (1990), *The Competitive Advantage of Nations*, Macmillan, London.

Porter, M.E. (1998), "Clusters and the new Economics of Competition", *Harvard Business Review*, Nov-Dec 77(1).

Sayer, A. and Walker, R. (1992), *The new social economy; reworking the division of labour*, Blackwell, Oxford.

Scott, A.J. (1988a), "Flexible production systems and regional development: the rise of new industrial spaces in North America and Western Europe", *International Journal of Urban and Regional Research*, vol. 12, pp. 171-86.

Scott, A.J. (1988b), *New industrial spaces: flexible production, organisation and regional development in North America and Western Europe*, Pion, London.

Scott, A.J. (1995), "The geographic foundations of industrial performance", *Competition & Change*, vol. 1, pp. 51-66.

Scott, A.J. (1996), "Regional motors of the global economy", *Futures*, vol. 28. pp. 391-411.

Scott, A.J. (1998), *Regions and the world economy*, OUP, Oxford.

Simmie, J. (1998), "Reasons for the development of 'islands of innovation': evidence from Hertfordshire", *Urban Studies*, vol. 35, pp. 1261-89.

Sjoholt, P. (1994), "The role of producer services in industrial and regional development: the Nordic case", *European Urban & Regional Studies*, vol. 1, pp. 115-29.

Smith, H.L., Mihell, D. and Kingham, D. (2000), "Knowledge complexes and the locus of technological change: the biotechnology sector in Oxfordshire", *Area*, vol. 32(2), pp. 179-188.

Storper, M. (1993), "Regional 'worlds' of production: learning and innovation in the technology districts of France, Italy and the USA", *Regional Studies*, vol. 27, pp. 433-55.

Storper, M. (1995), "The resurgence of regional economies, ten years later: the region as a nexus of untraded interdependencies", *European Urban & Regional Studies*, vol. 2, pp. 191-221.

Storper, M. and Walker, R. (1989), *The capitalist imperative; territory, technology, and industrial growth*, Blackwell, Oxford.

Sweeting, R. (1995), "Competition, co-operation and changing the manufacturing infrastructure", *Regional Studies*, vol. 29, pp. 87-94.

Thrift, N. (1994), "On the social and cultural determinants of international financial centres: the case of the City of London", in Corbridge, S., Martin, R. and Thrift, N. (eds), *Money, power and space*, Blackwell, Oxford, pp. 327-55.

Weber, A. (1929), *Theory of the location of industries*, University of Chicago Press, Chicago, Illinois.

Webber, M.J. and Rigby, D.L. (1996), *The golden age illusion: rethinking postwar capitalism*, The Guilford Press, New York.

Wood, P.A. (1991), "Flexible accumulation and the rise of business services", *Transactions of the Institute of British Geographers New Series*, vol. 16, pp. 160-72.

Wood, P.A. (1996), "Business services, the management of change and regional development in the UK: a corporate client perspective services", *Transactions of the Institute of British Geographers New Series*, vol. 21, pp. 649-65.

Wood, P.A., Bryson, J. and Keeble, D. (1993), "Regional patterns of small firm development in the business services: evidence from the United Kingdom", *Environment and Planning A*, vol. 25, pp. 677-700.

PART IV: CONTEXTS OF NETWORK STRATEGIES

13 Rural Entrepreneurs: Using Personal Networks as a Business Strategy

MAE DEANS

Rural agribusiness owners operate their firms in a complex web of social relationships. This chapter emphasizes the importance of the relationship that exists between social structures and entrepreneurial activity of rural agribusiness owners. Social relationships experienced by these owners are not fully understood, yet an extensive body of literature exists on networks and entrepreneurial activity. However, little of this research concerns the networking activities of agribusiness entrepreneurs located in rural areas.

To contribute to this relatively unexplored area, I focus on three networks used by agribusiness owners: family and friendship networks, broker networks, and volunteer networks. The research draws on the theoretical work of Granovetter and Aldrich, particularly their work on the strength of weak ties and the embeddedness of economic activity in social action. More specifically, we explore the question of how the proximity to personal networks, chosen by an owner, constrain or augment the ability of a firm to export regionally, nationally, and internationally.

Background and Significance

The restructuring of the Canadian prairie economy during the last fifty years is well documented. Globalization, elimination of the Crow rate, and subsidy reductions because of World Trade Organization negotiations have contributed to the change in the agricultural industry (Rutley 2000). Agriculture, once the primary industry on the prairies, no longer dominates the economic landscape. Innovations have given agricultural producers more flexibility in the land cultivated, commodities produced, and markets reached. Therefore, in place of agriculture and extractive activities, different forms of economic activity are emerging in rural areas: specialized government activities, tourism, agri-food processing, manufacturing or other business endeavors.

Alberta, one of Canada's most rapidly growing provinces supporting a population of almost three million, is experiencing unprecedented change. In Alberta 105 communities have populations between 1,000 and 15,000. More than 80 percent of these communities gained in population, contributing 34,204 new residents between 1991 and 1996 (Deans and Chambers 1997). This growth is occurring because of a robust economy fuelled by high oil and gas revenues, a burgeoning agri-food processing industry, and a strong communication and transportation infrastructure.

Until the last half-decade agribusiness owners had little choice where they worked. Their business had to be close to significant trade centers. Many business owners and workers engaged in a daily commute from their home to their workplace - often traveling more than an hour in each direction. Today, people no longer need to commute to metropolitan centers. Businesses now can operate in remote locations, yet still maintain contact with suppliers and customers thanks to FAX machines, E-mail and cellular phones. The cost of transactions across space has been lowered, at least for some types of work-related exchanges (Salent, Carley and Dillman 1996).

Operating a business in a rural area is fraught with enormous challenges. Traditional problems leading to social and economic isolation include declining populations or low population densities; these trends create low saturation points for absorbing goods and services. In turn, these factors create other issues for rural business owners; for instance an overworked and under-skilled workforce may culminate in a drop in the quality of work or the ability of business owners to engage in long-range planning (Aldrich and Auster 1986; Honadle 1983).

Yet what do we actually know about rural business owners who engage in business activities other than agriculture to supplement their agriculture activities? Studies suggest that rural businesses are unable to compete on price alone. These firms must take advantage of their geographic area, and the production of high quality, low volume, labor-intensive goods and services (OECD 1995). Business owners, using a valued-added strategy, may be more ready to compete and trade their product beyond the local market (Fossum 1993). Networks enable owners to identify services that they need, or to seek partnership opportunities with other firms especially when contracts are too large, too technically demanding or too distant for individual firms to undertake alone (Larson 1991).

One way to more fully understand the effects of social relationships upon business activities is to examine the importance of the relationship between social structures and entrepreneurial activity (Staber 1994). Business owners use social and personal networks to access know-how and resources they are unable to generate themselves (Larson 1991). Yet, Alberta business owners within the manufacturing sector have been described as having a solitary attitude toward business activities (Cameron 1993). In other words, these owners prefer to pursue business-related opportunities by themselves rather than in concert with others. These owners prefer to market, obtain financing, identify competition or initiate product development on their own.

Ultimately, the image of the self-sufficient rural business owner may be an idealized construct left over from memories of the opening of the Canadian Prairies by settlers. This myth may lead people to a delusion that they can do everything without benefit of counsel, advice and knowledge from others. This image may be obscure in the fact that pioneers operated their farms and businesses within a well-articulated network of social and economic ties. Still, whether or not businesses are found in rural or urban areas, people who forge social relationships operate businesses. Through these relationships they carry out transactions in the day-to-day activities of the firm. These businesses are not artificial constructs that emerge without some form of social interaction among society members.

Theory

The underlying assumption of business owners and their networks in this study is that the economic life of a business is embedded in the social relationships fostered by the business owners (Deans 1996). Anthropologist Fredrik Barth (1966) alluded to the notion of networks in his discussion of transactions. For Barth, entrepreneurs are inventors who seek to make profits. They engage in transactions for goods and services with others whom they had not been associated with previously. Therefore for Barth (1966, p. 18) entrepreneurial activity thus tends to make a bridge between what before was separated.

Granovetter (1974a) builds upon this notion of bridging in his sociological theory on the strength of weak ties. In his book *Getting a Job*, Granovetter believed that those individuals with whom one has the most contact would be the people who were most likely to be of help locating a job. The strong ties that Granovetter alludes to are those of family, friends and co-workers. These are the people who tend to interact with each other most often and in the most varied situations. However, the weak ties, those people who are less well known to each other, are more likely to divulge needed information to acquire work. As Granovetter (1974b, p. 54) noted "Acquaintances are more likely to pass on job information than close friends...".

In a business context, Aldrich et al. (1986) suggests that owners who are securely linked to a few sources of information may acquire superfluous or useless knowledge with unclear meaning. In a study of older married men and women, men were more likely to turn to their wives for assistance. Therefore there may be a tendency that one of the couple may have the same information and knowledge with only small amounts of new information infiltrating their network (Dykstra 1990).

Consistent with the notion of weak ties is the role of brokers in social networks. The function of broker networks is to link persons having complementary interests, transferring information, and otherwise facilitating the interest of persons not directly connect to one another (Aldrich and Zimmer 1986, p. 24). Today trade shows trade journals, conferences and the Internet are but a few of the broker networks that provide venues for entrepreneurs to access both customers and information about possible markets, technical knowledge and even competitors.

Studies suggest that business owners who work within embedded personal relationships can foster business opportunities (Staber and Aldrich 1995; Rosenfeld 1992). Three conclusions can be drawn from the available information regarding social relationships and business activities. First economic action (like all action) is socially situated and cannot be explained by individual motives alone; it is embedded in ongoing networks of personal relations rather than carried out by atomized actors (Granovetter 1992, p. 4). Secondly, research literature indicates that business owners use many avenues to acquire knowledge and information that will augment their business activities (Aldrich and Zimmer 1986). Thirdly, the social relationships or networking activities of rural Alberta business owners need to be documented including the reasons these owners choose to operate in locations far from Alberta's two major metropolitan centers: Edmonton and Calgary (Apedaile and Fullerton 1994).

There are several possible reasons for the operation of businesses in rural Alberta. Owners may wish to remain close to home; or an excellent physical infrastructure such as roads and communication systems allow for easy transport of goods and speedy contact with people distant from the home base of operation; or overall the negative effects of high location costs such as building rent and utilities deter movement to larger centers; or lifestyle and quality of life, and personal relationship ties prevail.

Study Area, Purpose and Methodology

The project area is the geographic area defined by the East Parkland Community and Business Development Corporation (EPCBDC) as at December 31, 1994. This area was chosen because of the following characteristics: its dependence upon the primary industries of agriculture, oil and gas, and mining and its distance from Alberta's two major metropolitan centers of Edmonton and Calgary. The EPCBDC is a Government of Canada initiative promoting valued-added businesses in economically depressed regions of the country.

The primary purpose of the project was to study how social networks of rural business owners either contribute or constrain those businesses from trading in markets beyond their home base of operation. The emphasis is place on non-agricultural businesses engaged in various types of manufacturing endeavors.

More specific questions answered through this project were these: 1) where do rural business owners receive most of their information about possible new markets? 2) what factors contribute to the beginning of the business? 3) who does the business owner consult when making business decisions and finally 4) what are the characteristics of the owner and the business?

Answers to these questions came from face-to-face interviews employing an interview schedule which together with business owners, the interviewer completed. We included two types of businesses in this study. The first were small businesses producing value-added products, but skewed toward those firms that were manufacturing products such as cattle handling devices, creep feeders, woodworking and fiberglass products. The second were businesses engaged in niche agricultural operations such as greenhouses, emu, ostrich or llama production. Eligibility for participation in the study required that the firm's product must be traded beyond the local area. For the trading sub-sample, the firm's product should be sold beyond the Alberta border.

We identified 112 businesses, 75 defined as non-agricultural and 37 defined as agricultural. The analysis emphasizes those firms that we identified as traders. These traders (17 non-agricultural and eight agricultural) market their project beyond the Alberta border and display a propensity to compete in a larger market segment.

Business directories and membership lists were used to find the firms. Owners of these sources may use marketing strategies or have contact to determine those businesses that are included in the directories. Therefore, caution must be taken in generalizing these findings because it is difficult to determine to what extend the sample represents the population of firms who are traders.

Results

Economic Aspects of Trading Businesses

Ownership of the trading firms is shown in Table 13.1. More non-agricultural trading (NAT) firms were incorporated than agricultural trading (AT) firms. Incorporated NAT firms accounted for 59 percent of the trading group, with 37 percent of the firms be owned with family members and 24 percent being owned with a non-family member. More AT firms were proprietors and partnerships than the NAT firms. Proprietorships account for 17 percent of the NAT firms. The AT firms showed fewer incorporations with 37 percent. Fifty percent were partnerships with family members and 13 percent proprietorships.

Table 13.1   Comparison of Trading/Non-Agricultural (NAT) and Trading/Agricultural (AT) Firms by Legal Ownership

Legal Ownership	NAT Percent of Respondents	AT Percent of respondents
Proprietorship	17	13
Partnership with family member	24	50
Incorporated with family	35	37
Incorporated with non-family	24	0
Total	100	100

Source: Original Data - NAT n=17; AT n=8

The mean age of the NAT and AT firms was 12.1 and 6.1 years respectively (Table 13.2). The largest percentage of new firms was the AT group with 63 percent. Twenty-eight percent of the NAT firms were in the age category of zero to five years while 63 percent of the AT firms were in the same age category. Thirty percent of the firms in the NAT group had been operating between twenty-one and twenty-six years, compared with 12 percent of the AT businesses.

Small business development is seen as an important component contributing to the growth and stability of rural economies by providing employment and income opportunities for community members (Dykeman, 1992). The NAT and AT firms provided employment for a total of 137 people (Table 13.3). The NAT firms provided full-time employment for a total of sixty-nine people, 73 percent were males and 27 percent females. The AT firms employed considerably fewer individuals: 11 full-time and 29 part-time positions respectively.

Table 13.2   Comparison of Trading/Non-Agricultural (NAT) and Trading/Agricultural (AT) Firms by Age

Age	NAT Percent of respondents	AT Percent of respondents
0 – 5 years	28	63
6 – 10 years	24	25
11 – 15 years	18	0
16 – 20 years	0	0
21 – 26 years	30	12
Total	100	100

Source: Original Data - NAT n = 17; AT n = 8

Seventy-five percent of the AT firms had sales of less than $CAN100,000 compared with 51 percent of the NAT firms (Table 13.4). Thirty-six percent of the NAT firms have gross sales of $CAN 400,000 or more, with 20 percent of those firms having gross sales of $CAN 500,000 or more. The NAT sample had twice as many firms with gross sales exceeding $CAN 500,000 than did the AT sample.

Table 13.3   Comparison of Trading/Non-Agricultural (NAT) and Trading/Agricultural (AT) Firms by Total Number of Full-time and Part-time Employees

| | Full-time | | | Part-time | | |
	Male	Female	Total	Male	Female	Total
NAT	45	13	58	35	04	39
AT	06	05	11	16	13	29
Total	51	18	69	51	17	68

Source: Original Data - NAT n = 17; AT n = 8

We also asked where these firms export their product (Table 13.5). NAT and AT firms both sold more than half of their product locally. Yet, these same firms are increasing their export radius beyond their local area. Eighteen percent of the NAT firms and 25 percent of the AT firms export off the North

American continent that is, outside Canada, the United States and Mexico. Although the AT owners rely more on exporting locally rather than aggressively venturing farther a field.

Table 13.4   Comparison of Trading/Non-Agricultural (NAT) and Trading/Agricultural (AT) Firms by Gross Sales

Gross Sales ($CAN)	NAT Percent of respondents	AT Percent of respondents
0 - $ 99,999	24	75
$100,000 - $199,999	17	13
$200,000 - $299,999	23	00
$300,000 - $399,999	00	00
$400,000 - $499,999	12	00
$500,000 – or more	24	12
Total	100	100

Source: Original Data - NAT n = 17; AT n = 8

Table 13.5   Comparison of Trading/Non-Agricultural (NAT) and Trading/Agricultural (AT) Firms with Sales Locally, within Alberta, Western Canada, United States and Mexico and Internationally

Export Area	NAT Percent of respondents	AT Percent of respondents
Local	65	75
Alberta	65	38
Western Canada	65	50
United States and Mexico	35	25
International	17	25

Source: Original Data - NAT n = 17; AT n = 8

Socio-Demographic Trading Owner Characteristics

Table 13.6 describes the characteristics of the owner including gender, age, marital status and education. Eighty percent of the owners of the NAT firms were male and 18 percent were female, compared to the AT firms with 50 percent male and 50 percent female ownership.

The NAT owners were older than the AT owners, with a mean age of 45.2 and 43.7 years respectively. The average age for these owners is slightly less than the average age of an Alberta farm operator in 1991, which was 49.0 years. (Alberta 1993). Thirty percent of the NAT firms had owners in the age range of 35-44 years, while 62 percent of the AT firm owners fell into the same category.

Table 13.6   Comparison of Trading/Non-Agricultural (NAT) and Trading/Agricultural (AT) by Owner's Attributes: Gender, Age, Marital Status and Education Attainment

Characteristics	NAT Percent of respondents	AT Percent of respondents
Gender		
Male	82	50
Female	18	50
Age		
25 to 34 years	12	00
35 to 44 years	30	62
45 to 54 years	47	38
55 to 64 years	11	00
Marital Status		
Never Married	12	00
Married/Common Law	82	88
Divorced/Separated	06	12
Widowed	00	00
Education – K –12		
Elementary or less	18	00
Some High School	18	38
High School Graduate	64	62
Education – Post Secondary		
Some College or Technical	24	25
Technical or College Degree	24	50
University Degree	17	00
No Post Secondary	35	25

Source: Original Data - NAT n = 17; AT n = 8

An equal number of NAT and AT owners have completed high school: sixty-four and 62 percent respectively. Eighteen percent of the NAT group has elementary schooling or less. Elementary means a grade eight education or less, for this study. Several interviewees had some form of secondary schooling. Twenty-four percent of the NAT group completed a college or technical degree and 17 percent have a university degree. Fifty percent of the AT owners had completed a technical or college degree. The post-secondary educational attainment for this sample was less than an Alberta study of small businesses by Steier and Greenwood (N.D.) Overall the NAT group was more comparable to Alberta farm operators than the AT group in educational attainment. In 1991, 26 percent of farm operators completed some form of post-secondary, non-university training and 11 percent had completed university (Alberta 1993).

We also asked why the business was founded. While the reasons varied among the respondents, five main categories emerged between the NAT and AT owners: personal interest, needed employment, farm diversification, health reasons and investments. Almost one third of the NAT owners started the business because they needed employment. For example, one NAT owner purchased the assets of the firm with unpaid wages, while another NAT owner indicated that all the doors seemed to close..."this was our last hope".

Still, one quarter of the NAT owners and two-fifths of the AT owners founded the business specifically as a farm diversification initiative. They cited the reason for this action as low and fluctuating grain and cattle prices including the need for a secure income. These owners wanted to be wage earners, rather than relying on a fluctuating income that is fixed to the market value, when selling cattle or grain. A secure income allows for some degree of personal financial planning especially for retirement considerations.

Personal interest in the endeavor was also high for both NAT and AT owners. One fourth of the AT owners diversified because of health reasons. These AT owners claimed that cattle were too dangerous and that they feared being injured while other owners suggested allergies or chronic health conditions as reasons for diversification. Thirty-five percent of the NAT owners were interested in a specific activity such as welding, computers or jewelry. These activities provided a basis for starting their current business.

Networks as a Business Strategy

The primary question explored through this research was what type of networks these traders used to augment their business activities. Three networks are discussed in this paper. The first network is broker networks or those networks that facilitate the economic activity of the entrepreneur (Aldrich and Zimmer 1986). The second network is the friendship network that provides solace, strength and support in times of crisis (Staber 1994). Finally volunteer networks are activities such as participation on government boards, churches or community activities that enable owners to bridge into social networks beyond their local area (Fischer 1982).

Broker networks include customers, trade shows, journals, auction sales, newspapers, suppliers and sales people and the Internet (Table 13.7). Correlations suggest that relationships exist between gross sales of the NAT firms and broker marketing networks for products sold to the United States and Mexico. These broker networks can provide specialized knowledge about culture, advertising strategies and customs regulations that enable international sales. These owners may acquire an abundance of knowledge and expertise from several broker networks that they are involved with.

Table 13.7 **Comparison of Trading/Non-Agricultural (NAT) and Trading/Agricultural (AT) Firms by Importance of Broker and Friendship Networks**

	NAT Moderate to V. Important	NAT Not Important	AT Moderate to V. Important	AT Not Important
Broker Network				
Word of Mouth	88	12	88	12
Trade Shows	65	35	88	12
Producers of Similar Products	59	41	50	50
Sales People	53	47	37	63
Newspapers	41	59	75	25
Suppliers	36	64	50	50
Trade Journals	24	76	75	25
Auction Sales	24	76	62	38
Conferences	24	76	62	38
Internet	00	100	00	100
Friendship Networks				
Friends	59	41	37	63

Source: Original Data - NAT n = 17; AT n = 8.

AT firms showed negative and non-significant correlations with broker networks (Table 13.8). Part of the reason for these negative correlations might be that these were infant businesses: the mean age was 6.1 years. Owners might be applying knowledge from the involvement in the grain and cattle industries. This knowledge of whom to contact, where to make contacts, what to ask or where to go for information may not readily be available through their current networks. Their current networks may be providing spurious information that is not pertinent to their new business endeavors however similar these new businesses may be to their former activities. Therefore their current knowledge is not appropriate for a new business activity that might function in a vastly different way.

Table 13.8   Correlations Measuring Ranked Associations Between Gross Sales and Broker Networks, Volunteer and Friendship Networks

	Broker Networks	Volunteer Networks	Friendship Networks
Trading: Non-Agricultural			
Gross Sales - Total	.24	.41*	-.03
- Alberta	-.12	-.03	.36
- Canada	-.07	.18	.32
- US and Mexico	.53*	.23	.43
- Other	.32	.15	-.20
Trading: Agricultural			
Gross Sales - Total	-.33	-	-.40
- Alberta	-.30	.12	.05
- Canada	-.07	.12	-.14
- US and Mexico	-.33	-	-.40
- Other	.45	.54	.27

Source: Original Data - NAT n = 17; AT n = 8; Significant at P<.05*; P<.01**

Friendship networks provide companionship for social activities or practical assistance (Fischer 1982; Shambly 1990). Friendship networks were weakly and negatively, but not significantly correlated with total gross sales and strongly and moderately correlated with sales beyond Alberta markets, Canada, the US and Mexico. The negative and weak correlations for friends and total gross sales might suggest that the more important owners believe their friends were providing information about marketing their product, the less likely their sales would increase (Table 13.8). These findings suggest that business owners use friendships for more personal activities rather than for business activities for both NAT and AT owners.

Friendships, while being a source of pleasure when sharing the positive aspects about the business, might be a source of pain especially when friends have declined or failed to provide the support and information that the owners anticipated. One business owner whose spouse was terminally ill indicated "since my [spouse] took sick, we don't have the friends come that we used to...they seem scared to come now". Another owner claimed that his interests had changed since he started the business. He expressed this sentiment "I'm sure that many of our friends feel neglected, but I just don t have the time and I m not sure they [friends] understand that".

Granovetter (1974a) suggests that close family and friends are the least likely to share pertinent information. Fifty-nine percent of the NAT owners felt that friends gave them some type of information that would help them market their product. Sixty-three of the AT owners indicated that friendships were unimportant when marketing their product. This research suggests that NAT and AT owners are "looking through rose-colored glasses" if they believe friends will provide support for their new business activity. As one NAT owner claimed "I'd be sitting by myself in a corner [of the coffee shop] if I talked about my business". These owners fear being isolated within their own personal community. Good friends and neighbors may be reluctant to say that prices are too high or too low, that the product quality is less satisfactory than they would like, that the product is becoming obsolete in the marketplace or that the business venture is rash. Friends may want to avoid being the bearer of bad tidings and want to maintain a relationship however fragile even if the owner's interest has changed from activities once done together, to a single overriding preoccupation with the business.

Membership in volunteer organizations by business owners is often a way to meet other community members plus individuals from outside their local geographic area. Volunteer organizations were moderately and significantly correlated with total gross sales for the NAT firms (Table 13.8). This suggests that the more the organization's owner was involved with volunteer organizations, the greater the gross sales of the business were likely to be. Thus, the chance of meeting people at meetings, conferences and social events might lead to unexpected relationships enhancing business opportunities.

One NAT owner was very involved with a government board. This person suggested that this organization was attempting to have his particular industry become more regulated. AI was asked to join the board and it's really helpful - you learn a lot and meet different people. Still, another NAT owner was asked to join a volunteer government board to set standards for the industry. This individual noted "I really enjoy being involved, but it takes time". An AT owner indicated that at the local association meetings, he learned what was happening in the industry. He claimed that the executive works closely with some government people, they report back to us - but I never talk to government people. These owners recognize that organizational volunteer involvement can and does take time away from their business activities while other owners prefer to concentrate their energy solely on the business.

Since many NAT and AT owners employed very few people, they perform many business activities themselves: product design, marketing, purchasing, and the plethora of day-to-day operating concerns and being active participants in community, professional organizations and the family. As one spouse indicated, "my husband thinks about this [the business] constantly. He takes the cell [phone] everywhere and phones back all the time. Even on holiday". So the many owners place the affairs of the business ahead of any social involvement. The business becomes a greedy institution consuming the owners whole being.

Discussion

This project provides some provocative insights into the operation of these firms. First, these firms are emerging as traders. They export beyond their local area, but mainly venture into areas that the owners understand: namely the rest of Alberta and Western Canada. As these owners become experienced exporters, they will gain experience to export aggressively into larger market segments.

Second, these rural business owners are far from being solitary and individualistic. Indeed they might be described as entrepreneurial, purposeful, relationship-building risk-takers. Both NAT and AT owners network with many people to operate their businesses. These networks or webs of personal relationships augment the business by marshaling resources and knowledge necessary for the business operation. The owners realize that to build a thriving business in a geographic area remote from major metropolitan centers, they require the cooperation and collaboration of many people both inside and outside their own industry. Yet, the use of these networks may not necessarily be an owner's personal choice, but a choice imposed upon the owner by geography, propinquity of certain people, the sense of community or the nature of the business.

Third, by virtue of the business ventures, these rural entrepreneurs are nonconformists. They have chosen not to go along with the norms and values of a community where traditional agricultural activities of cereal and livestock production dominate. Other community members may look upon these risk-takers as irrational because their diversified economic activities do not follow the norms of the community. Community members may view these relationship-building entrepreneurs with suspicion because their competition in the global market place leads them to bring new ideas, new people and new ways of transacting business into the community. Yet, these entrepreneurs have personal ties to the community. Therefore although they may be perceived as different from the mainstream community membership, they are less likely to antagonize the old-timers and over time they are more likely to have their ideas accepted and become formal and informal leaders in their particular local community.

Fourth, the owner's children are noticeably absent from the networks for either social or business support. Although questions were designed to elicit this information, children fail to be present in the business operation. A NAT owner claimed I told my son that he could take over the business if he could produce the quality of work that I do. He never tried and now he's doing something else - so I don't think he will take this over, while an AT owner noted "I wanted my son to get an education and get outta here". Without the active encouragement and apprenticeship of family members into the business, continuation of these businesses through more than one generation is questionable.

Continuation of the business raises several issues. One issue is the community's reliance upon the business. Many community members have become reliant upon these local businesses as a primary family income base. Occasionally the income might be the sole source of revenue for a family. In other instances the income may supplement a farming operation. In total NAT and AT owners employ 137 people. By using existing labor supplies in the community, owners have helped to raise or to maintain the standard of living for local community members. A second issue is educational opportunities. Staff are direct recipients of knowledge through hands-on training. In communities where training opportunities are limited, these owners are trainers in their own right by creating formal and informal apprenticeship activities. Moreover, the staff have access to learning opportunities such as workshops and seminars that would not normally be available if these businesses were not present within the community.

Finally, we want to place our findings in the larger context of economic development. We recognize that a major food processing or manufacturing plant can have an enormous economic impact on a small community. The benefits derived from tax and utility revenue, jobs and related spin offs for local businesses cannot be ignored by community leaders or economic developers and planners. Yet, for these businesses to be excluded from development strategies may be a significant oversight, since these firms complement and increase the viability of the community not only be providing specialized services to existing firms, but also by increasing the social value of the community itself.

NAT and AT firms, although operating within the same geographic area, are very different in their business activities. Therefore, they must be treated as distinct policy domains. Since, these rural firms use differentiated types of knowledge and expertise, economic development initiatives must consider this. Policy initiatives should enable NAT and AT firms to secure appropriate financing through access to low interest rates for start-up and venture capital, promote education and retraining opportunities for workers and owners alike. Just as extension activities support traditional agricultural diversification efforts through field excursions to test plots, so should non-agricultural activities be supported with field trips to activities supporting their particular industry. Rural business owners, too, need to take advantage of and foster networks with colleges, universities, provincial, federal and private research initiatives, to stimulate research and development that is expensive as an independent venture.

For rural business owners, choosing networks is a means of developing social and economic relationships that complement each other. Thus, opportunities are created to trade beyond the local market area. Whichever networks an owner chooses to use, the owner must realize that this is an important personal decision, for networks have both positive and negative attributes. Choosing a network does not suggest choosing between networks, but rather suggests developing conditions where separate networks can complement, inform, and shape an attitude conducive to enhancing the business activity.

Acknowledgements

The research reported here was funded through grants from Human Resources Development Canada, Agri-Food and Agriculture Canada – Rural Secretariat and Prairie Farm Rehabilitation Administration. This support is gratefully acknowledged.

References

Alberta (Agriculture, Food and Rural Development) (1993), *Agriculture Statistics Yearbook – 1993*.

Aldrich, H. and E. Auster (1986), "Even Dwarfs Started Small: Liabilities of Age and Size and their Strategic Implications". *Research in Organizational Behavior*, 8:165-198.

Aldrich, H. and C. Zimmer (1986), "Entrepreneurship through Social Networks" in *Population Perspectives on Organizations*. Stockholm, Sweden: Uppsala.

Aldrich, H. et.al. (1986), *Population Perspectives on Organizations*. Stockholm, Sweden: Uppsala.

Apedaile, L. and D. Fullerton (1994), *A Comparative Analysis of Tradeables as a Development Strategy for Rural Economic Systems: Alberta - Nebraska - Sonora. Project Report #2.* Department of Rural Economy, University of Alberta.

Barth, F. (1966), *Models of Social Organization.* Royal Anthropological Institute Occasional Paper No. 23. University Press. Glasgow.

Cameron, K. (1993), *Manufacturing Networks: For the Competitiveness of Alberta Manufacturing Industries.* Western Centre for Economic Research: University of Alberta. Information Bulletin No. 17.

Deans, F. M. (1996), *Social Networks and the Economic Life of Rural Business.* Masters Thesis. University of Alberta. Unpublished.

Deans, Mae and E.J. Chambers (1997), *Communications Technology and the Business Service Sector: A Renaissance for Alberta's Communities.* Western Centre for Economic Research, Faculty of Business, University of Alberta. Information Bulletin No. 47.

Dykeman, F. (1992), "Home-Based Business: Opportunities for Rural Economic Diversification and Revitalization", *Contemporary Rural Systems, Vol 2, Economy and Society.* I. Bowler, C. Bryant, M. Nellis, (eds) C.A.B. International, Oxon, pp. 279-293.

Dykstra, P. (1990), "Disentrangling Direct and Indirect Gender Effects on the Supportive Network" in *Social Network Research: Substantive Issues and Methodological Questions.* (eds.) Knipscheer, K. and T. Antonucci. Swets and Zeitlinger, Amsterdam, pp. 55-65.

Fischer, C. (1982), *To Dwell Among Friends: Personal Networks in Town and City.* University of Chicago Press, Chicago.

Fossum, H. (1993), *Communities in the Lead: The Northwest Rural Development Sourcebook.* North West Policy Centre: University of Washington.

Granovetter, M. (1974a), "The Strength of Weak Ties", *American Journal of Sociology.* vol. 78, no. 6, pp. 1360-1380.

Granovetter, M. (1974b), *Getting a Job: A Study of Contacts and Careers.* Cambridge, Mass. Harvard University Press.

Granovetter, M. (1992), "Economic Institutions as Social Constructions: A Framework for Analysis", Acta Sociologica, vol. 35, pp. 3-11.

Honadle, B. (1983), *Public Administration in Rural Areas.* Garland Publishing, New York.

Larson, A. (1991), "Partner Networks: Leveraging External Ties to Improve Entrepreneurial Performance", *Journal of Business Venturing,* vol. 6, pp. 173-188.

Organization for Economic Cooperation and Development (OECD) (1995), *Niche Markets as Rural Development Strategy.* Paris.

Rosenfeld, S. (1992), *Smart Firms in Small Towns.* The Aspen Institute, Washington, D.C.

Rutley, B. C. (2000), *Needs Assessment of Peace Country Agricultural Value-Added Entrepreneurs.* Prepared for Peace Agriculture Value-Added Strategy Group, October

Salent, P., L. Carley and D. Dillman (1996), *Estimating the Contribution of Lone Eagles to Metro and Nonmetro In-Migration.* Social & Economic Sciences Research Centre. WA. Technical Report #96-19.

Shamley, F. (1990), "Neighbours Helping Neighbours: Informal Support Networks", in *Entrepreneurial and Sustainable Communities.* (ed.) F. Dykeman. Sackville, NB. Rural and Small Town Research and Studies Programme, pp. 221-225.

Staber, U. (1994), "Friends, Acquaintances, Strangers: Gender Differences in Structure of Entrepreneurial Networks", *Journal of Small Business and Entrepreneurship,* vol. 11, no. 1, pp. 73-82.

Staber, U. and H. Aldrich (1995), "Cross-National Similarities in the Personal Networks of Small Business Owners: A Comparison of Two Regions in North America", *Canadian Journal of Sociology,* vol. 20, no. 4, pp. 441-467.

Steier, L. and R. Greenwood (No Date), *Priming the Pump: Promoting the Small Business Sector in Alberta.* University of Alberta, Faculty of Business, Unpublished.

14 Developing and Coordinating Regional Networks for International Competitiveness: The Case of Queensland Agribusiness Exports

SHEELAGH MATEAR, BRETT TUCKER, ANDREW McCARROLL
AND LES BROWN

The markets-as-networks approach offers a conceptual framework for managers to understand their competitive world (Easton 2000). In particular, it highlights the concept of context for decision-making, rather than environment (Jutter and Schlange 1996). The approach has been used to gain insight into how firms, particularly smaller firms, internationalize, suggesting that internationalization depends on the relationships that the firm (Coviello and McAuley 1999). In terms of policy support for internationalization, the network perspective has been applied to trade promotion policy, particularly the development of export groups (Wilkinson, et al. 1998; Wilkinson, Mattsson and Easton 2000) where it has been used to provide insight into group membership, inter-firm learning and targeting facilitation.

This chapter adopts a markets-as-networks perspective to examine the development of internationalization among a group of small agribusiness firms in Queensland, Australia. In contrast to many other export grouping schemes, which are often focused on one major product group, these exporters provide a broad range of products. These exporters have adopted a collaborative approach to overcome problems of critical mass, multiple contact points and product quality specifications. However, the network extends beyond the immediate group to create an inter-regional network, which further increases the volume of product available and, in the case of fresh produce, the time period for which it is available. A further unique feature of this case is the alignment of the network with the category management system adopted by one of the major customers. The collaborative efforts and network development have enabled these firms to compete successfully in international markets, in particular establishing supply relationships with major food retail conglomerates in Asia.

The processes through which relationships, and therefore networks, develop are complex and difficult to appreciate from an external analyst's perspective. This chapter draws from the action research report of the Senior Trade Development Officer who played a key role in facilitating the development of the network, plus archive files of the project, interviews with alliance members and multiple interviews with the trade development officer. The use of a single case is justified as the approach to international competitiveness reported here is unusual, if not unique, both substantively and in terms of the participant-observation nature of the data collection (Yin 1984). The participant-observation nature of the case, historical account, and retrospective nature of the analysis reflect a subjectivist approach to the research (Borsch and Arthur 1995), which together with a case study methodology are appropriate for studying network phenomenon (Easton 1998). The participant-observation approach has been particularly valuable in gaining access to the data contained in this case (Buckley and Chapman 1996). We are therefore able to offer rich and deep insight into the problems facing the exporters, the evolution of a collaborative approach and difficulties faced in establishing a collaborative network structure.

However, in order to appreciate the reasons why the exporters have adopted the network structure that they have, it is first necessary to examine the factors that contributed to the adoption of the collaborative approach. This is followed by an account of how the network was developed and how the local network extends into an inter-regional network. The analysis section, consistent with the inductive research tradition, then "enfolds" (Eisenhardt 1989) this account within the markets-as-networks, supply chain management and strategic management literatures in order to seek greater understanding of the competitive consequences of these decisions and structures. The chapter concludes with a discussion of the particular issues raised by this case.

Background

A number of factors, including poor and fluctuating domestic returns and government policy (e.g., Supermarket to Asia) encourage Australian fruit and vegetable producers (growers) to enter Asian food retail markets. Australian growers have significant advantages over their northern hemisphere counterparts in terms of their ability to produce counter-seasonally and relative proximity to these markets. Government support for this initiative includes facilitating buying missions by supermarket representatives.

The Senior Trade Development Officer in Queensland's Burnett region hosted two such buying missions by representatives of major Asian supermarket chains. In the first mission, the supermarket representative visited a series of tomato, capsicum, melon, avocado, vegetable and other tree crop growers in four regions. The representative acknowledged the quality of the produce and indicated an intention to launch a Queensland food promotion. The intention to hold the promotion was communicated to the Burnett region growers through the Queensland Government Trade and Investment office in Hong Kong. The supermarket directed their Sydney-based exporter to source produce from the Burnett region. However, the exporter was reluctant to accept this level of direction over their operations and appears to have been suspicious of the direct relationship between the supermarket and the growers. The exporter failed to source the product, citing problems with seasonal supply. The result was that no orders eventuated. Discussions with growers at this point revealed a growing sense of frustration, as they had been involved in previous unsuccessful missions.

In the second mission, the supermarket representative declined to visit individual producers and indicated that they wanted to meet with all potential suppliers as one group. This required a considerable change in attitude by the growers who traditionally operated on an individual basis and competed fiercely in the domestic market. Eleven grower representatives met with the supermarket representative who indicated that the supermarket would require a "whole basket of food products" for them to consider importing from a particular region. Their argument was that "suppliers are in a better position to take care of business in their own country than a buyer who purchases from all over the world". Further discussions with this supermarket representative confirmed that the supermarket wanted a central coordination point in the Burnett region and a sales and marketing plan to resolve the following issues:

- A full product range from the region with quality assurance.
- Coordination of product availability and management of supply logistics.
- Support for in-store sales promotion.
- A price advantage over other suppliers.

The request from the second supermarket focused the issue of international market development for the growers. Responding to these issues in order to compete in international markets would require significant attitudinal and operational changes. The growers' traditional view of international buyers was that they only sourced product intermittently (when domestic spot prices were low) and therefore international markets offered little basis for sustained business or market growth.

Alliance Development and Network Formation

The two supermarket buying missions had not resulted in any significant success in entering Asian markets although growers were slowly starting to develop more co-operative behavior. Following the first unsuccessful buying mission, growers arranged to visit other regions, which were exporting successfully. Funding for the visit was secured from the Queensland Department of Primary Industries (QDPI) under a "Doing More With Our Services" (DMWOS) initiative. This trip resulted in the development of an alliance between (fresh market) vegetable growers, a transport operator and other investors, which established a co-operatively operated central pack house facility. Traditionally fresh market growers operated their own (on farm) pack houses but very few of these were able to meet quality assurance and phytosanitary requirements for export. The modern packhouse (which operates as a cost-center) allows the produce to enter the cold chain as soon as it is delivered from the field. This has benefits for produce quality.

Other sectors (horticulture, beef, pork) followed this example and conducted visits to successful exporters with marketing groups emerging out of these collective experiences. These groups varied considerably in terms of their levels of formalization and activity but were organized around traditional single product groupings. While some groups were able to achieve export market success, they were still unable to respond to the opportunity and requirements for supplying Asian supermarkets.

Development of a "One-stop-shop" for Regional Exports

Two key growers in the region supported the emerging idea of a centrally co-coordinated regional export organization. A funding proposal ("An Export Supply Chain Co-ordination Initiative") to support the development of a Burnett region food alliance, which could deliver the regionally co-

coordinated response that the supermarkets were seeking, was submitted to a Queensland Department of Primary Industries (QDPI) horticultural export initiative. The proposal was not successful but was subsequently expanded to include beef, pork and seafood and presented to an Exporter's Regional Roundtable conducted by the Federal Secretary to the Minister for Trade. The proposal received support from the AUSTRADE and Department of Economic Development and Trade representatives at the Roundtable and subsequently received in principle support from QDPI.

Evidence of industry support was required for the in principle support to be converted into funding support. An expression of interest was circulated to all food companies in the region who had shown support for previous buyer missions. All but one company expressed an interest in exploring the idea of a regional food export alliance. An initial meeting of all members resulted in the formation of a small working group to develop the concept further.

The working group considered that the long-term viability of a regional export alliance could only be achieved by the development of trust between the region's food companies. This organization would involve individualistic growers relinquishing some control over the marketing of their product and relying on the negotiation and marketing ability of a traditional competitor. Face to face meetings were required in order to develop the level of trust needed to overcome traditional competitive attitudes. The working group did consider involving growers and producers from outside the region but decided that the face to face meetings were paramount for the development of trust and therefore membership would need to be restricted to companies who were within a "reasonable" traveling time for regular meetings.

Further, the working group determined that inter-industry conflict over supply could be resolved by giving one key company or organization (where marketing groups existed) in each product group responsibility for volume, quality and branding issues. Therefore, the South Pacific Melon Group was responsible for melon supply and CPH Fresh for capsicum, squash and eggplant supply, etc. Fourteen marketing groups or companies were allocated co-ordination responsibility for a range of products spanning fresh and frozen seafood, beverages, health and beauty products, pre-processed vegetables, meat and fresh fruit and vegetables (see Figure 14.1). A development plan was formulated to address the many other issues regarding the regional export organization, raised by members. The development plan remains private and confidential to members but follows a formal development process with concept development, market scoping, concept testing, test marketing and implementation stages.

During the development process, an opportunity to test market the concept of the one-stop-shop arose with a market mission to the Gulf States. Promotional materials, which included the proposed one-stop-shop organizational structure, were developed. The concept was favorably received with a UAE Chamber of Commerce representative stating "We have been waiting for Australia to do business this way for a long time. When can we start trading?" This favorable response also helped convince the alliance members who were part of the mission that they were on the right track and their commitment to the collaborative concept increased.

Following the success of the Gulf States market visit, a market visit to Asia was undertaken by the alliance. The alliance representatives had little previous experience in dealing with international retail buyers and were initially hesitant. However, their confidence grew rapidly with the enthusiastic response of supermarkets to the single point for regional food products. The market visit allowed the alliance members to gain a much greater appreciation of the difficulties faced by Asian supermarkets in maintaining shelf stocks and co-coordinating products from global suppliers. The alliance team identified opportunities for supply that would better support supermarket category managers. Reciprocal invitations were issued to all the supermarkets visited and the first orders were placed before the alliance members had returned home. A memorandum of understanding was signed with one of the supermarkets that had previously made an unsuccessful visit to the region. The development process continued after the market visit and the name Aus Food Exports (AFE) was chosen for the single contact point alliance. It should be noted that the alliance also operates as a cost center.

Another of the supermarkets visited by the alliance members had a procurement organization in Sydney. This supermarket indicated that they were interested in establishing a supply relationship with AFE but that the relationship should be co-coordinated through Sydney. Shortly after the return of the alliance team from Asia, a representative of this supermarket visited AFE. This was the third supermarket buying mission to the region. The procurement manager of this third supermarket confirmed that they were interested in establishing a supply relationship directly with AFE. However, they wanted AFE to support the supermarket's category managers. The supermarket was prepared to assist AFE to develop category management expertise. Shortly after this visit AFE commenced weekly trading with the supermarket and two months later the local newspaper reported that the Alliance had won a contract to supply a major supermarket chain in Hong Kong, with three containers a week leaving the region (*News Mail* 2000, p.11). The latest development of AFE has been the appointment of a dedicated international marketing manager.

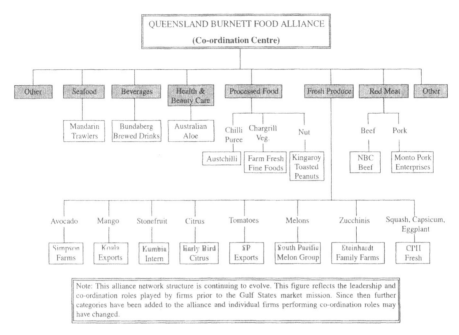

Figure 14.1   Alliance Network Structure

Development of an Inter-regional Network

The development of the inter-regional network began in parallel with the development of the AFE alliance. The Gulf States market mission had also been attended by the Queensland Minister for Primary Industries and the Minister had witnessed the positive and enthusiastic response to the one-stop-shop concept. On his return the Minister addressed a citrus industry conference and suggested that the approach adopted by Burnett region growers and producers offered potential benefit to other regions.

A consistent criticism of the AFE development had been that even acting collaboratively, the region still lacked the critical mass and continuity of supply to be able to compete effectively at a global level. The working group had previously rejected the inclusion of producers from other regions in the alliance as they would be unable to attend regular meetings and a decade of this type of inter-regional initiatives had not been successful. The success of the Burnett region alliance suggested that collaboration needed to be established at a local level first, before inter-regional collaborative behavior could occur. The model for the development of AFE is being replicated in other regions but will require time to develop. The level of collaborative behavior in other regions could be two to three years behind the Burnett. Further impetus for the development of other regional one-stop-shops is coming from AFE Directors, who are no longer considering growers in other regions as competitors but as a means of increasing their volume and product range and lengthening the supply period.

Analysis

The difficulties faced by these Australian growers are common to those faced by many small firms entering international markets. Within food retailing however, these difficulties, particularly the lack of critical mass, have been exacerbated by major structural changes in the food retail industry. There are few Asia-specific studies of supermarket retailing; therefore this analysis draws on research from other economies, predominantly UK and USA markets. As European supermarkets particularly expand into Asia, management practices are likely to be transferred and Asia will follow the trends in these other economies where the supermarket industry is considered to have reached a mature stage. These trends include industry consolidation, adoption of supply chain principles and a reduction in the number of suppliers, all of which have important consequences for suppliers.

Channel power has shifted · to the supermarkets (Greenley and Shipley 1992) and supermarkets use this power to leverage their suppliers (Cox 1999). In this case, supermarket power has been exerted to change the industry structure of the suppliers. Further, adoption of supply chain principles has led to supermarkets reducing their number of suppliers to deal with "fewer, larger, technically efficient and innovative suppliers" (Fearne and Hughes 1999, p.122). The modern packhouse provides the technical efficiency and there are indications of innovation with AFE members collaborating to produce pre-prepared meals from a combination of their products. The power of the supermarkets allows them to push responsibility (and cost) for quality control, assortment and logistics functions upstream to suppliers who are "rewarded" with increased volumes (Fearne and Hughes 1999). Again the pressure exerted by supermarkets to reduce the number of suppliers and push back functions are evident in this case. The supermarkets are also seeking closer relationships with their suppliers to improve information flow, which will in turn improve co-ordination of activities and the performance of supply logistics (Stank, Crum and Arango 1999) and help to develop the trust and commitment considered to characterize a valuable relationship (Hunt and Morgan 1994). Again, evidence of a developing relationship is provided, by the third supermarket being willing to share their category management knowledge.

A further trend relevant to this case is the increased use of own label strategies by supermarkets in order to differentiate themselves (Fearne and Hughes 1999). Fresh produce is almost exclusively own label, as is a large proportion of frozen and chilled meats and seafood. These products constitute "destination categories" for shoppers and growth in these categories is predicted to be based on ready-prepared fresh produce such as washed, peeled, sliced and grated vegetables, either singly or as part of an assortment (Fearne and Hughes 1999). As Asia follows lifestyle trends such as both adult members of the household undertaking full-time employment, it seems likely that trends towards greater convenience and ready-prepared foods will also follow. One feature that distinguishes Asian supermarkets from their western counterparts is a lack of warehousing, either owned or third party (Gray, Matear, Irving and Lim 1999). This places even greater emphasis on the ability of suppliers to be able to deliver frequently and reliably (considerable congestion occurs when delivery time slots are missed) to multiple stores.

Until recently these major changes in supermarket industry structure have had little impact on agribusiness supplier industries which remained characterized by open market, transactional trading. The fragmentation of supplier industries may not be surprising, given relatively low entry barriers, high transport costs, erratic supply and sales, diverse and variable product range and the presence of exit barriers (Mowatt and Collins 2000). Producers within these industries have traditionally been highly product oriented and received only limited market information through traditional distribution channels. The development of an alliance network industry structure has allowed these small companies to reduce their dependence on the open-market system and develop longer-term relationships with major customers. This structure also allows the alliance to compete with major food corporations (e.g., Sunkist, Chiquita) in terms of their product volume and range but without the generations of corporate development and investment and also without the costs associated with ownership. Nonetheless the cost of industry restructuring has been considerable and firms need to consider the costs and benefits carefully (Contractor and Lorange 1988).

In order to assess competitiveness, the sources of advantage resulting from this network structure need to be examined. The sources of advantage in this case are the ability to provide a consistent source of high quality produce and a category management competency. For these sources of advantage to result in a competitive advantage, they must be rare, valuable, difficult to imitate and non-substitutable (Barney 1991). The main sources of advantage, which the AFE alliance firms appear to have are, product quality, product range and the lower cost structure afforded by a network as opposed to a hierarchy. Considered individually, these advantages offer little potential for sustainability, as product quality is not based on proprietary technology, major food corporations can also offer a broad product range and transactional systems may offer cost advantages. Considered together however, the "bundle of resources" is more sustainable. The product range and quality are considered to be valuable and as the alliance has the opportunity to provide packaged assortments of vegetables in line with current trends, the product advantage is sustainable in changing market conditions. The network structure will take time to imitate although this is being actively encouraged as it will increase product related advantages. Additionally, the relationships (or supply chain positions), which the alliance has achieved, also constitute valuable resources. The intangibility of such resources makes them difficult to imitate and are therefore sustainable. Overall it seems that the AFE does have potential for sustained superior performance.

Discussion

This chapter has examined the development of a collaborative network of small producers, across a wide range of products using a case study methodology and suggested that this network approach does afford a sustainable base for international competitiveness. This discussion considers the particular issues raised by this case. The collaborative approach to international strategy (Contractor and Lorange 1988), the role of regional factors (Brown and McNaughton 2000; Brown and Bell 2000) and government in facilitating collaboration for internationalization (Wilkinson et al. 2000; Wilkinson et al. 1998) and collaboration in agribusiness supply chains (Fearne 1998; Stank et al. 1999; Katz and Bolland 2000).

The idea of a collaborative approach to international business is not new. Contractor and Lorange (1988) suggest that co-operative ventures can be broadly considered to create value through either vertical or horizontal arrangements. However, both horizontal and vertical aspects are present in this case. Producers acting together to produce sufficient volume are a horizontal arrangement but the development of the one-stop-shop with AFE performing assortment and consolidation functions suggests vertical co-operation also. The net effect however is consistent with Contractor and Lorange's (1988, p. 9) assertion that "the combined effects of all partners must add up to a value chain that can produce a more competitive end result". Collaborative approaches to small firm internationalization recognize that competitiveness depends not just on the efforts of an individual firm (Wilkinson et al. 2000) but also on the resources and skills that can be accessed through the network.

Brown and Bell (2000) and Brown and McNaughton (2000) consider the role of regional or locational factors in small firm internationalization. Specifically they consider the extent to which cluster programs deliver market-related benefits for firms (Brown and Bell 2000) and more broadly whether success of cluster programs have been over-stated by relying on correlational rather than causative analyses (Brown and McNaughton 2000). Brown and Bell (2000) found that members of an engineering cluster considered that they received very little marketing benefit as a result of membership. Although not considering a cluster as such, this case suggests that regionally based groups of firms can attain significant marketing benefits through collaborative activity. Cluster programs have tended to emphasize production-related benefits such as product innovation. However, the regionally based alliance network considered in this case was developed specifically to gain market-related benefits. Nonetheless, some production-related innovations and transfer of knowledge through shared problem solving have also occurred. The issue of attributing success based on correlation rather than causation is overcome in this case by a longitudinal study and the market success achieved by the alliance can be clearly attributed to the collaborative approach.

The issue of demonstrating results is also raised by Wilkinson et al. (1998) who suggest that the lack of concrete evidence of success can make it difficult to generate support for such schemes. While outcomes such as increased knowledge sharing and trust may have positive implications for future competitiveness, they are likely to be indirect, difficult to observe (if at all possible) and causally ambiguous. These may be desirable features in a source of competitive advantage (Grant 1998) but not in seeking support for further schemes. The concrete evidence of success of the network alliance in this case should help in gaining support for similar schemes. The role of government in facilitating and supporting the development of this alliance network has been critical. This study and that of Wilkinson et al. (1998) support the idea that networks can be facilitated. However, Wilkinson et al. (1998) caution that while networks can be facilitated, they cannot be controlled.

Collaborative approaches have also been investigated in agribusiness supply chains. Fearne (1998) comments that partnerships in these industries have been difficult to establish and slow to develop but that the competitive strategy of supermarkets have been a driver for collaboration. Both these assertions would seem to hold for this study. Horizontal collaboration not only allows the volume requirements of major customers to be met but also increases the bargaining power of suppliers (Fearne 1998). However, the majority of the examples in agribusiness industry collaboration continue to focus in single product examples (Katz and Boland 2000), rather than the product range examined in this study.

Conclusion

While it is now widely accepted that small firms compete within networks, less attention has been paid to the ways in which traditional industries may need to be restructured before network competition can occur. This chapter makes a contribution to understanding the context within which collaborative network approaches to international business can be developed and begins to address some of the antecedent conditions. These conditions include the need to develop collaborative attitudes and networking skills prior to alliance formation. The development of the inter-regional alliance relies on mature networking skills developed through the establishment of first single product groupings and then the multi-product alliance network. The ability of the alliance to compete internationally is based on its ability to co-ordinate activities within both local and inter-regional networks. Understanding markets-as-networks from an analytical perspective is considerably removed from facilitating the development of a network in industries that are not characterized by long term, relatively stable relationships (Turnbull, Ford and Cunningham 1996). This disparity may indicate bounds to the applicability of the paradigm or it may resonate with Easton's (2000) call for research into the context in which decisions are made.

References

Barney, Jay (1991), "Firm Resources and Sustained Competitive Advantage." *Journal of Management 17* (1): 99-120.

Borsch, Odd Jari and Michael B. Arthur (1995), "Strategic networks among small firms: implications for strategy research methodology," *Journal of Management Studies*, vol. 32, no. 4, pp. 419-441.

Brown, Peter and Jim Bell (2000), "Industrial clusters and small firm internationalisation," AIB Conference, UK.

Brown, Peter and Rod McNaughton (2000), "Cluster development programmes – panacea or placebo for promoting SME growth and internationalisation?" International Entrepreneurship Conference, Montreal, September.

Buckley, Peter J. and Malcolm Chapman (1996), "Theory and method in international business research," *International Business Review*, vol. 59, no. 3, pp. 233-245.

Contractor, Farok J. and Peter Lorange (1988), "Why should firms cooperate? The strategy and economics basis for cooperative ventures," in Contractor, Farok J. and Peter Lorange (eds), *Cooperative Strategies in International Business*, Lexington Books, Lexington, MA, pp. 3-27.

Cox, Andrew (1999), "Power, value and supply chain management", *Supply Chain Management*, vol. 4 9, no. 4, pp. 10.

Coviello, Nicole E. and Andrew McAuley (1999), "Internationalisation and the smaller firm: a review of contemporary empirical research," *Management International Review*, vol. 39, no.3, pp. 223-240.

Easton, Geoff (1998), "Case research as a methodology for industrial networks: a realist apologia," in Naude, Peter and Turnbull, Peter, W., *Network Dynamics in International Marketing*, Oxford, UK: Elsevier Science, pp. 73-87.

Easton, Geoff (2000), "Is relevance relevant?" IMP Conference, Bath, UK.

Eisenhardt, Kathleen M. (1989), "Building theories from case study research", *Academy of Management Review*, vol. 14, no. 4, pp. 532-550.

Fearne, Andrew (1998), "The evolution of partnerships in the meat supply chain: insights from the British beef industry," *Supply Chain Management*, vol. 3, no. 4, pp. 214-231.

Fearne, Andrew and David Hughes (1999), "Success factors in the fresh produce supply chain: insights from the UK," *Supply Chain Management*, vol. 4, no. 3, pp. 120-128.

Grant, Robert M. 1998. *Contemporary Strategy Analysis (3rd Ed.)*. London; Blackwell.

Gray, Brendan J., Sheelagh M. Matear, Gregory P. Irving and Tee Sern Lim (1999), *International Distribution Channels for Export Marketing Success*, Marketing Performance Centre, Department of Marketing, University of Otago, New Zealand.

Greenley, Gordon E. and David Shipley (1992), "A comparative study of operational marketing practices among British Department Stores and Supermarkets," *European Journal of Marketing*, vol. 26, no. 5, pp. 22-35.

Hunt, Shelby D. and Robert M. Morgan, (1994), "Relationship marketing in the era of network competition", *Marketing Management*, vol. 3, no. 1, pp. 18-28.

Jutter, Uta and Lutz E. Schlange (1996), "A network approach to strategy," *International Journal of Research in Marketing*, vol. 13, pp. 479-494.

Katz, Jeffrey P. and Michael Bolland (2000), "A new value-added strategy for the US beef industry; the base of US Premium Beef Ltd.," *Supply Chain Management*, vol. 5, no. 2, pp. 99-109.

Mowatt, Alistair and Ray Collins (2000), "Consumer behaviour and fruit quality: supply chain management in an emerging industry," *Supply Chain Management*, vol. 5, no. 1, p. 9.

Stank, Theodore, Michael Crum and Miren Arango (1999), "Benefits of interfirm coordination in food industry supply chains," *Journal of Business Logistics*, vol. 20, no. 2, pp. 21-41.

Turnbull, Peter, David Ford and Malcolm Cunningham (1996), "Interaction, relationships and networks in business markets: an evolving perspective," *Journal of Business and Industrial Marketing*, vol. 11, no. 3, pp. 44-62.

Wilkinson, Ian F., Louise C.Young, Denice Welch and Lawrence Welch (1998), "Dancing to success: export groups as dance parties and the implications for network development," *Journal of Business and Industrial Marketing*, vol. 13, no. 6, pp. 492-510.

Wilkinson, Ian F., Lars-Gunnar Mattsson and Geoff Easton (2000), "International competitiveness and trade promotion policy from a network perspective," *Journal of World Business*, vol. 35, no. 3, pp. 275-299.

Yin, R. (1984), *Case Study Research*, Applied Social Research Methods; vol. 5, Sage.

15 Integration in the Multinational Corporation: The Problem of Subsidiary Embeddedness

ULF ANDERSSON AND MATS FORSGREN

A major issue in the literature on the multinational corporation is management's need to find the right trade off between local adaptation and global integration (see e.g., Doz 1986; Porter 1986; Bartlett and Ghoshal 1989; White and Poynter 1990; Dicken 1992). Local characteristics and capabilities are seen as important resources of a firm operating in a large number of countries and should therefore be used to develop competitive advantages. Adaptation and entrepreneurial activity at the subsidiary level should be encouraged because the competence generated there may later become the core competence of the entire corporation. But to reach competitive advantage on the global scene, the firm also has to consider the advantages of economies of scale and scope which means combining local responsiveness with global integration. From this follows that the management of the multinational corporation needs to get the best out of two different principles simultaneously.

Different scholars have used different labels for the "new" multinational corporation depending on what characteristics they want to emphasize. For instance, the *global firm* (Porter 1986) co-ordinates the dispersed activities and thereby takes care of both economies of scale and location advantages. The *transnational firm* (Bartlett and Ghoshal 1989) is co-coordinating the innovation processes in the dispersed organization in order to harvest the multinational corporation's potential economies of scope and the benefits from worldwide learning. The *horizontal firm* (Poynter and White 1990) achieves both global and local advantage by connecting the dispersed subsidiaries by lateral decision processes. The *heterarchic firm* (Hedlund and Rolander 1990) is replacing the internal hierarchy with balanced interdependence between subsidiaries having different strategic roles concerning research, marketing, production etc. Finally, global competitiveness is also related to the ability of the multinational corporation to develop core competence, i.e. a collective learning process in the organization, especially concerning how to co-ordinate diverse production skills and integrate multiple streams of technology so that the corporation becomes something more than a collection of discrete businesses (Prahalad and Hamel 1990). Lately, the multinational corporation has been conceptualized as a *differentiated network*, in which integration and differentiation are the core design variables (Ghoshal and Nohria 1997).

Although these models state the importance of integration, they pay rather little attention to the problem of transforming the capabilities developed on the subsidiary level into competitive advantages of the whole corporation. Gupta and Govindarajan (1994) recognize multinational corporations as networks of different flows, where different subsidiaries play different strategic roles which can be organized by the management in order to fulfill certain strategic goals. This model does not take the subsidiaries external network into account and is therefore not recognizing the influence from important business counterparts on subsidiary behavior. For instance, why would a subsidiary use its resources for corporate needs instead of further enhancing its competence to meet local needs?

As has been observed by many scholars, multinational corporations belong to multiple business networks (e.g., Kogut 1993; Andersson and Forsgren 1996; Andersson, Forsgren and Pedersen 2001). These networks are first of all sets of exchange relationships in which the subsidiaries are embedded. The counterparts in terms of customers, suppliers, competitors, governments, trade unions, research bodies etc., exert influence on the separate subsidiaries through these relationships. This influence can, or cannot, be in accordance with the striving for integration and a coherent strategy from the top management. An analysis of both the needs and possibilities of integrating different units in a multinational corporation must take networks of business relationships on the subsidiary level into consideration. Business relationships develop over a long time and a subsidiary's role in such a network is formed in long-lasting interactions with other actors (Tichy, Tushman and Fombrun 1979; Forsgren and Johanson 1992).

Having this in mind, the issue of integration in the multinational corporation should perhaps be somewhat reformulated. It is not only a question of designing the organization in such a way that sufficient integration and co-operation among the units is reached, but also of obtaining flexibility and economy of scale and scope among a set of subsidiaries which are embedded in different business networks with different interests not always geared towards integration. This is in accordance with looking upon the multinational corporation as an interorganizational network (Ghoshal and Bartlett 1990). Take for instance the often advocated devices of creating lateral groups or task forces in order to enhance vertical and horizontal integration. The success of these devices is dependent on the operational structure of the multinational corporation and the characteristics of the different business networks surrounding the subsidiaries. The less the subsidiaries have in common among themselves and with the higher management levels in terms of technology, type of customer and supplier relationships, competitive situations, size of the market, profit level etc., the less effective these organizational devices will be. Integration is not free of cost and will therefore be supported by the subsidiary only if it coincides with its interests. To a large extent these interests will be reflected in the nature of the subsidiary's business. If the subsidiaries' businesses have very little in common, global integration will be difficult to reach.

The question of integration should therefore be extended to a question of embeddedness in networks *both* inside and outside the multinational corporation. The degree of a subsidiary's integration into a corporate system must be evaluated against its embeddedness in the external network of specific relationships (Andersson and Forsgren 1996). Moreover the integration into the corporate system must also be analyzed as a question of embeddedness into specific relationships. If a multinational corporation has a competitive strategy which requires integrated subsidiaries some of the subsidiaries' critical relationships consequently concern other corporate units.

This approach to the environment gives room not only for a discussion of the balance between corporate integration and the subsidiaries' involvement in external networks. It also contributes to an understanding of the possibility of reaching higher levels of corporate integration and competitiveness in specific situations.

In the following we will discuss the concept of embeddedness, thereafter we will classify the sample of subsidiaries into four categories, and then measure the subsidiaries' degree of external and corporate embeddedness.

Embeddedness

A subsidiary's environment is first of all its set of direct exchange relationships with other counterparts and indirect exchange relationships which are connected to the direct relationships. One way of defining the degree of embeddedness in such a set is to estimate the number of connections in relation to possible connections, often called density (e.g., Aldrich and Whetten 1981; Ghoshal and Bartlett 1990). Density measures to what extent each actor is linked to every other actor in the set. Even if density reflects the tightness of the set of relationships and therefore also to some extent an actor's degree of embeddedness in the network, there are two problems with this definition. First, it does not cover the *attributes* of the exchanges in terms of activity interdependence and adaptation between the actors. The stronger the specific activity interdependence between the sub-unit and other actors, the more they will be inclined to develop close relationships rather than conducting business through arm's-length negotiations. Inversely, two actors who are engaged in a close relationship will tend to strengthen their specific interdependence over time in order to raise the joint productivity of their activities. We can assume that the closer a subsidiary's relationships, the higher the subsidiary's degree of embeddedness because close relationships are more difficult to substitute.

Secondly, the concept of density assumes that an external observer would be able to estimate the number of actors and connections in a network. But networks in terms of exchanges are mostly enacted. They can only be subjectively defined from an actor's viewpoint and the border of such a network is vague in terms of the number of relevant counterparts. Therefore, a subsidiary's degree of embeddedness should be defined by letting the subsidiary estimate its relevant direct and indirect counterparts and the attributes of the exchange with these counterparts in terms of interdependence and adaptation.

It follows from the discussion above that the more transparent the counterparts are to the subsidiary, the more its behavior and activities are likely to be influenced by these network actors. The more dependent the subsidiary is on its counterparts to pursue its activities and the more adapted it is to its counterparts, the more embedded it is. If these counterparts in their turn are dependent on and adapted to the subsidiary, this is likely to strengthen the subsidiary's embeddedness because interdependence is more prone to produce long-term relationships. Therefore, the more pronounced the interdependence between the subsidiary and its counterparts, the more embedded the subsidiary is in its network.

It is not only direct relationships that influence a subsidiary's degree of embeddedness. Customers' customers, complementary suppliers, suppliers' suppliers etc. that strongly influence the subsidiary's direct relationships will also increase its embeddedness. The more prominent such indirect relationships are to the subsidiary, the tighter the structure of the network and thereby the more embedded the subsidiary is.

As can be seen in Figure 15.1, the focal subsidiary can be more embedded in some relationships than in others. It is the total degree of interdependence in all involved relationships that build up the focal company's embeddedness. As is indicated in Figure 15.1, it is not just the focal company's dependence on and adaptation to its counterparts that constitutes embeddedness but also the counterparts' dependence on and adaptation to the focal company. In other words, it is the strength of the interdependence that exists in the focal company's enacted network that constitutes the focal company's embeddedness.

Even if a subsidiary's embeddedness is constituted by both its dependence on business partners and the business partners' dependence on the subsidiary, these two dependencies are not unrelated. Based on network theory we would expect that if one actor over time adapts its resources and activities to some other actor a corresponding adaptation will also be carried out by the latter (e.g., Hallén, Johanson and Seyed-Mohamed 1991).

Corporate and External Embeddedness

Integration has been treated in different ways by different scholars: direct contacts, planning procedures, liaison roles, teams and matrix structures are administrative devices that can be related to integration (Galbraith and Nathanson 1978). These integrative devices are supposed to enhance information exchange and co-operation in the company. The more of these devices, the stronger the integration. The degree of integration can also be estimated more directly by mapping the proximity of the headquarters and the subunits (Egelhoff 1988). A more tangible way of estimating integration is to measure the actual flows of goods and services between the subsidiary and the rest of the company (Gupta and Govindarajan 1991). Even if administrative devices can be implemented to enhance such integration, it is the actual outcome of integrative efforts that is reflected in the flows between the subsidiary and the rest of the multinational corporation (Gupta and Govindarajan 1991).

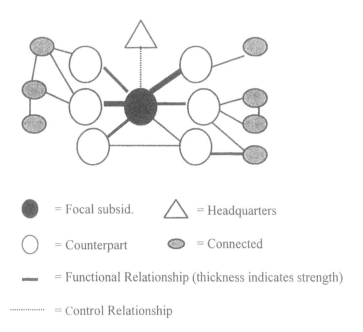

● = Focal subsid.   △ = Headquarters

○ = Counterpart   ◍ = Connected

▬ = Functional Relationship (thickness indicates strength)

⋯⋯ = Control Relationship

Figure 15.1   The Embeddedness of a Focal Subsidiary in its Network

In this chapter we define integration as a subsidiary's realized integration in terms of the flows of goods and services between the subsidiary and other corporate units. We call this corporate embeddedness. Corporate embeddedness shows how deeply a sub-unit is involved in its business relationships with its sister units. But we also have to consider that the subsidiary is embedded in specific business relationships with counterparts outside the multinational corporation. We call this external embeddedness. It is the configuration of the subsidiary's network and strength of its corporate and external embeddedness respectively, that determines the management's possibilities to enhance the integration of the subsidiary's activities with the rest of the multinational corporation (Andersson and Forsgren 1995, 1996).

Subsidiary Embeddedness: A Classification

There are almost infinite possible combinations of external and corporate embeddedness of subunits in multinational corporations, especially if we consider every possible type of relationship. Below four archetypes are identified based on the subsidiary's customer and supplier relationships (Andersson and Forsgren 1995). These archetypes reflect the degree of external and corporate embeddedness and the extent to which the foreign subsidiary's relationships cross the national border.

The classification is based on an identification of the subsidiary's counterparts in terms of business relationships and whether those relationships constitute links with external or corporate units. The degree of embeddedness may vary within each archetype.

The External Subsidiary

The *external subsidiary* (see Figure 15.2) is a unit whose relationships are dominated by business relationships with counterparts outside the multinational corporation. The connections with other corporate units are delimited to financial and administrative links. This structure characterizes the conglomerate or multi-domestic type of multinational corporation with little corporate embeddedness within the multinational corporation but with a varying degree of external embeddedness into its network of suppliers and customers. The possibilities for integration, and thereby increased economies of scale and scope, first of all depends on whether the changes imposed by increased integration are in accordance with the development of the subsidiary's network, and secondly on the strength of the external embeddedness. In a situation where the subsidiary operates under "market like" conditions, the external embeddedness will be limited, and the possibilities for integration propitious. In the opposite situation, the integrative efforts from headquarters can be counteracted by the conditions in the network of which the subsidiary is a part. A high degree of external embeddedness allows the subsidiary's counterparts to exert influence on its activities.

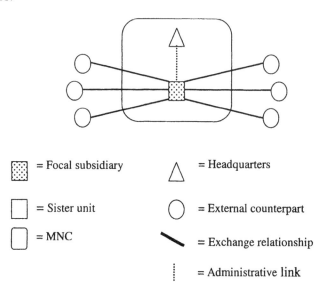

▦	= Focal subsidiary	△	= Headquarters
☐	= Sister unit	○	= External counterpart
⬭	= MNC	╲	= Exchange relationship
		⋮	= Administrative link

Figure 15.2   The External Subsidiary

The Semi-vertical Subsidiary

In the *Semi-vertical* subsidiary the exchange relationships are predominantly external. But there are also exchange relationships with other corporate units which separate the Semi-vertical subsidiary from the External subsidiary (see Figure 15.3).

The structural situation in the Semi-vertical subsidiary implies that it is at least to some degree corporately embedded. It is important to point out that it is not only the number of relationships that are important but also the degree of embeddedness. This means that one single relationship to a corporate unit in which the subsidiary is to a high degree embedded can outweigh several external relationships in which the subsidiary is less embedded. In a multinational corporation where the integration is limited to certain semi-finished goods or services while other important inflows originate from external suppliers, the subsidiaries have this structure. For example, some subsidiaries in the car manufacturing industry are assembly units which, for instance buy the engine from other corporate units but the chassis and chariot from external suppliers. In this case the possibilities to increase the integration of the subsidiary further is dictated by the strength of its corporate and external embeddedness respectively.

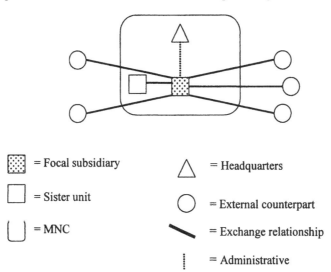

▨ = Focal subsidiary		△ = Headquarters	
☐ = Sister unit		◯ = External counterpart	
⊔ = MNC		╲ = Exchange relationship	
		┊ = Administrative	

Figure 15.3   The Semi-vertical Subsidiary

The Vertical Subsidiary

Subsidiaries that function as outlets or long arm to the parent company or other corporate units production for local or international markets we call *Vertical subsidiaries* (Figure 15.4).

The vertical integration dominates the subsidiary's input-side while the output-side is directed toward external customers locally or internationally. This type of subsidiary has similarities with the *Implementor* type of subsidiary in Gupta and Govindarajan (1991). There is also the possibility that the subsidiary's output is directed towards sister units while its input comes from external sources. This category has similarities with the subsidiary labeled *Global Innovator* (Gupta and Govindarajan 1991).

In this type of subsidiary the corporate embeddedness is clearly more accentuated than in the semi-vertical type. The vertical subsidiary is highly adapted and dependent on its corporate counterparts to conduct its business. Headquarters could anyhow be constrained by a high degree of external embeddedness if the strategy of the multinational corporation is influencing the subsidiary's relationships to external counterparts in a negative way.

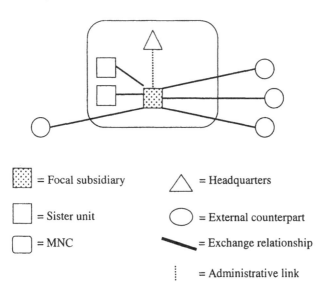

Figure 15.4   **The Vertical Subsidiary**

The Integrated Subsidiary

The fourth type, labeled the *integrated subsidiary,* is much more integrated into the corporate system because not only its input-side *or* its output-side, but both the input *and* the output sides are directed toward units within the multinational corporation (Figure 15.5). They are highly integrated systems where economies of scale in for example production, marketing or R&D are the main features. As an example consider SKF, the Swedish ball-bearing company. It manufactures different qualities of ball bearings in specialized subsidiaries, but each subsidiary is selling the whole range of products in its local market. This system implies a high degree of internal buying and selling between the subsidiaries.

Assuming that it is easier for the headquarters to control and influence a corporate relationship than an external relationship, they can in a situation like this influence from both the input and the output sides. The integrated subsidiary is probably the most common subsidiary in the theory of the modern multinational corporation. But how common is this type of subsidiary in reality?

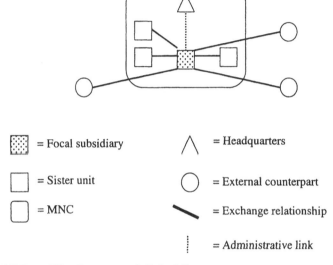

Figure 15.5   The Integrated Subsidiary

The perspective behind the classification is that influence is highly dependent on exchange relationships. Actors in a network can affect each other through interdependence in exchange relationships. To understand the behavior of the subsidiaries of a multinational corporation, and the possibility for the management to control and influence them, we need some comprehension of the subsidiaries' networks. The classification above can be used as a first approximation of how the networks are configured, where the basic indicator is the degree of corporate embeddedness of the subsidiaries. In the first two groups the corporate embeddedness is non-existent or limited. In subsidiaries with this configuration the corporate management competes with external suppliers and customers for influence over the subsidiary. If the exchange relationships are dominated by a few relationships on which the subsidiary is highly dependent it is possible that the external actors influence the subsidiary to a higher extent than the corporate management. The first group is similar to what has often been called the multidomestic organization, in which the management control consists mainly of financial control systems (see e.g., Bartlett and Ghoshal 1989). In the second group the management control can be sustained by exchange relationships with other corporate units. But these relationships are limited to some of the important relationships on the input *or* output side, while the other relationships are external.

In the third and fourth groups the corporate embeddedness is higher. In the integrated subsidiary the exchange relationships with other corporate units dominate and the management can probably exert considerable influence over the subsidiary through these relationships. This situation has certain similarities with what is sometimes called the transnational company where the subsidiaries are interdependent and specialized (e.g., Bartlett and Ghoshal 1989). In the vertical subsidiary the subsidiary is very much dependent on other corporate units on the supply side while dominant customers are external or *vice versa*. This is a more "balanced" type of situation in which the content of the relationships in terms of dependence and adaptation will determine which actors have the strongest influence over the subsidiary.

In the next section the subsidiaries in the sample are assigned to their respective archetype and then we particularly estimate the subsidiaries degree of external and corporate embeddedness.

Corporate and External Embeddedness in the Different Archetypes

The complexity of the multinational corporation as an organizational form, i.e. its multidimensionality in terms of multiple geographical markets and its multiple product lines, makes it particularly difficult to study and manage (Doz and Prahalad 1993). One tendency in international firms to cope with the increasing complexity has been to decentralize the decisions for global strategic issues down to the management level responsible for operational decisions, i.e., the division. This tendency to strengthen the position of the divisions has been observed in Swedish multinational corporations by Hedlund and Åman (1984). The reporting from the subsidiaries is to an increasing degree directed towards the (Global) Divisional management rather than to the chief executive office of the multinational corporation. Therefore, we are in this study investigating the integration between the division and its subsidiaries.

A number of the largest and best known Swedish companies, representing the pulp and paper industry (three divisions), transportation (one division), industrial supplies and equipment (ten divisions), computer software (one division), management education and sales training (one division), telecommunications (three divisions), and chemical industry (one division), are included in this study. The companies investigated are highly internationalized and have a very long history of business abroad. Only four of the 20 divisions have less than 50 percent of their employees abroad (14, 22, 24 and 38 percent respectively) while the others have between 50 and 97 percent. The turnover ranges from nearly $US 66 million to about $US 2.9 billion. The mean share of turnover coming from foreign units is about 70 percent but, the percentage of employment abroad varies from 28 to 97 percent. The subsidiaries are primarily located in western European countries and all headquarters except one are located in Sweden. Together we have conducted interviews in 95 subsidiaries in these divisions.

Our aim has been to collect data from all subsidiaries in a division, but time and limited resources have forced us in a number of cases to exclude some of the smaller subsidiaries. For example we have excluded small sales units in divisions with mainly production subsidiaries. Subsidiaries located in Europe have been given priority to subsidiaries overseas. In general, the subsidiaries can be said to be representative for the divisions' activities, at least when it concerns Europe.

Data have been collected through personal interviews with two respondents in each subsidiary, the sales manager and the manager responsible for purchasing. All in all we have conducted 190 interviews. The respondents, i.e. the sales manager and the managing director of purchasing, have been asked to evaluate the importance of and adaptation in each of their three most important supplier and customer relationships, respectively. First they were asked to indicate whether the relationship concerned a corporate unit or an external organization. Second, the respondents were asked to estimate the degree of interdependence in these relationships. In order to do so we have used 28 indicators that cover different aspects, for instance sales, purchase, technology, information about the market and business condition. For a description of the indicators see the Appendix.

As said above, the respondents were asked to choose the most important relationships. In order not to overestimate the degree of importance and adaptation in each relationship the original scale, a five-item Likert-type scale ranging from "not at all" to "very high", was dichotomized by letting the answers "high" and "very high" be 1 and the other answers 0. This means that a score above 0 in a relationship indicates at least some degree of interdependence. It would be theoretically possible but not very likely to have a score of 28, meaning that the counterparts are reciprocally important and adapted concerning each and every possible aspect we have asked about. Already having a score of 1.0 in half of the aspects, that is a total of 14, can be considered a very high degree of interdependence in a relationship. Based on a relatively high Cronbach alpha (K-20 for dichotomized variables) for the indicators used (0.85), the items were combined to a single measure of interdependence in each customer and supplier relationship (Nunnally 1978). A score for a subsidiary's total embeddedness was obtained by combining the measures of the subsidiary's interdependence in each of its relationships. Measured in this way the degree of embeddedness in the 95 subsidiaries varies from 0 to 85.

Our use of the concept embeddedness in the empirical analysis can be referred to as a vertical actor-network embeddedness. This implies that the network is identified in terms of supplier/customer relationships and viewed from a certain actor, in this case the subsidiary (Halinen and Törnroos 1998).

Result

The degree of embeddedness among the subsidiaries is illustrated in Figure 15.6. Some important conclusions can be drawn from this figure. First, the degree of embeddedness varies substantially between the subsidiaries. Some subsidiaries on the left-hand side of the figure show a low degree of embeddedness in their networks. It is a "market like" situation in the sense that the counterparts are relatively easy to substitute. This "market like" situation indicates a relatively low degree of adaptation and importance between the subsidiary and its counterparts. On the other hand some subsidiaries are highly embedded in its' networks.

Secondly, the relative importance of corporate and external embeddedness differs between subsidiaries. In some of the subsidiaries the business relationships with external counterparts dominate, while integration in terms of corporate embeddedness dominate in other subsidiaries. Thirdly, the figure indicates that, in general, it is more common with a high degree of external than corporate embeddedness in the investigated subsidiaries. This means that the highly integrated subsidiary with "market like" relationships with external customers and suppliers does not seem to be such a common case. In many instances the network structure is quite the opposite, that is, the subsidiary is highly "integrated" in business relationships with external counterparts while corresponding relationships with corporate units show a high degree of substitutability. This indicates that the influence from external network counterparts on the subsidiary could very well be an obstacle for the headquarters if increased integration is desired.

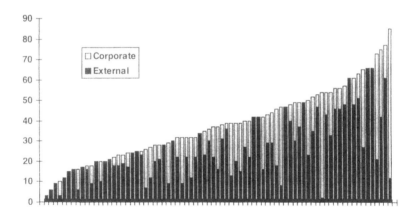

Figure 15.6   **The Subsidiaries' Degree of Corporate and External Embeddedness in Ascending Order**

Figure 15.7 shows the extent to which the subsidiaries' external embeddedness is dominated by local partners or counterparts outside their home country. The figure reveals that an overwhelming part of the subsidiaries' external embeddedness is local, even though some subsidiaries' customer and supplier relationships are more international than local. This implies that in most cases it is the local counterparts that exert influence on the subsidiaries' behavior.

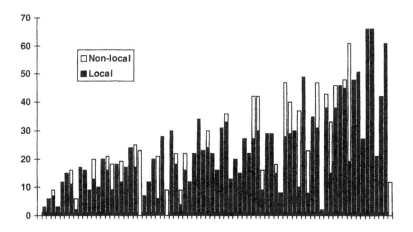

Figure 15.7   The Local/Non-local Aspect of External Embeddedness

In Table 15.1, the subsidiaries have been allocated according to the four different archetypes. The *Integrated subsidiary,* that is a subsidiary with important corporate counterparts on both the input and output side, is not a very common case among the investigated subsidiaries. Only nine percent of the subsidiaries investigated belong to this category, while 33 percent of the subsidiaries are *External subsidiaries*, that is they have no important business relationships with corporate units whatsoever. Subsidiaries with more than one corporate relationship on the input or the output side, *Vertical subsidiaries*, account for 18 percent in this sample. The *Semi-vertical subsidiary* dominates the sample, that is 44 percent of the subsidiaries are dominated by important business relationships with external counterparts in combination with one important corporate relationship, mostly with a supplier.

All in all, more than two thirds of the sample consists of subsidiaries with no or only one important corporate counterpart. As was concluded earlier, the highly integrated "ideal" type of subsidiary, described in much of recent literature, is quite a rare phenomenon in this sample.

Table 15.1   Distribution of External and Corporate Embeddedness in the Different Categories

	No.	EMBEDDEDNESS External Average	Corporate Average	Total Average
External	32	8.9	0	8.9
Semi-vertical	38	7.1	8.9	8.0
Vertical	16	9.0	10.9	10.0
Integrated	9	9.4	13.4	11.4

The averages in Table 15.1 reflects the average embeddedness in each relationship, i.e., in the category *Vertical subsidiaries* the average external embeddedness in the relationships is 9.0 compared to 9.4 in the category *Integrated subsidiaries*. Some interesting results emerge from this table. First, the average degree of embeddedness in each relationship increases as the archetypes get more integrated, except for *semi-vertical subsidiaries* which has a lower average embeddedness in the relationships (8.0) compared to *external subsidiaries* (8.9). Second, the degree of embeddedness seems to be higher, on average, in corporate relationships compared to external ones. Looking at the different archetypes the average degree of embeddedness in external relationships is approximately the same, except for the semi-vertical subsidiaries which has a considerably lower average degree of embeddedness. This has as a consequence that even if there is a rather high degree of integration, as in the vertical and integrated categories, the degree of external embeddedness stay the same. The external embeddedness does not decrease as the structural integration increases. This means that the more a subsidiary is integrated into the corporate system of flows of goods and knowledge, the more it can be stuck in the middle, between two forces influencing their activities and behavior. On the other hand this can enhance the possibilities to share knowledge developed in the external relationships with the also, highly embedded, sister units.

Table 15.2 shows that 13 of the 20 divisions have subsidiaries belonging to more than one category, although only six divisions have subsidiaries in more than two (divisions C, E, F, G, P and T). None of the investigated divisions have subsidiaries in all four categories, while there are seven divisions with subsidiaries in only one category (divisions J, N, O, R and S are of the external type, and divisions H and M are of the semi-vertical type).

Table 15.2   The Distribution of Archetypes in Each Corporate Division

Division (subs)	External Sub-sidiary	Semi-vertical Subsidiary	Vertical Sub-sidiary	Integrated Sub-sidiary	Mean Embeddedness in Division		
					Total	External	Corporate
Div. A, (9)	1	8			39.3	34.0	5.3
Div. B, (4)			2	2	48.8	20.2	28.5
Div. C, (3)	1	1		1	50.7	30.0	20.7
Div. D, (6)	3	3			48.5	43.0	5.5
Div. E, (7)	2	2	3		36.0	25.4	10.6
Div. F, (6)		1	2	3	47.2	18.2	29.0
Div. G, (4		2	1	1	38.0	17.2	20.8
Div. H, (3)		3			32.3	20.0	12.3
Div. I, (4)		1	3		37.5	25.5	12.0
Div. J, (3)	3				31.0	31.0	0.0
Div. K, 6)		3	3		42.0	23.7	18.3
Div. L, (5)	2	3			30.4	24.4	6.0
Div. M,(7)		7			33.4	21.3	12.1
Div. N, (4)	4				51.8	51.8	0.0
Div. O, (7)	7				11.4	11.4	0.0
Div. P, (5)		2	2	1	56.0	34.2	21.8
Div. Q, (3)	2	1			34.3	30.0	4.3
Div. R, (2)	2				52.0	52.0	0.0
Div. S, (4)	4				36.8	36.8	0.0
Div. T, (3)	1	1		1	63.3	43.7	19.7
Total subs 95	32	38	16	9			

It is much more common with a higher average on external embeddedness than on corporate embeddedness among the investigated divisions. There are only three cases with a higher average on corporate embeddedness, viz. in divisions B, F and G. Divisions having subsidiaries of the integrated type have, on average, the highest degree of corporate embeddedness in the sample. Both the highest and the lowest average degree of external embeddedness are in divisions that comprise only subsidiaries of the external type.

Concluding Remarks

A multinational corporation's corporate or divisional management exerts control over the subsidiaries in different countries through hierarchy and knowledge about the different units' business conditions. But corporate control always competes with the influence from other interest groups in the subsidiaries' environment. In this chapter we have claimed that influence over the subsidiaries' behavior can be analyzed through the business networks in which the different subunits are embedded. These networks consist of activity interdependence between the subsidiary and other actors on which influence can be based. As these activity interdependencies are of many different kinds, endless, dynamic and formed by the views of the involved actors rather than by some intrinsic technical imperative, the delimitation of the network is arbitrary (Håkansson and Johanson 1993). The aim of this chapter is to design a classification based on a few simple network indicators which can be used to differentiate between subsidiaries in different situations of realized integration, or to put it differently, various situations of corporate and external embeddedness. Implicit in this classification is the subsidiaries' own views about important customer and supplier relationships and the extent to which the partners in these relationships belong to the same corporate system. The last criterion is selected because we believe that the hierarchy in an organization matters even if it is only one of several possible mechanisms for influence. Based on legitimacy the management is in a better position, ceteris paribus, to control and influence corporate units than external units. But this influence is exerted in a structure where other actors also have a say. Suppliers and customers are such important actors. The management will be in a different position if some suppliers or customers are corporate units than if the subsidiary is the only corporate unit in its network.

The degree of external embeddedness is a continuous variable. In the classification, however, it has been reduced to four groups. The first group includes the subsidiaries in which the network of customers and suppliers are totally external. These subsidiaries are the least integrated in the corporation and have therefore probably the greatest autonomy in relation to corporate management. In the second group, the semi-vertical subsidiaries, the subsidiary network is mainly external but includes some form of supplier or customer relationship with another corporate unit. The third group, the vertical subsidiaries, includes situations in which the subsidiary functions more as a long arm to other corporate units and are supplied more or less totally from the corporate system, or functions as a Global Innovator (see Gupta and Govindarajan 1991). Finally, in the fourth group, the integrated subsidiaries, the exchange relationships with the rest of the corporate system includes both the supply and the customer side. In this situation the network is more corporate than external and the subsidiary autonomy is probably more restricted than in the other three categories. Within each archetype we can also identify to what extent the network is national or international.

In our sample of 95 subsidiaries belonging to highly international Swedish corporations, the degree of embeddedness in the subsidiaries networks is estimated. It is found that the degree of embeddedness varies considerably among the subsidiaries, from more or less "market like" situations to highly structured networks with high degrees of embeddedness. The empirical result also indicates that the external embeddedness is at least as important as the corporate embeddedness for the subsidiaries, or expressed differently, the "integration" with external counterparts is as important as integration within the multinational corporation.

We can assume that it is not enough to look only at the structural configuration to evaluate the possibilities for further integration. A more qualitative estimation of interdependence and adaptation in each relationship is needed. This can be done by assessing the degree of corporate and external embeddedness of the subsidiary in question.

To the extent that important customer and supplier relationships are representative of the network and the sample is representative of subsidiaries in Swedish multinational corporations, we can conclude that the highly integrated subsidiary, a form which is often discussed as an "ideal" type in the transnational company (e.g., Bartlett and Ghoshal 1989), is an exception rather than the rule. Further, the degree of external embeddedness seems to be more or less the same irrespective of how integrated the subsidiary may be.

Acknowledgement

The financial support from Jan Wallanders research foundation, Handelsbankens forskningsstiftelser is gratefully acknowledged.

References

Aldrich, H. E. and Whetten, D. A. (1981), "Organization-sets, action-sets and networks: making the most of simplicity", in P. Nyström and W. Starbuck (eds), *Handbook of Organizational Design*, Free Press, New York, pp. 385 408.

Andersson, U. and Forsgren, M. (1995), "Using networks to determine multinational parental control of subsidiaries", in S. J. Paliwoda and J. K. Ryans (eds.), *International Marketing Reader*, Routledge, London, pp. 72-87.

Andersson, U. and Forsgren, M. (1996), "Subsidiary Embeddedness and Control in the Multinational Corporation", *International Business Review*, vol. 5, pp. 487-508.

Andersson, U., Forsgren, M. and Pedersen, T. (2001), "Subsidiary Performance inmultinational corporations: the importance of technology embeddedness", *International Business Review*, vol. 10, (forthcoming).

Bartlett, Ch. A. and Ghoshal, S. (1989), *Managing Across Borders - The Transnational Solution*, Hutchinson Business Books, London.

Dicken, P. (1992), *Global shift: the internationalization of economic activity.-2nd ed.*, Paul Chapman Publishers, London.

Doz, Y. (1986), *Strategic Management in Multinational Companies*, Pergamon Press, Oxford.

Doz, Y. and Prahalad, C. K. (1993), "Managing the DMNCs: A search for a new paradigm", in S. Ghoshal and E. Westney (eds) *Organization Theory and the Multinational Corporation*, St. Martins Press, New York.

Egelhoff, W. G. (1988), *Organizing the Multinational Enterprise - An Information-Processing Perspective*, Ballinger Publisher Company, Cambridge, MA.

Forsgren, M. and Johanson, J. (1992), *Managing Networks in International Business*, Gordon and Breach Science Publishers, Philadelphia.

Galbraith, J. R. and Nathanson, D. A. (1978), *Strategy Implementation: The Role of Structure and Process*, West Publishing Co, Minnesota.

Ghoshal, S. and Bartlett, Ch. A. (1990), "MNC as an Interorganizational Network", *Academy of Management Review*, vol. 15, pp. 603-25.

Ghoshal, S. and Nohria, N. (1997), *The Differentiated MNC. Organizing Multinational Corporation for Value Creation*, Jossey-Bass Publ., San Francisco.

Gupta, A. K. and Govindarajan, V. (1991), "Knowledge Flows and the Structure of Control within Multinational Corporations", *Academy of Management Review*, vol. 16, pp. 768-92.

Gupta, A. K. and Govindarajan, V. (1994), "Organizing for Knowledge Flows within MNCs", *International Business Review*, Vol. 3, pp. 443 – 457

Håkansson, H. and Johanson, J. (1993), "Networks as a Governance Structure", in G. Grabher (ed.), *The Embedded Firm: On the Socioeconomics of Industrial Networks*, Routledge, London.

Hallén, L., Johanson, J. and Seyed-Mohamed, N. (1991) "Interfirm Adaptations in Business Relationships", *Journal of Marketing*, Vol. 55, pp. 29 – 37

Halinen, A. and Törnroos, J.-Å. (1998), "The role of embeddedness in evolution of business networks", *Scandinavian Journal of Management*, vol. 14, pp. 187-205.

Hedlund, G. and Åman, P. (1984), *Managing Relationships with Foreign Subsidiaries - Organization and Control in Swedish MNCs*, Sveriges Mekanförbund, Stockholm.

Hedlund, G. and Rolander, D. (1990), "Actions in heterarchies: new approaches to managing the MNC", in Ch. A. Bartlett, Y. Doz and G. Hedlund (eds), *Managing the Global Firm*, Routledge, London.

Kogut, B. (1993), "Learning, or the Importance of being Inert: country Imprinting and International competition", in S. Ghoshal and D. E. Westney, (eds), *Organization theory and the Multinational corporation*, St. Martins Press, New York.

Nunnally, J. C. (1978), *Psychometric Theory*, -2nd ed., McGraw-Hill, New York.

Porter, M. E. (1986), "Competition in Global Industries: A Conceptual Framework", in M. E. Porter, *Competition in Global Industries*, Harvard Business School Press, Boston.

Prahalad, C. K. and Hamel, G. (1990), "The Core Competence of the Corporation", *Harvard Business Review*, May, June pp. 79 - 91.

Tichy, N. M., Tushman, M. L. and Fombrun, C. (1979), "Social Network Analysis for Organizations", *Academy of Management Review*, vol. 4, pp. 507 - 19.

White, R. E. and Poynter, T. A. (1990), "Organizing for world-wide advantage", in Ch. A. Bartlett, Y. Doz and G. Hedlund (eds), *Managing the Global Firm*. Routledge, London.

Appendix

"To what extent is this customer/supplier
important to the subsidiary concerning..."

...product development
...production development
...continuity/security in delivery
...sales volume
...technological information
...information about governmental restrictions
...information about market activities
...maintaining important relations with other corporate units
...maintaining important relations with external organizations
...new important business contacts

"To what extent has the relation with this customer/supplier
caused adaptation for the subsidiary concerning..."

...business conduct
...product technology
...production technology
...organizational structure

The answering alternatives to these questions are
from 1=Not at all, to 5=Very high

Note that the respondents have also been asked "To what extent is the subsidiary important to this customer/supplier concerning..." with exactly the same alternatives as above. The same goes for the questions about adaptation.

For Product Safety Concerns and Information please contact our EU representative GPSR@taylorandfrancis.com Taylor & Francis Verlag GmbH, Kaufingerstraße 24, 80331 München, Germany

T - #0081 - 160425 - C0 - 219/154/21 - PB - 9781138716797 - Gloss Lamination